MOVEMENT
DISCOVERY

PHYSICAL EDUCATION FOR CHILDREN

Andrea Boucher, PhD, MEd
Towson University

Evelyn Wiseman, MEd, MDiv
Formerly of Western Washington University

JONES AND BARTLETT PUBLISHERS

Sudbury, Massachusetts

BOSTON   TORONTO   LONDON   SINGAPORE

World Headquarters

Jones and Bartlett Publishers
40 Tall Pine Drive
Sudbury, MA 01776
978-443-5000
info@jbpub.com
www.jbpub.com

Jones and Bartlett Publishers Canada
6339 Ormindale Way
Mississauga, Ontario L5V 1J2
Canada

Jones and Bartlett Publishers International
Barb House, Barb Mews
London W6 7PA
United Kingdom

Jones and Bartlett's books and products are available through most bookstores and online booksellers. To contact Jones and Bartlett Publishers directly, call 800-832-0034, fax 978-443-8000, or visit our website, www.jbpub.com.

Production Credits
Publisher, Higher Education: Cathleen Sether
Acquisitions Editor: Shoshanna Goldberg
Senior Associate Editor: Amy L. Bloom
Senior Editorial Assistant: Kyle Hoover
Production Manager: Julie Champagne Bolduc
Production Assistant: Jill Morton
Associate Marketing Manager: Jody Sullivan
V.P., Manufacturing and Inventory Control: Therese Connell
Composition: Arlene Apone
Cover Design: Todd and Andre Stringer
Title Page Design: Scott Moden
Associate Photo Researcher: Sarah Cebulski
Cover Image: Courtesy of Gerstung Intersport
Printing and Binding: Courier Stoughton
Cover Printing: Courier Stoughton

Library of Congress Cataloging-in-Publication Data
Boucher, Andrea.
  Movement discovery : physical education for children / by Andrea Boucher and Evelyn Wiseman.
      p. cm.
  Includes bibliographical references and index.
  ISBN-13: 978-0-7637-5041-1
  ISBN-10: 0-7637-5041-7
  1. Physical education for children—Curricula. 2. Physical education and training—Study and teaching—Curricula. 3. Movement education—Curricula. 4. Physical fitness for children—Curricula. I. Wiseman, Evelyn. II. Title.
  GV443.B68 2010
  796.07—dc22
                        2010001807

6048

Printed in the United States of America
14 13 12 11 10   10 9 8 7 6 5 4 3 2 1

Dedication

Dedicated with gratitude to Elizabeth (Betty) M. Barwell (1910–1999) and Agnes M. Whyte (1910–2008), pioneers in movement/teacher education. They knew about individual differences and the value of encouragement.

Contents

Chapter 11

Chapter 12

Preface

The prevalence of overweight and inactive children and adults in Western society has reached crisis levels. Many factors contribute to this sad state of affairs, and few can deny its truth. And yet, in marked contrast to this trend, babies are born with an urge to move. They seem to enjoy the physical sensations of moving, and they extend their world by activity. They are skill hungry. Constant exploration seems to be very enjoyable and utilizing emerging and increasing capacity deeply satisfying. "Look at me! I can . . ." is perhaps a faint echo caught from the joy, laughter, and expression of a happy infant.

The Physical Education profession needs to look closely at current practice in early childhood education and elementary school Physical Education if it is to play a role in stemming the tide of obesity and inspiring children—who grow into adults, of course—to engage in healthy lifestyles throughout the life course. *Movement Discovery: Physical Education for Children* is written in the belief that the best way to improve the present crisis situation is to ensure that all early childhood and elementary school teachers themselves experience and value simple, strenuous, and enjoyable activity and know which material will enable them to give such experiences to young children. Creative, challenging, and interesting Physical Education lessons in preschools and elementary schools are essential.

Movement Discovery highlights the history of Physical Education to provide an understanding of why programs are as they are, shares information about child development and skill development to give guidance to teachers, and offers plenty of material to start an ongoing Movement Discovery program that capitalizes on the innate human urge to discover one's physical capacities and enjoy them. This can be done by encouraging children to make decisions about their possible responses and the

most efficient use of time and equipment available. In this way, children assume partial responsibility for their own learning. If this happens on a regular (preferably daily) basis, teachers will then be freed to observe, interact, reflect, evaluate, improve, and perhaps enjoy their work more. If children experience strenuous and enjoyable lessons, if they can derive satisfaction from their increased skills, and if these skills have an obvious link with their future education and the world in which they live, there is at least a good possibility that physical activity will continue throughout life. This kind of experience will involve interaction with others, participation in mixed-gender activities, the use of local facilities, and support from the home. This text focuses on these objectives.

Movement Discovery includes material to help the pre-service student, the graduate student, and the in-service teacher examine their own attitudes, the influence of their previous experiences, and the ways in which this material links with other courses in their teacher preparation program. The suggested activities included within the text are based on current psychomotor developmental theory. Many examples of practical activities have been included for college students and teachers to try for themselves. Any teacher education course that includes work with children is by far the most beneficial. Student interns can work with children on a one-on-one basis as well as in small groups, while taking time to observe the children and practice some of the teaching techniques this text recommends. Information and suggested assignments geared to those who conduct such courses at the college/university level are included.

The material provided in this book covers interdisciplinary lessons for very young children as well as the curricular areas of expressive movement and creative dance, developmental games and pre-sport games experiences, track and field, and body management/educational gymnastics. Guidelines are included to help teachers ensure that their program is physically demanding enough to develop fitness. Advice on water activities is also included for those who can access appropriate facilities. Many children with special needs are integrated into school classes, and there is specific material included for them; however, the discovery teaching method allows for individual responses and its content is applicable at *all* levels.

Throughout the book, personal anecdotes are included to provoke discussion, to stimulate observation, and to aid greater understanding of the teaching process. Many chapters also begin with a number of questions designed to begin discussion sessions. It is recommended that most, if not all, theory sessions begin with in-class discussions because this is an important process that will involve students more deeply and increase the pace of learning. Partner and small-group discussions work well, too, and whole-class discussions can help the professor monitor the progress of the course. Some of these opening questions could be used as assessment measures as well.

For those new to Movement Discovery, a description of the method is included as well as suggestions for its introduction in a new situation.

References at the end of each chapter have been deliberately restricted to a select few. They mostly refer to "classical" writings that uncovered new insights and spurred a widespread shift in understanding of the educational process. It is important that students recognize how the material presented in this text links with other courses in pedagogy included in their preservice teacher education preparation. Students should use the Internet to look at recent research worldwide. Additional helpful Web sites for students and instructor resources, such as PowerPoint presentations, TestBanks, and an Instructor's Manual are available on the book's Web site: http://health.jbpub.com/movement.

This book will be a valuable tool for change. Much of the terminology has been used before, albeit superficially or even misapplied. We can no longer afford to spend time on practices dear to tradition but whose effectiveness is unsupported by research. The opinions of skilled and experienced teachers who have the courage to learn from one another and from the children they teach will be increasingly valuable in proving the worth of the approaches described here.

All material in this text is designed to be personalized at the students' individual level. Discovering new information on one's own generally leads to better retention, and is more interesting, than simply being told to do something. University teacher education courses still deal with groups of students who differ widely from one another and whose individual potential sometimes outstrips that of professors.

In a crisis situation, we may need to change attitudes and teaching behaviors. We also need to apply practices that will lead to lifelong learning and participation. We must help future teachers to be flexible and resilient in the face of our classrooms' vast diversity and to have the confidence to develop their own unique gifts. The text is structured to do this, and we look forward to seeing the contributions to be made by the next generation of teachers.

About the Authors

Andrea Boucher, PhD, MEd, Diploma in Physical Education, Diploma in Teaching (Early Childhood), NDT certified (Neuro-Developmental Treatment Theory)

Andrea Boucher is a professor of Physical Education in Teacher Education at Towson University, Baltimore, Maryland. Andrea has spent 40 years of her career in higher education in the United States. Prior to coming to this country, she worked as a classroom teacher in both Australia and Canada. Before leaving Australia, she was an itinerant advisor for early childhood physical education in the state of South Australia for 3 years, working with classroom general educators. In this capacity, she taught hundreds of preadolescent children in a variety of urban and rural settings.

Andrea's scholarship (presentations, publications, research) has focused on preschool and elementary aged children, including those with disabilities. Her presentations number more than 180 and have been given both nationally and internationally. Andrea has also produced two films: *Movement Toward Control* and another for Disabled Sports USA. Both films demonstrate how children with disabilities can be integrated into Movement Discovery programs. *Movement Toward Control* was a federally funded project to produce a 30-minute film depicting children with disabilities working with able-bodied children in Physical Education. Andrea was the project director, and Eve Wiseman worked as a consultant and teacher in the film.

Andrea served a 4-year term on the Council of Physical Education for Children (COPEC), National Association of Sport and Physical Education (NASPE), and American Alliance for Health, Physical Education, Recreation, and Dance (AAHPERD). She is a recipient of the AAHPERD/COPEC "Margie R. Hanson Distinguished Service Award," the Eastern District AAHPERD "Outstanding Professional Award in Physical Education," and the Maryland Association of Health, Physical Education, Recreation and Dance's (MAHPERD) "Simon McNeely Award" for Higher Education in Physical Education.

Reverend Miss E. D. Wiseman, MEd, MDiv

Evelyn Wiseman is a former associate professor at Western Washington University (WWU), Bellingham, Washington. While teaching at WWU, Eve obtained a U.S. federal government grant (Title IX) to develop a Movement Discovery curriculum minimizing sex-role stereotyping in elementary school Physical Education (Project Active 1979). WWU instituted a major in Elementary Physical Education in which Eve also taught.

Eve was educated in England and gained her original training and focus on children at Homerton College, Cambridge. While teaching in "tough" schools, Eve learned early on that permanent learning takes place only when the learner is actively involved in his or her own learning. After several years teaching children aged 5–15 years, she joined the faculty of the University of Birmingham when it was the only university in the United Kingdom at that time offering an undergraduate degree in Physical Education. Her colleagues there included David Munrow, Peter McIntosh, and Barbara Knapp—all published authors who had great influence on Physical Education both in England and internationally.

Eve emigrated to Canada in 1959, and while based at the University of British Columbia–Vancouver, she worked with practicing teachers and students and gave demonstration lessons with children for the school districts and Department of Education personnel.

Eve and Andrea began their close professional relationship at WWU and were pioneers in Movement Education for nearly 40 years. Both gave presentations, demonstration lessons, and published articles for AAHPERD, NAEYC, and the Canadian Association of Health, Physical Education, and Recreation (CAHPER).

In 1984, Eve was ordained in the Anglican Church of Canada.

Reviewers

Thank you to the reviewers of this edition for their valuable feedback, comments, and suggestions:

Helene Afeman, MS
Kinesiology, Louisiana State University

Weiyun Chen, PhD
University of Michigan

Brian D. Clocksin, PhD
Hofstra University

Joyce A. Ellis, PhD
Fort Hays State University

Claudia Maria Guedes, PhD
San Francisco State University

Dr. Kath Howarth
Professor, Physical Education
SUNY Cortland

Joe L. Jones
Assistant Professor of Health and
  Physical Education
Cameron University

David G. Lorenzi, EdD
Indiana University of Pennsylvania

Rip Marston, PhD
University of Northern Iowa

Johnny Newsome, PhD
Morehead State University

Dr. Heidi Henschel Pellett
Minnesota State University

Jon R. Poole, EdD
Associate Professor
Radford University

Robert J. Rausch Jr., PhD
Westfield State College

Ann-Catherine Sullivan, PhD
CAPE, Saginaw Valley State University

Virginia L. Trummer, MS
Physical Education, University of Texas
  at San Antonio

Discovering Roots

"The time for extracting a lesson from history is ever at hand for those who are wise."
—Demosthenes Philippicus (384/383–322 B.C.)

"Those who cannot remember the past are condemned to repeat it."
—George Santayana (1905)

QUESTIONS TO DISCUSS

1. Why do you want to become a teacher?

2. What do you hope to get out of this course?

3. Why do you think your professor has chosen this text?

4. Why do you think this course is required? (Or, if it is not required, why have you chosen to take this course?)

5. Can you remember anything significant from your elementary school Physical Education program?

6. What attitudes do you, your parents, or your friends have toward physical activity? What attitudes does your community have?

7. Why do you, your family, or your friends participate in vigorous and strenuous physical movement?

8. Where in your community is most physical activity to be seen?

9. Describe any prejudices you may have against some activities.

10. Do you enjoy or prefer some aspects of physical activity but not others? Explain.

11. Which sports or physical recreation activities do you enjoy? Why do you enjoy them?

12. Did you ever encounter a situation where physical activity was prescribed as a punishment? Describe it.

There are always antecedents to any situation in which we find ourselves. It is very important to discover why things are the way they are and to reexamine our current practice in the light of present and future needs. As stated in the preface to this book, the prevalence of overweight and inactive children and adults in Western society today has reached crisis levels. Valuable lessons can be learned from our history—as a profession and as individuals.

Most readers of this book have probably already read something about education, physical activity, schools, or children. You may have chosen your present institution or course for a reason. You will already have some understanding of what to expect from other students, other courses, your own past experiences in school or sports, and so on. At some point you probably experienced Physical Education classes in school or in a church or a recreational facility.

Write a brief personal history of your own Physical Education experience in school.

Start an anecdotal "observational journal" of young children moving.

If our life experiences have been vivid, hurtful, or pleasurable, we often have strong opinions or attitudes and may judge other individuals' ideas in the light of that experience.

Working with a partner will extend your learning and make it more relevant and interesting. Choose a partner from your class who is very different from you if possible. Gender differences, age differences, and cultural differences often lead individuals to have very different perspectives on the same issue. If your chosen partner lives near you or in an adjacent location, this proximity could enable you to increase your informal learning time. If necessary, switch partners during the course to facilitate your learning.

Complete Assignment 1–1 and exchange your response with your partner. As you consider your own history, try to become aware of how it may be influencing you (or your partner). Realize that you may not have a completely open mind (Everyone is prejudiced to some extent!) on some things but also that you may have insight and understanding beyond the rest of the group or the professor. You have something to offer as well as to receive. For this reason, you are encouraged to take responsibility for your own learning by participating in discussion, interaction with your partner, and linking of this material with what you learn in other preservice courses.

Be aware of your institution's history with reference to Physical Education and Early Childhood/Elementary teacher preparation. Discover the recent trends nationally in Physical Education at the pre-K and elementary levels.

Remember that observation will be crucial to your success as a teacher of Physical Education. Movement is

evanescent; it does not remain. We need to develop a trained eye that sees what children do and a "movement memory" that will form the basis of comparison. This does not mean that we compare individual children to others, but rather that we compare the "now" with "previously." This practice is the very basis of "assessment." The focus for teachers is to encourage children, approve of their new capacity, and help all children to develop confidence. Children need to feel they are getting somewhere. They are skill hungry and approval hungry. Although you will certainly increase your understanding of capacity at different maturational levels and between individuals, it is even more important to understand the progression of learning and the development of skill within individual children. Developing this understanding will take time, however.

It is recommended that you begin training your observational skills now. Keep a journal of your observations. For the first three weeks, observe children only when adults are not present. Children are to be found on public transport, in the family (Do you have young siblings or young relatives?), and elsewhere in your community. Look in the neighbors' yard and at churches, schools (recess, before and after school), playgrounds, parks, swimming pools, and open spaces. Many stores, shopping malls, markets, and large restaurants have play areas for young children. Record the date, time of day, and gender and approximate age of the children, and describe what they were doing and anything else you notice. It is also possible that your professor or institution will invite children to visit campus so that you can observe them.

You are probably already interested in children—if you were not, you would not be reading this book! It is normal to feel apprehensive about your future role as a teacher, as there are so many other adults involved who will be interested in you and your work: the students' parents, the principal, the mentor teachers, supervisors, college professors, other teachers in the school, and so on. This interest

A physical education teacher had lost touch with a Greek couple with whom she had stayed five years previously. While driving through the Greek countryside near the town where they lived, she passed a woman dressed in a long dress with a large hat (no features were visible) working in an olive grove. The sight was momentary but something about how the woman moved as she threw a branch aside reminded the driver of her friend. She called at the house but no one was home. On impulse, she went back to the olive grove and stopped. Three friends were reunited because of the teacher's movement memory.

Participate in some form of strenuous physical activity. Try to experience the euphoria that comes afterward or find others who have. Explore the Internet for such responses to physical activity, marathons, and other types of strenuous exercise. It is possible to get a "high" from exercise.

Assignment 1-4

Discover recent national trends in Physical Education at the pre-K and elementary school levels. Explore the Web sites of the National Association for Sport and Physical Education (NASPE)/ American Alliance for Health, Physical Education, Recreation, and Dance (AAHPERD), Centers for Disease Control and Prevention (a U.S. government agency), P.E. Central, and Center for Advancement of Standards-Based Physical Education.

in children is basic to your future success. You are not being trained to teach Physical Education so much as to teach children; think about the implications of this statement. Another basic requirement for future success is your own enjoyment of strenuous physical activity. Are you personally physically active or do you want to be?

Your interest in children and in movement for its own sake will sustain you as a teacher. You will enjoy interaction with individual children as they discover more and more of their physical capacities. This observation and interaction will become the basis of progressive teaching and assessment. The variety and skills that children show in both performance and personality will challenge and delight you for the rest of your life. If you enjoy teaching, it is more likely that children will enjoy your lessons. It is a privilege for a teacher to participate actively in their lives. Of course, strenuous physical activity is also essential to good health. It stimulates further physical and cognitive development as well. Ultimately, enjoyment is the strongest motivation and society's greatest aid in producing physically active adults.

You may find it interesting to look at some selected historical influences to try and imagine what the motivation underlying these beliefs would have been. Additional historical material can be found in Appendix 1.

Recent History in the United States

The United States developed college education for all at an early stage. Democracy, so dear to the American heart, had its influence on the development of college education. A largely immigrant society often places its hopes for the future on opportunities for children to better themselves through education. In 1890–1920, when the U.S. population grew by 68 percent, high school enrollments increased by 986 percent (Skinner & Langfitt, 1937/2006). By the end of the nineteenth century, the United States had developed a system of college education—sometimes

using private benefaction—that was the most advanced in the world. Part of that rapid expansion featured development of physical plant and facilities for Physical Education that would be considered palatial by European standards.

The U.S. emphasis on Physical Education has had an enormous impact on the Physical Education profession around the globe. Professionalism in sport has developed worldwide, and professional athletics, international competition, and the Olympic games have expanded to the point that they have global political and financial implications.

Locally, at a grass-roots level, the fortunes of the local college or professional team often dominate American communities, affecting both facilities and programs. Gate receipts from sporting events produce steady revenue for many colleges, some of which finds its way to Physical Education departments that carry out research. Most of these funds are used to upgrade facilities. Unfortunately, many abuses and problems are also associated with the system of athletic scholarships, the use of academic appointments to support coaches, and unequal divisions between programs for men and women.

Many prominent leaders have old college loyalties. For example, President John Kennedy appointed a university football coach in 1961 to advise him on a youth fitness program for the nation.

In the past, many women physical educators in the United States opposed such competitive intensity. As a consequence, some paid more attention to younger children and to dance and the process of teaching, rather than to the sports themselves. This influence was especially notable among women college educators in the late 1920s and early 1930s.

In 1932, Ruth Glassow published *Fundamentals in Physical Education,* a seminal work in Physical Education. Glassow had spent some years observing movement visually and attempted some kind of classification, which included a category of basic body movements that were labeled "fundamental." Movement Fundamentals became a subject widely taught at the college level, often replacing formal drills and calisthenics. It seemed to meet a need for participation in physical activity that was required at the college level, yet was perhaps more feminine and included academic content. Such courses included simple locomotor movements and body actions, which were linked with good posture and health and even relaxation and simple hygiene. The courses often emphasized the feel of a movement, sometimes linked with music and rhythmic activities. Interestingly enough, the words used in the first chapter of Glassow's first book to describe these movements were "speed, strength and direction." Glassow wrote:

> A classification of activities is valuable because it tends to show that many forms of movement are fundamentally the same. What has been learned in one form of work or sport may be applied in another. (Glassow, 1932, p. 20)

The emergence of Movement Fundamentals also had an effect on the Physical Education of young children. During the 1930s and 1940s, simple activities such as walking, galloping, and swaying were sometimes linked with music when teaching children. In one book published in 1968, for example, one finds the following suggestion: "In all activities strong emphasis should be placed on proper body mechanics and on fundamental skills of running, jumping, throwing, catching, striking, kicking, etc." (LaPorte & Cooper, 1968).

Recent History in the United Kingdom

Two highly significant historical influences imported from the United Kingdom also emerged largely from the work of women physical educators. These concepts supported and led to the development of Physical Education programs in U.S. elementary schools.

As described in the additional historical material found in Appendix 1, there is often a close connection between military physical training and educational programs in schools. Both of these British influences really came about as a result of World War II. During World War II, military leaders recognized that there was a need for a different kind of soldier. Infantry drill training requiring a mass instant and unquestioning response to the commands of a superior officer was superceded in some situations by development of the "commando"—the secret agent who, undetected by the opposition, infiltrated enemy lines or stealthily performed acts of sabotage or otherwise prepared the way for later military assault. Commandos were individuals trained to use their initiative, make decisions, and be inventive. Sometimes operating in small groups, they needed to be physically tough and cooperative, ingenious and very versatile physically as well as mentally. To develop these skills, a different kind of training was developed. Skills were developed in climbing, hanging, balancing, and maneuvering the body in these training courses. A rope, a tree, a cargo net, a fence, a tunnel, a hill, a ladder, a pole, and so on challenged the individual to overcome the obstacles in his or her own way.

As an outgrowth of this military training, the jungle gym became widely used in early childhood centers and playgrounds. It has some limitations, however. The cargo net was used in early commando military training because it could be folded and carried. A soldier could climb to the top of a cliff or barrier, secure the top, and let the net unfold; many soldiers could then scale the cliff. The net could be retrieved and used somewhere else. In contrast, in an activity room, apparatus that moves can be hazardous (and challenging!).

There was no time for a system to be developed, such as Cargo-Net Climbing Level I, followed by Cargo-Net Climbing Level II and so on; the need was urgent. Europe was occupied by an efficient "fit" German army, and British troops had to be evacuated from France. During this time, a demonstration of commando training was presented to a group of physical educators. Mostly women in senior positions watched the young men in action. What struck the observers was the zest and enjoyment the soldiers displayed: Army training is not always enjoyed.

There is a direct link between this event and the development of climbing apparatus for children used in the British infant school (children aged 5–7 years) and later the junior school (children aged 7–11) , thereby ensuring that many children aged 5–11 years had a challenging individualized activity program. Sometimes the apparatus was permanently erected in the school playground; sometimes it was made so that children in a hall or classroom could easily assemble it. There was only one rule applied: Children were required to work alone and could not touch anyone else. The child was not expected to copy others, and each individual was encouraged to work at his or her own level and invent his or her own activities. Activities were *not* taught, and no child was required to do a specific activity. This practice had major implications for safety. If a child did not choose to use the equipment, other choices were available. It was realized from the outset that children are safe if allowed to work individually at their own level and speed without teacher intervention, compulsion, or assistance. Later, as confidence developed (both by the children and by the teachers), children were challenged to link skills together, to vary their responses, and to use more parts of their bodies.

As part of this training, children were expected to look after themselves at all times, not to interfere with or help another child even if asked to, and to solve any difficulties themselves. Many critics of this practice predicted that such freedom would be dangerous. In the army, even the military hierarchy itself predicted an increase in accidents. But it was wartime, and the need for physically fit soldiers was urgent. Surprisingly, the predicted accidents did not occur. In fact, the level of accidents dropped. It looked as if the soldiers were learning to be safe as well as skilled.

Physical Education, a compulsory subject in state schools at this time in Great Britain, followed a government syllabus for young children in the British infant schools and junior schools, known as the *Syllabus of Physical Training 1933* (His Majesty's Stationery Office [HMSO], 1933). This syllabus, which was widely used, was based on the Swedish system of compensatory activity to remediate the effects of sedentary living. The 1933 syllabus contained a wealth of strenuous and enjoyable activities, with resistance for strengthening exercises obtained by using partners, manipulating the body weight, lifting and carrying another body, and engaging in contests and small-group activities (three or four people) in competitive situations. Classroom teachers who received compulsory physical training taught lessons in a formal fashion. Drills, teams with appointed captains (usually boys), competitive group games, and relay races were widely used.

As tentative experiments began in the 1940s using large climbing apparatus and improvised equipment by teachers of young children, concerns about the safety of these practices grew. It was believed that there was a need for compensatory activity and fitness provided by the current 1933 syllabus, which was still in use during this era. Prudent teachers wondered if children would really think of something to do if not told explicitly which activities were appropriate. Would children simply play and waste time? Would small children simply be bored? It is fascinating to read contemporary accounts of concerned professionals:

> Before the children used the apparatus, lists of possible and probable exercises for each part of the apparatus were made. Exercises for Infants and exercises for Juniors. We have however never needed to use these lists, except to add to them exercises the children themselves had evolved that we had not thought of. . . . within a few days we saw all the exercises we had prepared, and many others we had not thought of and not one single exercise had been suggested or taught. (Ricks, 1947)

Later in the same article, the author refers to the progression exhibited by students:

> Watching a given class for many sessions, it was very clear that the individual child gradually attempted different and more varied exercises, exercises higher up the apparatus, exercises combining two or three previous movements and so on. (Ricks, 1947)

Catherine Cooke, working in Bristol, England, was another pioneer during this era. She tells an interesting story:

> Members of the American Army interested in schoolwork kindly came one day to make further suggestions. A few children were shown how to "flip" over the top, but as the mesh was six inches wide and their heads were rather small, this activity was not encouraged and it was thought wiser to keep to the children's own inventions. . . .
>
> Suggestions that they might now like to come down were treated with a pitying smile. . . . Later, as they got older, progression took the form of working in couples or making a pattern with the whole group using the ropes. (Cooke, 1946)

Cooke (1946) also reported "over a period of two years no accidents have occurred in any of the schools using climbing apparatus." The ideas by Cooke were obviously novel, as one of the photographs included with her article was printed upside down!

Traditionally, many female Physical Education teachers at that time had been trained in sports, swimming, and gymnastics, which had derived from the Swedish and German systems. There was much emphasis on "good posture" as a product of gymnastics and the use of calisthenics to compensate for the effects of a largely sedentary life on the human body. If dance were included, it would have been folk dance.

Compulsory public education included many children from deprived and poor areas. The Industrial Revolution

An observer watched two boys aged approximately 12 years using a climbing frame, climbing up and jumping off. One boy went confidently to the top and jumped to the ground. His friend was jumping from lower down. "Come on up," said the one and the second (halfway) boy did. "It's easy," said the confident boy and jumped. The second boy looked and hesitated. The confident boy repeated the activity. The second boy again hesitated. "Chicken," shouted the confident boy. The second boy looked around as if admiring the view and then climbed down to the halfway bar where he had been previously and jumped from there.

Discuss the previous material with your partner. Mention any aspect that connects with your personal history in Physical Education.

had created crowded and often unsanitary living conditions for many workers in the United Kingdom. Schools were also concerned with discipline, and it was not uncommon for mass drill of the whole school to be conducted in the schoolyard as a means of training and developing the body for good posture, control, health,

and fitness. Control and discipline were often linked with this mass drill, just as they had been in military training. In addition, extra physical activity was sometimes used as a form of punishment. That Physical Education was primarily intended to serve disciplinary purposes was underlined by the fact that in 1895, English lawmakers decided a higher grant (of money) would be paid only to those public schools that provided instruction in Swedish or other drills or suitable physical exercises.

Although many teachers from women's specialist Physical Education colleges taught only girls and in private schools, the local education authorities appointed some of these women to supervisory and consultant positions in the public school system. In this way, the needs of younger and deprived children (boys and girls) were forcibly brought to their attention. Postwar Britain was characterized by major changes in social and other structures. As mentioned earlier, army training (commando style) was one key influence at the time. The second major influence that was developed in Britain and was exported to the United States was an outgrowth of Laban's work; Laban had previously had an influence on American modern dance but not on U.S. elementary schools.

Rudolf von Laban de Varalja (1879–1958), a Hungarian working in Germany, fled from Nazi Germany to England in 1938. Laban was a very idealistic and charismatic person. He had a wide background in artistic circles and had developed a system of movement notation, called Labanotation. In Manchester, England, he opened a studio and advertised a course in Modern Dance. Couples arrived in evening dress expecting to learn ballroom dancing. In response, Laban decided to change the title of the course to Modern Educational Dance; he used the same phrase as the title of his book on the subject when it was published in English in 1948 (the work had previously been called *Central European Dance*).

The female inspector of physical education in Manchester at that time, Myfanwy Dewey, was most interested in Laban's work and involved her senior colleague Ruth Foster in

Describe incidences you have encountered of physical activity being used as punishment. Discuss this topic.

bringing this new venture to the school system. Prior to that time, the training of most women Physical Education specialists had not included much in the way of dance. When students engaged in such freeing movement, creative dance often provoked a very emotional response. The artistic and freer forms of movement that Laban used were very attractive, however, and Laban himself had a very strong personality that inspired others to follow his example.

With top-level support, there were soon many opportunities for physical educators to discover modern educational dance. Indeed, many specialist Physical Education teachers attended short courses led by Laban. The teaching method was direct and formal, with Laban himself or his assistant Lisa Ullmann directing groups of dancers. Themes were usually "heroic": conflict, reconciliation, differences resulting in harmony and sometimes drama. Individuals were expected to move freely in their own way but to be part of a group that had a specific theme. Usually the performances took place outdoors. Dartington Hall, an arts center in Devon, was a favorite place for these activities, as its beautiful gardens added to the overall effect of the dance. Many games and sports enthusiasts discovered a new dimension to life! Laban himself believed sincerely that war would cease if people learned to move in harmony with the group (yet retaining their individuality in how they expressed their feelings). Not surprisingly, many teachers were anxious to pass on their experiences to children.

The new U.K. government publications that were developed to replace the 1933 syllabus were called *Moving and Growing* (HMSO, 1952), *Planning the Programme* (HMSO, 1953) and later *Movement: Physical Education in the Primary School* (DES, 1972). They included beautiful photographs of young children using the new experimental gymnastic apparatus as well as dancing. The 1950s was a time when international travel was resuming after World War II; as part of this trend, exchange teacher programs flourished. The type of Physical Education emerging from British primary schools (ages 7–11 years) during this era attracted worldwide interest. Special workshops were held, including those involving U.S. women physical educators from colleges, school districts, and government supervisory positions. Readers can find reports of these workshops in the AAHPERD publications.

With such exciting work being developed by classroom teachers in terms of Physical Education lessons in elementary schools, it is not surprising that secondary school teachers were forced to take notice. A secondary school gymnasium in the United Kingdom usually included larger apparatus developed from the Swedish/Danish system. There were wall bars, also called rib stalls, along side walls; gymnastic benches with hooks to provide inclines; adjustable balance beams with small "saddles" fitting over the curved side; climbing ropes that could also swing; a padded vaulting box; and sometimes a climbing ladder and a pom-meled horse. With government persuasion from His Majesty's Inspectors of Schools, the U.K. teacher training colleges—and particularly the private colleges for women, which prepared women specialist teachers in Physical Education—began to develop new content material that spread into the secondary schools. Many state secondary schools were single-sex institutions, and the influence of the new movement was strongest in work targeting girls and women. The work was usually called Educational Gymnastics or simply Movement Education. Foremost in this development was the I.M. Marsh College in Liverpool, whose senior lecturer Ruth Morison published a small booklet titled *Educational Gymnastics* in 1956.

How the Laban movement came to be adopted as a framework for this new work is difficult to discover. Certainly it was not due to Laban himself. At one conference in the 1950s, one of your authors remembers vividly an incident where a questioner asked, "Mr. Laban, when you apply your work to . . ." Laban interrupted her angrily and said, "I apply nothing. I make the discovery. It is you people who apply" (Wiseman, 1950).

Whereas a child-centered approach suited young children, it was more difficult to justify at a secondary level. Surely specialist teachers should have something to teach, rather than simply allowing students to invent their own activities?

Laban movement was called an analysis of movement (recall that English was not Laban's first language) and seemed to some to provide a legitimate framework on which content could be based. It was not uncommon at this time to see dance and dramatic movement performed on apparatus. Many men Physical Education teachers at the secondary level did not like this development and insisted that Newtonian physics was more relevant to gymnastic movement; the performer's feelings were not. The U.K. National Physical Education Professional Association (called the Ling Association) was largely composed of women at this time. No matter how enjoyable Laban movement was to the performer, the men teaching at the tertiary and secondary levels insisted that gravity, body management, and skill development should be the focus when using large apparatus and in the teaching of tumbling activities.

The women turned to Laban movement to provide content and structure to the new child-centered activities, which were emerging at a rapid pace during the 1960s. Often movement themes were presented as challenges, and students were expected to develop individual responses, even while using large apparatus.

Current Influences in the United States

During the 1970s and later, another development occurred in tertiary education that has continued to influence the development of elementary school Physical Education programs even today. With the growth of feminism, the interaction between men's and women's programs increased. Many institutions amalgamated what had hitherto been separate men's and women's departments. More men began to be involved in elementary Physical Education, and various systems of movement and pedagogy emerged. Texts for elementary school Physical Education began to be written by both men and women authors, who often contributed different perspectives.

Further anomalies exist in the actual elementary school programs and the systems that helped them to develop. Recall that Glassow used the words "strength, speed and direction" in her first work on Movement Fundamentals; Laban used the terms "space," "weight," and "time" to describe basic elements of movement. "Basic Movement" was a term used on both sides of the Atlantic, referring perhaps to content. The phrases "Movement Exploration," "Movement Training," and "Direct and Indirect Methods" were also used in both the United Kingdom and the United States, referring more to the teaching

method employed. *Movement Education—What it is and What it is Not! What's in a Name?* (Wiseman, 1967) addressed this issue. In terms of teaching method, this text obviously favors "discovery" as the term best fitting the needs of children as individuals, with different capacities emerging at different rates. Discovery offers the greatest hope that physical activity will be lifelong.

In terms of content, some confusion regarding the profession needs to be clarified. The two attractive descriptions of movement—(1) Glassow's strength, speed, and direction; Movement Fundamentals; and basic locomotor skills; and (2) Laban's space, weight, time, and flow—are just that, descriptions. We need to examine more carefully how they provide useful content material for skill learning. Some difficulties arise when these descriptions, based on visual observation, are used as analytical tools and claimed to provide a logical sequence of skill development (see Chapter 3, Discovering Capacity). For example, "[d]espite the hesitancy of many teachers to undertake the teaching of effort concepts, there is agreement that an applied understanding of these concepts is essential in skill development, from beginning to advanced levels" (Graham, Parker, & Holt-Hale, 2006, p. 269). Also, "[s]kill themes are initially practiced in isolation; as youngsters develop their motor skill they are practiced in sports, games, gymnastics and dance contexts" (Graham et al., 2006, p. 15). But is there evidence to support these practices?

If teachers apply Laban efforts to games and gymnastic skills, it could be dangerous. Free Flow is defined by Laban as movement where an external force is in control. In a school situation, a performer should be in control of his or her body at all times. Skill learning activity should be a result of intended, planned, thoughtful action or reaction initiated by the performer.

The Physical Education profession needs to devise new methods for developing physical skills as well as allowing children to develop their interests and work at their own individual levels. Much work has already been done in motor learning; in particular, Piaget's work in this area is considered seminal (see Chapter 3, Discovering Capacity).

The history of Physical Education, like the history of most other fields of learning, contains many instances of cherished beliefs being abandoned in favor of "a new way." In ancient Greece, for example, the broad jump was performed holding heavy weights in each hand (Halteres). It was believed that if the athlete released the weights after take-off, he or she could travel farther. This practice was eventually abandoned, as was swimming land drill. Indeed, the "correct" way to perform a skill is frequently abandoned by top performers. In the 1950s, for instance, the breaststroke kick was taught by spreading the knees wide apart, with the ankles together, and sweeping them straight, thereby squeezing water out from between the straightened legs. This was abandoned for the "dolphin" kick, in which

---

Anecdote 1–4

A demonstration of Movement Discovery was being given, and any interested professors, students, teachers, principals, supervisors, and interested professionals were invited to attend. During the demonstration, a class of first-grade children was observed just finishing a lesson; the children were separated into four groups, with each group using different small apparatus. A middle-aged woman walked in and sat down to watch the "chaotic" scene. After approximately three minutes she approached the teacher and said, "This is what I want my teachers to do. Where can I find out about this?"

the knees are pressed together. Similarly, a two-handed backhand in tennis is still considered "incorrect" by some teachers. And who invented the basketball "slam dunk"? Today's high jumpers typically go over the bar when the back arched beneath them (the Fosbury flop); in the past, however, many teachers had taught a rolling or straddle action, in which the stomach was placed lowest to the bar.

And consider soccer, which is a game of educated and versatile feet. One simply cannot say what is the correct way to kick for all people and every situation. Studying the experts (not college professors, but top-level performers), one sees a very great variety. Even if there were a "correct" way, it would be predictable—and unpredictability is a valued asset in soccer offense and a very real hazard in defense. The most successful players often use unorthodox techniques.

We all know something about individual differences and pay lip service to their existence. The reality is that because of them, there is unlikely to be a single correct way to perform physical skills that applies even to a small group of individuals—and most teachers have classes containing 25 or more students.

It is likely that most of the shots that experienced tennis players produce are never executed exactly in the same way.
—Schmidt & Wrisberg (2004, p. 146)

Many teachers also have a preconceived idea of what teaching is. To many, it is telling or explaining and then watching to see that the instructions are carried out. In this text, teaching is defined as the causing of learning. This may happen just because the student is ready; or it may be initiated by a cue given by the teacher, the environment, or other students; or—most likely of all—it may flow from practical physical experience and an assessment of what is effective by the performer.

Movement Discovery as a teaching method is based on the application of individual differences. It emphasizes the learner doing, discovering, and problem solving. It requires being an active and engaged learner, rather than the teacher telling the student how to do the movement and when to do the action. Although there is no one correct way to perform skills, common scientific factors and the composition of individual bodies are taken into account. Environmental clues will be vital in sports' skills (see Chapter 2, Discovering Differences, and Chapter 3, Discovering Capacity). Many chapters in this text contain suggested material to use if you wish; they offer examples of cues, challenges, and problems that can be applied in a variety of classrooms and PE settings.

Movement Discovery allows and encourages children to find the best way for themselves as individuals to perform a variety of the skills that so many of them are eager to try. Our experience suggests that progress is rapid and satisfying as children cooperate enthusiastically.

Summary

One cannot use an intelligent approach to any situation without some knowledge of why things are the way they are. Historical developments are fascinating in this sense, as is the personal history of each learner. Students need some appreciation of the way these factors have interacted in the past and can be manipulated. Notably, the differences in the Physical Education profession and in educational pedagogy have resulted in anomalies, which need to be addressed.

The skill of observation is essential to all teachers of activity. Learning will progress more rapidly when teachers and students cooperate actively and monitor their own progress.

In Physical Education directed toward meeting military needs, separate programs for men and women have had enormous effects. Movement Fundamentals and Laban movement have dominated many programs, as has the need for safety in school-based programs.

There are many exciting opportunities for research in both motor learning and educational psychology to be applied to the Physical Education field.

References

Cooke, C. E. (1946, March). Bristol climbing apparatus. *Journal of Physical Education, XXXVIII*(113).

Department of Education and Science. (1972). *Movement: Physical education in the primary school*. London: Author.

Glassow, R. (1932). *Fundamentals in physical education*. Philadelphia: Lea and Febiger.

Graham, G., Parker, M., & Holt-Hale, S. (2006). *Children moving: A reflective approach to teaching physical education* (7th ed.). New York: McGraw-Hill.

Her Majesty's Stationery Office (HMSO). (1933). *Syllabus of physical training 1933*. London: Author.

Her Majesty's Stationery Office (HMSO). (1952). *Moving and growing: P.E. in the primary school part one*. London: Author.

Her Majesty's Stationery Office (HMSO). (1953). *Planning the programme: P.E. in the primary school part two*. London: Author.

LaPorte, W. R., & Cooper, J. (1968). *The physical education curriculum* (7th ed.). Los Angeles: NCPEAM College Bookstore.

Morrison, R. (1955). *Educational gymnastics*. Liverpool: Speirs & Glendale.

Ricks, E. N. (1947, November). The Southampton apparatus. *Journal of Physical Education, 118*.

Santayana, G. (1905). *Introduction and reason in common sense*. London: Archibald Constable & Co.

Schmidt, R. A., & Wrisberg, C. A. (2004). *Motor learning and performance* (3rd ed.). Champaign, IL: Human Kinetics.

Skinner, C. E., & Langfitt, R. E. (Eds.). (1937/2006). *Introduction to modern education*. Boston: D. C. Heath.

Wiseman, E. D. (1950). Personal anecdote.

Wiseman, E. D. (1967, April–May). Movement education— What it is and what it is not! What's in a name? *Journal of the Canadian Association for Health, Physical Education and Recreation, 39*(4), 18–20.

Discovering Differences

"This above all, to thine own self be true; thou cans't not then be false to any man."
—William Shakespeare

"If we cannot end now our differences, at least we can help make the world safe for diversity."
—John Fitzgerald Kennedy (1963)

QUESTIONS TO DISCUSS

1. Consider your own body and decide if you have a tendency to linearity (ectomorphy; long limbs, narrow chest, long spine). Or are you broad shouldered, narrow hipped, muscular, and short in stature (mesomorphy)? Perhaps you are more pear-shaped, narrow shoulders, broad hips, and fatter (endomorphy). Assess your partner and discuss your shapes.

2. Recall any unusual circumstances or irregularities in your own growth process. Did these issues affect your acquisition of any physical skills?

3. Relate prowess in specific skills to physique. (Watch a top athletic competition such as the Olympic Games.) Do offensive and defensive line players in American football all have a similar body type? In rugby, do the players on the front row all have similar body types?

4. State your experience and opinion of fitness awards. Think about the motivation for winning awards.

5. Can you recall or observe a situation where physical capacity in one skill is a disadvantage in another (e.g., a loose wrist in badminton, which is not strong enough for success in tennis)?

6. Mention and criticize play areas used by children in your home district. Recall play activities that were strenuous and absorbing to you when you were a child.

7. Copy all articles in your local newspaper over a period of two weeks that deal with sports and politics or sports and culture.

8. Mention any instances you can recall of physical skill being used to establish superiority.

9. Check your local community for the provision of opportunity and/or encouragement to be active for (a) the elderly, (b) females, (c) males, and (d) children.

10. In your experience of elementary school Physical Education, have you ever encountered instances where the need to drink water or visit washrooms was restricted? Discuss these events.

Spend a day observing a baby. Notice all movement and record the number of minutes when the infant is free to move without restrictions. Modern babies are often confined to car seats, grocery buggies, or plastic carry seats, all of which may restrict the use of arms or legs and keep a child in a supine position. Often an adult takes a child into the fresh air, but in a pouch or sling. Record the time when a baby is on its tummy and unrestricted. Notice if clothing (sun hats, heavy coats or sweaters) restricts activity.

Reflect on your observations. Can you see any evidence that an urge to move comes from within the child? You will see many instances of an adult or sibling trying to elicit a response. Does the adult select the response most of the time? Does the adult physically manipulate the baby? Does the adult encourage some actions at the expense of others? Basically does an adult encourage what originates within the baby or impose/change the activity?

Try to record instances when a baby seems to enjoy "purposeless" movement (e.g., waving arms, kicking, turning the head, putting hands in mouth). Does being on the tummy restrict action or promote other kinds of movement? Notice eye movements in different positions.

Are there any times when the baby is naked? Are there any times when the baby is in water? Does the baby receive tactile sensation from stroking, tickling, or touching? Is the baby cuddled or held to experience different pressures? Which movement reactions do you observe when sound/noise or music is present?

There is so much to observe and your skill in observation will be crucial in your future success as a Physical Education teacher. In infancy as in childhood, movement may indicate highly significant learning. Share your observations with a partner.

Chapter 1 focused on historical factors, which will have produced many differences in attitudes and experiences among you and your classmates. Ideally, you will have realized that what you need to learn about teaching Physical Education to young children is not necessarily the same as someone else needs to learn. Take responsibility and initiative for your own learning.

Differences are built in to our world. Variety is part of creation. We do not live in a closed system. Instead, we must learn to accommodate others' differences while developing our uniqueness—by building our self-confidence,

self-esteem, self-actualization, integration, meeting our emerging needs, and so on. It is as if multiple dynamics exist within each person (and they may be different from the dynamics inside someone else), which push that individual to develop in a particular way. Conversely, all of us encounter some hard facts of life from the environment, both physical and human. The result of these two forces—nature and nurture—can be called education. Move this encounter of who we are and where we live into the realm of young children, and the dynamics that confront a teacher are born. Just as important as the needs of society, parents' expectations, and the requirements of the system are children's need to discover their capacities, their identities, and their potential. If education does not enable children to learn, it has failed. Likewise, if teachers inhibit or squelch the drive to learn, they do not fulfill their function and may inflict lasting damage on their students.

How should a teacher of young children in the area of Physical Education function? There is a potential conflict with the competing influences of the nature of the child (what is within) and the pressures or demands from the profession, the system, the parents, society and the future (what is without).

For many years, the teaching profession has insisted that the whole child comes to school. Of course, all children are individuals, differing from other children of the same age and gender. They have differing capacities and attitudes and so on. The "rule of thumb" statement presented in Chapter 1—"If all children are doing the same thing in the same way at the same time, it represents uneducational practice"—applies. We cannot continue to divide children into groups (classes) and make learning relevant to some 25 or 30 individuals at the same time.

Despite these difficulties, it *is* possible to individualize a program of Physical Education. In this chapter, we look in more detail at some factors that will guide us to do a better job of synthesis while balancing children's needs and capacities with the requirements of the educational system.

Body Type

If you look around your own group of classmates, you may be able to distinguish different types of bodies. Some useful information resulted from the work of William Sheldon (1940/1963), who developed somatotyping in the 1940s. Sheldon classified human physique using three components: endomorphy (pear-shape, narrow shoulders, broad hips), mesomorphy (broad shoulders, narrow hips, bulky muscles), and ectomorphy (long spine and limbs, narrow chest). In regard to these components, most people fall in the middle of the continuum and not at the extremes.
 and Carter (1967) have refined the classification process and produced an instruction manual that interested readers can use for this purpose. Parnell (1958) related

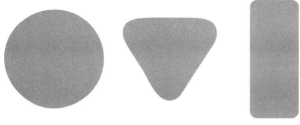

3 Body Shapes

Body Proportions

While being classified as having a particular body type, a child may exhibit other individual differences. Body proportions, for example, may cause variations in the center of gravity. Race or ethnicity may also come into play: For example, Malina et al. state that black children tend to have longer lower extremities compared to their non-black counterparts (Malina, Bouchard, & Bar-Or, 2004, p. 567).

somatotype to behavior and suggested that a high correlation exists between ectomorphy and intelligence; he further suggested that mesomorphic men tend to marry mesomorphic women and produce more male children than female children (a decidedly odd idea). Is the Physical Education profession dominated by mesomorphs?

These symbols for three body shapes are obviously extremes. Most people would be considered "mid-types."

The most important fact to remember is that body type is largely inherited (compare yourself to your parents). No matter how hard we try or work, a long-limbed individual cannot turn into a chunky, broad-shouldered person. Some activities favor some body types; for example, a long-spined linear child may have great difficulty doing a forward roll. Mesomorphs have a tendency to mature more quickly, whereas ectomorphs are often slow developers. A chunky female at age 8 years may excel at basketball, yet become totally outclassed at age 17 years by her friends who are linear and grow much taller. Height is at a premium in basketball. A push-up presents a totally different challenge to a muscular body or a linear one, and the endomorph is at a disadvantage in many gymnastic skills. The center of gravity will be in different places in different bodies—a factor that will affect all gymnastic and body momentum activities.

With children, one can teach tolerance for differences in others. More generally, however, children have to learn their own individual capacities and accept themselves as they are. They may also learn to use their individual differences and exploit them in a competitive situation.

Do not despair. Physique is not everything. *All* bodies have unrealized potential. Ways to increase physical capacity will be described subsequently. Some information on physical growth follows, in recognition of the fact that the children we teach will be growing at different rates.

Growth

Perhaps it is easier to observe some of the individual differences in children's bodies that are physical. In the past, teachers have been handicapped by the concepts of "normal" and "average" standards. These concepts derive from the many cross-sectional studies done on children at different stages of growth, in different environments, and so on. More difficult to obtain are data from longitudinal studies; such research is expensive to conduct and takes longer to produce results.

Pioneering work on growth-related differences was done at the Tavistock Clinic in London, where J. M. Tanner (1961) electrified many in the teaching profession with his findings. In the 1930s, Myrtle McGraw (1989) did groundbreaking work on the neuromuscular maturation of babies. Her twin studies showed there was little value in giving special instruction before a child was ready to tackle the skill—in this case, riding a tricycle. In McGraw's work, the twin who was trained before he was ready did learn to ride a tricycle eventually, but the untrained twin very quickly caught up to his level. The trained twin showed some adverse effects of the long period of frustration, while the untrained twin showed much more enthusiasm for riding. Also, the activity persisted for longer in the untaught twin. Consider your own experience of being "put-off" by an overzealous teacher or an ambitious parent?

Bowditch conducted the first longitudinal growth study in the United States in 1872. In another demonstration of growth-related differences, Tanner (1961) published a photograph of two boys who were the same height, one of whom was aged 11 years and one of whom was aged 17 years.

Although a common sequence of growth and development has been identified for humans, the tempo of this process varies greatly among individuals. Motor development proceeds from the head down the spinal column (the cephalo-caudal principle). Also the mid-line of the body develops ahead of the extremities (the proximal-distal principle); think about the implications of this point. In addition, gross motor development precedes fine motor control—and most "games" activities require fine motor control. Perhaps some "inadequate" fine motor control

---

Assignment 2–2

Look for achievement in Physical Education that relies heavily on physique. Can you discern dominance of certain body types in swimmers, sprinters, gymnasts, marathon runners, and football players?

(such as using pens and pencils) requires better development in the shoulder and arms.

Teachers can improve the gross motor experience of children in a wide variety of ways and provide a better basis for *many* skills. Consider the following example: A speech therapist came to observe a Movement Discovery program (Boucher, 1977). She wanted to know which kind of movement program could provide such positive results in such a short time with one of her clients. One of the teacher's students, a first-grade girl, had made dramatic improvements in her articulation. In the Movement Discovery program and with the additional help from a neurodevelopmental treatment (NDT) therapist, the child learned new ways to twist and rotate her body while balancing, hanging, and climbing on large apparatus. She had previously moved her body "all in one piece," without any rotational movement. The development of lateral movement of the tongue follows movement around the body's axis.

Similarly a second-grade boy who displayed a flaccid/floppy upper body, due to very low muscle tone, was in danger of failing his year due to "atrocious" handwriting, as described by his teacher. In body management sessions, he was asked to take the weight of the body on his hands and allowed to use climbing apparatus for hanging and swinging. As his shoulder girdle strengthened, his writing improved dramatically—and he passed his year.

Assignment 2–3

Research any recent study you can find on the effects of "special teaching" and "neglect" of some skills.

A key principle of motor development is that control of the body proceeds from the proximal body to the distal body; in this boy's case, as the shoulders and upper body were stimulated and strengthened, improvements in his control of the fingers and hands followed.

Tanner (1961) identified that females develop earlier than males. Girls are ahead even at birth (some two weeks in advance) and reach adolescence some two years ahead of boys.

The secular trend toward earlier adolescence has meant that a teacher may face a class in which girls who are physically young women are being taught Physical Education alongside male children. Teachers must recognize and address differences in the students' physical characteristics, changing body weight distribution, shifting of the body's center of gravity, growth spurts, and development

of binocular and peripheral vision, in addition to emotional and social characteristics. Body proportions change in adolescence.

What are some ways in which capacity can be increased in all bodies? All bodies have unrealized potential. Muscles can be strengthened—many muscle fibers normally go unused. All joints have a range of motion that can be increased. Our bodies usually respond to stress during the growth period by becoming more capable. Cardiovascular function can be increased. Teachers will need to know enough to ensure that the activities they develop for students promote progressive physical benefits.

Strength

Strength (meaning "muscular strength") has traditionally been one of the objectives of a Physical Education program. The fighting soldier of earlier generations had to be physically strong as well as skillful in battle. The objective of increasing strength as part of Physical Education typically wins the whole-hearted support of most male members of the population, because strength is frequently equated with masculinity and is beloved by the body-building community.

The question of how much strength is appropriate has never been satisfactorily answered, however, and trends emphasizing this characteristic in Physical Education have varied. For example, sufficient strength to produce good posture was one quantitative measure; later, the increase of strength to improve function and performance was valued. There is currently much emphasis on strength training—and one is tempted to believe this trend largely reflects the fact that strength is easily measured. After all, convenient experiments that suit thesis requirements can easily be devised, and results can accrue relatively quickly. The current emphasis on strength training may also reflect the widely held belief that such activities burn more calories. Some teachers may be tempted to measure strength because it is relatively easy to assess and one can readily show improvement in an individual. (As always, to use such a result to compare different children is wrong.) Nevertheless, improved strength should not be valued in isolation, but rather assessed in relation to improved capacity or function. Depending on the person's body type, the "Superman" physique may be completely unattainable for many individuals.

The earliest work on increasing muscular strength was based on the principle of overload, which was first stated by Lange in 1917. The harder muscles are forced to work, the stronger they will get. A muscle works when its fibers contract, so the process of strengthening is a question of calling into play more fibers. In contrast, to speak of "stretching" a muscle is inaccurate. Traditionally, strengthening activities forced muscles to work (contract) against resistance; sometimes weights were used to provide this resistance. The amount of weight can be altered to suit individual levels. Obviously, all individuals do not possess the same degree of strength. Likewise, if muscles must work at their greatest capacity, this level will vary between people. The body itself can also provide weight as part of strengthening activities. A curl-up, raising the knees to the chest, will place different demands upon the abdominal muscles depending on whether it is performed while standing, lying on the back, or hanging from a bar.

Various forms of activity have been developed to capitalize on differences in the manipulation of the amount of resistance, the time involved, and the number of repetitions of a movement. Delorme formulated the principle underlying this practice, which is generally known as progressive resistance.

Sometimes research has yielded conflicting results on the effectiveness of certain approaches, and many practitioners in the Physical Education profession have long prescribed differing programs. Nevertheless, all tend to prescribe increased effort of some kind as a means of strengthening the body. Be aware that isolated strengthening exercises do not always improve performance in skilled activities requiring strength, even when the particular muscles concerned have been strengthened. We must always ask about the goal of such activities, "Strength for what?" A strong isometric contraction in one position does not necessarily mean as strong a contraction of the same muscle in a slightly different position. Consider the shot-putter who resorted to weight training to improve performance: He gained muscle strength as a result of this activity, but was unable to put the shot any farther.

Repetition of one type of movement does not increase the strength of the performance of a different type of movement. As a consequence, the results of strengthening activities are highly specific. Teachers would do well to examine the purpose and function of activities before they devise and use artificial means of producing strength either

Assignment 2–4

Stand. Raise one knee waist high, then the other. Repeat. Try to be aware of the effort involved. You can hold on to something to help your balance.

Lie on the floor on your back. Repeat raising the knee to waist level. The lying position enables you to raise both knees at the same time. Again, be aware of the effort involved.

Hang from a bar supported by the arms alone. Repeat the preceding exercise using first one leg, and then both legs.

with weights or specially designed exercises (e.g., sit-ups, push-ups).

Another crucial factor in encouraging children to work with increased effort is motivation. Much of the emphasis in a modern society is geared toward eliminating effort. Historically, many individuals did not consider physical labor to be a worthy activity. Girls and women, in particular, were often taught that perspiration and the strain of working toward the limits of physical capacity were undesirable or unladylike. Even in modern-day Physical Education, specially designed strengthening programs are unlikely to succeed unless the individual concerned wants them to.

When working at the limits of human capacity, fortunately a very strong self-preservation instinct comes into play. This factor may have a stronger effect in women than in men.

The key to increasing strength may be experience, since you never know what you can do until you try, and increased awareness of capacity results in increased capacity. If we wish to improve the muscular strength of children's bodies, we should seek to stimulate their effort at the limits of their existing capacity. Our challenge will be not to impose hard work, but rather to organize our lessons so that the children want and are able to extend themselves. The activities we devise will need to be varied if we want to encourage all-round development. Ideally, these activities will be performed frequently in normal life and be both interesting and challenging to children. After all, there would be little purpose in performing sit-ups unless sit-ups were a normal part of adult life (in which case children may be expected to attempt them whether we teach them or not).

As a profession, we may not yet know enough about the normal physical life of young children. Perhaps school-based Physical Education programs should make provisions for different forms of locomotion, using the body in a variety of ways, such as rolling, jumping, crawling using the hands to support the body weight, upside-down activities, curling up and stretching out, twisting the body, arching, bending, rotating, rocking, climbing, hanging, swinging, dropping, running, dodging, chasing, wrestling, lifting, holding, pulling, pushing,

Assignment 2–5

Do a literature search for research studies that relate to the acquisition, retention, and loss of physical capacity.

spinning, sliding, throwing, kicking, catching, striking, and bouncing.

Children may also invent new activities if given an opportunity to do so. A wide experience is a prerequisite for a wide capacity; intensive experience would create intensive capacity. Lifting the total body weight (as in climbing), supporting a partner, resisting a partner, and manipulating the body weight in a variety of suspended positions are all activities that demand a great deal of strength; therefore, attempting them will create the strength to the level at which they are performed. Of course, limitations of strength

will be different in different individuals, so it will be essential to use a teaching method in which individual children work on their own at different levels of achievement, ideally at the upper limits of what they are capable. Material on this issue is presented in Chapter 10, which covers body management and gymnastic movement. Teachers have a responsibility to encourage maximum activity to the limits of their students' capacity. To do so, Physical Education professionals will need to make careful observation of young children in a natural, stimulating environment and determine the ways in which their interest is piqued by strengthening activities.

The ability to support the body weight by reflexive grasping is present at birth. Photos have been taken showing a 5-day-old baby girl hanging from a horizontal rope and lifting straight legs (or at least holding them in an extended position nearly parallel to the floor). If you performed Assignment 2–4, you would know how difficult this task is! Presumably, if this capacity were exercised, it would not disappear. All children, including very young children, will climb if given an opportunity.

The reader is reminded, however, that a self-protective mechanism cannot operate fully unless a child is allowed to choose and is not forced to attempt activities. Perhaps the safest program for the next few years would be to emphasize activities that are invented and chosen by the children rather than imposed by adults, given that our knowledge of the physical capacity of young children remains very limited.

Danger could arise if children feel under any pressure to attempt particular feats. Experience with climbing apparatus has shown that, when left to go at their own pace, children select activities within their own capacity. As strength improves over time, children increase their capacity accordingly.

The task for the teacher is to stimulate working at the upper limits of capacity, while still allowing the child the choice of activity. It is also important to realize that in the artificial situation of a school and within the short period of time devoted usually to intensive physical activity, there will be a very definite role for a teacher who wishes his or her students to increase muscular strength.

In the school context, the environment is largely under the control of the teacher. It may be possible to manipulate the environment so that strengthening opportunities are increased. The provision of climbing apparatus, ropes, hills, trees, car tires, and large apparatus such as boxes, bars, trestles, ladders, benches, tables, and tumbling mats will undoubtedly stimulate the strengthening activities of climbing, hanging, swinging, running uphill, jumping, lifting, carrying, pulling, and pushing. Some German schools have installed large sand pits, reflecting the belief that running in sand is more strengthening. Other schools have natural climbing obstacles readily available, such as rocks, tree stumps, trees, fences, walls, and posts. A tetherball area may not cause much strengthening activity if

the ball is used; if the post is strong enough and no hooks protrude, however, it makes an excellent piece of equipment for the would-be climber.

Discrimination is needed: The jungle gym usually has too many bars; some apparatus is not high enough off the ground to allow taking the weight on the arms alone; and the overhead ladder will be better used if the children do not follow one another in sequence, thereby limiting the invention and amount of time spent by the child in front. It will be more strengthening if children are allowed to pull themselves up a slide as well as to slide down it. If swinging is available, then removal of seats or knots in ropes would be more strengthening.

Sitting still or holding a stationary position while apparatus moves is passive and presents hazards in the control of momentum. A net, for example, may be moved or jerked by other children. Although the rule of "no touching" may be practiced, children also have to learn that what they do may affect others, especially if they are close by. Overcrowding on large apparatus must not be allowed. Swinging on ropes is a very popular activity—but if a row of climbing ropes is available, for example, children must learn to swing straight or to control their swinging action so that it does not impede others. Collisions should be avoided. To stay passive on a moving apparatus requires strength.

If heavy pieces of apparatus such as benches are available, then children can be encouraged to carefully and slowly push, pull, lift, and carry this equipment. Older children can lift and carry each other if sensible enough to cooperate. In addition, contests between evenly matched pairs are very strengthening and can be done in a great variety of ways. Consider the following activity: Find a partner your own size. Shake hands and grip tightly. Then try to pull them across the room. Put both hands flat together and push against your partner. Try using your side (or back, feet, hips, and so on).

Even in a classroom, the teacher can engage students in strengthening activities. "Let's push the walls down!" for example, has proven very popular with children. If teachers realize that the overload factor is necessary to increase strength, ample opportunities can be found to include other strengthening activities in the classroom. Of course, care will be needed to ensure safe procedures and responsible activity. This includes responsibility not only for self but also for others.

When a muscle is not working, it relaxes. This relaxation normally results from a process of reciprocal innervation when the opposing or antagonistic group of muscles contracts. Utilizing this principle can often relieve cramp in a muscle. A cramp in a calf muscle, for example, can be relieved by pushing the heel down and lifting the toes.

Stronger muscles can mean muscles that relax more. At some time in a Physical Education program, it may be a good idea to teach relaxation or "going floppy" to young children, although this idea will probably be easier to grasp after students have engaged in strenuous activity or when the lesson is linked with going stiff or clenching muscles.

Strictly speaking, one does not want relaxation when landing from a height, or at least the amount of "give" needs to be carefully controlled and related to the speed, force, and angle of the landing and the weight of the performer. It will probably be more helpful to talk about "give" and "control," and bending the knees or hips rather than pointing the toes and landing lightly. Noise is a good guide to a teacher as far as controlling the body on landing is concerned. A well-controlled landing lessens impact and avoids jar; it can be practiced in a variety of ways and situations.

Traditional gymnastic or conditioning programs frequently exercised the body in sections to ensure a balanced development. In contrast, modern conditioning programs tend to overemphasize abdominal strength. In view of the number of minor injuries and the widespread incidence of lower back trouble later in life, perhaps programs should emphasize back-strengthening activities. Lying on the tummy and arching the back, and rocking on the tummy are both good back-strengthening movements. Whole-body activities, which focus on function in a variety of situations, are likely to produce the kind of all-round development that traditional programs value. Some of the most crippling injuries that adults frequently sustain are whiplash effects, which involve the spine. Teachers have a duty to help children to develop strong backs and to become interested in activities that can maintain this condition if possible. Turning and rotating one part of the body upon another should be included in the program for this reason.

Even in the 1960s the importance of early strengthening work was valued for its long-term results:

> In the light of recent findings, strength development is not as transient as was previously believed. Since increased strength may become permanently anchored, so to speak, it appears important that all children should begin participation in vigorous muscular activity at a very early age and continue this activity throughout their lifetimes. This is perhaps the greatest justification for programs of muscular activity for the optimum development of the human organism. (Davis & Logan, 1961, p. 61)

Assignment 2–6

Find a recent study on the development of muscular strength in young children or elementary-aged children. Report your findings.

Flexibility

Flexibility refers to the range of movement possible in the joints of the body. The standard teaching of anatomy for many years has been that muscles both cause and limit movements, but that the ligaments take on this second function in emergencies. This also happens when movements are unexpected and muscles are relaxed, as well as when muscles are fatigued and no longer capable of controlling movement. Normally, if the performer is working at his or her own pace, this point of fatigue is not reached. However, momentum and weight of the human body can often place pressure on ligaments. A good example is the exercise, now largely abandoned, where a performer bent the arms and then opened them out in a side-backward direction upon receiving the command "Arms apart, fling." The flinging action used momentum. To prevent injury to the shoulder joint, most performers instinctively contracted their muscles to minimize the jar at the end of the "fling," thereby strengthening muscles but not improving flexibility.

To improve flexibility one should go to the end of the possible range of motion, hold, relax, and then gently make small pressing movements to stretch the ligaments. An easy experiment for you to try is to bend or turn to the limit. Turn your head sideways, for example, and go gently as far as you can. Hold the position and relax. You will then probably find that you can go considerably farther.

To a certain extent, the process of improving flexibility goes against the natural development of the human body.

After all, the function of ligaments is to bind together and stabilize joints. Human infants have a large range of movement available to them, which decreases as the body grows older. If you had continued to suck your toes, which you did in infancy, you would still be able to do so! The goal of teachers should be to maintain good range of movement by using the capacity so that it does not deteriorate. In cases where the range of movement is already limited, caution must be exerted so that stretching does not take place vigorously. Use gentle pressing movements in the end position.

Greater stretching of ligaments occurs when muscles are relaxed and when children use climbing equipment and hang in a variety of positions; the weight of the body will cause passive stretching of ligaments. Parents who swing young children holding only their hands should be cautious, however, because shoulder joints can be overstretched.

We do not know enough about the relationship between flexibility and performance of skilled movements. Certain ranges of movement at joints are crucial to some skills, while hypermobility can produce problems of dislocation. For example, badminton requires flexible wrists; tennis does not. Forward and backward rolling movements are contraindicated for some students with Down Syndrome who have atlanto-axial instability of the cervical spine. A backward roll requires a good degree of flexion in the cervical spine. If required to do this maneuver, many people will turn the head and roll on the shoulder because the neck is stiff. In contrast, skating and skiing require an outward rotation of the hip, which is frequently not maintained or acquired in a school program.

If a teacher is aware of specific needs, they can be met by taking the movement required to the end of its possible range and then performing gentle pressing movements in the end position. The performer must be active, if possible, in a relaxed way; thus, for purposes of motivation, explanation may be required. It is in the fields of dancing, gymnastics, swimming, and track and field athletics that some of the extremes of flexibility are required. This need goes beyond what is required of both a physical education and a classroom teacher, although some young children are seriously involved in extracurricular activities.

If teachers provide a wide range of activity, encourage a wide variety of body management, use a large apparatus, and prescribe gymnastic movement, flexibility will be maintained at a level that is more than adequate for good health. Allowing children to work at their own level and choose what they do capitalizes on the natural urge to do more—to go farther, higher, or for longer than previously—without injury. The teacher's role is to encourage but not require. Approve of hard, strenuous work and increasing capacity, but do not give grades or rewards based on this type of effort. Encourage children to notice their improvement.

Endurance

Endurance can refer to different kinds of physical capacity. There is muscular endurance, which is localized and affects the ability to do strenuous muscular work. It is noticed particularly when the muscular work is static or a fixed position needs to be held. Local endurance is related to the strength of a muscle, but can be produced by specific training.

There is also the kind of stamina, which is really willpower, where the human body continues fairly moderate activity for a considerable period of time, often against severe climatic conditions, lack of food, or other challenges. Such endurance is perhaps best described as resilience in the face of adversity or a good reaction to stress. In other words, it is a psychological capacity rather than strictly a physiological effect.

A young woman and an experienced pilot lived forty-nine days without food before they were rescued. Not only were they in remarkably good physical condition, but they did not even describe their total experience as horrible. (Glasser, 1965, p. 7)

In this case, the couple never "lost faith" that they would be rescued.

For the purpose of affecting young children's bodies in a school Physical Education program, the primary concern is with cardiovascular endurance—that is, stamina where the physiological basis is cardiovascular. With this type of activity, the heart, lungs, and circulatory system will all be affected. The heart is a muscle, so it will respond similarly to other muscles in the face of overload. The venous circulation is sometimes referred to as a peripheral heart, and obviously the function of the lungs is related to the whole system. In traditional programs, breathing exercises or respiratory gymnastics were used as means to increase cardiovascular endurance. Unfortunately, giddiness was often caused when students took several deep inhalations without need for them. Breathing exercises have since largely disappeared from school Physical Education programs, although they remain a feature of some systems of yoga.

By paying attention to breathing, classroom teachers have a readily available guideline to know if they are affecting children's cardiovascular systems: Children should be exercised to the point of being breathless. Often children can notice that their heart is beating hard, that they are sweating, or that they have red faces. Approve and encourage these observations, as they provide a means of assessment for both teacher and children.

Astrand carried out important research related to the work capacity of children of different ages in the 1950s. His more recent recommendation about physical activity is summarized in the following quote:

The intensity should be sufficiently high to cause a moderate degree of breathlessness, which represents a level of 50%–60% of one's maximal capacity. . . . In the case of most people, the more vigorous and prolonged the activity, the greater are the health benefits, provided that the increments in activity level are not too abrupt. (Astrand, Rodahl, & Stromme, 2004, p. 542)

When strenuous demands are placed upon the body, the initial reaction is to use energy that does not require oxygen—that is, anaerobic activity. Glycogen in the muscle is used as the energy source in such a case, and lactic acid is produced. Oxygen is then required for synthesis of glycogen to replace the amount removed. Anaerobic activity builds up an oxygen debt such that if activity is continued, a balance will be required between oxygen intake and oxygen requirement. This second kind of activity, known as aerobic activity, establishes a steady state.

In 1970, one of this book's authors conducted a research study on the ability of 5- and 6-year-old children to prolong physical activity. The heart rate response to that activity was measured. Study subjects could run, jump, hop, and skip as they pleased, but walking was not allowed. The children participating in this research clearly understood the purpose of the activity, which was to keep moving for a very long time! They were given frequent verbal encouragement but minimal equipment (e.g., a few hoops were provided to prevent boredom). The results amazed all concerned: Three children kept going without stopping for more than two hours! (Boucher, 1971). Our knowledge of young children's capacities is still very limited. As Riddoch (1988) commented, "Whereas much is now known about the benefits and hazards of physical activity in adulthood, in comparison, there is relatively little known about children and young people's physical activity."

Many kinds of activity can cause children to become breathless. The natural means usually exploit various forms of locomotion such as running, jumping, dodging, chasing, skipping, and hopping. Many dance activities cause breathlessness if continued long enough, as does playing games if the children are active enough. Some children have an interest in jogging, cycling, or swimming that can be exploited for endurance training.

As with flexibility and muscular strength, it is important to work at the limits of capacity when promoting endurance. Children should be encouraged to keep going a little bit longer, to go just a bit further than previously.

The initial reaction of the cardiovascular system to this type of activity is to speed up; the heart beats more quickly and the rate of breathing increases. Later, the heart is forced to beat more strongly and a greater portion of the lungs is used. Over a period of time, the heart muscle can become strengthened and enlarged; the circulation can become more efficient with the possibility of increased capillarization of the muscles. The diaphragm is also strengthened and the capacity of the lungs increased. Possibly more alveoli in the lungs are produced, and the whole cardiovascular system can become more adaptable and capable of withstanding greater demands. This increased fitness or efficiency of the cardiovascular system should result in a lessening of the resting heart rate. Lungs with an increased capacity and a large, strong heart will not need to function so often to supply the body's demands at rest. One simple way to determine this status is to measure the resting heart rate, indulge in strenuous activity, and see how quickly the body returns to the normal heart rate. Schools that already use heart rate monitors will find them useful in Movement Discovery lessons for this reason. Notably, when fitness tests are administered, children in a strenuous Movement Discovery program often tend to score highly.

Teachers can confidently cause and encourage breathlessness in normal healthy children. Although the main physical effects of exercise have been discussed, other physical effects of strenuous activity will, of course, be evident.

For instance, it is likely that the body temperature will rise. This means that activity can safely be taken outdoors in many climates, although the initial effect is chilling. To warm children quickly, isometric contractions of large muscles and friction—rubbing particularly the extremities—can be very effective. Normally, heavy clothing, sweaters, jackets, and other apparel should be removed so that it can be worn when the body cools off after exercise. In terms of hygiene, one of the reasons for wearing special clothing for Physical Education is to absorb and remove perspiration; this effect happens only if the clothing next to the skin is changed.

During strenuous activity, all body systems will be stimulated and muscular contractions of the abdominals can have massaging effects on the intestines. Children may want to visit washrooms and drink fluids after engaging in such exercise. Premenstrual cramps may be relieved.

Exercise can have a very slight effect on reducing body fat. Although exercise burns relatively few calories (it would take 7 hours of mountain climbing—with an empty stomach—to consume 1 pound of body fat), the daily difference in physical activity between active and sedentary habits can easily amount to 500 calories. In one week, this mild extra activity would consume a pound of fat.

What is perhaps more relevant in the case of obese children is that regular enjoyable physical activity may help to break a sedentary pattern of living. Obese children tend to be inactive. Similarly, a pattern of life that includes physical activity may help to delay the onset of degenerative diseases, or at least reduce stress.

An increasing body of evidence suggests that physical activity brings about direct health benefits for young children, some of which may persist into adulthood. In young children, skeletal health and bone mineralization and bone density are boosted by all kinds of weight-bearing activities (Kemper, 2000; McKelvie, Kahn, & McKay, 2000). It has also been suggested that this enhanced bone mass from physical activity has the potential to reduce the risk of osteoporosis and associated fractures in later life (Boreham & Riddoch, 2001).

It cannot be emphasized too strongly that while benefits can be acquired in terms of increased flexibility, endurance, and strength, they can also be lost. Benefits likely build up gradually over a period of time and, if acquired while the organism is young, will be retained longer than those acquired quickly in adulthood. Nevertheless, teachers will fail in achieving their physical objectives for children unless they take steps to ensure that physical benefits are maintained over the lifetime. Adults may indulge in strenuous physical activity for a variety of reasons. For example, some activities lend themselves more easily to male/female activity and family physical activities. Conversely, the availability of facilities, cost of equipment, transportation, and time available are all factors that may make participation more difficult. Probably the most powerful factors relate to skill and enjoyment of the ac-

tivity—and we must not fail to promote these incentives in school programs. To do so, teachers must eliminate students' boredom and frustration.

Many young people leave school or college with a desire to develop their personal choices, to make independent decisions, and to get away from a subordinate position. We believe that if a discovery approach has been a feature of teaching, such that choices and independence have been incorporated in Physical Education programs, young adults will retain interest in physical fitness. Confidence and self-esteem often result from development of a skill. Likewise, the physical pleasure and euphoria associated with strenuous physical activity are powerful motivators. The rush of adrenalin is often a part of competition, and endorphins released in the brain during strenuous exercise contribute to a feeling of well-being. The "high" associated with strenuous physical exertion needs to be more widely appreciated by our young people, and firsthand experience is the best teacher.

Cultural Diversity

Today many cultures tend to contribute to the local community and be present in our classrooms. More needs to be known about differences based on culture, if only because culture impinges upon sensory input. Hall (1966, p. 125), for example, describes how a Japanese person can look at the living room of an American family and see it as bare because although furniture is present, it is arranged around the sides and the center of the room is empty. Native American, Inuit, Mexican, and many European cultures all exhibit different child-rearing practices. The previous sensory experience that children have may well influence their responses in Physical Education lessons; the shape of the eyeball may interfere with skill acquisition.

Gender equity is assumed in all the suggested activities. Many cultures have deeply engrained attitudes about

---

Assignment 2–7

Try to notice, observe, and record differences in behavior in a group of children that you think may be due to cultural influences. Watch out for stereotypes like these:

- "Black girls love to dance."
- "Asian boys are very industrious."
- "German children like to know the rules."

Find others!

Very often, "folk wisdom" and "prejudice" are based on such differences. The movie *My Big Fat Greek Wedding* highlighted how "cultural differences" can bind together (and separate) individuals.

suitable activities for males and females, however, which could limit the sensory experience of girls and boys.

Obesity and Body Composition

Many factors have contributed to the staggering obesity levels currently found in U.S. society. The plain truth, however, is that whatever the history of Physical Education is in the Western world, it has *not* produced widespread participation in physical activity for its own sake. Most people are inactive through choice. Obesity in the Western world has reached crisis proportions, and educators, healthcare providers, and others all recognize that we must develop a society that is physically active. Layden wrote an article entitled "Get Out and Play!", in which he reported, "Like the rest of Americans, school-age children are becoming overweight at an alarming rate" (2004, p. 81). Layden also notes, "In this changing culture children who once were viewed as fat—and teased about it—are now considered ordinary" (p. 84). Malina et al. (2004) discuss obesity at length, stating that "the role of the school is especially important for children and adolescents. Because school attendance is mandatory, programs that can be carried within the school setting are a logical focus of efforts to reduce obesity" (p. 546).

Enjoyable participation in strenuous activity and the development of skills in lifelong activities at least offer a familiar context for the control and prevention of obesity.

Summary

We all have a personal physical endowment, whose facets depend very largely on heredity. Our previous physical experience and our cultural background are also relevant in determining our physical capacity. These factors affect our learning of new material and can be both positive and negative forces in driving us to achieve. Most human beings—and particularly children—are more comfortable with uniformity than with difference. When considering the physical factors in human bodies, we need to look at growth and physical development, at the variety in the growth process, and at the different ways bodies respond to training. In this chapter, simple descriptions were provided to help teachers observe and guide the increase in physical capacity among their students. Teachers will be responsible for ensuring that the benefits acquired through physical activity during youth are not lost in adulthood. In addition, in our present culturally diverse society, teachers need to be guided by the children they teach.

Today, the obesity problem has reached crisis proportions in the United States. Teachers must help children to develop intrinsic motivation to engage in strenuous, enjoyable physical activity so that its benefits will remain available to them throughout the life span.

References

Astrand, P., Rodahl, K., Dahl, H., & Stromme, S. (2004). *Textbook of work physiology: Physiological bases of exercise, fourth edition.* Champaign, IL: Human Kinetics.

Boreham, C., & Riddoch. C. (2001). The physical activity, fitness and health of children. *Journal of Sports Science, 19,* 915–929.

Boucher, A. (1971). *Prolonged activity and heart rate response in five and six year old children.* Thesis, Western Washington State College.

Boucher, A. (1977). *Movement toward control* [film]. Funded by a grant from U.S. Office of Education, Bureau of Education for the Handicapped, Washington, DC.

Bowditch, H. (1872). Comparative rate of growth in the two sexes. *Boston Medical and Surgical Journal, 10*(434), 35.

Davis, E., & Logan, G. (1961). *Biophysical values of muscular activity.* Dubuque, IA: Wm. C. Brown.

Glasser, W. (1965). *Reality therapy: A new approach to psychiatry.* New York: Harper & Row.

Hall, E. (1966). *The hidden dimension.* New York: Doubleday.

Heath, B., & Carter, J. (1967). A modified somatotype method. *American Journal of Physical Anthropology, 27,* 57–73.

Kemper, H. (2000). Physical activity and bone health. In N. Armstrong & W. Van Mechelen (Eds.), *Paediatric exercise science and medicine* (pp. 265–272). Oxford, UK: Oxford University Press.

Kennedy, J. (1963, June 10). Commencement address at American University, Washington, DC. Public Papers of the Presidents of the United States: John F. Kennedy.

Layden, T. (2004, November 15). Get out and play! *Sports Illustrated,* 81–84.

Malina, R., Bouchard, C., & Bar-Or, O. (2004). *Growth, maturation, and physical activity.* Champaign, IL: Human Kinetics.

McGraw, M. (1989). *The neuromuscular maturation of the human infant (Classics in developmental medicine).* Philadelphia: J.B. Lippincott.

McKelvie, K., Kahn, K. M., & McKay, H. A. (2000). Is there a critical period for bone response to weight-bearing exercise in children and adolescents? A systematic review. *British Journal of Sports Medicine, 36,* 250–257.

Parnell, R. W. (1958). *Behaviour and physique.* London: Arnold.

Riddoch, C. (1998). Relationships between physical activity and physical health in young people. In S. Biddle, J. Sallis, & N. Cavill (Eds.), *Young and active? Young people and health-enhancing physical activity: Evidence and implications* (pp. 17–48). London: HEA.

Sheldon, W. (1940/1963). *The varieties of human physique.* New York: Harper Bros/Hafner.

Tanner, J. (1961). *Education and physical growth.* London: University of London Press.

Discovering Capacity

"Tomorrow's students must be problem solvers, persons able to make good choices, to create solutions on the spot."
—A. W. Combs (1981)

QUESTIONS TO DISCUSS

1. Can you recall difficulties in learning any physical skill that others did not share? Were you "the odd one out" in any Physical Education learning situation?

2. Can you recall "catching on" quickly in learning any physical skill and not understanding why others had difficulty with it?

3. Were there any situations in your Physical Education history where you were asked to learn a skill you already possessed? Explain. If this was true, what were your reactions or any later effects?

4. Select a physical activity that you are good at. Can you identify a "key component" that helps you perform well? Perhaps there is a thought, idea, attitude, or state that means you do better—for example, "I play a better game when . . ."; "I am at my best if . . ."; "To do well I need to . . ." Discuss with your partner.

5. Recall any major failures you experienced in performance. State how you reacted and describe any consequences.

6. "If a thing is worth doing, it is worth doing badly." Discuss this statement with your partner.

7. In observing professional or highly skilled performers, can you identify why you think some individuals are better than others? Does your partner agree with your choices?

8. In your observation of children, have you noticed any incidents of experimentation with size (e.g., fitting shoes, putting big things in small holes), distance (e.g., how far, long, or short), classification (e.g., by color, shape, or size), or sequence (e.g., this comes first, this comes last)? Describe them.

9. Try to interact with a young child (younger than 8 years) in a simple skill such as catch, throw, kick, or hit. Ask questions about "outcomes" (examples: "What happens if . . ."; "Where will it go?"; "How can you make it . . . ?"). Compare your findings with those of an interaction with either a younger child or a more mature child.

10. Were you ever taught a skill by teachers who could not perform that skill themselves? Did this affect your learning or motivation?

11. While a young child is playing, put a new item within his or her field of vision. Watch and describe what happens. (This may take time. Allow for no initial response.)

One interested observer and colleague once said to one of your authors: "You find out what children would do naturally if left alone and then make a profession out of it."

There should be a great deal of truth in this statement. Unfortunately, historically speaking, it sometimes seems as if the Physical Education profession has tried to prove that it is academically respectable, that children's play or games or natural climbing activity is worthy of study, and so on. In fact, any subject is worthy of study. What academic educational environments should do is develop the process of thinking, the integrity and honesty of fact finding, unbiased thought, the discipline of study, the discovery of where to find knowledge, and so forth. The reason a golf ball has dimples relates to aerodynamics. Watching humming birds can lead to the development of a helicopter.

The modern tendency to absorb knowledge from a teacher, to think the same way as current dominant fashions, is basically noneducational. That is why an attempt

has been made here to encourage you to take the initiative in your own learning, to realize that you are unique and will work better if you believe in what you do and know why you are doing it. You can contribute to the future improvement of teaching. Observe children while you are yourself a student, but also continue to observe them as a teacher. Constantly reevaluate your program as you see the results of your work.

The previous chapter insisted that children are not miniature adults, but rather individual bodies whose activity creates their future capacity, both physical and cognitive. Physical (body) activity is cognitive (mental) in nature; sensory input develops brain cells and organization of the brain and is thought. It is as if the physical activity room, playground, or gymnasium is a laboratory for life and development. Before children reach adolescence, however, assessments focus on only their behavior and performance (meaning "doing," and not "telling"). We cannot

expect children of this age to answer questions verbally about their activities except in a superficial way. The significance and understanding of performance may not yet be known; it is buried in the individual developmental process. For this reason, you should be cautious of assessment activities that require only verbal or written answers.

The Acquisition of Physical Skills

Before you try to meet the practical needs of a teacher in games or pre-sport activities, you can take one step that would be most beneficial: Learn a new physical sport such as riding a bike, water skiing, juggling, snowboarding, swimming, snow skiing, a new racket sport, and so on. Think about the process as you learn your new skill:

- Would you rather be left alone for a short time with the equipment or special situation of the sport, or would you rather be shown what to do?

- If you try to learn to swim, for example, would you like time on your own in the water?

- Do you feel a need for instruction right away? Why?

- How long do you want to be left alone?

- What about boredom? Frustration?

- Do you need to know the rules of the sport or the objective of the activity?

- What about skills needed that involve no other people?

- What about skills needed that are related to what another player does?

- Where does "improvement" lie?

- Is "competition" a factor, either against yourself or against others?

- What constitutes "success" or "motivation" for you?

- How would you (or do you) feel if there are observers?

- Do you want your instructor to be an expert or at least able to perform the skill?

- Do you want to feel you can ask questions when you are ready, or would you rather be told what to aim for?

The following subsections describe some factors that have been deemed relevant to the acquisition of physical skills. Research often isolates actions and measures a variety of factors.

MOTIVATION

No matter how good the teacher, the equipment, the conditions, and other factors, if an individual is not interested in learning a skill, little progress will be made. Enthusiastic teachers sometimes assume that learners will be motivated (here we are talking about being motivated in the skill or sport, not being motivated to please the teacher). Teachers should use the longer-lasting intrinsic motivation to encourage development of a skill. If the motivation is too intense, however, it may actually interfere with learning. Some extrinsic motivation can be very intense, such as the need to please a parent, teacher, or another person, or the need to earn a high grade. Fear of failure can produce anxiety in such cases.

If previous activity has been restricted, the body's need for "therapeutic" activity may override the ability to focus. For example, limited previous physical activity may have prevented the necessary neuromuscular physiological development needed to support learning a skill. This is a very complex consideration—but think perhaps of a learner who has never seen snow and tries to put on skis. Many adults regret starting a new sport "too late" in life. They may learn the skill, but probably will not reach the level of expertise that might have been attainable with earlier experience. Think of a lifelong ice hockey player who is given a soccer ball on a grass field, the person might be highly skilled in one sport, but how "clumsy" would his or her initial soccer playing be? And for how long?

Upsetting experiences will obviously affect motivation. The effects of early "mistakes" can prove very off-putting, more so for some people than for others. If other people watch or see the individual's initial attempts at a new skill or if the learner is too self-conscious, progress will be inhibited.

If there is no guidance or instruction, a learner often continues with a method he or she happens to hit on at

---

Assignment 3–1

Find a piece of research relating to the development of skill in your "new" sport.

first. If this behavior becomes "grooved," it may be extremely difficult to change later on. Often beginners at tennis face the net to hit the ball; swimmers attempting to learn the breaststroke may develop a "screw kick," a kind of scissors action. As these examples suggest, early experience can be misleading as well as helpful.

QUALITY INSTRUCTION

No instruction can be preferable to wrong instruction, provided that the desired outcome of a skill is presented. If a learner has an idea of the game of tennis, sees a film or high-level game, and knows that the ground strokes are quick, strong, and placed carefully, attempts to replicate this model would probably prevent the person from facing the net and playing "pat-ball"—that is, lobbing the ball over the net with a scooping action. If no expert knowledge is available, a variety of techniques should be encouraged so that later expert instruction can build on flexible behavior. This is an important consideration for classroom teachers.

We have also realized that individual bodies vary and that the best technique may not be available to some learners. There is a long history in sport in which an expert's best technique is abandoned in favor of a new expert's best technique. For a short period of time, for example, a roll or straddle technique was taught in the high jump event—until a top athlete (Dick Fosbury) cleared the bar by going over backward. Now the "Fosbury flop" is the norm in this sport.

Who discovered a slam-dunk in basketball?

Who first used a double-handed backhand in tennis?

Which expert first used a straight-arm stroke recovery in back crawl swimming?

Even the way to hold the special equipment may represent a fashion rather than the best technique for a particular individual. In the past, a practice has often been presented as the "one correct way," to be passed down from professor to teacher to children without regard to its effect on top-level performance and the individual's capacity. Thus a teacher might stop a child from using a two-handed backhand in tennis because it is seen as in-

Assignment 3-2

Find several examples of a new best technique replacing established practice.

correct, even though it is widely used by top players. What is now the best way to serve in tennis? Watch the top players. Technique relates to an individual body and skill. As a consequence, a particular technique does not always adapt well to another person.

Any top-level performer also needs to be prepared for failure. It is possible that the learning process should include deliberate mistakes to enable the student to learn the limits of his or her effectiveness.

Many years ago, instructors believed that going through the motions of an action slowly would facilitate analysis and learning. Swimming was even taught using the arm and leg actions on land and not in the water ("swimming land drill"). Coaches sometimes guided the action by physical assistance, by guiding while holding the performer.

Skill is highly specific. Not only is it specific to a learner and the learner's particular body, but it is also specific to a real situation and the equipment used. The overhead smash in badminton is a different skill from the overhead smash in tennis. A mid-air somersault is different from a forward roll, even though the body action may look similar.

A learner of a new sport will need some kind of model. If you have never seen the new sport you are learning, being successful in the new sport will be more difficult. In today's world, top-level performance is familiar to many. Nevertheless, to help a learner, the teacher may have given a demonstration. This type of modeling has very limited

Anecdote 3-1

An adult gave a light, small, plastic hockey stick and ball to a 6-year-old girl and said nothing. Initially the little girl used the stick as a fishing rod behind a sofa. She later swung it and in the space of three minutes discovered what an adult would call "dribbling" (hands apart on the stick), hitting (hands together), hitting for distance, and aiming for a target.

Anecdote 3-2

A frustrated track and field coach described teaching a 12-year-old boy to high jump. The youngster was a "natural" with tremendous ability to use his body, even though he could not read or write. The objective was to learn the Western roll technique (the strategy used before the days of the "Fosbury flop"). Everything had been tried—watching an expert, drawing a diagram, practice galore with a reasonable response, holding the "position" in a stationary position on the floor, and so on. Finally, the coach said, "Reggie, next time you do it, kick your chin with your knee and reach with your arms for my hankie." He put his handkerchief in the appropriate corner of the pit. Result: a "perfect" Western roll.

value. A demonstrated skill is simply not the same as the real thing in performance: Even an excellent technique can be used inappropriately in the context of a particular activity. Often attempts are made to give cues when teaching. It is vital that these cues focus on the end result of the action. Cues also need to take a form that can be understood and have meaning for the performer. We vary widely in our ability to interpret instruction.

Direction, speed, and strength are usually important when acquiring a new skill, although what the body does to achieve these characteristics relates more to Newtonian physics, individual neuromuscular development, and physique than to any simple cue a teacher may give. "Watch the ball" is probably a useless cue. Instead, there are many clues to the behavior of an approaching ball that relate to the visual environment and the actions of the thrower that have more importance. Likewise, "Watch the ball on to your bat" is misleading; no expert ball player ever does this. Manual guidance also gives false kinesthetic sensation and never occurs in the real-world situation.

As you struggle to learn a very great deal in a short time (because success in the sport or activity itself pushes you onward), you will need the real equipment to use while learning. Of course, real equipment is usually expensive. If you are forced to learn in a large group (class) and if the real equipment is not available, it will mean dividing the large group into smaller subgroups and rotating equipment. Real equipment is typically made for adults. Imagine the difference it would make if there were child-sized basketball courts with lower baskets and smaller soccer fields with smaller goals. Shots on goal and goalkeeping skills, for example, both relate to the size and shape of the goal.

You must have practical experience. Being told what to do will not change your skill level.

Skilled actions are those that produce the desired effect. It is not helpful to practice an action where knowledge of the results of that action is not immediately available. Practicing an action must be the real action in terms of its result—not the pattern of the movement or the way it looks to an observer. Dribbling around traffic cones for any sport is not what is required. Although dribbling may be used to deliberately slow the pace of a game so that players can get into position, a basketball travels faster when it is passed. In fact, good passing is a far more crucial activity in many team games. Successful passing does not depend on the body action used to send the object away, although good skill is desirable. The far more important skills to be learned are the timing so that the object will be where it is needed when the moving player gets there and the kind of pass used relative to the skill of the receiver. Also, one does not have to make judgments only relative to the situation and one's teammate, but must also take into account the likely responses of the opposing team, its situation, those players' skill in interception and blocking spaces, and whatever other difficulties present themselves in the course of fast-moving competition.

Thus practicing passing, and passing slowly to a teammate with no opposition has limited value.

The condition of the surface on which the contest is being played—including the weather, temperature, and wind direction—also has effects. Apart from outwitting the opposition, skills must often be adapted to external conditions.

As you progress in learning your new sport, you will need and want to practice. Periods of practice should be short and intense, rather than longer and half-hearted. Practice at the speed required in the game if possible. An action performed at top speed is not the same as one performed slowly.

You may find it encouraging to know that mental practice can be effective—but the image you practice mentally must be a good one. Replay that marvelous moment in your mind. You will need to know exactly what was marvelous, which means that feedback from a reliable source is essential.

You will probably want to know some rules of your new sport, if they exist. It will be helpful to think of ways to be "clever" while still conforming to the rules.

So often in the past, we have focused on the learner and how he or she performs, rather than taking note of the results of the learner's actions. Essentially, sports involving other players require complicated and instant decisions based on changing situations. If the structure of

Assignment 3-3

Identify the least helpful incidents or instructions in your new sport. Mention anything that interfered with your progress in learning your new skill.

the game is understood (the "whole"), skills will develop more quickly. If reactions to plays can be predicted, and if the opposition can be deceived or fooled, this is good. Team sports are essentially an intellectual activity: One team outwits the opponent, although occasionally superior skill is all that is required.

If you are learning a new skill, you will be gaining insight into the complex process involved—and this is with your mature body. As an adult learner, you can think and apply your thoughts to the work at hand. Your eyes are mature and give consistent observations. Peripheral vision is developed, and you may already have some physical skills. In contrast, children have immature bodies (see Chapter 2), a factor that must be taken into account when gauging their learning.

Psychomotor Learning and Children

For many years, educators talked about mind and body as if they were separate entities—a healthy mind in a healthy body. Physical growth in children is certainly obvious, but it was many years before it was linked with the developmental nature of thinking.

As mentioned earlier in this book, the many cross-sectional studies conducted in the realm of Physical Education provided little information of value for teachers. We are not concerned here with averages or class standards, after all. In contrast, longitudinal studies brought about new insights that allowed teachers to teach children, rather than a curriculum subject called Physical Education. A similar development happened in education when the actual process of learning finally became the focus of instruction.

Much of the new understanding developed from the work of Jean Piaget, a Swiss epistemologist. Piaget was interested in the structure of knowledge and the process of development and learning within an individual. He initially used his own children as subjects, conducting perceptive and exact observations of them from their birth. As part of his study, he looked at the process of reasoning used by children before they developed language. Along the way, Piaget realized that children simply think differently from adults.

If teachers are to achieve more than incidental learning on a "hit or miss" basis, they must have knowledge of the

nature of children's intellectual processes and some understanding of the sequence in which such development occurs. All knowledge that we wish children to acquire or all curriculum content will have to be translated into that which children are capable of learning. Importantly, teachers must realize that process will vary among individuals.

We have also discovered that *all* learning is physical in young children. When dealing with children in the elementary school, Physical Education as a subject in a curriculum really does mean education. The basis of the developmental sequence is a continuous expansion from simple sensory-motor differentiations and experienced realizations of performance to active operational experience of the environment. Gradually external actions become symbolized and internalized, and the development of language occurs. It takes several years for a child to develop an internal system for mentally experiencing the world of his or her physical existence, and the organization of this understanding continuously depends on action and activity. Not until adolescence does the child become able to function in the abstract and "think" in the traditional sense of the word.

Recognition of this fact necessitates changes in teaching methods and curriculum content in our schools. Although many children may superficially conform to adult standards, give right answers, and "learn" abstract concepts, we must look deeper for genuine understanding. To do so, teachers may need to alter their assessment of intelligent

Anecdote 3-5

Julie, a fourth-grade student, asked a classroom teacher about how worms reproduce. Julie had noticed baby worms in the classroom wormery on the science table. The teacher showed her the chart on the wall above the wormery showing the internal organs of a worm and carefully explained it. "But that's not a worm," Julie objected. The teacher persisted and Julie considered the evidence. Finally, she stated firmly, "No! That's not a worm. It's too big."

behavior in children. It is intelligent for a child, possibly aged 6 or 7 years, to look at two equal quantities of modeling clay and say that one is larger than the other when one of the two quantities has been rolled into a long sausage. If the child is in the intuitive stage of thought and has not yet established a realization of the conservation of matter, the sausage looks longer, a fact that may mean "more" to the child. The senses provide information that is believed, and the sausage looks like "more" because it is longer.

Piaget has also delineated certain logical operations such as classifying, grouping, ordering in series, differentiating, and coordinating, and has shown that these abilities also follow a sequential development and constitute much of the basis of thought. This notion suggests exciting new possibilities for teachers, who often find it beneficial to focus on operations or functions rather than on subjects and content. It also suggests that teachers could use the normal content of children's Physical Education lessons as an important basis for later learning of an academic nature. There will be many opportunities during Physical Education lessons, if children are continuously active on their own initiative, for a teacher to question handling of materials; anticipated outcomes of actions; experiments by children in manipulating speed, size, weight, area, themselves, others, round objects, and linear objects; and so on. Much will be learned about the stage of individual children's thinking, which may assist a teacher to match better teaching materials and technique to the individual child. What many Physical Education teachers take for granted—namely, the tremendous variety of experience included in lessons—may, in fact, be of vital importance to intellectual development. Requiring the child to take the initiative to think, to plan, to interact with a variety of objects, situations, and other children is readily available in a Physical Education lesson using a discovery approach. It is also crucial to later development. "When children engage in varied practice, they are able to develop a general capability for producing many different versions of the movement" (Schmidt & Wrisberg, 2008, p. 146).

Piaget describes the overall process of intellectual development as equilibration. In equilibration, the organism constantly tries to balance the intrusions of the social and physical environment with the internal structures, which may be genetically determined, the result of maturation, or part of the emergent organization of previous experience. Equilibration is a dynamic process of interaction. At one extreme, children may use assimilation to bend the world to themselves; at the other extreme, they may use accommodation when they conform to or imitate reality. The child is always the agent. Sometimes the child assimilates the world, absorbing and organizing experiences around the activities that produce them. At other times, the child accommodates to reality and the environment, such that the "within" interacts with the "without."

Assignment 3–4

[T]he greater the variety of situations to which the child must accommodate his behavioral structures, the more differentiated and mobile they become, the more rapid is his rate of intellectual development, and the greater is his range of interests in the novel and the new.
—J. M. Hunt (1961, p. 259)

Relate this statement to current educational theory and practice. Collect at least six similar statements from different current authors.

It is vital that we give young children adequate time and experience to learn new skills. They need to work on their own. They should be allowed and encouraged to change, reorder, invent, revise, and extend their interactions and encounters with the world. It is this constant balancing of assimilation and accommodation that can give the satisfaction of understanding and learning.

The process of development is a continuous one and does not proceed in a series of jumps. As always, there will be great variations between individuals in terms of how they work their way through this sequence. Nevertheless, the concrete operational stage of development will be observed among most of the children in elementary education. The youngest children in our program—those in preschool and the primary grades (preK–3)—will most probably exhibit characteristics of symbolic preoperational and intuitive thought.

Many researchers in education have modified and expanded Piaget's work. As a consequence, what you learn in other teacher preparation and educational psychology courses is very important. The kind of program recommended here for the Physical Education of young children can be seen as a powerful tool to enhance the total education of individual children.

Classroom teachers are ideally placed to discern this level in the many interactions in an active Physical Education lesson. Children can be encouraged verbally to think, experiment, and interact both with the teacher and with other children: "Discover what happens when the ball is bigger? If the bat is heavier? When you kick a ball upward or faster? Roll your body sideways! Curl up while you are hanging!" and on and on, as far as the teacher's ingenuity goes.

This recommendation should not be interpreted as meaning that much time should be spent on talking, telling, or verbalizing, however. The essential point is that different activities will present the child with different information—sensory, muscular, vestibular, tactile, proprioceptive, kinesthetic, and so on. The child will balance the "within" and "without" over a period of time. Teachers should see repetitive patterns, a growth in confidence, and consistency in performance as the child matures both physically and mentally. Roughly at age 7 years, structural thought begins developing, which brings an awareness of reversibility of actions and the understanding of conservation.

Classroom and Physical Education specialist teachers have a wonderful opportunity to enrich the lives of their students and affect their lifelong learning. To do so, however, they must recognize that logical operations and abstract thought need a basis of concrete operational activity. It seems likely that the quality of this more adult thinking will depend on the quality and variety of the concrete activity that precedes it. Remember: "The greater the variety of situations to which the child must accommodate his behavioral structures, the more differentiated and mobile they will become" (Hunt, 1961, p. 259).

The organization of the brain is mainly dependent upon the sensory input it receives. Teachers using physical activity as part of the educational process can deliver a wide range of stimulation and sensory input that would not otherwise be made available to children. Adaptability

Anecdote 3–6

Andrew (aged 3 years) was sent to his room after misbehavior when company was present. After a while (while his mother and two adults watched with astonishment), Andrew emerged from his room with his eyes shut. He headed for the door into the garden. When he bumped into a sofa, he opened his eyes. Upon seeing the adults, he was "horrified" and quickly closed his eyes again before continuing out. Andrew believed he could not be seen if he could not see.

Assignment 3-6

Relate two or three major concepts from your studies in learning, child development, or educational psychology to any part of a Physical Education lesson.

Some Factors Affecting Individual Differences in Learners

Interests

Prior movement experience (e.g., opportunities with parents, recreation programs, community competitive sports)

Learning styles (e.g., preference for kinesthetic, auditory, or visual learning)

Self-confidence

Cognitive capacity

Fitness levels: a continuum from very fit to very poor levels of fitness

Strength: a continuum from very strong to very weak

Flexibility: range of movement, from stiff to loose

Cardiovascular endurance

Muscular endurance

Coordination

Body type (e.g., tall, short, muscular, thin, stocky)

Emotional differences

Motivation

Previous social experience

Cultural background

Attitudes

Sensory integration

is a feature of the highly skilled person in some types of skilled performance.

Of course, we do not yet know enough about the process through which child development occurs. Possibly repeated stimuli may create cell assemblies in the brain, which later develop into larger association areas. Phase sequences may develop as a result of repeated sensory stimulus. Repetition, however, is clearly a key function in children's learning. They love to repeat newly acquired skills and learned responses. It is possible, too, that children "try things out" while this organization of the brain is emerging; to facilitate this process, teachers must allow their students a lot of free practice with any activity and skill. Tolerance for mistakes can be developed. The means available to children for the gathering and coordination of information is activity—and that means physical activity.

There is also a motivating factor here that might be termed appetitive behavior. As organization, assimilation, and sensory input cause structural neurophysiological changes in the developing brain, the child develops a need for "more." That is, the brain constantly seeks stimulation; the effects of learning cause more learning; emerging capacities push us to do more. Although capacity precedes function, the earlier activity causes the physical basis of the capacity to be developed. In other words, function precedes structure.

Many educators have built on Piaget's work through their own research. One interesting blend of theories is known as constructivism. By the 1980s, the research of Dewey and Vygotsky had blended with Piaget's work in developmental psychology into the broad approach of constructivism. "The basic tenet of constructivism is that students learn by doing rather than observing. . . . Active practice is the key of any constructivist lesson. To make an analogy, if you want to learn how to ride a bike, you don't pick up a book on bicycle theory—you get on the bike and practice it until you get it right. It is this repetition of practice and review that leads to the greatest retention of knowledge"(Carvin, 2009).

Students will find many similarities between Movement Discovery and the 12 principles called essential to constructivist teaching as enumerated in J. G. Brooks and M. G. Brooks (1993), *A Case for Constructivist Classrooms.* Brooks and Brooks assert that the need for constructivist

Assignment 3-7

A bird does not fly because it has wings; it has wings because it flies.
—R. Ardrey (1966)

Discuss this statement in the light of your views on evolution.

Assignment 3-8

Add to the preceding list of factors affecting learning from your own reading, your observations, and information learned in other courses related to child development, motor learning, psychology, or pedagogy. Compare your list with that compiled by your partner.

classrooms is much stronger and more critical today when so much emphasis is placed on assessment and accountability in test results. You will notice parallels to these principles suggested throughout this text.

It is essential that you link the information in this chapter with your learning in educational psychology classes and other courses involving pedagogy.

to occur, the active learner needs to develop his or her own understanding and knowledge of results. Teachers of children in the elementary school grades must have an awareness of the complex process underlying the development of neurophysical organization in the brain, individual differences among learners, and the experiential nature of learning. To be effective, a teacher needs to develop children's confidence in themselves. To do so, the teacher must adopt a pedagogy that involves the children in their own learning, allows for individualization of content material, and taps into the joy of discovery.

Summary

Great insights into the teaching of skills can come from our own learning process. The quality of instruction is crucial and needs to be based on each particular learning situation. The overall most powerful factors are maturation (readiness) and motivation. Intrinsic motivation is preferable, and one person's interest and enjoyment are often contagious. Much time has been wasted when teachers insist on teaching a hypothetical "correct way" to perform physical skills. More attention should be paid to physical and maturational cognitive capacities, the proper context for performance, and the desired outcomes.

Many traditional cues, manual guidance, and practice conditions are used inappropriately. For effective learning

References

Ardrey, R. (1966). *The territorial imperative.* New York: Delta/Dell.

Brooks, J. G., & Brooks, M. G. (1993). *In search of understanding: The case for constructivist classrooms.* Alexandria, VA: Association for Supervision and Curriculum Development.

Carvin, A. (2009). *Constructivism basics.* Retrieved October 11, 2009, from http://www.edwebproject.org/constructivism.basics.html

Combs, A. W. (1981). What the future demands of education. *Phi Delta Kappa, 62,* 369–372.

Hunt, J. M. (1961). *Intelligence and experience.* New York: Ronald Press.

Schmidt, R. A., & Wrisberg, C. A. (2008). *Motor learning and performance* (4th ed.). Champaign, IL: Human Kinetics.

Discovering
Movement Discovery

We shall not cease from exploration
And the end of all our exploring
Will be to arrive where we started
And know the place for the first time.
—T. S. Eliot, *Little Gidding* (1942)

Exploration "Play Rules"
These rules can be stated as follow:
(1) you shall investigate the unfamiliar until it has become familiar; (2) you shall impose a rhythmic repetition on the familiar; (3) you shall vary this repetition in as many ways as possible; (4) you shall select the most satisfying of these variations and develop these at the expense of others; (5) you shall combine and recombine these variations one with another; and (6) you shall do all this for its own sake, as an end in itself.
—Desmond Morris, *The Naked Ape* (1967)

QUESTIONS TO DISCUSS

1. Reread your journal of observations of children. Outline some suggestions for a teaching method that would incorporate what you have learned from these observations. (Work with a partner if you like.)

2. Consider your personal experience of teachers who have taught Physical Education. Try to discern any personality traits or character of those you deemed to be successful.

3. Describe conditions in a school situation that might cause a teacher to be dominant and use a teacher-directed method in Physical Education lessons.

4. Justify your opinion of whether Physical Education in the elementary school should be taught by classroom teachers or Physical Education specialists.

5. Observe Physical Education lessons in two different schools. With a stopwatch, time the actual amount of physical activity in them.

6. State whether you consider noise to be permissible in an activity room. Define the kinds of noise you would find acceptable.

7. Mention any instances where in your opinion "freedom" was harmful or unhelpful to children. Justify your opinion.

8. Describe any skills that are outside the traditional Physical Education program but that you think should be included in this program. Justify your opinion.

9. Describe what you consider to be good relationships between teachers and children. Focus on Physical Education lessons.

10. Recall any instances of "lining up" and "waiting for a turn" in your own experience of Physical Education lessons. Discuss ways of teaching responsible self-management.

The previous chapters of this book tried to raise awareness of the individual nature of learning and the physical bases in young children that are foundational for all growth and development. It is essential that you relate this material to your current studies in the fields of pedagogy, psychology, motor learning, and child development. For example, the physical effects of exercise were mentioned in Chapter 2. In April 2009, a study on this topic that was conducted in Canada and the United States was featured on Canadian National Television (CBC); search the web to find it (Ratey & Hagerman, 2008). (One hopes you will have a richer understanding of "exercise" than using weights and treadmills!) Chapter 3 described the "revolution" in research triggered by Jean Piaget (1896–1980) when he published his studies about the intellectual development of children. Claims have also been made that multiple intelligences develop in early childhood. For example, Gardner (1983/2003) has proposed the existence of 11 types of intelligence: linguistic, logical–mathematical, musical, bodily–kinesthetic, spatial, interpersonal, intrapersonal, naturalist, spiritual, existential, and moral. Gardner uses the phrase "individually configured education" to describe what has traditionally been called "child-centered" or "individualized" instruction.

Whatever the label used, it is clear that learning takes place at an individual level. This is inevitable.

Put another way, if we do not allow individual responses, we will not meet the needs of children, and the children will lose out on many learning opportunities. Active learning—in which the child is allowed to take the initiative—capitalizes on natural drives to explore and to follow interests. Intrinsic motivation is highly effective in this regard, and can be used to appreciate differences in others. It can also allow choices where some responses and skills are developed at the expense of others. Tolerance of self and others is more likely to develop where differences are welcomed and honored. If children are self-motivated and allowed to develop much of the content material in education, a teacher is freed to focus on other important tasks. A teacher controls the environment in which children will learn; a teacher helps a child to develop self-confidence;

a teacher communicates pleasure in achievement and a sense of adventure in learning; a teacher supports, stimulates, and helps children to make the many adjustments required when working in a large group of other children.

Of course, classroom teachers are also individuals. Their work is profound and demanding. A good teacher gets to know the individuals in a class in a way that many parents cannot. Apart from the wide range of curriculum encountered in most elementary schools, the class has its own unique social dynamics, usually of both genders. Home background, culture, and family relationships may all contribute to or work against learning.

Truly both teacher and learner are caught up in a process of discovery. This text is titled *Movement Discovery*, in recognition of the recommended teaching method in which teaching becomes the causing of learning.

Human movement begins in the womb. Mothers of more than one child often comment that knowledge of differences in children was communicated to them by differences in the children's prenatal activity. The ways in which a fetus moves often prepare the mother for future characteristics of personality, gender, and difference from the child's siblings. Does developmental capacity create activity or does activity create capacity? (See Chapter 3.)

Certainly movement is a powerful medium. Life is inconceivable without movement. Movement is action, movement is activity, movement is active, movement is not still, and movement is not stationary. Movement is doing.

Movement and action are a means of learning about the self and the world in which we live. Through movement, one encounters others. Movement precedes words.

In the recent history of Physical Education in the elementary school, the word "movement" has been used for 50 years—in fact, more often than the term "physical education." As curriculum and teaching methods have changed, "movement" has sometimes been used to encompass the whole program, usually referring to content or "subject matter." You will probably have encountered terms such as Movement Education, Movement Exploration, and the Movement Approach, among others. You may also have heard of Educational Gymnastics, the Indirect Teaching Method (often combined with the Direct Teaching Method), Expressive Movement, Objective Movement, and Inventive Games. Likewise, the word "creative" has appeared frequently in the literature over the decades.

In truth, both content material and teaching methods have changed over the years. Those (often highly skilled teachers) who have valued sports, gymnastics, and dance skills have sometimes thought time spent on exploration and indirect teaching to be wasted time. One of the reasons this text uses the word "discovery" is to highlight the positive outcomes and results of exploratory activity. Children do learn through exploration, and the teacher will profoundly influence what they learn.

Discovery is a result of exploration. One searches, explores, invents, tests, and creates in an effort to find out

what was previously unknown. Cynics may say, "There is nothing new under the sun," but the key point is that the knowledge is new to the learner. Having been discovered by the learner, it is also more likely to be retained. Importantly, as Chapter 3 mentioned, sensorimotor learning has significant effects on the neurological organization of the brain and physical growth and development, and it is likely that variety and having a wide range of experience are vital for that maturation.

In a strange environment, a person's initial exploration may be timid, even fearful. As familiarity is established, however, the process often continues with interest and curiosity and a relaxed enjoyment of opportunity.

A confident learner is often someone who has successfully discovered something about self, the environment, or the world of relationships.

The teacher of young children has a major role to play in helping individuals to develop self-confidence and make realistic assessments of their own and others capabilities. Movement Discovery is an inevitable, powerful teaching method for both children and teachers.

> Movement Discovery presents a paradox. A teacher tells children what to do without telling children what to do.

This is the essence of "open-ended" instruction. Enough guidance and focus are given to stimulate a response, but there will be many ways to comply with the instructions. Children will be able to choose those responses that are at their own level of ability, but not necessarily the same responses demonstrated by other children.

Movement Discovery Defined

This section outlines the Movement Discovery teaching method. It has been defined as including five stages (levels) that are visually displayed as **Figure 4–1**: Movement Discovery Model:

1. Exploration

2. Variety

3. Sequence/extension

4. Synergy—working with others

5. Performance/peak/mastery

Although the Movement Discovery method attempts to delineate stages in progression, progression will, of course, happen at variable rates in individual children. In any one class of children, much overlap will inevitably be seen and different levels must be expected. Transition between stages and progression at individual rates will not be sudden, but rather gradual. This type of development is cumulative and may not take place at an even pace. During a time of overlap, a child may show inconsistencies in achievement. No step-like pattern is intended to be

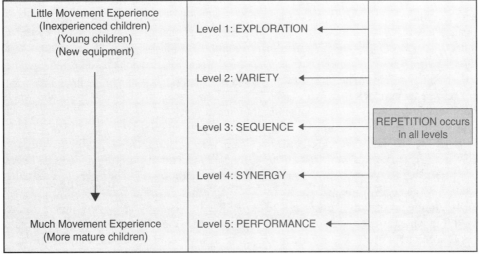

MOVEMENT DISCOVERY MODEL: FOR DEVELOPING A PROGRAM

Little Movement Experience
(Inexperienced children)
(Young children)
(New equipment)

Level 1: EXPLORATION

Level 2: VARIETY

Level 3: SEQUENCE

REPETITION occurs in all levels

Level 4: SYNERGY

Much Movement Experience
(More mature children)

Level 5: PERFORMANCE

FIGURE 4–1 Movement Discovery Model: For Developing a Program

implied here; rather, progression occurs continuously through the levels, which merge into each other.

LEVEL 1: EXPLORATION

Exploration is a natural reaction in normal children. Most creatures feel ill at ease in strange surroundings. In Movement Discovery, the unfamiliar may be represented by a piece of apparatus, a large empty space, or a large group of people. As children grow in self-knowledge, they will also want to experiment and see what their bodies are capable of doing and to discover many ways of interacting with other people. The initial use of small objects should be exploratory. It may also be that children have previously been confined to a small room or desk and need free vigorous activity.

The exploratory level will be prolonged if climbing apparatus is used, as such apparatus provides such a variety of activities to discover. It is essential that children become confident and experienced on apparatus before limitations or challenges are set. At first, manipulating the body while taking the force of gravity into account is quite enough of a problem. This experience will be foundational for future safety, as children need to develop self-confidence in body management.

Younger children will use exploratory movement nearly all the time. It is only as their maturing coordination develops that they become capable of more things. Finding different things to do with a hoop or ball can last a long time with preschoolers and first-graders, for example. All children should have an opportunity to work with all equipment. Even when all children are using the same piece of equipment, teachers can be deceived into thinking that because such a great variety of activities has been observed, the children have done many things. In fact, any one child may have had a chance to do only one thing.

If this teaching method is new, even older children may need a time of exploration.

The exploratory level serves several functions. First, it can show a teacher that children have a much greater potential than was realized.

Second, it enables the teacher to observe and establish modes of behavior. It is important to see whether children are capable of working sensibly on their own. If freedom to work alone represents a very great change (e.g., if the class is used to formal instruction), it is probably unwise and unproductive to give students complete freedom. Until the teacher is sure that children can work sensibly alone, perhaps large apparatus work should be restricted or avoided. This step is only necessary as a temporary measure, however; normally, young children can be given freedom to climb and explore with complete confidence. They do it in parks, in trees, at home, and in many situations, as your record of observations will show. If there are many children and only a few pieces of some apparatus, a routine of exchange and organization will need to be established.

Third, a teacher can observe something of the level of children's' response. For example, it is highly interesting to observe differences of response. Some children react slowly and extend their range of activity only gradually. Others have a "try everything once" attitude and sometimes need to be persuaded to return a second time to discover more possibilities.

Fourth, teachers may stimulate exploration by asking questions: "What else can you do?" "Try using a new piece of equipment . . ." "Find out what you can do with . . ." "Where else can you . . . ?" Teachers may also need to caution the careless: "Try not to interrupt anyone else." "Work alone without touching anyone." "Keep spread out." "Always work in a space."

Fifth, the teacher will need sensitivity to decide how much and when exploration is needed. These decisions will be easier if an abundance of equipment is available. Children cannot be expected to "wait for a turn." Waiting a turn when a child is in the prelogical state of development is wasting time.

Sixth, working at the exploratory level enables a teacher to reorganize and adapt the physical environment. A simple rearrangement of the environment can stimulate many new responses. It is not always possible to anticipate children's use of space or equipment, so apparatus may need to be relocated or additional items provided. Space is very important to make good use of some apparatus. Balls and hoops roll; hitting and striking activities need more space; a run-up may be needed to go "over" a piece of equipment; "swinging" space must not impinge on others; and so on. Activity on the floor or mats often requires its own dedicated space; frequently a stage or platform can be used for this purpose. Walls can be used as apparatus. Teachers may need to control the use of space at this level.

Seventh, use of Movement Discovery at the exploratory level enables a teacher to facilitate the development of self-responsibility in the children. A teacher cannot deliberately challenge students to strive for greater achievement until the students accept a large measure of responsibility for themselves. Particularly on climbing apparatus, a child will need to feel confident enough to reject a teacher's suggestion if he or she feels that the new skill is beyond his or her capacity.

Eighth, children have a chance to try everything out to see what they can do. Many different kinds of games can be played with the same equipment. For example, kicking balls leads to a different kind of game than hitting balls with a bat. Using rackets, paddles, and hockey sticks of different weights and lengths allows children to experiment with how these hitting implements can be used. With small equipment, the admonition "Keep it up" represents a challenge in its own right.

Exploration is also appropriate for older children, particularly when they are presented with the use of new or unfamiliar equipment. It may also be needed when trying out ideas in relationship to another child or group of children. Repetition will be a feature of all levels.

Repetition in Level 1

Level 1 is the stage at which teachers will need to stress repetition the most. Simply saying, "Can you do it again?" may present a major challenge at the exploratory level, because young children are not always aware of what they have done. As young children respond to inner urges and environmental factors, the memory of movement patterns and pathways may not be present. Encourage and affirm repetition, and do not be impatient to ask children to try another way. Sensory input requires stabilizing. Much learning results from repetition at the preschool and kindergarten levels.

1. Sheer repetition often happens naturally during the exploratory period when some children discover pleasurable skills or sensations. The ability to repeat requires some accuracy and memory.

2. This level also tends to facilitate learning from others, because a repeated pattern is more likely to be observed or noticed. Emerging capacity needs repetition to become stabilized.

3. It is important that the child selects what is to be repeated from a wide range of experience. Simply doing the same thing over and over could represent rigidity or lack of ideas. Similarly, there may well be "copying" at this stage from other children. If this action represents an extension of the individual's repertoire and is not merely a passive following, then it is good. If a child complains that another has copied the individual, suggest that the action must have been a very good idea to be worth copying.

4. Although children naturally repeat some activities, at some point they should be asked to focus on one particular response and repeat it. This may require a deliberate re-creation of a chance action. Such repetition will lead to more discoveries either as parts of the movement achieve significance or as time is spent with the same piece of apparatus and previously unrealized possibilities become apparent.

5. Practice on landings, footwork, and good spacing can be included at the exploratory level if the teacher determines that it is necessary for safety reasons.

LEVEL 2: VARIETY

The function of the variety level is to enlarge the movement vocabulary of all children by increasing the quantity of different movements each child can do with and without objects and equipment.

A deliberate attempt should be made in all areas of the curriculum to increase the repertoire of different responses: "How many different . . . ," "Try to vary . . . ," "Try other ways to . . . ," "How many other ways can you find?" "Try another way to . . . ," "Do as many different things as you can." The teacher should use challenges, tasks, or instructional cues to push children into discovering new activities. These tasks must be sufficiently open-ended to offer several different possibilities.

In creative dance and gymnastics, the teacher should seek to extend the range of the body's capabilities.

It takes time for children to try a great variety of skills. Do not rush through this level. Suggestions can be made to do a certain number of different things on a piece of apparatus or with equipment. Teachers can encourage children to "Find some more things to do with . . ." Individuals sometimes have movement preferences or habits and may be challenged to try "another way."

A great aid in this process is to use a variety of equipment. Additional small equipment can be invented and acquired. Large apparatus can be varied, and the availability of many different configurations presents an opportunity for a greater variety of responses.

It is during the variety stage that a great opportunity exists for the teacher to make inquiries of individual children as to what are anticipated outcomes of their actions and to deliberately suggest "experiments"—for example, "If you kick it harder, will it rebound quicker?" "Is it easier to swing your legs up or to pull yourself up by your arms?" "Why do you make such a bang when you drop off the bar?" "Can you see where the ball will go if you spin it?" The content material in Chapters 6, 8, and 10 describes how to do this.

Repetition in Level 2

Variety and repetition can lead to an extensive understanding and awareness of ways to use movement effectively and skillfully. Possible outcomes and desired effects will vary in their application. There is a wealth of content material contained in Chapters 6, 8, and 10, and this level may be targeted by the bulk of any Physical Education program at the elementary school level.

At the variety level, children are asked to increase their knowledge and versatility quite extensively. Repetition helps the teacher and other children notice this variety. The greater variety of activities, when combined with repetition, extends learning. These effects are increased even further when apparatus is used. The availability of small apparatus and recognition of the effects of how it is used open up many possibilities for future sports activities. For example, an understanding of what the body can do to produce specific effects is crucial to later skill development in dance and gymnastics as well as sports.

As activities are repeated, the teacher also has an increased opportunity to interact with children.

LEVEL 3: SEQUENCE/EXTENSION

The function of the sequence level is to have individual children work to link and join movements together to form a series of longer phrases or patterns. When children have selected and practiced a response, they can be asked to extend it. Simply adding a beginning and a finish can be sufficient. Alternatively, the teacher may stipulate the inclusion of a variation in speed or a specific part (for example, "Include a 'held' position") or ask children to join two different movements together. With apparatus, an approach can be added, as well as a dismount or landing.

At the sequence/extension level, movement becomes more significant, and the child makes a real attempt to compose or invent something that will be satisfying to perform. Instead of isolated and short responses, an attempt is made to join things together, to increase the length of the activity, and to keep moving from one part to another.

Games will become more complex. Simple skills need to be performed continuously or "on the move." Consequently, the purpose of games' sequences needs to be addressed. Cooperation and competition may also change the way skills are performed. Some children may use another child to extend the sequence, particularly in sport skills.

If children choose to work on a sequence with a partner, they should be allowed to do so. In doing so, they will learn to respect the other person's skill level, which may be either lower or higher than their own.

With sequence/extension activities, the character of the lesson changes and becomes more a "working out" period where the teacher is less obvious but very necessary in an advisory and facilitative capacity. While individuals are absorbed and busy, the teacher can watch for those students who need help. Individual differences become more apparent, and great variation in the quality of movement is usually seen.

In dance and gymnastics, combinations of movement can turn into an individual performance linking various parts into a smooth whole. Toward the end of the linking process, the teacher can coach good-quality movement, varied compositions, fluidity, poise, control, and good form. A sequence should look good and feel good.

It is at this stage that sensible tasks and challenges really stimulate good work and persistence and thoughtfulness produce satisfying results.

Repetition in Level 3

Repetition is inevitable at the sequence/extension level. At this level, phrases and patterns in gymnastics and dance, together with strategies in sport, are extended and sustained over a longer period of time.

LEVEL 4: SYNERGY: CHILDREN WORKING TOGETHER

This level serves several functions. Specifically, it involves one child now combining to work with another child or a group of children. Activities geared toward this level will produce good work only if the previous levels have not been hurried through. Children are not ready to combine with others or manipulate several ideas or challenges until they are confident and experienced.

Different partners and different members of a group will present new challenges of adaptation. Working with others can sometimes be left to choice; at other times, it may take place at the suggestion of the teacher. Mixed-gender groups can be required as well as same-gender groups. Each grouping of individuals will offer new and different problems to solve.

When older children are working with a partner or in a small group, adaptation and alteration may be necessary. Variety may be increased. Likewise, interaction and discussion should increase. One will need to turn a movement vocabulary into a verbal one. It is important to realize that a unison response is not necessarily required. Although simultaneous movements can differ, they still need to be planned and coordinated.

In games skills, the child's activity will need to be extended to include one or more other players. After all, relatively few games are played alone. Skills become much more complex when another person has to be taken into account. This requires cooperation and "looking ahead"— a feat that may not be possible until children reach grade 5 or 6. Games involving competition or a "team" of two or three players should be attempted. Methods of scoring and restricting skills should make rules appear (for example, "Feet only; no hands to touch the ball"). The pattern of the game will be established, and children should realize that offense and defense require very different skills.

Sports and games combine different kinds of response to other people or events that occur. A sudden switch from offense to defense may be required. Over time, games will become more complex, combining different skills, including more players (games in elementary school are rarely effective if they combine more than four students per side), defining boundaries and playing areas, introducing positional play, marking or checking opponents, and delegating different functions to specific players.

In gymnastics or dance, children may be asked to combine a number of different ideas. Small apparatus can be combined with floor work; one child can combine with a partner. This type of collaboration requires cooperation with others and coordinating movements that must be adapted to others' skill levels. In addition, the inclusion of different partners will stimulate different ideas. Three persons can be asked to combine, or a small group can be formed. For the group as a whole to be successful, individual preferences may have to be sacrificed to the needs of the group. However, the advanced skills of a few should not be squelched—but neither should they dominate. Gymnastics activities will probably include some students with quite advanced skills and a range of large apparatus, floor work, and aerial skills.

In dance, movement can be combined with many different areas, music, drama, and art. Longer compositions may not suit all students, however. Children can begin to dance in relation to others or a theme or a drama.

Much interaction will be needed to integrate individual performances into a pleasing group whole. All members of a group are important and may choose to contribute in different ways. This may be very difficult for some children, and they may choose to continue work on their own or with a partner. Offer choices, but recognize that coordination of the parts of the whole is a real challenge.

Repetition in Level 4

Repetition here may be extensive but it is incidental to the problems posed by combining different factors and experimenting with ways to accomplish this goal. The repetition will need to adapt to changing circumstances, events during play, or the cooperation and inclusion of other people.

LEVEL 5: PERFORMANCE/PEAK/MASTERY

There seems to be a natural pleasure in achievement and "mastery." Movement has many different purposes, but the work that has gone into the earlier levels in the Movement Discovery method needs to be recognized: It represents a climax or peak for previous work. There is pleasure and satisfaction in achievement and growth of skill in many areas. The pursuit of excellence or mastery is important. Even though it may be a temporary thing appropriate to the level of the children and the context of the children, it still represents "the best" of which we are capable at this time.

The final level in the Movement Discovery method has been called "performance," although this term does not necessarily mean performance for an audience to see. Rather, it means a way of suggesting completion, fulfillment, achievement, and appreciation by self and others. The purpose of this level is to encourage refined, controlled, skilled movements that can be reproduced at will, even under different conditions or in different situations.

Dance offers an opportunity to be "me" and to become wholly absorbed in a subjective experience. This self-knowledge may be communicated to others through the movements of the dance. The composition and execution of a pleasing whole will be important in both dance and gymnastics.

Gymnastics is to be done well. Achievement in this area is very satisfying, but discipline and technique are essential for success. Gymnasts should produce good style and show polished performance.

In games and sports, by contrast, the purpose is usually to outwit the opposition during the course of play. Games players must constantly adapt and overcome difficulties. In sports, a match against another class or another group can be arranged. The results of sporting contests are important, and lessons learned during these events can be applied in the future.

With children, we sometimes have an opportunity to see the results of sustained effort. It is *not* always necessary to provide an audience. Instead, the value of this type of activity lies in the doing. It is often sufficient for the teacher to deliberately "watch" or for children to watch one another. Sometimes a few minutes can be spent where half the class performs for the other half.

Repetition in Level 5

Repetition at this level will be incidental. To obtain a pleasing "whole," repetition and practice will be needed. There is an important role here in pre-sport games to analyze results and decide which strategies or learnings were effective.

Repeat the whole for sheer pleasure. The "whole" may indeed be greater than the sum of its parts.

Characteristics of Movement Discovery

Movement Discovery is an individualized teaching method. As such, it will assume characteristics that may vary from teacher to teacher. The processes of discovery, exploration, experimentation, and invention by the children are central to this method.

A casual observer cannot help but be impressed by the tremendous variety of activity that results once a class of children start to work on even a simple movement task or challenge with ample choice. It can be overwhelming to a teacher used to traditional teaching.

Another usually obvious characteristic is how absorbed the children are in producing this variety. Because the children are required to think about the task, their bodies, the space, and the possible ways of moving, there is often quite a low level of noise. A good deal of concentration, problem solving, and decision making is evident, sometimes of quite an intense nature.

The activity is often initiated and pursued by the children as the teacher plans age-appropriate choices. This assumption of responsibility by the students leaves the teacher freer to observe them. Movement Discovery incorporates varying degrees of freedom and choice for each child, along with suitable amounts of direction or structure provided by the teacher as needed.

Another characteristic of Movement Discovery is that teachers can get to know individual children better, observing their personalities, attitudes (toward self and others), self-confidence, and physical skills. The teacher can relax and observe both personal characteristics and social skills evident among the students. Anecdotal notes by a teacher can be useful over time and can uncover needs not previously revealed by children.

Children are free to learn at their own pace and ability level in Movement Discovery. As a consequence, the teacher frequently sees new facets of the children during the lesson.

Most teachers who use a Movement Discovery approach are amazed by the abilities of children to move safely and confidently in such a variety of ways. This recognition can give great pleasure to a teacher and generate excitement about the amount of significant learning obviously taking place.

As one teacher commented, "This [Movement Discovery] really puts the fizz into phys ed!"

Movement Discovery often gives teachers confidence to know that children can, and do, take the initiative in their own learning and follow their interests and needs. They are obviously able to work at the upper levels of their capability. For this reason, all teachers—whether specialists or nonspecialists, experts or novices—can use a discovery teaching method.

For children, the sheer amount of time spent in physical activity is usually much greater in a Movement Discovery lesson than in a lesson taught in the traditional fashion. (This is easy to measure with a stopwatch and detached observers.)

Similarly, skill and fitness gains are often greater, as children are inspired to push themselves further. To confirm this progression, the teacher may choose to give any of the currently available, easy-to-administer fitness tests; comparison groups are also readily available in most schools. In one experimental Movement Discovery project, known as Project A.C.T.I.V.E., the use of a pre- and post-test design to quantify students' improvement showed that although fitness of the participating students increased, they made even greater gains in self-concept and social maturity (Arnett, 1979, pp. 47–48).

After several weeks of a Movement Discovery program, it is possible to notice more subtle differences among children. It is not just the simple variety of activities that becomes apparent, but also the many different ways in which children demonstrate their individuality, even while engaging in similar activities.

Movement Discovery focuses on the development of cognitive as well as physical capacity—indeed, on all aspects of a child's development. Classroom teachers are ideally positioned to use this growth in understanding in all other areas of the educational curriculum. As discussed in Chapter 3, many experts in early learning suggest that

Anecdote 4–2

A professor was giving a demonstration lesson with kindergarten children, who were individually exploring large apparatus and a climbing frame. Preservice college students sat around the walls watching and taking notes. A worried student who was looking for the professor approached her to ask a question and was incredulous when he received the reply, "I'm busy." The student merely saw children playing in a gym.

an extensive variety of physical activity is crucial to driving other types of development. Given this relationship, Movement Discovery has a profound and extensive ability to influence all learning.

Lesson Plans

Teachers will probably be required to produce lesson plans to show what use is being made of the time allocated to Physical Education. Local requirements vary, whether by county, by school district, or sometimes at the request of a principal. A number of external conditions may also affect the conduct of the lesson. Despite these differences, the Movement Discovery teaching method lends itself very easily to the simple, consistent outline that is provided in this section. This outline is only a suggestion, of course, and should be adapted by individual teachers to meet their class's particular needs. Sample lessons in different content areas are included in Chapters 7, 9, and 11 for your consideration.

The suggested framework for Physical Education lessons is as follows:

1. Free practice (optional)

2. Introductory activity (some form of vigorous locomotion mainly for endurance (breathlessness)); often to make a connection with a prior lesson; sometimes to do a quick assessment (and with younger children to learn spacing)

3. Individual activity (for strengthening, flexibility, or skill effects)

4. Group activity (climax)

5. Final activity to transition to the next class

If children arrive at the activity area in ones and twos, it will clearly be a waste of time to have them sit or wait for the rest of the class to arrive. Sometimes a class arrives together, but some children will work in bare feet (no street shoes should be worn) and time will be needed to remove shoes and socks. It is usually the keen students who are ready first—and it would be a pity to penalize their enthusiasm. If there is something to do for the early birds, it may speed up the emergence of the rest. Perhaps the teacher is busy preparing the area or arranging apparatus; in such a case, it will be very helpful if lessons are self-starting. Children will probably have come from a sedentary activity and their bodies will need to get moving. Preventing them from doing so may build up unnecessary tension or excitement. For all these reasons, children need to be trained to get busy as soon as possible.

Free practice enables the lesson to start promptly. Possibly the children can be told what to do before leaving the classroom. Free practice must be purposeful activity. Previously learned skills can be practiced, small apparatus may be used, or children can teach one another known activities. During this period, children can show how much they have remembered from previous lessons.

Sometimes the class may arrive as a group so that the lesson can begin at once. Free practice can still be allowed in these circumstances, although a teacher may feel time is wasted in getting out and putting away equipment that will be used later in the lesson anyway. Some groups may get too noisy and dispersed if left undirected. If control is a problem, it would be wisest to draw the group together with an *introductory activity*. This activity should be simple and easy to perform, because no group of children newly arrived at a large space wishes to listen to instructions. One or two words is often sufficient to initiate activity (e.g., run, jump, hop, skip, dodge, run and jump). Activity should be vigorous and continue until the children are breathless. This can be helpful to a teacher with a talkative class; if repeated regularly, the activity may also improve students' endurance. If children are made to think "how" they are performing, this process may help organize them when control is difficult and lead to harder physical work and more repetition.

During these kinds of activities, children will need to learn how to move vigorously in a space with others. Much valuable safety training can be included here. For example, children may be asked to run in and around others without touching. They can be given an opportunity to learn how to find a space that is adequate to the needs of the activity. Young children will need practice at keeping "spread out," a task that will sometimes be made easier if the teacher deliberately moves around and does not stay in one place.

If control is difficult, jumping or hopping and skipping can be substituted for running until control improves. If children get breathless and breathe more deeply, it would be best if fresh air could be inhaled. Either make sure windows are open or take this part of the lesson outdoors.

If the children have worked very hard, they may be unable to continue running or engaging in other vigorous activity, yet still not be warmed up. If they are working in bare feet, their feet may be cold. Friction can warm the skin and stimulate superficial circulation; the extremities (including hands and feet) can easily be rubbed and shaken. Isometric static contraction of muscles is quick to perform and is very warming. Simply "stiffening up" and relaxing several times can be very helpful in this regard. Working the large muscle groups in strengthening activities is both strenuous and important, as is maintaining and increasing the range of movement in the joints of the body.

Assignment 4–1   Part I

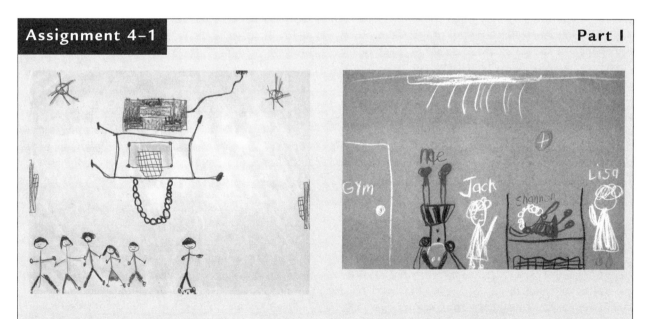

Study the two pictures, which were drawn by third-grade girls in different schools. The girls were asked to create a picture of their Physical Education lessons. Discuss what you observe with a partner. Once you have completed this activity, turn the page.

As emphasized throughout this book, these kinds of activities must take place at the limits of individual capacity. The next suggested type of activity is, therefore, *individual activity*. Individual activity can be chosen by the teacher for many different reasons, but over a period of time a balance and variety should be offered that include strengthening and flexibility activities. All the child requires is space. If the class is spread out after the introductory activity, simply asking the children to sit or work on the spot can be a quick and easy transition to the individual activity. A well-run lesson depends very much on the smoothness of links between one activity and the next. Teachers should plan transitions and the distribution and return of small apparatus before the lesson begins.

The floor is a very useful piece of apparatus; when working outside, individual mats allow the ground to be used. (The mats are easily stored in twos, dirty side against dirty side, and can be carried out for each lesson.) These mats also serve as a focus of activity and can be used to space out the members of the class and stimulate ideas. Using the floor or ground allows gymnastic tumbling skills to be attempted and facilitates a great variety of supported activities using different parts of the body. An attempt should be made in every lesson to include an activity where the hands take the body weight. Even when no mats are available outside and the ground is wet, the hands are easily washed and can be used. (One kindergarten teacher used old magazines to put hands on. The dirty page was torn away afterward and the booklets reused.)

Teachers should particularly encourage children to extend and arch the spine and strengthen the back muscles. To counteract the effects of too much sitting, twisting the body should be included. Partners can be used as resistance if no apparatus is available, a practice that allows for gymnastic agility work in twos if children are old enough. If large apparatus is available, much of the strengthening and flexibility effects can be achieved there, so it might suit the situation better if skill activities were done in this section.

To focus on pre-sports skills, small apparatus may be used; individual activity is necessary to become skillful at any sport. Technique practices in dancing also need to be done on an individual basis. Several different activities can be included or time taken to develop one idea or sequence. Sometimes this effort can link with the introductory activity or group activity so that one part of the lesson flows into the next.

Group activities and learning centers give the opportunity to bring the lesson to some sort of climax. To show to or work with a partner can be very satisfying. Large apparatus would have to be divided out and used on a small-group basis. Sometimes a dance lesson is very satisfying when group composition is possible, such as individual activity to music or a theme. Children younger than 7 or 8 years of age will probably still need to work alone but can be divided into groups using different ap-

---

Assignment 4–1 | **Part II**

The left picture on the previous page was drawn by a girl in a traditional Physical Education program; the right one was drawn by a child in a Movement Discovery program. In the left picture, the girl did not label herself; when asked, she said she was the girl in the skirt.

When looking at pictures children draw of themselves in their Physical Education lessons, do you get a feeling for

- The number of children in the class?
- The variety of activity?
- Any gender differences in activities or interests?
- The amount of time available to the child for detailed observation (i.e., the amount of time spent waiting)?
- The ratio of apparatus to children?
- The variety of apparatus used?
- Any interaction between children?
- The child's awareness of the teacher?
- The use of space?
- The variety of body action?
- The child's perception of himself or herself as active and involved?

Revise your observations in light of these questions.

---

paratus individually as a basis for later skill development. The fact that a group works on one piece of apparatus need not mean they perform an identical activity or work with one another. Older children sometimes enjoy working out a group pattern. More groups and smaller groups are needed in large classes. When equipment is limited, it is sometimes possible to initiate parallel games and gymnastic activities (for example, one group on the climbing frame, one group using ropes, one group using mats on the stage or in a corner, and one group working in twos with hoops). In this situation, the group apparatus and any special tasks or challenges used in each group would be kept constant and the groups of children rotated so that all get an opportunity to try all activities. Achieving this goal may take several lessons.

Group work is important, of course. If large apparatus is available or small-group games are being played, this type of activity should account for at least half the lesson or more, unless a teacher particularly wants to work on individual floor sequences. Much relevant lesson material can be found in Chapters 7, 9, and 11.

In some schools, sufficient large apparatus is available so that all children can use something and assignments to specific groups need not be adhered to so rigidly. If they are well taught in the early stages, children can soon learn to organize their own group work. Climbing apparatus must not be crowded during its use by groups, however. If in short supply, this type of equipment should probably be used in every lesson for at least one group. Children can also learn to organize their own apparatus.

To finish the lesson, apparatus must be put away, unless an arrangement has been made with another teacher to maintain it in its current location. It may be necessary to draw the class together for another teacher or a different kind of lesson to quiet them after exciting activities. If there has been adequate and satisfying physical activity, no special exercises to do so should be necessary. However, sometimes teachers like to draw attention to relaxation, foot exercises, and good posture; these steps can be included in a *final activity* as necessary. This may take the form of a reflection/assessment or planning activity for the next lesson but must be short.

Teachers should feel free to adapt any program to the needs of a particular group, to the time of year, and to the local situation. There is no reason why an activity area and apparatus should not be in constant use throughout the school day, as well as before school and at recess. Many schools do allow this kind of ongoing use.

Promoting Variety and Difficulty in Movement Discovery

Although the word "levels" was used in the definition of Movement Discovery, in no sense should the various types of operations be separated. Progression is a continuous process that is "built into" a Movement Discovery method. After a period of initial adaptation, children work at the upper limits of their capabilities; as they attempt more and more, they become capable of more and more. A good teacher will get good results. If teachers stay alert for opportunities to refine and improve control, continuity of movement, precision, and form, then a high standard of work will result. Whatever the teacher encourages will reappear. Even if a simple challenge is given, the response can be "advanced." Over a period of time, the responses children make increase in difficulty. Skills may become more complex and take more factors into account; the games children invent will bear more resemblance to known sports. In gymnastics and dance, more speed and momentum can be exploited, more differentiation and sensitivity of the body should be seen, more complicated movements should appear, and greater elevation of performer and apparatus should be enjoyed.

Of course, one would not expect to see the same response to a challenge from fourth-grade children as from preschoolers. Nevertheless, it is a characteristic of Movement Discovery that very often the identical task can be presented at different levels to different students. Pro-

gression emerges from the nature and level of the response, rather than from the specific material that is presented. This represents a complete change from much traditional teaching.

> Progression in Movement Discovery emerges from the nature and level of the response, rather than from the specific material that is presented.

A teacher of Movement Discovery will have to learn to take more pleasure in the children's capacity to learn than in his or her own power to teach. One of the interesting features of Movement Discovery is that teachers can see a progression in behavior. Young children at the exploration level need little direction or limitation from the teacher. A period then follows where challenges, problems, and tasks are very helpful because they inspire the children to increase their variety of responses and extend their repertoire of skills. Children enjoy working hard. Over time, as the children become increasingly more self-directed and experienced, they need less interruption from the teacher and become capable of organizing themselves and their apparatus to produce good work. In fact, a group with several years' experience almost runs itself. In addition, a few children may become interested in specific coaching and extra work out of school.

With the youngest children, a simple way to stimulate an active program and ensure progression is to provide learning centers—perhaps using the four corners of an activity room, using a stage, or marking a particular area of a playground using traffic cones, blocks, markers, or tapes. Floor markings in an activity room can be helpful, as can a suitable blank wall. Large apparatus should be used as much as possible, because it allows a great variety of positions and the weight of the body provides overload for strengthening or improving flexibility. Examine your

facilities carefully. Once the area is divided into centers, perhaps with small equipment available in one or two areas, your lessons can follow a regular pattern. Use whatever space is available to get children breathless. With older children, perhaps you may want to assign them to each learning center. Preschoolers can be left to use what is available as a choice.

All children should get an opportunity to use all centers, though it may take several lessons before this goal is achieved. Keep the organization simple. There must be enough apparatus and space so that activities are not restricted and children are safe to work alone. Check that all children have an opportunity to use everything over several lessons. Observation of what children discover will provide a teacher with material to suggest to other children. If children do not maintain interest after several weeks, simple variations in the arrangement of apparatus and the use of different small equipment will stimulate new ideas.

Young children naturally extend the range and difficulty of their activities. If a teacher wishes, however, sim-

ple suggestions can ensure this extension. It will be helpful for novice teachers to know that they can think up suggestions easily. Some examples follow.

The initial exploration can be **extended and varied** by:

Changing the speed

Changing the direction

Changing the level

Working on the "spot"

Moving

Varying the shape

Varying the body position

Changing the pathway

"Prepositional" variation

At the same time children are extending and varying their skills, they should be encouraged to improve the quality of their work.

The initial exploration can be **improved** by making it:

Smoother

Higher

Lighter

More controlled

Bigger

Clearer

Teachers using the Movement Discovery approach might find it helpful to reflect on the various ways they can state the movement tasks they plan and then implement with children. As the teacher's confidence improves, his or her repertoire of teaching skills will naturally expand. A teacher should be able to generate many, highly diverse movement tasks over a long period of time. Because many programs use a lot of small apparatus, the list in Assignment 4–2 might spark some new ways of presenting tasks to children.

This assignment challenges the teacher to invent movement tasks. For each of the 12 general ideas listed here, write out a sample learning experience/ movement task in any area of Physical Education. More than one response must be possible, because you will be telling children what to do without telling them how to do it. The task might be explored alone, in pairs, or in a small group.

1. FREE CHOICE of activity to do with small equipment
2. Practice ONE activity with equipment
3. Practice something DIFFERENT with equipment
4. Invent DIFFERENT WAYS to use the small equipment
5. Practice ONE movement and IMPROVE it
6. Practice ONE movement and VARY it
7. Practice ONE movement and ADD another to it
8. CHANGE from one body action to another using the small equipment
9. Make a PATTERN of the SAME type of movement with the equipment
10. Make a PATTERN of different types of movements
11. VARY the ORDER of your PATTERN
12. IMPROVE the FLOW (or linking of the movements) of your PATTERN

In a small group of peers, teach some of the tasks you have invented.

It is helpful when using the Movement Discovery method for the teacher to be able to readily think of, and facilitate where necessary, some ideas and variations that are possible in response to the planned learning activity. Consider the following activity:

In a group playing 2 versus 2, find ways to get away from a person who is guarding you closely so that you receive the ball from your teammates successfully. Dodge away, fake it, be quicker than them. Remember to switch players.

- Try this experiment with a ball.
- Try this experiment with an oval ball.
- Try when the ball comes in high.
- Jump to get it; reach to get it.
- Try this experiment with a stick and puck/ball of some kind. Find out what you need to do to succeed.

Try to invent more variations and types of extensions that will elicit the skills necessary for soccer, field hockey, football, lacrosse, rugby, basketball, and other sports.

Here is another example in the developmental games and sports area:

Approach the basket from five different angles and try to get the ball through the hoop. Fake a shot, but wait until you are free to shoot. Do this with a partner who tries to block your shot. Switch roles with your partner.

- Travel at different speeds as you approach the goal.
- Use a jump, and shoot while you are in the air.
- Use right, left, or both hands.
- Spin the ball to get it through the hoop.
- Use the backboard sometimes; at other times, do not use the backboard.
- Shoot from far away.
- Choose a shot close to the basket.
- Try a "new" way.

Playing one-on-one allows all kinds of "intercepting" and shooting experience. (Switch players.) There is limited value in shooting when there is no opposition.

In addition to generating many task variations, it is helpful for the Movement Discovery teacher to challenge children to share their knowledge of the discoveries they have made. This is also a skill that young teachers might practice. Examine the following learning experience for possible questions:

Find the most effective ways of throwing a ball over a variety of distances to a friend. Be sure to investigate both short- and long-distance throws. Choose the ball you wish to use for this practice.

1. Show what you discovered about throwing at different distances with your friend.
2. Find what is effective at all distances. Notice which differences in performance are needed.
3. Show how you had to alter your throwing action when you had to throw very far versus making a short throw.

Try to think of other possible challenges the teacher could use with children to encourage them to think about and discover some of the important elements of effective throwing skills.

For each of the games and sports learning experiences listed here, plan two possible questions you could ask children to check their understanding or knowledge of the skills involved in each:

1. In a small group, practice "batting" using a paddle or baseball bat and ball. Discover what produces a strong hit. What works for you? Show a friend.
2. Experiment in small groups to discover what determines the direction of a ball when it is hit. Use any ball, any bat, or any body part. Vary the swing, the grip, and the speed. Hit a ball close to and ahead of you.
3. Working in twos, find out where the ball has to be placed if a running player is to receive it in such a way that he or she can throw or hit the ball back to you almost immediately.

PREPOSITIONAL TASKS

Prepositional tasks can be used effectively in all curricular areas. In the early stages of Movement Discovery work, it is easy for the teacher to focus on just one preposition (e.g., "over," "into"). Short movement tasks can be planned and implemented, such as "Move *along* . . ." and "Get *on* . . ." Later, combinations such as "on and off," "around and through," and "up and down" can be used to extend exploratory work even further. These learning experiences give children many choices and the freedom to use a variety of body actions or parts of the body, choice of speed, varied shapes and directions of movement, and different levels and pathways to follow. The prepositions in **Figure 4–2** are provided to design a host of individualized learning experiences.

Assessment

The main characteristic of Movement Discovery is that it is child centered. In contrast, traditional programs are often teacher centered. As part of the traditional approach, teachers often rate skills in terms of difficulty (for whom?) and

PREPOSITIONS

BALLS (all shapes, sizes, and weights)	IN	MATS
BATS and other hitting implements	OUT ACROSS AROUND	BARS (all heights, lengths, and combinations)
	OVER	BOXES
ROPES	UNDER ON	
HOOPS	OFF	BENCHES
BOWLING PINS	UP	BALANCE BEAMS (different widths)
NETS (high, low)	DOWN ALONG	LADDERS (high, low, sloped)
TARGETS (all shapes and sizes)	BETWEEN THROUGH	SLIDING SURFACES
BEAN BAGS	INTO	
SIMPLE IMPROVISED EQUIPMENT OF ALL KINDS	OUT OF INSIDE	BARRELS and CARDBOARD BOXES
BUILDING BLOCKS	BELOW ABOVE	CLIMBING APPARATUS OF EVERY VARIETY

FIGURE 4–2   Prepositions

then rate progress on the achievement of specific skills. To see progression in Movement Discovery, however, one needs to allow several lessons or weeks to elapse. Pre- and post-learning observations must be compared if evaluation is required. The value of informal, anecdotal observations taken regularly is that such comparisons are readily available if specific evaluation is required of a teacher. Formal assessment using health-related physical fitness tests, skill tests, and social maturity tests can be undertaken at any time if required, though time should also elapse between tests to allow for assessment of progression. It is most important to assess an individual child's progress over time, rather than to compare that child's performance to the performance of other, different children—a consideration that has sometimes been ignored in traditional teaching.

Previous chapters have shown the bases of individual development and emphasized their importance in learning. The present crisis of overweight, inactive adults in society may have some of its roots in the "fitness test" era that prevailed in the U.S. school system in earlier years. From your observation of children, it is hoped that you will realize that children normally do seek the upper limits of their capacity and extend them. This process apparently gives great satisfaction and sustains interest. In fact, it is observable throughout the entirety of the animal kingdom. In this sense, Movement Discovery is a self-testing program. An observant teacher will probably become involved in the children's learning in a profound way.

In contrast, the system of tests, grades, and comparison of personal achievement against wider (usually national) norms is based on extrinsic motivation. There is no evidence to support its value either as a stimulus for children or as a satisfying result for parents. Education research confirms that intrinsic motivation is superior and has longer-lasting effects. If teachers want to ensure that their students mature into adults in society who choose to be strenuously active and who enjoy this type of exertion, they must do everything possible to offer enjoyable strenuous, physical activity to children. The best way to do so is to provide climbing apparatus and sports equipment and to allow children to progress in dance, body management/educational gymnastics, and pre-sports activities during their earliest years of life. (There is a great deal of teaching material related to this point in Chapters 6, 8, and 10.)

There is no evidence to support the claim that testing programs promote skill and enjoyment. Statements such as the following are untenable:

> We know that learning is most effective when learning goals match both assessment and instructional practices. This suggests that you "tell students what is important for them to know and be able to do, teach them what you told them they would learn, design appropriate tasks that allow them to practice what you taught them and assess them on what they have been practicing (Tannehill, 2001, p. 19).

For example, if you want to teach kids to learn to skip, teach them essential components of skipping, let them practice skipping, and then assess how well they can skip (National Association for Sport and Physical Education [NASPE]/American Alliance for Health, Physical Education, Recreation, and Dance [AAHPERD], 2004, p. 3).

The tail is wagging the dog!

Movement Discovery professionals would insist that children are individuals presenting at different levels of development and capacity. Whether children skip will be decided by them at an appropriate time; the teacher may not know the "essential components" needed to reach this stage of development. Who decides what is essential? How these activities are presented should be individualized, because not all children need the same teaching. Likewise, not all teachers teach in the same way: Teaching, too, is a creative process. The context and purpose of skipping are highly relevant to the activity, and the way it is performed may need to be adapted for different uses, again on an individual basis.

One can only conclude that those who follow the teaching pattern outlined in the earlier quote are following a "teacher-centered" approach. It might be easier to feel satisfaction in one's own teaching skill if matters were as straightforward as presented in the quote, but in the real world teachers need to produce satisfaction in the children, not in themselves. To repeat, in a Movement Discovery program, teachers may need to learn to take more satisfaction in the children's learning achievement than in their own teaching ability. Children's achievements often surpass teacher's expectations. Indeed, where Movement Discovery is continued over a period of time, the inventive and creative responses of children will delight the experienced teacher both in variety and difficulty.

Parents do have a right to know the teacher's opinion of their child's achievement and to receive assurance that their child is not wasting time. An informal, recorded anecdotal system is recommended here. Some schools may require that grades be based on more formal, objective tests. Some simple tests for this purpose are provided at the end of this chapter. To allow an assessment program to take time away from Physical Education lessons or to let tests dictate the content of a teaching program is wrong. There is also a danger that such a program will send children the wrong message: that physical activity is not worthwhile unless it is measured. To repeat, if a thing is worth doing, it is worth doing badly. (Just do it!)

All testing programs tend to provoke comparisons. In this sense, the superior achievement of one child—which may ultimately be due to greater maturation, physique, genetics, or previous experience—may debase the achievement of another child. *No* comparisons should be made between children with any assessments used. Unfortunately, this dictate has sometimes been ignored in traditional teaching. All assessments, both formal and informal, should focus on individual improvement only. (Pre-test students, allow time to elapse, and then give a post-test.)

There is no evidence that verbal or written descriptions of skills enhance subsequent learning or that recording feelings or stating "knowledge" about activities by the learner improve performance. Movement is action; one demonstrates progress by doing. *Do* the activity, rather than telling, talking, explaining, or writing about it.

Teachers must observe individual performance (gathering anecdotal evidence that is at least consistent to an observer). These observations must be recorded as they occur, and an effort made periodically to check these notes to ensure that all children have a record. Children themselves usually know when they are improving. Some will derive satisfaction from this knowledge, but others may not. Some children may become competitive ("How many times did I hit the target in 10 tries?"), but not all children are competitive. What matters for lifelong learning and satisfaction is that children have pleasurable, interesting, and enjoyable experiences and learn to see themselves as skilled, capable, and able to tackle new physical experiences. Their confidence in themselves and what their bodies can do is crucial to future activity.

A lack of strong negative memories will help in this regard. Teachers should rightly be fearful that the experiences they offer young children may have negative results. Unfortunately, in the past, where skill practices and fitness training have been dominant, negative attitudes have been developed. Perhaps the worst sin a teacher can commit is to put children off learning for the rest of their lives. Human existence—at all phases of the life course—should include activity and pleasure in moving.

The process of discovery is natural, individualized, and safe. It can be profoundly enjoyable and satisfying. It can teach children self-acceptance, tolerance of others, and community awareness as well as improving fitness, social maturity, and skill.

Following are some examples of simple tests of interest and participation, change of attitude, and growth of self-confidence. To verify their appropriateness, it may be helpful for a teacher to have a friend observe and fill

out checklists. It is also possible to ask children to evaluate themselves.

Bear in mind that the objectives of a program such as Movement Discovery are to produce lifelong enjoyment and participation in physical activity, which may take years to achieve. Progression centers on the growth of skill, learning, social adjustment, self-responsibility, tolerance of differences, belief in self, fitness, interest in and enjoyment of vigorous physical activity, and self-concept (seeing oneself as active, capable, and skilled in many different contexts). Anecdotal comments can reflect these objectives. Although anecdotal comments should be recorded about children as they are noticed, it might be wise for a teacher to review these comments every few lessons and make a special effort to observe those children who have received no comments. Read the following suggestions and devise your own means of assessment.

A simple survey of children's interests follows (**Figure 4–3**). The best information from its use may be obtained if it is given before a Movement Discovery program is introduced and then repeated several months later, perhaps at the beginning of the school year and at the end of the school year. There are no right or wrong answers. Add or omit items if you wish.

Teachers may like to ask children to add an additional "comment": "What I like best is . . ." or "One thing I don't like in Physical Education is . . ." One third-grade girl reported, "I have lots of friends now that we have Physical Education lessons." These kinds of comments are important, because a teacher cannot always predict children's reactions.

Preschool children are not usually given formal tests. Nevertheless, the wise teacher will want to ensure that progress is made among children of this age. Children of all ages enjoy achievement and a feeling of success, and early failure or success often dictates their attitude toward school for years ahead.

ASSESSMENT OF TEACHERS' SKILLS AND BEHAVIORS

Teachers should also make progress in administering the Movement Discovery approach, though this evolution will vary among individuals. Progression in teachers' observational skills is the key to better Movement Discovery programs. Teachers will develop their observational skills as experience allows. It is most important that practice in observing active children, recording simple anecdotal data, and comparing one's skills with others' skills happens as soon as possible. Personal and informal observation has already been suggested as a means of self-reflection, but teacher preparation courses often offer an explicit opportunity to address this need. If groups of teacher-education students cannot be taken to local schools to observe Physical Education lessons, it will be important to bring groups of children to the college campus. In fact, children often enjoy the use of different apparatus during these outings,

---

Assignment 4-4

Write a brief account of your experience of being tested in Physical Education lessons. Did you undergo fitness tests or perform a skill required by a teacher? Discuss your experience with a partner, and list any advantages and disadvantages that you see linked to tests, grades, and teacher's reports. Did you experience any problems with a teacher's subjective opinions?

and local "master" teachers enjoy the opportunity to share their skills with novices.

Observations can also be shared among college students. When two observers choose to follow the same child, comparisons of "noticed" and "missed" incidents can be very helpful in honing observation skills. If possible, observation of a sequence of lessons where one child is observed in a group over time reveals a great deal and is likely to stimulate many questions.

When observing a lesson, an attempt can be made to notice specific things. The following list of questions might be helpful:

1. Are the children at the same or different developmental levels? Assess levels of functioning.

2. As the children solve the problems of movement posed by the teacher/therapist, which "movement answers" are similar? Which are different? In what ways are they different?

SURVEY OF CHILDREN'S INTERESTS

Child's Name:_____

ACTIVITY/SPORT	I do not want to play	I might want to play	I definitely want to play
Basketball	☐	☐	☐
Floor Hockey	☐	☐	☐
Soccer	☐	☐	☐
Square/Folk/Line Dance	☐	☐	☐
Table Tennis	☐	☐	☐
Softball/Baseball	☐	☐	☐
Riding a bike	☐	☐	☐
Skateboarding	☐	☐	☐
Tennis/Badminton	☐	☐	☐
Swimming	☐	☐	☐
Roller-blades/roller-skating	☐	☐	☐
Yoga/Judo/Tae-Kwando	☐	☐	☐
Rugby	☐	☐	☐
Volleyball	☐	☐	☐
Water-Skiing	☐	☐	☐
Track and Field	☐	☐	☐
Gymnastics	☐	☐	☐
Football	☐	☐	☐
Frisbee	☐	☐	☐

FIGURE 4–3   Survey of Children's Interests

3. How much variety do you note in the movement responses? In other words, how many *different* ways do the children use their bodies?

4. How *well* do the children move? Note the quality of their movement.

5. How well can the children use the space of the room without bumping into one another?

6. When experimenting with apparatus/equipment, which different uses can the children find for each item?

7. How confidently do the children move when asked to work off the ground (e.g., on ladders, tables, bars)?

8. Which children need constant encouragement and guidance?

9. Are the children experiencing success?

10. How well do the children change their direction and level of movement?

11. When asked to use different parts of the body, which are used and which are avoided or not used?

12. What evidence do you see that children are aware of the variety of shapes their bodies can make (e.g., wide, long, stretched, curled)?

13. Which different types of movement are tried (e.g., jumping, balancing, twisting, bending, throwing, catching, kicking)? Do the movements use the *whole* body or just *parts* of the body?

14. Do some children always prefer to move quickly? Slowly?

15. How easily can children link movements using different body positions?

16. Do children move at a similar pace throughout the lesson?

17. How aware are children of others around them?

18. Do children "watch" and "copy"?

As adult role models, teachers convey unstated or "hidden" messages to children about the value of physical activity or about the growth expected of children. An observer may help uncover what some of these hidden messages are. The following checklists may be helpful. Suppose, for example, that a teacher participates actively in bat-and-ball activities, showing great enthusiasm, but stands to one side during jump rope, showing only mild interest. Children may then begin to work harder on bat-and-ball skills than on jump rope. Of course, teachers cannot be equally enthusiastic about every area in the

curriculum, nor is it suggested that they ought to be. Rather, it is suggested that teachers become more aware of the unstated messages they convey so that they can increase their positive and conscious choices about which messages they wish to continue to convey and which ones they wish to change. Stereotyping can be one kind of hidden message. One female classroom teacher was observed in high heels; she gave directions to the class but did not herself engage in movement. Was she fitting all too closely the stereotype of the nonathletic, inactive woman whose clothes limit her possibilities for activity? What was she suggesting to the girls about their future as adults or to the boys, about what to expect of women?

Teachers are often unaware of how they present themselves. It might be helpful to ask a friend to observe you teaching and fill out one of the checklists, such as the one in **Figure 4–4.**

There are many ways to assess progression and teacher effectiveness in a program. A teacher may need to identify objectives/lesson outcomes beforehand and simply check on their achievement at the end. Ask a friend to do this. Read the following suggestions and devise your own means of assessments. Some teachers may prefer to use the Self-Assessment Checklist 1: Assessing Outcomes (see Figure 4–4) to aid self-assessment. Fitness levels will increase if limits of existing physical capacity are reached frequently—a factor that can be measured. An increase in social maturity can also be measured.

The Short Teacher Checklist 2 (see **Figure 4–5**) or the Teacher Checklist 3 (see **Figure 4–6**) may be completed with either an experienced teacher or a trusted, critical friend observing you. If you do get an observer and use the checklist, be sure to use it on several occasions, certainly for more than one lesson or with more than one class.

ASSESSMENT OF CHILDREN'S SKILLS AND BEHAVIORS

In situations where formal assessment of children is required, the tests described in this section could be used. A simple test of self-concept and social maturity is the Self-Observation Scale (SOS; Katzenmeyer & Stenner, 1973). Teachers can research the wide variety of tests available and select those that are most appropriate for their own unique situation.

One of the most commonly used fitness tests is the FITNESSGRAM. This can be used as a pre- and post-test assessment. Teachers may elect to select their own fitness test items, but they must be consistent in applying the same items during the pre- and post-test situations. FITNESSGRAM is a health-related physical fitness assessment developed in 1982 by leading scientists in physical activity and fitness assessment at the Cooper Institute in Dallas, Texas. It includes a computerized reporting system. According to AAHPERD (2009), "The FITNESSGRAM/ ACTIVITYGRAM assessment program complements the

Self-Assessment Checklist 1: Assessing Outcomes

In the columns below, on the left are listed some of the major outcomes to include in a successfully individualized program; on the right are listed outcomes to avoid or minimize. As programs achieve desired outcomes, teachers will observe everyone's increased interest and enjoyment in physical education. They will also observe wider ranges of physical skills. More children will do more things as progression takes place; fitness levels will increase, and more advanced skill levels will be evident.

OUTCOMES TO INCLUDE	OUTCOMES TO AVOID OR MINIMIZE
The focus is on the child. The child is doing; the teacher is observing and guiding.	The teacher is demonstrating, dominant, or talking too much.
All children are active most of the time.	Children are wasting time in line-ups, waiting for a turn. Timid children are passive.
The child chooses to compete. Competition is not imposed by the teacher.	The child competes only because of peer pressure or group competition imposed by the teacher.
Progression in skills is apparent. Activities are purposeful.	Activities are isolated. There are repetitive drills without obvious goals.
Equipment is cared for, handled, and stored neatly.	Equipment is lying around and untidy, causing problems with distribution or storage.
Children cooperate with others, are tolerant of them, and respect their needs.	There is pushing or other physical disruptions; arguing instead of discussing, and discriminatory behavior.
Inclusive behavior: Children are willing to include others, cooperate, and share. Supportive statements are common.	Exclusive behavior: Participation is limited to boys or girls or "just us," "not you," "we were here first," and so on. Other children are seen as rivals.
Children think and plan for themselves and with others.	The teacher tells the children what to do and how to do it.

FIGURE 4-4 Self-Assessment Checklist 1: Assessing Outcomes

SHORT TEACHER CHECKLIST 2

Observer's Name _____

Check only those items which are applicable.

5—Outstanding, **4**—Very Good, **3**—Effective, **2**—Needs Improvement, **1**—Unsatisfactory

1. Teacher used learner's names. Showed interest in individual children.	1	2	3	4	5
2. Organized class to provide for maximum participation, that is, all students were actively involved most of the time.	1	2	3	4	5
3. Demonstrations by learners were effective, not too frequent.	1	2	3	4	5
4. Lesson activities gave children a chance to be creative on an individual basis and sustained their interest.	1	2	3	4	5
5. Teacher observed learners and moved around working space with confidence.	1	2	3	4	5
6. Teacher demonstrated enthusiasm (a) for physical activity and (b) progression.	1	2	3	4	5
7. Instruction was appropriate for the various levels of student performance.	1	2	3	4	5
8. Equipment dispersal and collection quick, safe, and orderly. Equipment in good shape and clean.	1	2	3	4	5
9. Children were not waiting or inactive.	1	2	3	4	5
10. Teacher's enthusiasm was spread over a wide range of different activities.	1	2	3	4	5
11. Teacher's comments spread at all ability levels, focusing on application and used with different children.	1	2	3	4	5
12. Noise level appropriate for the activity.	1	2	3	4	5
13. Asked questions which were appropriate for young children. Not too many questions.	1	2	3	4	5
14. All children expected to clean up, tidy up, and set apparatus straight.	1	2	3	4	5
15. Specific appropriate feedback given, not just "good job"!	1	2	3	4	5
16. Voice—audible, expressive, clear, articulate, appropriate speed and volume. Teacher not too dominant.	1	2	3	4	5
17. Professional behavior, dress, appropriate use of good English.	1	2	3	4	5
OVERALL EVALUATION	1	2	3	4	5

COMMENTS:

_____

_____

_____

FIGURE 4–5   Short Teacher Checklist 2

TEACHER CHECKLIST 3

Observer's Name: _____

Teacher's Name: _____

Type of Lesson: Educational Gymnastics/Developmental Games & Sports/Creative Dance/Combination

Date: _____

Place: Indoor/Outdoor/with apparatus/without apparatus (Circle as appropriate)

Length of Lesson: _____ mins.

5—Outstanding, 4—Very Good, 3—Effective, 2—Needs Improvement, 1—Unsatisfactory

1. Instruction allowed for varied responses at the level of most students.	1 2 3 4 5
2. Organized class to provide for maximum participation, that is, all students were actively involved.	1 2 3 4 5
3. Teacher observed and interacted with timid or less skilled children.	1 2 3 4 5
4. Teacher gave the children positive reinforcement.	1 2 3 4 5
5. Teacher moved around the working space with confidence.	1 2 3 4 5
6. Teacher's attention was not limited to certain activities.	1 2 3 4 5
7. Teacher allowed the students to develop self-management and care for others at all times.	1 2 3 4 5
8. Children were not waiting or inactive.	1 2 3 4 5
9. Teacher's enthusiasm was spread over a wide range of different activities.	1 2 3 4 5
10. Teacher showed no more interest in one activity or another.	1 2 3 4 5
11. Teacher used learners' names and gave attention to individuals.	1 2 3 4 5
12. Teacher showed support for leadership roles and initiative taken by children.	1 2 3 4 5
13. All children expected to clean up, tidy up, and set apparatus straight.	1 2 3 4 5
14. Equipment dispersal and collection quick, safe, and orderly.	1 2 3 4 5
15. Voice—audible, expressive, clear enunciation, appropriate speed and volume.	1 2 3 4 5
16. Asked appropriate questions that make children think (avoided those with YES/NO answer only).	1 2 3 4 5
17. Children used to demonstrate sparingly and at different levels of skill.	1 2 3 4 5
18. Specific appropriate feedback given, not just "good job"!	1 2 3 4 5
19. Teacher stood near, watched, smiled, or gave some kind of positive support.	1 2 3 4 5
20. Teacher did not make negative comments. Children behaving badly are dealt with on a one-to-one basis.	1 2 3 4 5
21. Teacher inclusive of student exceptionalities.	1 2 3 4 5
22. Evaluate the activity area for visual stimulus. Charts, pictures, children's drawings, photos, gender equality.	1 2 3 4 5
23. Teacher's clothing was appropriate for the activity.	1 2 3 4 5
24. Professional behavior, appropriate use of good English.	1 2 3 4 5
Overall presentation of lesson	1 2 3 4 5

FIGURE 4–6 Teacher Checklist 3

Physical Best educational program." The test items are shown in **Table 4-1**.

Teachers interested in using these assessments can find more information about them on the Internet site "FitnessGram."

Sometimes teachers may use informal assessments for their own benefit (i.e., the results are not given to the children). These serve as markers to support an opinion and are based on comparisons. Some samples of simple qualitative rating scales, similar to a Likert scale, are shown in **Figure 4-7**.

One advantage that many classroom teachers have discovered while using a Movement Discovery approach to teaching Physical Education is that they get to know the children very well. There is such a wide range of individual differences to be seen in many different activities. There is also a wide variety of vocabulary used in activity and a large number of challenges that can be used with children in the later stages of skills development. Children tend to get very absorbed and involved in their discovery, and there are many opportunities for a teacher to stimulate thinking.

It is perhaps most obvious that creative dance and expressive movement can be linked with music, poetry, art, language, and other classroom subjects. Nevertheless, a great deal of sports preparation and gymnastic activity on apparatus uses vocabulary that can stimulate classroom work. Children encounter science in a very meaningful way—for example, momentum, balance, center of gravity, weight, angles, directions, speeds, levels, variations in sequence and composition. Different relationships are forged with other individuals. Rich, meaningful, oral language emerges that can be used in many ways in the classroom, such as accounts of invented games, descriptions of body management/gymnastic sequences, and so on. Classroom projects often benefit from students' engagement in an active, challenging Movement Discovery program. Distance, accuracy, timing, speed of performance, amount of time used, subtle variations, and skills adaptations to different circumstances and performance are the very essence of skills development. If a teacher wishes, these aspects of the program can be used as an interesting and meaningful focus for almost any classroom "subject." Each child is unique, and Movement Discovery provides teachers with a wonderful opportunity to fully appreciate and enjoy this individuality. Through this teaching method, they can watch the development of a child in character and personality.

Many classrooms have optional materials available for keen students to use. Simple recordings of performance may attract some children. "My Book of Games" can be a challenging language project. "Getting Better in Skills," in which students maintain records of self-administered and invented performance tests (measuring accuracy, speed, distance, time taken, and so on), is interesting for some children (and their parents!). Simple technology to enhance these efforts—such as heart rate monitors, stopwatches, and pedometers—is readily available for those who wish to use it.

TABLE 4-1   Fitnessgram Test Items

Aerobic Capacity (Select either one.)	Body Composition (Select either one.)	Muscle Strength, Endurance, and Flexibility
1. The Pacer: a 20-meter, progressive, multistage shuttle run set to music	1. Percent Body Fat: calculated from triceps and calf skinfold measurements	1. Abdominal Strength: curl-up test
Or	Or	2. Trunk Extensor Strength and Flexibility: trunk lift
2. One-Mile Walk/Run	2. Body Mass Index: calculated from height and weight	3. Upper Body Strength (select one out of the three options): • 90-degree push-up • Flexed-arm hang • Modified pull-up Flexibility (select either option): • Back-saver sit-and-reach • Shoulder stretch

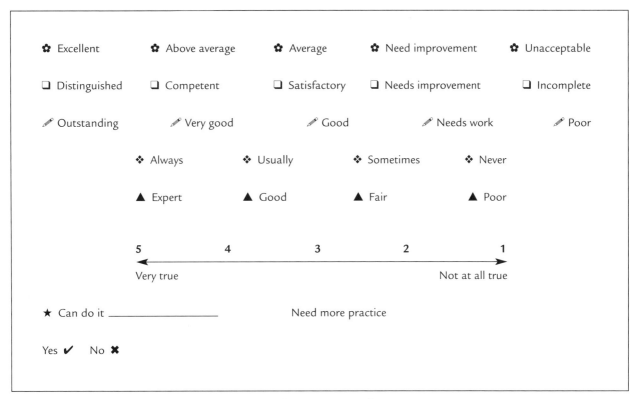

FIGURE 4–7 Samples of Simple Qualitative Rating Scales

The overall purposes of Movement Discovery are geared toward both the present and the future and should reflect a child's' interests and enjoyment. The interdisciplinary links mentioned previously are a welcome by-product of this kind of program. The tests or recorded achievements, if included, should be choices undertaken by individual children. They are mentioned here to reassure teachers and suggest ways of enriching children's experience of life. Remember, however, that some assessments and tests may have a negative effect on some children.

Summary

Physical Education is for EVERYONE.

EACH CHILD NEEDS the satisfaction of skilled performance.
EACH CHILD NEEDS to know what his or her body can and cannot do.

EACH CHILD NEEDS to feel comfortable with his or her body.
EACH CHILD NEEDS cooperative interaction with others.

EACH CHILD NEEDS to learn independence.
EACH CHILD NEEDS to increase his or her physical fitness level.

EACH CHILD NEEDS the confidence to grasp an opportunity when it occurs.
EACH CHILD NEEDS to learn assertiveness.

EACH CHILD NEEDS the benefits of leadership experience.
EACH CHILD NEEDS the "give and take" of teamwork.

EACH CHILD NEEDS the refreshment of just moving for the sake of moving.
EACH CHILD NEEDS to know his or her body as a means of artistic expression.

EACH CHILD NEEDS the physical release of emotion.
EACH CHILD NEEDS the euphoria of physical fatigue.

EACH CHILD NEEDS to be able to manage his or her body safely in a new situation.
EACH CHILD NEEDS to increase his or her self-confidence.

Your observations will have shown that young children are almost continuously active if allowed to be so. All school days should include at least one period of strenuous activity. As early as the seventeenth century, the poet John Milton (1608–1674) recommended three and a half hours each day for exercise (as cited in McIntosh, 1963, p. 43). Naturally, schedules permitting adequate physical activity within the school may be difficult to organize. Nevertheless, teachers could make more use of outdoor areas and improvised equipment as the need arises. Even strenuous activity within a classroom is possible.

In 2009, the National Association for Sport and Physical Education (NASPE, 2003b) issued a position statement that "All children birth to age 5 should engage in daily physical activity that promotes movement skillfulness and foundations of health-related fitness." At the same time, this organization published some physical activity guidelines geared toward meeting those goals and which reflect the best research and thinking of motor development, movement, and exercise specialists about young children's physical activity needs during the first years of life. Guidelines have been developed for three age categories, namely, infants (birth to age 12 months; see **Table 4–2**), toddlers (age 12 to 36 months; see **Table 4–3**), and preschoolers (ages 3 to 5; see **Table 4–4**).

TABLE 4–2 Guidelines for Infants

Guideline 1	Infants should interact with caregivers in daily physical activities that are dedicated to exploring movement and the environment.
Guideline 2	Caregivers should place infants in settings that encourage and stimulate movement experiences and active play for short periods of time several times a day.
Guideline 3	Infants' physical activity should promote skill development in movement.
Guideline 4	Infants should be placed in an environment that meets or exceeds recommended safety standards for performing large muscle activities.
Guideline 5	Those in charge of infants' well-being are responsible for understanding the importance of physical activity and should promote movement skills by providing opportunities for structured and unstructured physical activity.

TABLE 4–3 Guidelines for Toddlers

Guideline 1	Toddlers should engage in a total of at least 30 minutes of structured physical activity each day.
Guideline 2	Toddlers should engage in at least 60 minutes, and up to several hours, per day of unstructured physical activity and should not be sedentary for more than 60 minutes at a time, except when sleeping.
Guideline 3	Toddlers should be given ample opportunities to develop movement skills that will serve as the building blocks for future motor skillfulness and physical activity.
Guideline 4	Toddlers and preschoolers should have indoor and outdoor areas that meet or exceed recommended safety standards for performing large muscle activities.
Guideline 5	Those in charge of toddlers' well-being are responsible for understanding the importance of physical activity and promoting movement skills by providing opportunities for structured and unstructured physical activity and movement experiences.

TABLE 4–4 Guidelines for Preschoolers

Guideline 1	Preschoolers should accumulate at least 60 minutes of structured physical activity each day.
Guideline 2	Preschoolers should engage in at least 60 minutes, and up to several hours, of unstructured physical activity each day, and should not be sedentary for more than 60 minutes at a time, except when sleeping.
Guideline 3	Preschoolers should be encouraged to develop competence in fundamental motor skills that will serve as the building blocks for future motor skillfulness and physical activity.
Guideline 4	Preschoolers should have access to indoor and outdoor areas that meet or exceed recommended safety standards for performing large muscle activities.
Guideline 5	Caregivers and parents in charge of preschoolers' health and well-being are responsible for understanding the importance of physical activity and for promoting movement skills by providing opportunities for structured and unstructured physical activity.

NASPE (2009b) released the guidelines, displayed in **Table 4–5**, for older children, ages 5–12. The purpose of these guidelines is to provide information for parents, physical education teachers, classroom teachers, youth physical activity leaders, administrators, physicians, health professionals and all others dedicated to promoting physically active lifestyles among children.

TABLE 4–5   Physical Activity Guidelines for Children Ages 5 to 12 Years

Guideline 1	Children should accumulate at least 60 minutes, and up to several hours, of age-appropriate physical activity on all or most days of the week. This daily accumulation should include moderate and vigorous physical activity, with the majority of the time being spent in activity that is intermittent in nature.
Guideline 2	Children should participate in several bouts of physical activity lasting 15 minutes or longer each day.
Guideline 3	Children should participate each day in a variety of age-appropriate physical activities designed to achieve optimal health, wellness, fitness, and performance benefits.
Guideline 4	Extended periods (periods of two hours or more) of inactivity are discouraged for children, especially during the daytime hours.

References

American Alliance for Health, Physical Education, Recreation, and Dance (AAHPERD). (2009). *FITNESSGRAM.* Retrieved December 28, 2009, from http://www.aahperd.org/naspe/professionaldevelopment/physicalBest/resources.cfm

Arnett, C. (1979). *Project A.C.T.I.V.E.: Developing sex equity in elementary school physical education, final report.* Washington, DC: Women's Educational Equity Act Program, U.S. Department of Health, Education, and Welfare.

Gardner, H. (1983/2003). *Frames of mind: The theory of multiple intelligences.* New York: Basic Books.

Katzenmeyer, W., & Stenner, A. (1973). *Self-observation scale.* Durham, NC: National Testing Service.

McIntosh, P. (1963). *Sport in society.* London: New Thinker's Library, Watts.

Morris, D. (1967). *The naked ape: A zoologist's study of the human animal.* New York: McGraw-Hill.

National Association for Sport and Physical Education (NASPE). (2009a). *Active start: A statement of physical activity guidelines for children birth to five years* (2nd ed.). Reston, VA: American Alliance for Health, Physical Education, Recreation, and Dance. Retrieved December 28, 2009, from http://www.aahperd.org/naspe/standards/nationalGuidelines/ActiveStart.cfm

National Association for Sport and Physical Education (NASPE). (2009b). *Physical activity for children: A statement of guidelines for children ages 5–12* (2nd ed.). Reston, VA: American Alliance for Health, Physical Education, Recreation, and Dance. Retrieved December 28, 2009, from http://www.aahperd.org/naspe/standards/nationalGuidelines/PA-Children-5-12.cfm

National Association for Sport and Physical Education (NASPE)/American Alliance for Health, Physical Education, Recreation, and Dance (AAHPERD). (2004). *Moving into the future: National standards for Physical Education* (2nd ed.). Reston, VA: AAHPERD.

Ratey, J., & Hagerman, E. (2008). *Spark: The revolutionary new science of exercise and the brain.* New York: Little, Brown.

Introducing the Movement Discovery Approach

Society is always taken by surprise by any new example of common sense.
—Ralph Waldo Emerson (1803–1882)

Common sense is genius dressed in its working clothes.
—Ralph Waldo Emerson

QUESTIONS TO DISCUSS

1. Control will depend on whether children choose to cooperate with a teacher. Discuss this issue with your partner. List factors that would cause children to want to cooperate.

2. Recall any accident you observed or experienced in Physical Education and try to pinpoint its causes. Share this information with your partner.

3. Can you recall any instances where the intervention of an adult caused children's behavior to get worse? Describe them.

4. Try to identify your reaction to aggressive children.

5. Do you think boys exhibit more aggression than girls? When answering this question, think about younger children, not adolescents.

6. Do you think frustration is involved in some cases of bad behavior? Explain.

7. Mention any learning program you have encountered where the objective is to cause behavioral changes. Describe the means used to achieve this goal.

8. What is your own reaction to conflict? When you meet with an antagonistic response, do you tend to withdraw or persist? Would your reaction differ with children versus peers or adults?

9. Have you ever encountered a class of children who seemed to behave badly just to break the monotony (i.e., because "It's boring")? Discuss with your partner.

10. Keep a tally of Physical Education classes that began with activity and not lengthy instructions. Describe the situations that made this approach possible.

11. What makes a good teacher? Try to record vivid memories of "good" and "bad" teachers from your experience as an elementary school student. Identify your reasons for making these judgments, and share them with at least two other members of your group. Try to list at least five characteristics of a "good" teacher.

Previous chapters have highlighted some of the reasons why an individualized program in Physical Education is essential. Ideally, your observations will have convinced you that the Movement Discovery approach to teaching physical skills is consistent with children's ways of learning. Also, you should have noticed that children enjoy physical activity and manage their bodies safely in a great variety of ways and in many different situations.

These factors are great assets in an "artificial" situation, such as a school, in which there is an arbitrary grouping of young children into a large number with others, usually based solely on chronological age. The fact is that society requires children to attend school. Unfortunately, sometimes children become alienated from their natural interests, familiar adults, and self-chosen friends in this educational environment, though much depends on the ethos of a particular school.

Many children expect that the teacher will like them and be a person who cares about helping them to develop and learn. Although they quickly learn that they cannot receive the full attention of a teacher all the time, most children feel more comfortable if a teacher is "accessible" (warm and friendly toward them). Children need to feel that they are valued for who they are. They often expect to be treated equally; as a consequence, one of the most devastating criticisms of teachers by children is that teachers show favoritism. Children are sensitive to atmosphere and body language. They often doubt their own abilities to please a different adult but can relax quickly when they are appreciated for their differences and accepted.

The noun "education" derives from a Latin verb *educare*, meaning "to care for." Our responsibility as teachers of young children is to care for them. This relationship is normally interpreted as being "in loco parentis." In court cases, this duty has been interpreted to mean that teachers must show toward children that care and interest which can be expected of a wise and prudent parent. Of course, there may be pressure on children from their actual parents to "get on," "do well," obey or listen to a teacher, and so on. Attitudes toward schooling vary in different cultures, however.

Most elementary school staff members seek to develop happy places where children are supported, challenged, and enjoyed for who they are. The extent to which this goal is realized depends on many factors, but especially the school principal and the particular group of teachers involved. Most principals expect that their teachers want to interact with and engage young children, that they like children, and that they have the experience, interest, and knowledge to do so gained from their academic preparation. School principals who are in the same school for many years usually have the greatest knowledge of individual children, simply because they observe and interact with the children in their school over several grade levels. Responsibility for setting the "tone" and level of discipline found in any particular school rests ultimately with a

principal, but strong teachers in individual classrooms have a great influence on the school atmosphere.

Teachers are often unaware of their personal attributes and gifts that cause children to behave well and work for them. Many beginning teachers worry whether they will be able to control classes and produce good work. The requirement in this helping profession is to like children and to want to care for them. Teachers need to establish a positive relationship with all members of a class, regardless of the diversity that exists. Teachers of Physical Education need to recognize the difficulties inherent in organizing purposeful activity, using apparatus efficiently, managing time wisely, and covering the content material in their subject area. (In this text, content material is divided into three areas: creative dance/expressive movement, body management/educational gymnastics, and games/pre-sports activities.) Because Physical Education can include risk, teachers need to know how to create safe working spaces and how to develop safe practices in an activity area.

Preservice Teachers

Having considered the general situation, readers now need to look at themselves as future teachers and develop confidence. As is to be expected, no two preservice students will be alike. Many will not experience difficulty in becoming an authority figure and will easily lead children into a satisfying and effective Movement Discovery program—indeed, into any learning situation. It is recommended that preservice students have an opportunity to observe children in Physical Education lessons and have initial experience teaching a small group of children. Share your experiences, doubts, failures, and successes with your fellow students. All teachers need to reflect on their experiences, and a great deal can be learned from others.

OBSERVE, OBSERVE, OBSERVE.

It may require an effort at first to focus on the children and their individual, unique responses. Manner and body language are powerful communicators. Deliberately project an expectation that the opportunities and material that you are presenting will be enjoyable, productive, and appropriate to the child's level of ability. Because you will be offering the child choices in activity, this belief is likely to be upheld. If a teacher enjoys the process, the children will, too. A tense, nervous teacher can easily inhibit children's responses, whereas an enthusiastic, friendly teacher can inspire interest and enjoyment.

The preceding advice applies to the introductory phase of teaching. In the longer term, the intrinsic attraction of content and method should ensure learning and permanent skills development.

Scattered throughout this text is a variety of assignments and discussion topics intended to help teachers improve their own skills in using the Movement Discovery teaching methods. You are strongly advised to use these learning aids, and always to review material in the light of your own experience with children. Listen to others and experts, but ultimately adapt the material and insights to fit your own personality and skills. Reflect, observe, and assess your own teaching skills and do not be afraid to try something new.

Some material offered here will have been used effectively by other teachers in their own situations. You may be a better teacher and may not need any of the following suggestions. Have the courage of your convictions, and take control of your own learning and development.

Introducing Movement Discovery

Briefly, if a Movement Discovery approach is new to a class, a teacher would do well to assess the situation and discover something about the expectations the children have regarding the program. An interesting way to uncover children's expectations for an activity session or Physical Education lesson is to ask each child to draw a picture of a Physical Education lesson that includes a picture of themselves. Look carefully at the responses.

A principal or school may have organizational structures already in place. For example, there may be established procedures for using facilities. Notice the behavior in school corridors, and most significantly at bus assembly areas, if they exist. Before- and after-school behavior and conversations with bus drivers and supervisors can be very revealing. Remember that staffroom conversations are often a way of letting off steam and relaxing from the very demanding nature of good teaching—so do not be misled by negative comments about certain classes or specific individuals. You may not provoke the same reactions as other teachers.

Children do not like to be preached at, nagged, or told things they already know. It may be worthwhile ignoring

> ### Anecdote 5-1
>
> A beginning teacher had a class of 12-year-old students. When recess came, the teacher allowed them to go out into the hallway without lining up. The principal happened to see unruly behavior and brought them *all* back to line up (complaining to the teacher). The teacher apologized and said she would do something about it but asked the principal if she could do things her way. Because the teacher agreed the children had behaved badly, the principal grudgingly agreed.
>
> The teacher made sure the children were busy on individual activities when the bell rang for recess. Ignoring it for a few minutes, she said, "If you have finished your work, you can tidy your desk and go out to recess." (One or two rushed out.)
>
> After a few weeks the teacher checked with the principal if "her" class was behaving well in the hallways. (By this time, she sometimes had to insist that students go out to recess instead of continuing to work.) The principal agreed her class behaved well but said, "I could have done it more quickly." Later, when writing a recommendation for this teacher, he said, "She prefers the unorthodox approach."

a less-than-perfect response to an introductory activity so as to get going quickly and improve the response later when at least some of the class is busy and beginning to get interested. "I'm waiting," when said to a restless class, is rarely effective. "Let's do it again and see if we can improve" would be better if children know a normal noise level is expected and neater or more careful action or better concentration is required. A "slightly" surprised teacher (or a shocked one) can be effective if the children know that the teacher is normally friendly and welcoming. Sometimes giving the problem to the children generates a useful response ("I would like to use more equipment but I'm not sure how we can best get it out"). Equipment should always be in good condition (e.g., no deflated balls, broken hoops) and plentiful.

A discovery teaching method has been, and is today, widely used in preschool, nursery, and kindergarten education. We are familiar with a group of young children busy on their own in a variety of situations and not all doing the same thing, in the same way, at the same time. Even so, a unison response and a "neat" formation (e.g., lines, squads, rows) have traditionally become associated with good control, especially in Physical Education; the model is a military one. Some parents, other adults, and traditional teachers, principals, and supervisors may look at a discovery session and perceive it to be merely "play" or even "chaos." Such a session does not look orderly; in fact, it is sometimes difficult even to see the teacher, as he or she is not dominating the lesson. In a discovery session, the teacher may look like one of the children, possibly participating with a group of students or involved with one individual child, but certainly not always obvious. And yet there is much to do to establish a discovery program that is purposeful and well controlled. The goal is for the children to develop self-control; the children will have taken over the responsibility for much of their own learning.

If you are the person introducing this situation, you might like to prepare your justification for what you are doing. Be ready to point out to an observer the significant aspects of the process.

The role of a teacher when introducing Movement Discovery in the early stages is to circulate among, affirm, and encourage the children; to help them to develop self-confidence; to suggest further variations; and to make children think about what they are discovering and concentrate on what they are doing. Teachers may need to challenge the confident to exert greater effort and enjoy their achievements, encourage the timid, befriend the nervous, become more familiar with individual differences and the capacities of all children, and remember what comes next in the lesson and how to make a smooth transition. You will be busy! The following chapters of this book give examples of quite specific comments that a teacher might use as part of a discovery approach. You will, of course, need to develop your own way of commenting on children's work. The reward is that, apart from enjoying the process and the children, teaching becomes easier day-by-day. Classroom management can even reach a point where the children hardly need to be controlled by

a teacher. "I know I have done a good job," said one teacher, "because I can leave the room and nothing will change." Legally, you are reminded, you have a duty of continuous supervision. You must remember that it might take time to introduce a Movement Discovery program.

In Movement Discovery, where small groups are used often, there are many opportunities for leadership. Although both boys and girls often need support as leaders, traditionally many more girls than boys have found it difficult to accept and exercise leadership. In the past, girls were seldom chosen by their classmates to be, say, team captains. Even when the teacher assigned girls to be team captains, often a boy took over the job. Teachers need to give active support to children so that they can learn effective leadership skills.

If children refuse leadership, accept their refusal but ask them to do it "another time." ("I'll help you." "Well, do it just for now.") Switch the area of request. Reinforce good action or management first and then request leadership. "I knew you could do it." When children "show," prepare the class to appreciate the performance, and acknowledge the effort. ("Good try!") Ask for an activity in twos, where one student will be the leader and the other student will copy; then switch leadership among the pairs. Sometimes ask good performers, on a gender-equal basis, for permission to use them as demonstration. Allow volunteers to "show."

If there is a particular child whom no one will choose as partner, try to arrange activities so that you are free to work with that child. Call the student to you quickly before he or she gets left out. You will need to do this several times in a row. As the teacher, you may start out with this child, but then trade partners with another pair so that you get to work with "someone else for a little while"; next, make another trade so that you work with a third child. Another way to approach this issue is (privately before the lesson) to ask a good-natured child to choose the isolate as a partner. You might also want or allow the isolated child to play alone and give him or her frequent attention. In the long run, you will need to find out the reason behind the child's isolation.

Teach an awareness of how physical differences can affect leadership or success in physical activities. Help

children understand that they are their own best judges, and that what they are judging is their own progress. The tall child has more weight when climbing rope, the short-legged child is more likely to knock the hurdles down, the child with a long spine finds it hard to roll, and so on. Can you do more now than you could? Good! Hot and sweaty? Good! Encourage doing it "differently." Praise creativity and originality.

DEMONSTRATIONS BY CHILDREN

Sometimes a good demonstration by a member of the class inspires others to emulate it. The things to aim for should always be pointed out in a demonstration, and the other children should immediately be allowed to try the activity again. The Movement Discovery teacher does not demonstrate, but rather distributes the privilege of demonstrating fairly and equally among the children.

This is a way to share the ideas children generate. Other ideas for making demonstrations by children more effective so that children notice more include the following:

- Select children who are doing UNUSUAL movements.

- Select one to three children doing movements WELL (good control/polish).

- Highlight SIMILARITIES and DIFFERENCES.

- Make demonstrations BRIEF but INFORMATIVE.

- Direct attention to CONTRASTING movements, positions, or shapes.

- Select ALL ABILITY LEVELS, not just the "best" movers.

- Check the children's understanding by using QUESTIONS.

- Over time, plan for EVERY CHILD in the class to demonstrate something.

- Allow half the class to OBSERVE the other half and comment positively.

- Arrange for OBSERVATION in pairs.

Organization

Organization is best thought out beforehand. Teachers need to take into account the environment, safe uses of space, and the likely responses of children. Children need choices. They must develop their own ideas and be allowed to improve both variety and skill. Have brief stopping signals. A gym or activity room represents a classroom or laboratory, and a clear, well-articulated human voice should be sufficient to get attention.

POSSIBLE SIGNALS FOR STOPPING AND STARTING ACTIVITIES

If possible, use one-word commands or very brief instructions.

Signals for Stopping

"Stop!"
"Freeze!"
"Hold it!"
"Sit down!"
"Finish."
"Finish up now."
Handclap
Whistle (short, sharp blast)
Drumbeat (clear and quick)
"Stop and sit."
"Stop and jump up and down."
"Stop and stretch high."
Make a preliminary warning sound and "Stop!"
"Aaaaaaaaaaand, stop!"
"All right and stop!"
"And rest."
"Slow down, slower, and stop."
"Okay, everybody stop."
"Finish off what you are doing and stop."
"Stop and come and sit here."
"When the music stops, sit down."
"When you've had one more turn, I want you to put the apparatus away."
"Have your last turn, then come and sit down."
"You have 10 seconds to finish."
"Five, four, three, two, one, and finish."
"If you are climbing high, start coming down slowly because in a minute we are going to stop."

Signals for Starting

"Run!"
"Spread out and run."
"Off you go!"
"Begin."
"Go!"
"Are you ready?"
"Start moving."
"Get busy."
"Start as soon as you're ready."
"When you are in a space, begin."

SOME WAYS OF ORGANIZING EQUIPMENT

As a general rule, to help with organizing their classes, some teachers prefer to keep all small equipment (hoops, balls, bean bags, jump ropes, small bats) in boxes or milk crates with separate compartments that are always placed near the periphery of the area. If all equipment is divided into four to six boxes, then there are several places where any item is available. This spread-out arrangement can reduce crowding. Some teachers paint each box a different color and divide children into permanent color groups so that on any occasion children know where to fetch and return equipment.

Pay attention early on to the dispersal and collection of all equipment. Smooth organization and no wasted time will repay you later.

- Equipment could be spread out along the perimeter of the working area.

- Have children fetch equipment by color of clothing, if their name starts with "S", if their birthday is in December, and so on. The ultimate goal is to teach the children to walk—not rush—to collect equipment.

- If children collect individual mats or any other equipment from a single source, try to allow access from all sides.

- Care should be taken to see that equipment is handled sensibly and put away properly.

- Have children collect the equipment and take the closest piece to them. (Discourage grabbing.) There is enough for everyone to use or share.

- Put the equipment on the floor and rest your foot on it.

- Encourage children to "Show me that you're ready to use the equipment by taking it out properly."

- If all teachers use the same facility, agree with another teacher to use the same apparatus or equipment and split the organization. One teacher can get out apparatus and leave it out at the end of the lesson. The next teacher can then use the same apparatus and put it away at the end of his or her lesson.

- Consider whether an area with permanent climbing apparatus could be made available for all classes.

- Using equipment may pose problems of organization, but it usually increases children's interest. Especially with difficult classes, all children must have an item. Expecting badly behaved children to wait for a turn is likely to increase any difficulties; the passive or timid need the stimulus and opportunity to use equipment.

- When using small equipment, state or suggest the activities to be performed before the apparatus is obtained. Teach personal responsibility.

Anecdote 5–3

An elementary Physical Education teacher was offered $5000 by a climbing apparatus company representative to buy climbing frames, such as A-frames, trestles, and other portable hanging, sliding, swinging, and climbing equipment for his son's elementary school. The Physical Education teacher declined the offer, saying all he wanted was some more balls, not trestles and bars. The teacher ended up with nothing new. The school had no educational gymnastic equipment at all.

- A general rule to establish is that upon getting apparatus, the child must take the item to a space (away from the container) before it is used. If behavior is not good or the apparatus is not properly treated, then it should be put away again. This can be done on an individual basis or on a class basis as necessary, but it is important to give children another chance to show improvement if they really are unfamiliar with procedures.

- Teachers should not tackle the use of large apparatus or group work until they are confident that they can control children in an active situation. When children can work sensibly, without interfering with others, and when a teacher can stop a group on demand, then large apparatus can be explored.

- When children are climbing on apparatus, give them a warning and never make them hurry to get down and off it.

- Prepare challenge/task cards and place them at the apparatus or in learning centers/stations. This step eliminates the need for some of the teacher's explanations and allows for more effective use of time.

- Use concrete objects to establish areas for teaching: markers, ropes, hoops, vinyl spots, traffic cones, and so on.

Anecdote 5–4

An elementary school principal was given $1000 to spend on Physical Education equipment. He had noticed that when playing softball, many students were afraid to catch the ball. He decided to buy enough softball mitts so that every child in the class could have one. When asked how many balls were available for softball, he replied, "Two."

Ways to Choose Partners or Groups

- Choose a variety of equipment and use it. Later choose a partner who has the same equipment as you.

- Choose a partner who is the same height (or weight) as you.

- Get the closest person to you and sit down.

- Choose a partner with whom you have never worked before.

- Choose a partner whose name begins with the same letter as yours (or color of eyes, color of clothing, and so on).

- Choose a partner you think you could help.

- Choose a partner who can do the same skill as you.

- Choose a piece of equipment you would like to use and sit in that station (equipment previously distributed).

- The teacher may privately prearrange for some children to "help" others.

- The teacher may establish a policy that each member of the class works with everyone else before the end of the term.

- Choose same-gender partners. Later include a group-of-four activity, and include a girl couple and a boy couple in each group.

- The teacher may assign partners—either ahead of the lesson or while children are getting equipment. If there are any objections, tell the students, "Try it first and see me later."

- Find a partner before the teacher counts to 5.

- Sometimes partners can get equipment and begin, while the rest sit until the teacher assigns them to an activity.

- Mix boy/girl partners.

- Work with a partner who lives near you.

- Use color or number cards that are randomly distributed. Ask each child to find the child with the matching color or number.

- Require mixed-gender teams (no more than four per side). The teacher may establish a policy that groups or teams formed by children are to include equal numbers of boys and girls.

> One of the bitterest memories retained by some adults of their Physical Education lessons is "I was always last to be picked. No one wanted me on their team."

Ways to Increase Active Learning Time

- Reduce the amount of time spent in transitioning from one activity to another.

- Reduce the amount of time spent in giving instructions for tasks.

- Spend as little time as possible organizing partners and small groups.

- Distribute all small equipment as quickly as possible.

CONTROL

Current educational practice urges teachers to focus on children and follow individual interests and capacities. Chapters 2 and 3 in this text have shown how essential this approach is. Even so, a discovery method may represent a change in teaching method for some teachers or some schools. Following is an attempt to offer some help where this is the case. This help may be limited in value, however: Discipline and control are always personal issues. What has helped some teachers in some situations may not be useful in all cases. Behavior management and motivation for learning depend on many factors, so readers are advised to spend some time examining their own skills and approach to teaching. "Teachers are born, not made" and "Leaders are born, not made" are familiar phrases that may contain a grain of truth.

Many teachers have reported that discipline improves when the Movement Discovery teaching method is used. They also find that because they are freer to observe, they are able to be more proactive and can intervene in potentially disruptive situations before they become full-blown problems. The following material describes some ways in which some teachers have solved problems related to behavior management. You may not need them.

The objective of Movement Discovery is responsible self-management and awareness of others. Here, however, the focus is on introducing the program in a situation where it has not been used. It is also true that Physical Education lessons offer a very rich environment for the personal development of teachers as well as children. It is no accident that many directors of education, supervisors, consultants, and principals started their careers as Physical Education teachers: They learned and honed their skills by managing groups of active children before they used those same skills to manage systems and larger numbers of people.

Experience in teaching even just a few children to discover physical skills and activities will be valuable, as it allows beginning educators to discover some of their own limitations and gifts in teaching. Children appreciate a teacher who is interested in them personally and

First-grade boy to visiting Physical Education teacher: "Miss, I think you're a good teacher." "Thank you, Johnny. Why is that?" "Because you always use lots of stuff."

who is fair to all (no "favorites"). Children respond well to being trusted.

The Movement Discovery teaching method seeks to follow the natural process through which children grow, develop, and learn. When this aim is achieved, the teaching method will not be difficult to implement. Children should find it to be simply an extension of the current "modus operandi." Teachers, however, may find it different from their experience or the ethos of a school. Beginning teachers particularly may be unsure of the kind of responses they will get. Even having taught part of a lesson or a small group of children will give the novice more confidence when using this teaching method.

It will be important to learn which kind of activity lessons and Physical Education programs the children have experienced in the past. Movement Discovery expects the individual student to demonstrate a high degree of self-responsibility and self-control, even when activities take place in the midst of other children. If this requirement is not mandated elsewhere in a school (children must line up in hallways, not run at recess, and so on), care should be taken to introduce Movement Discovery gradually.

In this situation, for safety reasons perhaps large apparatus should not be used until control is established. Such apparatus is naturally attractive to children and focuses their attention immediately. Hula hoops, scoops, and bean bags are easier to control than balls that bounce and roll and jump ropes that "entangle." Teachers must judge each situation for themselves. Benches and mats on the floor could precede trestles, bars, and climbing ropes.

If there is large apparatus in the playground, a teacher can observe how well children use it before including the equipment in a lesson, but it should be used if available. It might be possible to take part of a Movement Discovery lesson outdoors for vigorous running and then come indoors for subsequent activity. The overload benefits to the body of using large apparatus are highly valuable, and all children should have an opportunity to use it.

The key to control and discipline with a class of children is the students' relationships not only with the teacher, but with one another. These relationships reflect basic processes in the educational system, several of which have been highlighted in previous chapters. Most normal children want to learn, enjoy the learning process, and welcome gifted and caring help from a qualified adult who is interested in them. Children can distinguish the kind of interest that is self-seeking from the kind of interest where the other person genuinely wants to help; in turn, they often respond differently to individual teachers. Unfortunately, supportive factors are sometimes lacking in children's lives, placing the children in jeopardy when we group them and develop a system of schooling. Children sometimes learn in spite of schools, in spite of teachers, and even in spite of themselves and their families. Society, of course, seeks to enable and develop the fullest potential of its younger members, with adults often projecting onto youths their own aspirations and failed accomplishments. As teachers, we must never order our educational systems to squelch the thirst for knowledge and skill in a misguided attempt to cater only to those who have been damaged (though remedial work needs to be included); conversely, educators must not allow the difficulties of group instruction to detract from or inhibit the process of nurturing individual abilities.

While recognizing the difficulties of developing individual teachers' gifts and competencies, it is essential to encourage personal confidence and effectiveness before allowing neophyte teachers to experience the problems of school situations where control and discipline have already broken down. Teachers must develop their own ways of inspiring and motivating children, and there are many factors to be borne in mind when doing so.

Consider these discussion questions in relation to the following anecdotes:

1. Do children enjoy learning material that is topical, relevant, and useful to them?

2. Is the focus on activity, not behavior?

3. Do children learn more from attitudes than from direct teaching?

4. Do children want to be treated fairly—that is, the same way as everyone else?

Consider the following anecdotes carefully. Each has profound implications.

A young second-grade teacher was hired in the middle of the school year to take over a class whose teacher had resigned upon becoming pregnant. The principal warned the new teacher that it was a poor class; there was much absenteeism, lateness, and lack of enthusiasm for school. The county supervisor told the teacher that the students' reading ability was very poor and below level. When a reading lesson was announced, the children asked, "Do we have to?"

The teacher had enjoyed good success previously in teaching Physical Education with a discovery approach. Although the school's facilities were poor, she managed to obtain enough small balls for the class to play with them, and she took the children to a park adjacent to the school. When it snowed, she obtained sheets of plastic so that the class members could slide down inclines.

Avoiding the use of reading books, the teacher introduced morning and afternoon lessons in Physical Education, enriching the lessons with much oral language, art, and movement. It was the time of the first moon walk, so the class made lunar module constructions with toothpicks and orange peel and looked at the pictures the teacher obtained from NASA. Much discussion and excitement were generated in the classroom, and absenteeism and lateness improved greatly. After about a month, more formal reading materials were gradually introduced and the children eagerly participated in lessons.

When the county supervisor came to observe near the end of the school year, she complimented the new teacher by saying she must be a magnificent reading teacher: The children were now reading at or above grade level and showed interest in learning. The new teacher responded by saying she was not a great teacher of reading, but rather cared more that children were interested in school and learning.

5. Do the appearance and manner of a teacher inspire some children?

6. Do positive comments eliminate some undesirable behavior?

7. Should "problem" children be dealt with on an individual basis?

8. Is novelty attractive to children?

A beginning teacher went to the fully equipped gym at her new school—a school that took many children who were refused entrance to other schools on the grounds of bad behavior—to teach her first Physical Education lesson. When she arrived, she discovered that the boys had not been told that their lesson that day was to take place in the hall. The two mixed classes of 11-year-olds had taken out all available large apparatus and were using it vigorously with a great deal of pleasure and noise.

Slamming the door, the teacher announced in her loudest voice, "Stop what you are doing and stand still!" There was no response; the teacher doubted that she had even been heard. Discarding the thought "What do I do now? They never told me about this at college," she proceeded to the row of climbing ropes that bisected the room and physically dragged them to the sides. (Various students dropped off the ropes during this process.) It made a noise and some students became aware of her presence, a new teacher neatly dressed in her gym uniform. When all students were sitting on the floor, the novice teacher sent the boys to the hallway, where their own teacher awaited them. She then got the ropes out again, required all girls to attempt to climb them, and encouraged much activity on all other apparatus. After several minutes when the girls were visibly tiring, she put apparatus away and sat the class down to introduce both herself and the program. Safety and the conduct of a Physical Education lesson were included.

PREVENTIVE TECHNIQUES

Sometimes a proactive teacher prevents situations from developing. Children need to know that bad behavior has been noticed. Sometimes just a look from the teacher or the mention of a name is enough to check the child. Walk closer to a child who is not working well and watch for a few moments. If a normally friendly and interested teacher turns a little "cool" toward specific behavior or undue noise, that is often enough to stop it. It is important for a teacher not to get emotionally involved in a more difficult situation, but rather to calmly suggest that a child or a small group take a "time-out." The teacher can continue positive reinforcement with the rest of the class.

Often, asking the offending child to sit out and watch temporarily is very effective. Allow the child to decide when to rejoin the group. ("I want you to sit and watch

Paul, aged 12 years, caused major disruptions in class. The class "clown," he had recently failed an examination that would have set him on the road to follow his father into the police force. Paul dropped books, fell off his chair, made smart comments, and generally wreaked havoc in the classroom, much to the delight of his classmates, who responded uproariously and egged him on.

Shortly after the beginning of the school year, Paul got sick and ended up in the hospital. The teacher made all classes write letters to Paul, which she promised she would deliver without reading. (She later discovered that one letter began, "Dear Paul, I am writing to you because Miss Blank says we have to.")

When Paul returned to school, he began to work and by the end of the year earned good grades. His parents thanked the teacher with tears in their eyes for turning Paul around. The teacher said she had done nothing other than to treat Paul the same way as the other children.

how others are behaving, and when you think you can behave more sensibly or settle down [or work properly] you can join in again.") Keep an eye on the offender; if he or she does not rejoin the class after a few minutes, more investigation may be required.

It is more effective to question children than to reprimand them: "Why are you not working properly? Is it too difficult for you? Are you not interested in . . . ?" The aim is to inspire and stimulate cooperation from the child; to show flexibility rather than rigidity often accomplishes this goal. A good feature of the Movement Discovery approach is that it allows each child to function at his or her own individual level and, therefore, can be interesting to everyone.

Some children are easily distracted in the early stages of a discovery program if too many "attractive nuisances" are present. This problem can usually be solved by a specific, direct request from a teacher to a particular child. At any time a teacher can be direct and tell a child what to do if needed.

Overall, the best way of preventing disruptive behavior is to present interesting material at the child's level that has some relationship to "real life." Children always appreciate a teacher who cares.

Proactive, effective teachers often use the following techniques to prevent undesirable behaviors from occurring:

- Have sufficient small equipment so that children don't have to wait for their turn.

- Avoid the need to share small equipment, particularly with the youngest children.

- Maximize activity time; minimize talking/listening time.

- Avoid line-ups where children have to wait for their turn to move or use apparatus.

- Give choices. Choice promotes cooperation and helps prevent uncooperative behavior.

- Be aware of readiness for competitive activities. When children can handle competition, it naturally emerges in their behavior. In contrast, when competition is imposed by the teacher, some children who find it too difficult may misbehave to avoid it.

- Be alert to pairing unsteady children with each other.

- Check the responses to content material and the children's interest levels.

- Be neutral (or unemotional) in attitude rather than emotional in potentially argumentative or explosive situations.

- Send a warning look without using any words.

- Walk close to the child who is exhibiting the behavior that is not appropriate or desirable and stand still, again with no verbal interaction.

- Remove "attractive nuisances" that distract children.

- Use a "self-help/time-out." During this short time period, the child—not the teacher—chooses to sit out of the lesson until he or she is steady and ready to work again.

- Remind the child about what he or she should be doing: "Your job now is to . . ."

- Withdraw warmth and praise in situations where teacher is usually very positive.

- Listen to both sides of a dispute and ask children how they think it should be solved fairly. Alternatively, state, "I'm sorry, but I haven't time to deal with this issue now; if you can't sort it out fairly, perhaps you had both better sit out for this activity." (If children do sit out, try to get over to them before long and help.)

- Ask misbehaving children, "If you both want the same piece of equipment , then perhaps neither of you should have it?" If the teacher is really busy, he or she can take the piece under dispute, and both children can get something else to use.

During the semester when you are observing and working with experienced teachers, make notes on the things they do and say to effectively obtain and maintain children's interests and cooperation.

The most powerful technique a teacher can use to improve behavior is positive reinforcement. Look for the good behavior you want to strengthen, and then verbally praise or say "very good" in many different ways. Some suggestions follow.

Examples of Verbal Praise

I'm proud of your work today.	You're doing a good job.
That's a big improvement.	Now you have it.
You're thinking!	Clever!
You made it look easy.	Look at you go!
That's coming along nicely.	That's an interesting shape.
That's a good landing.	Keep trying.
That's hard work.	Outstanding!
You did it that time.	Way to go.
I knew you could do it.	Well done.
Excellent!	That's an interesting pattern.
You're working hard.	I like what you're doing.

Examples of Nonverbal Praise

Winks	Head nods
High five	Thumbs-up signal
Tap on the shoulder	Mimic applause
Facial expression	Smiles

The emphasis throughout this text has been on the individual. Each child is different, which means that the basis of learning and physical development is individual and personal. This point applies to both teachers and students, of course. It has also been suggested that the development of confident, skilled, and self-reliant children is a natural process that will proceed in an orderly fashion if allowed to do so. This development can be encouraged, even perhaps challenged and stimulated. Your own observations of children should have convinced you that safety, discipline, tolerance, and self-motivation really are present in most children. The focus now is on the perhaps artificial situation of children in schools, however. There the grouping of children according to chronological age and the logistics of organization of large numbers of children and

teachers in a restricted environment must be considered in terms of how they affect children's development. Discipline and control are concerns of most neophyte teachers, and it is not surprising that the development of such skills and self-confidence in teachers also proceeds in a uniquely individual fashion. One of the best means of preparation for a beginning teacher is to work initially with small groups of children and to develop familiarity, confidence, and skill in content areas.

The specific suggestions included here reflect the skills and experiences of a variety of individuals. Even so, these recommendations may not apply to the specific group and the particular individual who is preparing to become a teacher of young children in physical activity. As before, anecdotes are included to emphasize the key points, along with questions intended to provoke thought and reflection. While there is no substitute for experience, each experience is inevitably personal and individual.

Many teachers believe that it is better to start a program with strict expectations that can be relaxed later as mutual respect develops. Others trust and lead children to expect good behavioral responses from the outset. Children's cooperation may need to be won, and enjoyment and interest are powerful factors in persuading children to cooperate. In contrast, the imposition of rules and restrictions often prevents children from realizing the full value of content material. Each situation must be evaluated and considered as it arises. The basis of noncooperation, bad behavior, or disruption of a group is best tackled on an individual basis by the particular teacher.

Disruptive students may be striking out at what they perceive as a hostile world, seeking attention, or expressing inner hurt, frustration, or boredom. The intervention in these situations can only be personal, caring, investigative, and individual (and perhaps implemented in private). Children always resent the class being punished because of the actions of a few. They also often react badly to rules and restrictions for which they see no need or purpose. Conversely, children respond well to being trusted and expected to behave sensibly. When this type of bond exists, learning can become a partnership with a teacher, with mutual respect and the natural "give and take" of human relationships. Teachers are privileged to be given the trust of such a variety of individuals during their growing years. They really do need to enjoy this diversity and to show their enjoyment of it, as this joy can help to prevent "burnout." In a Movement Discovery program, the opportunities for lifelong influence, help, and inspiration are many and always very exciting. The "problem" of bad behavior in children is actually a wonderful opportunity for good teachers to help youngsters in very significant ways that can affect their whole future lives.

Teachers should take time to discuss the questions of control and discipline whenever they are working with groups of children, but especially when physical activity is involved. Experience working with small groups of children should be offered in the initial teacher preparation courses. In the long run, the ways in which teachers will inspire and control children are personal and can be achieved in a tremendous variety of situations in many different ways. Confidence in personal teaching ability to control and guide may also need to be nurtured in many different ways.

NOTES ON CLASS CONTROL

In general, many teachers agree that it is easier to set firm guidelines for behavior that can later be relaxed. An "easy" or "informal" relationship between children and teacher, in which children are expected to behave responsibly, depends much more for its success on the personality of the teacher. Children can be prepared for this expectation before they enter the activity area, and boundaries may need to be set in advance.

Children's interest in this material is the best guarantee of good control. Nevertheless, unless a teacher is a sufficiently good disciplinarian to get started, the interest and attention of the class in the content material cannot be aroused.

Make sure that the children know that you really do want them to invent their own activity. Be supportive and encouraging, and give clear tasks or challenges. As Strain and Hemmeter (1999, p. 24) state, "Children often exhibit challenging behaviors because they don't know any other way to respond to a situation."

If the initial response is unruly or uncooperative, identify one or two children who have responded well; praise them, possibly let them show how they perform, and repeat the activity. Try to get children to engage in vigorous activity such as jumping before asking for "stop." Then simply repeat the activity or something similar until behavior improves and the "stop" response is better. Activity calms the energetic and arouses the passive—and it is certainly better (and more effective) than talking or nagging. Indeed, it is the rare child who responds well to being "nagged" or shouted at.

The best way to persuade children to change their undesirable behavior is to "withdraw" approval, to become a little "cold." This tactic will not work unless the children are used to a warm, friendly, and helpful teacher who approves of and encourages good behavior, hard work, vigorous activity, creativity, new ideas, thoughtfulness for others, and so on. If praise and encouragement are common and easy to "earn" in the classroom, then the disappointment of the teacher is usually sufficient to cause children to improve their behavior. Persistent individual problems should probably be dealt with out of lesson time.

Even at the expense of some noise and chatter, activity is essential. When it is present, the teacher is in a position to withhold further activity unless the noise level or participation improves. This is very difficult to do unless a start has been made. "I'm waiting" may work with unso-

phisticated groups, but it is not effective in many cases. Activity without apparatus is simpler to begin with and offers an incentive. (When a beginning activity is well done, then apparatus can be added!) With small children, much of the noise is a natural release with vigorous activity; more activity is needed to reduce the noise level.

Instead of dealing directly with undue noise, silliness, careless performance, or nonparticipation, an improvement can often be obtained by concentrating on "how" the activity is being performed: "I want to see your knees bend when you land." "The feet should be stretched in the air." "I can see two people really jumping high in the air." This type of comment, plus the mentioning of specific individuals for commendation and encouragement, will do much to improve concentration, thereby eliminating some poor behavior. Encourage the children to show good responses: Positive reinforcement really does work best.

If children fidget a great deal, you may be talking too much. Use eye contact and your eyes effectively, instead. Often a "straight" look at the child, perhaps with a "query" expression, is enough to check a child. This nonverbal behavior will only work if the child is aware of expected behavior, however. Even just the mention of a name could help: "Susan?" (The implication here is that you know Susan normally behaves well and you are a little "surprised.")

You can also ask open-ended questions to check a child, but only if you have a normally good relationship with the child: "Jimmy, do you think that is a good thing to do?" Questions work better than reprimands.

Sometimes a calm assumption that all is, and will be well, is the best approach and permits a slightly pained surprise if anyone should behave carelessly or noisily. As many teachers realize, children are particularly sensitive to tone of voice, manner, and bearing (teachers' posture), and they often pick up and respond to these kinds of nonverbal cues without realizing it. Speaking quietly to a group often reduces noise level.

Anecdote 5–9

A 12-year-old girl began to cause disruption in the class whenever a particular new teacher taught. The new teacher was very overweight, and the student had a mother who was "fat." The girl was a leader in the class. When asked why she caused so much trouble (she had been sent to the principal by the new teacher), she replied, "Because she's fat." (The student was ashamed of her mother.) Later the girl admitted that the new teacher had tried to befriend her and the student thought this was wrong; the girl believed that a teacher should treat all students in the same way.

Safety

In the early stages of developing Movement Discovery, there was much concern for safety. Many feared that accidents would increase if children (also young soldiers) were allowed freedom to use large apparatus without benefit of instruction. (See Chapter 1.) As is so often the case in education, a "problem" can also represent an "opportunity" for learning. Do we want young children to learn to be safe in a variety of physical activities? If so, then we must, "as wise and prudent parents," allow them to extend their experience. In present-day culture, one might even suggest that it is a violation of human rights to prevent children from climbing trees and exploring the environment (gates, fences, and ditches), and not to allow them to experience a sense of adventure in tackling the new and the unknown.

One early court case in Great Britain in 1954, when Movement Discovery was being developed, included a statement from the judge about the use of climbing apparatus. Mr. Justice Cassels (P.E. Association, n.d., p. 9.) stated, "This equipment in schools takes the place of what is available to the country child, who has trees and fences to climb." If you have observed children consistently, you will already have an opinion about this issue.

Consider for a moment a simple activity such as running. When children learn to walk, they attempt to run. Running presents greater hazards than walking and introduces the possibility of greater injury if not performed well. Should parents forbid running? Would it change the child's behavior if it were forbidden? When the forbidding adult was not present, it is likely that the child would attempt to run anyway—but perhaps this

---

Anecdote 5–10

A new teacher found no climbing equipment at her school, so she proceeded to have a fund-raiser to buy it. Within three months she had purchased and was using in her lessons the wall frames, trestles, bars, and some mats. The teacher enthusiastically started teaching educational gymnastics. Her supervisor of Physical Education came to observe and told her that using the apparatus was dangerous. The new teacher was distressed and asked one of her former professors to come and evaluate what she was doing. She was told she was doing an excellent job. After a year, the teacher transferred out of the county school system and into the school system of an adjoining county. She proceeded to do another fund-raiser for climbing apparatus at her new school. She went on to be a State Elementary Teacher of the Year in Physical Education.

---

time with fear of being discovered or guilt at disobeying instructions. Concentration would be impaired. If the internal pressure to run had been inhibited for a long period of time, it is possible the excitement level would be high and the resultant attempt even less controlled.

At the other end of the scale, imagine two excited young parents who are so thrilled that their child can walk that they each hold a hand and make the child run with them faster than the child would choose if left alone. Because the hands are held, the child cannot use them to protect the face, head, and neck if a fall takes place. The basic "safety (protective extension) reflex" has been inhibited.

In both of these cases, the child's learning has been inhibited and "unrealistic" sensory input may interfere with normal learning. If it is decided that running in a restricted space when others are present is hazardous, then the adults in society may decide to organize this activity for the children. Rules could be applied to restrict the direction of running, the pace, the length of time, and so on. Of course, children have individual capacities, so it would be very difficult to organize the activity to suit all of the individual levels of ability. Should the activity of running be banned? Perhaps running should be allowed only if it is not over the ground but rather is "stationary" or "on the spot." This idea may sound ludicrous today, but running on the spot has featured in past physical training programs, particularly in a military context.

The "problem" of many children running in a confined space can offer teachers the opportunity to teach responsible self-management while becoming aware of the needs of others. As a matter of fact, children have considerable experience with this type of limitation, as your observation of children will undoubtedly confirm. Look particularly at your observations of children when no adults are present. Self-preservation and the avoidance of injury really do seem to be a part of human nature. Depth perception (motion parallax) is present in very young children (as evidenced by the famous "visual cliff" experiments); babies only days old can support their body weight by hanging using the arms alone. Children chase and run at recess, in parks, and in sports. Even young children often simply run "for pleasure." Children do learn to run safely without the benefit of adult instruction and can control their bodies and apparatus in an extraordinary range of situations. We should encourage this exploration and provide many opportunities for learning this safety at an early age in a group situation. This is the emphasis in Movement Discovery.

> "Yes, we had P.E. at my other school
> but all we learned to do was stand in line."
>
> —Second-grade girl

There are several important factors to be considered. Children will move and climb if given the opportunity to do so. It is impossible to predict what children will do when exploring and inventing activities, so spotting is impossible and inappropriate. It is safe to allow this activity, and teachers should not be tempted to impose their ideas on children. In fact, if teachers do require children to perform imposed activities, they must be prepared to provide "spotting" assistance or safety precautions for error. This requires special training and is outside the mandate of a Movement Discovery teacher. To repeat, children should be left alone to work at their own level of competence.

For children, there is only one rule: "You may have a turn, but look after yourself and do not touch anyone else." "No touching even if asked to."

It is the teacher's responsibility to ensure that the physical environment is not crowded. There should be no "line-ups" that put pressure on those who are active. Line-ups also waste valuable time that could be spent in activities.

LEGAL LIABILITY

It was mentioned earlier that the definition of the word "education" comes from a Latin verb meaning "to care for." This notion is particularly relevant when one comes to consider the question of legal liability. Legally, teachers are required to exert that care for students which could be expected from a wise and prudent parent. The law does recognize that there is something called an accident, and there is no penalty attached to a pure accident. Legal cases are also decided on a basis of precedence, however. For this reason, it is important for a local school district and the professional teachers associations to keep records of previous court cases.

If liability is to be proven, negligence must be proved and the onus of proof is on the plaintiff. The best defense against a charge of negligence is to prove "contributory negligence," which shows that the victim was partly responsible for the event. This is one reason why Movement Discovery insists that children should be allowed to choose their activities and to work at their individual level of competence. Individualized instruction presents a sound educational goal with lifelong benefits. It requires students to take responsibility for their own actions and allows the natural self-preservation instincts to flourish.

As indicated in the section on safety, if a teacher does decide to impose a skill or performance on a student, adequate "spotting" and safety precautions must be taken. To teach specific skills can imply coercion. Spotting requires training, however, and such training is rarely provided for classroom teachers in their one or two Physical Education preservice courses. Spotting also requires the teacher to be involved, because children should never act as spotters. Children have a slower reaction time and are not physically mature enough to take that responsibility. If a teacher is required to be spotting, he or she is unavailable for supervision and observation. A study of legal precedents in Physical Education will reveal that most frequently liability applies to coercion, lack of supervision, and inadequate instruction.

> The skill level within the average Physical Education class varies greatly from student to student. Depending upon the activity, it may or may not be reasonable to expect all students to perform at the same level or even perform the same task. Individualization of instruction not only makes good sense educationally, but also makes for good practice from a liability standpoint.... (Oregon State Department of Education, 1988, p. 21)

> [E]ach Physical Education class is characterized by variances in size, experience and in some cases age. These variances can be extreme in some instances. It is the responsibility of the physical educator to make accommodations for these variances. . . . (Oregon State Department of Education, 1988, p. 22)

A SUMMARY OF SAFE PRACTICES

1. Try to give children an opportunity in the Physical Education program or classroom experience to learn to move among others without touching or bumping. Perhaps start with a slower speed. (Use hopping, skipping, or jumping instead of running. When children are more experienced, include running, dodging, and change in direction.)

2. Chasing is difficult to do safely and should be avoided. Races and beating the clock activities, if included at all, are best left until children are experienced in the activities and have performed them among other children.

3. Young children need the experience of barefoot work. This type of activity exercises the small muscles of the feet and can improve strength and flexibility in the foot and ankle joints. Street shoes should never be allowed, although tennis shoes and sneakers are permissible. No socks or tights should ever be allowed because this apparel inhibits traction. In fact,

<table>
<tr><td>Assignment 5-3</td></tr>
</table>

Study the recent litigation in your school district that refers to physical activity in schools. List five guidelines for safe practices as a result of your study and compare your list with a few fellow students' lists. Discuss the suggestions provided in this chapter and be critical of their implications.

many schools prohibit children from using climbing equipment in socks or shoes. Bare feet only are seen as safe because children can grip more effectively with the soles of their feet and toes.

4. Heavy and restrictive clothing should be removed before the lesson begins. It is then available after strenuous activity and can be needed during the cooling-off period.

5. Remove all jewelry, as it can present a hazard to the equipment as well as the child.

6. Avoid running toward walls.

7. Do not allow unnecessary noise. An interested, absorbed, and busy child is not usually very noisy. Teachers are advised to obtain a low-enough noise level such that the human voice can be heard.

8. No yelling or shouting should be allowed. Stress that children should speak normally to someone who is near them. Helpful comments might include these:

    • "Yelling instructions to someone doesn't help. They have to learn what to do for themselves."

    • "Leave them alone. Let them do it in their own way."

9. Teach children to "find a space" before starting an activity.

10. Avoid an "audience" situation to discourage showing off or pressure.

11. Do not always impose competition. Some children may choose to be competitive, but many children do not. Competition against oneself is encouraged. Many children take pleasure in cooperative and pattern games.

12. Try to teach and expect as much responsibility from children as possible. Children can get out and put away apparatus, handle themselves in a variety of situations, teach one another simple movement patterns, and keep an eye out for careless organization, leaving apparatus out, not setting up equipment sensibly, and other problems.

13. Teach and expect children to think about what they are doing and how well they are doing it. Concentration prevents much carelessness. Expect high standards of control and behavior, and be quick to get involved early before a dangerous situation develops.

14. Using and knowing a child's name is very helpful. If children feel that they really are expected to improve and perform well and that the teacher is interested in them personally, this perception helps control. The use of just a name can often check a child who looks to be unsafe.

15. Be aware of the position of the sun when working outside. The teacher should face the sun rather than the children.

16. Make sure there are no children behind you. Stand outside the groups of children to observe them—*not* in the middle.

PRACTICES TO AVOID

There are no good reasons for the following practices:

1. *Never* double-up classes for Physical Education lessons. In the case *Harrison v. Montgomery County Board of Education,* brought in 1983 in Maryland, the issue at hand was inadequate supervision. There were excessive numbers of students in a gym due to inclement weather–specifically, 63 students and 3 Physical Education teachers together in a gym where students were participating in a "free exercise day" (Oregon State Department of Education, 1988, p. 24).

2. *Never* impose group elimination games.

3. *Never* have children sitting watching while others are active.

4. *Never* have lines of children waiting to have a turn.

5. *Never* shame a child in front of others.

6. *Never* insist that students perform an activity if they are afraid or unwilling. Legally, this act is called coercion.

7. *Never* play relay races. They usually use atypical skills in a totally artificial context and cause much competitive excitement and noise. Besides, only one child in the team is active!

Teachers should not demonstrate skills because this practice can inhibit children's creativity and can give the impression that some skills are more important than others. Similarly, teachers should avoid using children to demonstrate only traditional skills, because it implies that some skills are more highly valued by the teacher and, as mentioned previously, can inhibit creativity. Creative children will often produce unusual responses, which can be shown for interest but need not necessarily be copied by other children. The teacher's way is only the "correct way" for that individual.

Ways to Improve Class Participation

Establish class procedures and rules. To do so effectively, teachers must have some knowledge of the previous experience of the children. They will need to know something of the children's attitude toward the subject or activity, and they will need to have a good idea of the kinds of behavior that can be expected from them. In planning actual lessons, it is also necessary to know the established procedures, if any, for changing clothing and organizing the process of getting out apparatus. Which apparatus is available and which areas of space are free to be used? Is a whistle normally used? What is the usual "stop" signal? A quiet signal will often cause children to listen for it.

In planning lessons, it is sometimes more important in Physical Education lessons to plan the transitions from one activity to the next than to plan the activities themselves. Good lessons will depend on the smooth linking of the various parts. Several lessons can be taught using the same outline and procedures so that these processes will become familiar.

Many procedures are common not only to Physical Education lessons but also to any situation in which individual children need to move about and control themselves and possibly apparatus (e.g., science, music, drama). There will be an obvious link with the way children are controlled or expected to behave when they move about the school building carrying books. The "discipline" and tone of school and classroom will be reflected in the gymnasium and on the games field.

First and foremost then, a teacher needs an appropriate and well-planned lesson; the ability to get going quickly is a key secondary consideration. The time for explaining what is planned or what will be covered or for soliciting children's ideas and opinions is after vigorous and demanding activity. Teachers might do well to cut out nearly all preliminary talking for the sake of "Let's get started." During the introductory activity, for example, this tactic allows further interaction to take place and leads to an improved response. Explanations should always be very short. Descriptions of movement tasks should be worded concisely.

Have a clear, brief "stop" signal. If the noise level is well controlled, the human voice should be sufficient for the purpose. After all, what goes on in a gym should be a lesson just as in any other room where the voice is normally used. Physical Education lessons are not recess periods, and no undue noise is necessary. However, a whistle or other signal may be necessary when the class is performing outdoors. When trying to establish the "stop" response, it is sometimes helpful to change the activity first. The instruction "Stop and sit down" sometimes helps children to be more aware of the teacher, who remains standing, and it also prevents much incidental movement and fidgeting (particularly when apparatus is used).

Keep children working individually until their behavior is sensible. Locomotion around the room may need to be eliminated in very difficult cases.

If children can be made to think, their responses usually improve. Therefore, any teaching that links the activity with skill or in which the activity is being performed or (sometimes) asking the children to think up ways of doing the same thing will help to establish a more thoughtful response. Sometimes allowing children to teach one another helps class control if they will tackle the task seriously.

It should be emphasized that most children enjoy physical activity and will be pleased to have lessons that are *active*. Many teachers find that this material commands initial attention simply because it is new and different and often seems more "natural" to the children. If teachers can show enthusiasm about a subject, they will often easily carry the children along.

Soliciting the children's help to try something new, or challenging them to perform above their level, is often a good technique for improving response. Certainly there are many problems of organization and techniques of teaching that cannot be realized until they have been attempted.

The teacher should circulate during activity, observing, encouraging, complimenting, and helping children who need it. This causes children to be aware of the teacher's presence and interest. Classroom teachers may find it helpful to change into suitable clothing or footwear so that you can join in with the activity. Talking while children are active often causes "listening."

Designate the area to be used for an activity before going outside, if you will be working outdoors.

Have something worthwhile to say when you stop children's activity. If children are very slow to stop playing, you may be stopping them too frequently.

Make positive comments so that all children can hear them:

- "You have a good idea."
- "Keep a 'bubble' around you when you move."
- "Spread your eyes, and look for a space."
- "Can you turn around in your space without touching anyone?"

It is more important to follow children's interest and activity than to keep to time allocations in a lesson plan.

Respond to those who tell tales—for example, "How do you know? You should be busy working." Accept suggestions for activities from the children with comments like these:

- "Remember what you did for the next lesson."
- "If you have a good idea, come and tell me so that we can all watch or try it."

Many small groups are always better than one large group when children are in their early years.

Help young children spread out to use their general space better. For example, say, "Find your own spot on the floor by the time I count to 3!"

Addressing Gender Equity

There is another aspect of introducing Movement Discovery that needs to be mentioned. Movement Discovery as described and practiced is gender neutral. Since 1972, the Title IX legislation has made it illegal to discriminate on the basis of gender in the United States.

> The Title IX statute generally prohibits sex-based discrimination in education programs or activities receiving Federal financial assistance. Specifically, it states that no person in the United States, on the basis of sex, can be excluded from participation in, be denied the benefits of, or be subjected to discrimination under any education program or activity receiving Federal financial assistance. (U.S. Department of Education, Office for Civil Rights, 2002, p. 31102)

> Current Title IX regulations generally prohibit single-sex classes or activities. The regulations in 34 CFR 106.34 state—A recipient shall not provide any course or otherwise carry out any of its education program or activity separately on the basis of sex, or require or refuse participation therein by any of its students on such basis, including health, physical education, industrial, business, vocational, technical, home economics, music, and adult education courses. (U.S. Department of Education, Office for Civil Rights, 2002, p. 31102)

In 2006, amendments were made to Title IX "pertaining to the provision of single-sex schools, classes and extracurricular activities in elementary and secondary schools" (U.S. Department of Education, Office for Civil Rights, 2006, p. 62530). This applies to your lessons, too.

If you are introducing Movement Discovery in a new situation, you may well encounter stereotypes and different expectations for boys and girls both within yourself and from other children. For children to be truly free to follow their own interests and to develop their individual gifts, you may need to check for sex-role stereotyping. Traditional Physical Education programs often divided content material, skills, and expectations based on male/female traditions, but the similarities between males and females in preadolescent children are actually greater than the few obvious differences. To avoid creating stereotype-based programs, you may want to use the Checklist 1 of Recreational Activities (**Figure 5–1**). The same instrument may also be used as an assessment tool if used at the beginning and end of a semester.

Project A.C.T.I.V.E. (Arnett, 1979) focused on ways to minimize sex-role stereotyping in elementary Physical Education lessons. It included some good diagnostic exercises for the teacher. Try using Checklist 2, Teacher–Student Interaction (**Figure 5–2**). Ask a friend to score it for you.

Children are aware of group memberships (gender, race, ethnicity) and tend to associate the mention of an individual with an expected characteristic of the group. For that reason, it is important to commend girls for as wide a variety of behaviors as boys. Avoid reinforcing any idea that boys are expected to be good at some things, girls at others. The expectation is that individuals will do their best, regardless of gender. The stress is on each child achieving his or her full potential.

Teachers inevitably convey unstated messages, and if you have different expectations of boys and girls, you may communicate these without knowing it. Read Checklist 1 and think about whether you, as the teacher, see any activities as more suitable for girls or boys. Would you perhaps think of kicking balls as more for boys and jumping rope as more for girls? When you introduce discovering rope activities, watch carefully to see if some girls are not good at it and if some boys are. Check your prejudices.

Sex-role stereotyping is often prevalent in a teacher's attitude toward behavior. One kindergarten teacher asked for "three strong boys to help put the mats away." With the secular trend and the fact that many girls mature more quickly than boys, she might have had more help if she had asked for "three strong girls"—in fact, she should have asked for three strong individuals ("people").

Some research indicates that even when girls and boys are reinforced an equal number of times, boys are more likely to be praised for skill or achievement, whereas girls are more likely to be praised for behavior (e.g., cooperation). Sometimes girls are more likely to be criticized for deficiencies in skill or achievement, whereas boys are more likely to be criticized for behavior. What might be the long-term effects of these patterns? Are boys or girls more likely to develop self-confidence, a belief in their own skills, and a willingness to try hard to achieve? Keep a log of what you praise or criticize, as well as how many of these interactions take place.

Research has shown that many teachers who believe they are "gender blind" and treat boys and girls equally do, in fact, interact more often with one sex than with the other. This tendency may be hard to appreciate unless an actual count of gender-based interactions is made, in more than one class period. Unless there is a teacher aide or teaching intern in the room, it can be difficult to find an observer to keep a record of such interactions. Some teachers keep their own diary or log, using brief free moments during the day to jot down every interaction they can remember. They do this for a day or two, stop for a few weeks, and then try it again. Is the total number of interactions different for the two sexes? Are there any particular categories of interaction in which sex differences are apparent? Which changes can be made so that boys and girls receive equal attention and reinforcement from the teacher?

Remember that visuals also serve as role models. If appropriate commercial posters are unavailable, use clippings from sports magazines and newspapers. Visuals should also be inclusive with regard to race, ethnicity, and disability. Try to provide a gender balance in the size,

CHECKLIST 1: RECREATIONAL ACTIVITIES

Place a (X) mark in the blank if you think that the activity is only a boy's activity, or only a girl's activity, or is an activity for both boys and girls.

Place only one (X) mark on each row.

ACTIVITY	BOYS	GIRLS	GIRLS AND BOYS
Bicycling	_____	_____	_____
Basketball	_____	_____	_____
Climbing Playground Apparatus	_____	_____	_____
Floor Hockey	_____	_____	_____
Football (Flag)	_____	_____	_____
Gymnastics	_____	_____	_____
Jogging—running	_____	_____	_____
Jumping Rope	_____	_____	_____
Hopscotch	_____	_____	_____
Skateboarding	_____	_____	_____
Soccer	_____	_____	_____
Softball	_____	_____	_____
Square and Folk Dancing	_____	_____	_____
Swimming	_____	_____	_____
Track and Field	_____	_____	_____
Trampoline	_____	_____	_____
Volleyball	_____	_____	_____
Roller-blading	_____	_____	_____
Snowboarding	_____	_____	_____
Other Games such as tag and dodge ball	_____	_____	_____

FIGURE 5-1   Checklist 1 of Recreational Activities

CHECKLIST 2: TEACHER–STUDENT INTERACTION

Tally the number of interactions or incidents you see.

DOES THE TEACHER:	BOYS	GIRLS
1. Use the child's name?	_____	_____
2. Praise the child?	_____	_____
3. Stand near, watch, smile, or give some kind of support?	_____	_____
4. Make negative comments, change the child's activity, ask the child to move, put apparatus away, give a stern look, etc.?	_____	_____
5. Make use of a "helper"?	_____	_____
6. Assign children to clean up, tidy up, set apparatus straight, etc.?	_____	_____
7. Make use of a leader, choose someone, have children already assigned for particular functions?	_____	_____
8. Support any kind of leadership role or initiative?	_____	_____
9. Fail to support any kind of leadership role or initiative?	_____	_____
10. Use child to demonstrate or model?	_____	_____
11. Have visuals (pictures, charts, awards) that show males/females/children with disabilities?	_____	_____
12. Have children choose apparatus?	_____	_____
13. Have children waiting or inactive?	_____	_____
14. Have children choose partners? (Record gender mix, able bodied/differently abled couples, boys couples, girls couples.)	_____	_____
15. Interact with timid or less skilled children?	_____	_____
16. Encourage out of school participation, use of recreational opportunities, show interest in out of school opportunities for physical activity?	_____	_____
17. Comment on any incidents of discriminatory behavior by the children?	_____	_____

FIGURE 5–2 Checklist 2: Teacher–Student Interaction

vividness, and visual interest of the posters or clippings, as well as in the numbers of men and women and in the range and variety of activities. If visuals of men are smaller and less active or dramatic than visuals of women, for example, they may convey the hidden message that women's sports are more highly valued than men's sports, and vice versa. Are there pictures of males dancing, females doing strenuous team sports, and other "nontraditional" images?

Teachers frequently find that children show gender differences in their choices of apparatus, partners or groups, levels of activities or skills, and participation in out-of-school recreation and physical activities. Children cannot exercise "free choice" in such areas, however, unless they are free enough from sexual stereotyping to have acquired the experience, skill, and self-confidence necessary to make genuinely individual choices. For this reason, it is essential that teachers learn how to observe both gender and individual differences in their students—and that they help their students make the transition from choosing "what the other girls do" or "what the other boys do" to choosing "what *I* want to do."

Teachers should also intervene, of course, when children show sex discrimination in their comments or behavior. Respect, tolerance, and group loyalty should be expected of all.

When you read the children's responses to Checklist 1, you may notice that several children believe certain activities are not for their gender. In such cases, teachers will need to be more careful when they introduce that kind of activity. Perhaps a change in vocabulary will help (change "dance" to "movement," or "jump rope" to "rope skills").

In some classes, but perhaps especially in grades K–2, sex mixing may be spontaneous and un-self-conscious. When asked to choose partners, some girls will pick girls one day, boys the next; some boys will pick boys at times, girls at others. You may also observe that some children seldom or never pick partners of the opposite sex, or that they always pick partners of the opposite sex. Or perhaps most children in your class habitually choose only same-sex partners. In those cases, the teacher needs to intervene to help children have constructive, successful experiences with members of the opposite sex (or the same sex, if they consistently select partners of the opposite sex). Sometimes this is best done very directly, by telling the children what you want and expect: "In this class I want girls to work with girls and also with boys. And I want boys to work with boys and also with girls. So this time, when we choose partners, if you're a girl, look for a girl. If you're a boy, look for a boy. Do an activity. Now, change partners. Girls look for boys; boys look for girls."

At other times you may not want to draw attention to the gender of partners or groups, but rather want to encourage children to work with a wider variety of partners or to develop a greater appreciation of one another's skills, interests, and other characteristics. In this scenario, you may want to use a number of "indirect" techniques that do not in themselves guarantee sex mixing but do increase the variety of partnership or group combinations.

In group participation, sex differences and sex stereotypes are only one reason why children may not be welcomed or effective. Sometimes there is a place for permanent mixed-gender groups. Then one can simply say, "Go to your group places." When free choice of groups or apparatus is allowed, check that it really is a choice and that the choices were not limited because some children felt unwelcome. (Many children do not want to be the only girl or boy in a group and, therefore, will choose not to join that group, even if they would like to use the apparatus or equipment.) Be aware of any unwritten rules at recess (e.g., girls use bars, boys play square ball), and plan ways to encourage gender integration and equal skill development in both girls and boys.

Deepening Your Understanding of the Movement Discovery Teaching Method

When the behavioral responses in Movement Discovery have improved and lessons run smoothly, there are still ways in which beginning teachers can improve the response to the content material used with this teaching method. Children and teachers may take time to deepen their involvement and engage with cognitive factors. The following activity is suggested for preservice students as a means to deepen their understanding of the process involved. The purpose is to work with another student or a few friends and record ideas and ways in which a teacher extends what the performers do. One needs to be able to build on what children do, to see ways of extending the variety and enlarging the range of different experiences. This process cannot be preprogrammed because one does not know how children will respond to a particular challenge or task. Instead, the teacher has to observe and think. Sometimes realizing what is *not* being discovered

Assignment 5–4

Try to produce nine sheets similar to the ones reproduced here. Plan three sheets for each of the content areas—dance, gymnastics, and games—covered in Chapters 6, 8, and 10, respectively. First decide on the task/challenge, then analyze the decisions made by the teacher, and finally look at the choices available to the children. The number of choices available to the children should be greater than the number of decisions made by the teacher.

can help the teacher add more ideas (e.g., "I like all those ideas but they are all done in the same direction. How about including a change of direction?"). If you come up with lists of variations, remember the purpose of the activity is to give you confidence, not to impose your inventions on the performers.

To complete this activity, invent a task or challenge that can be given to children and ask a few friends to respond to it. Observe what your friends do and try to analyze how the amount of teacher direction limits the choices available to the children.

To be successful with the Movement Discovery teaching method, you will need to be confident in your ability to extend and vary a simple response. If children are very unused to Movement Discovery and have always been told what to do and how to do it, it may take time for them to start creating their own interesting activity and to value the many variations that can be discovered. Begin-

ning teachers need practice at observing and extending children's activity. Remember to notice what is not being done. **Figures 5–3** through **5–9** are samples of tasks that can be presented to children on activity cards.

Games/Pre-Sports Tasks for Pre-K Through Grade 1

TASK: You have about 10 minutes to try different things with any of the balls that are in the containers.

(Types of balls provided: small tennis balls, softball-size whiffle balls, 5" diameter vinyl balls/foam balls, 6" playground balls, 8–10" light volleyball trainers, medium-size beach ball)

CHILDREN'S CHOICES
- Any type of ball
- How long to stay with the same ball
- How long to work on the same skill
- Type of skills to try: roll, kick, hit, throw, catch
- Where in the space to try things including the wallspace

TEACHER'S DECISIONS
- Selection of ball types
- Activity to last 10 minutes
- Children can use any skills with balls

FIGURE 5–3   Games/Pre-Sports Tasks for Pre-K Through Grade 1

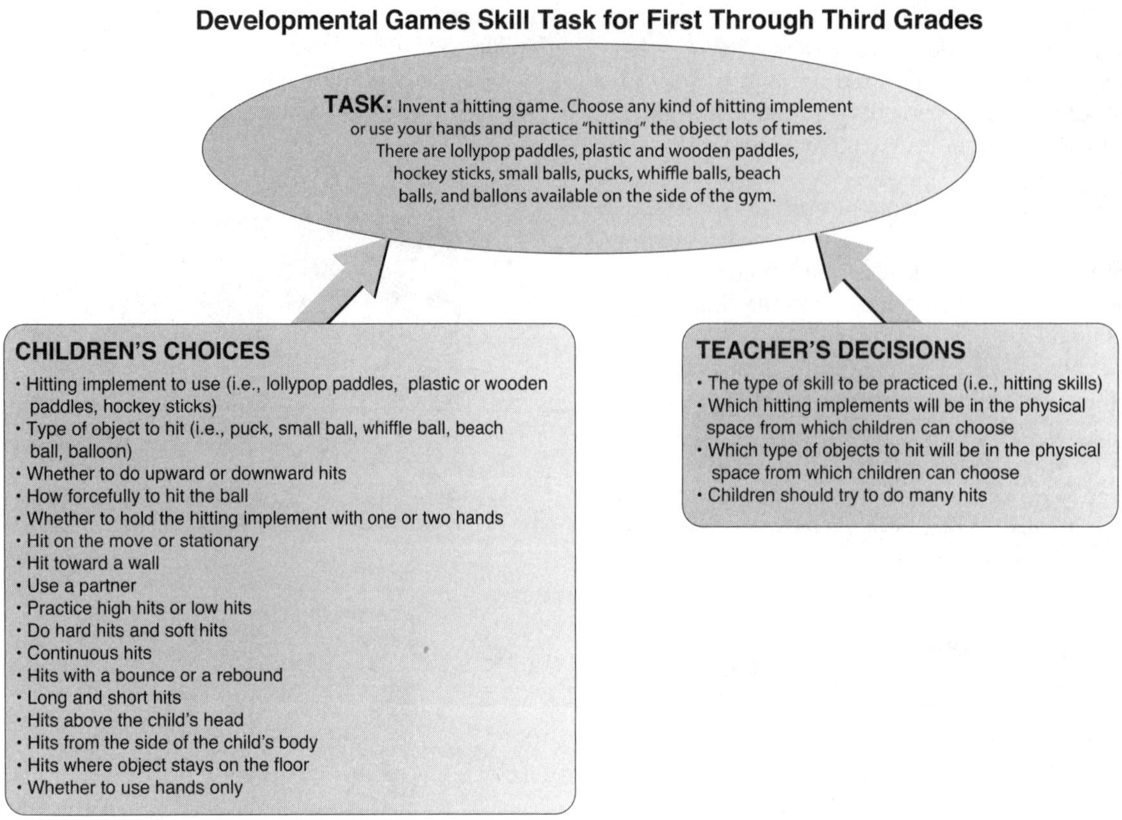

Developmental Games Skill Task for First Through Third Grades

TASK: Invent a hitting game. Choose any kind of hitting implement or use your hands and practice "hitting" the object lots of times. There are lollypop paddles, plastic and wooden paddles, hockey sticks, small balls, pucks, whiffle balls, beach balls, and ballons available on the side of the gym.

CHILDREN'S CHOICES

- Hitting implement to use (i.e., lollypop paddles, plastic or wooden paddles, hockey sticks)
- Type of object to hit (i.e., puck, small ball, whiffle ball, beach ball, balloon)
- Whether to do upward or downward hits
- How forcefully to hit the ball
- Whether to hold the hitting implement with one or two hands
- Hit on the move or stationary
- Hit toward a wall
- Use a partner
- Practice high hits or low hits
- Do hard hits and soft hits
- Continuous hits
- Hits with a bounce or a rebound
- Long and short hits
- Hits above the child's head
- Hits from the side of the child's body
- Hits where object stays on the floor
- Whether to use hands only

TEACHER'S DECISIONS

- The type of skill to be practiced (i.e., hitting skills)
- Which hitting implements will be in the physical space from which children can choose
- Which type of objects to hit will be in the physical space from which children can choose
- Children should try to do many hits

FIGURE 5–4   Developmental Games Skill Task for First Through Third Grades

---

Developmental Games Skill Task

TASK: With a partner, invent an "up-in-the-air" game in a square-shaped playing area. We are going to work outside on grass. Invent a way of scoring.

CHILDREN'S CHOICES

- The partner
- The small equipment they want to use (e.g., hoops, markers, cones spots)
- The size of the square where the game is to be played (i.e., a large or smaller area)
- The type of playing surface outside (i.e., blacktop or grass)
- Types of actions to use in the game (e.g., kicking, throwing, striking)
- Whether parts of the body can be used and how
- Whether to use any implements such as paddles or rackets
- Which object will be propelled into the air (e.g., birdie, small/large/beach ball, ring)
- How to outline the square playing field (e.g., with markers, ropes, lines)
- Any rules they want to use to make their game work well
- How to score in their game
- How the game starts and ends

TEACHER'S DECISIONS

- The type of game to be played (i.e., "up-in-the-air")
- The number of players (2)
- The playing area shape (a square and surface)
- Children will keep score

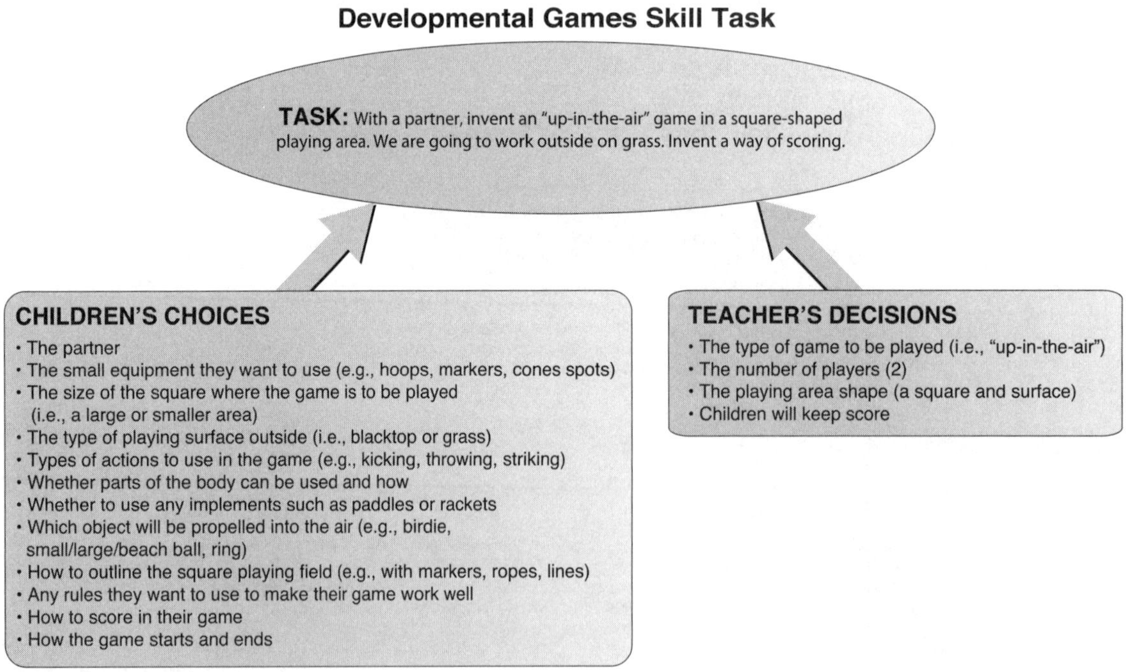

FIGURE 5–5   Developmental Games Skill Task

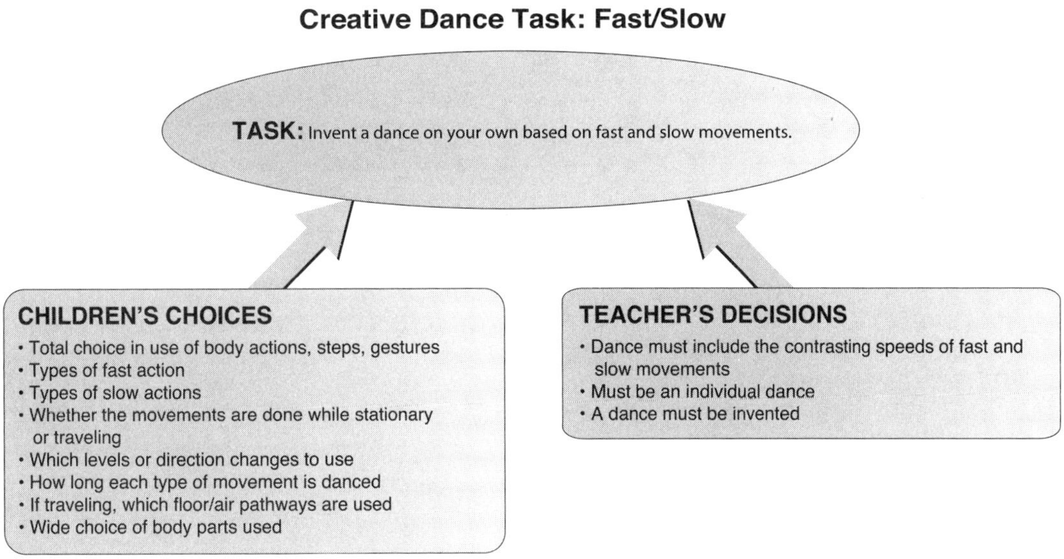

Creative Dance Task: Fast/Slow

TASK: Invent a dance on your own based on fast and slow movements.

CHILDREN'S CHOICES
- Total choice in use of body actions, steps, gestures
- Types of fast action
- Types of slow actions
- Whether the movements are done while stationary or traveling
- Which levels or direction changes to use
- How long each type of movement is danced
- If traveling, which floor/air pathways are used
- Wide choice of body parts used

TEACHER'S DECISIONS
- Dance must include the contrasting speeds of fast and slow movements
- Must be an individual dance
- A dance must be invented

FIGURE 5-6   Creative Dance Task: Fast/Slow

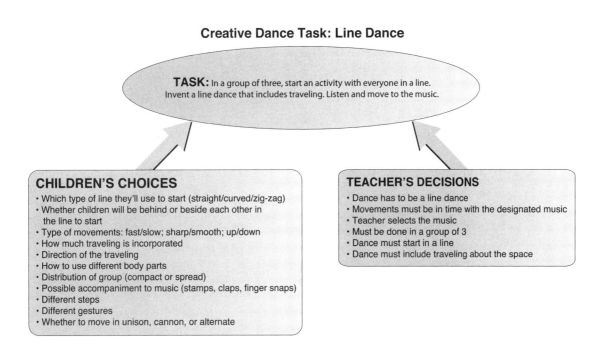

Creative Dance Task: Line Dance

TASK: In a group of three, start an activity with everyone in a line. Invent a line dance that includes traveling. Listen and move to the music.

CHILDREN'S CHOICES
- Which type of line they'll use to start (straight/curved/zig-zag)
- Whether children will be behind or beside each other in the line to start
- Type of movements: fast/slow; sharp/smooth; up/down
- How much traveling is incorporated
- Direction of the traveling
- How to use different body parts
- Distribution of group (compact or spread)
- Possible accompaniment to music (stamps, claps, finger snaps)
- Different steps
- Different gestures
- Whether to move in unison, cannon, or alternate

TEACHER'S DECISIONS
- Dance has to be a line dance
- Movements must be in time with the designated music
- Teacher selects the music
- Must be done in a group of 3
- Dance must start in a line
- Dance must include traveling about the space

FIGURE 5-7   Creative Dance Task: Line Dance

Task for Educational Gymnastics

TASK: Travel about the general space on hands and feet with feet sometimes together and sometimes apart.

CHILDREN'S CHOICES
- The position of the body as they travel on hands and feet (stomach up, back up, side up)
- Hands could lead the way
- Feet could lead the way
- Travel on one hand and one foot only
- Speed of the traveling movements
- Travel forward, backward, sideways
- Switch directions
- Amount of time to use for travel with feet together
- Amount of time to use for travel with feet apart
- Pathway of travel about the general space (e.g., zig-zags, curvy, straight)
- How far apart the feet should be
- Whether to move on hands only for some of the time

TEACHER'S DECISIONS
- Traveling must be in general space on the floor
- Hands and feet only should be used
- Feet should move together and apart as the child travels

FIGURE 5–8   Task for Educational Gymnastics

Educational Gymnastics Challenge for Third Through Sixth Grades

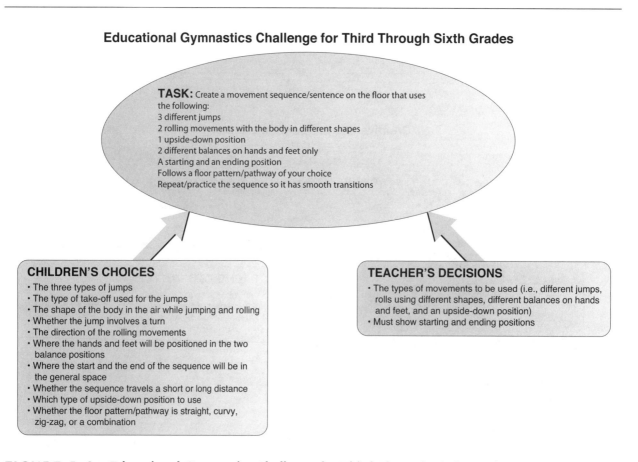

TASK: Create a movement sequence/sentence on the floor that uses the following:
3 different jumps
2 rolling movements with the body in different shapes
1 upside-down position
2 different balances on hands and feet only
A starting and an ending position
Follows a floor pattern/pathway of your choice
Repeat/practice the sequence so it has smooth transitions

CHILDREN'S CHOICES
- The three types of jumps
- The type of take-off used for the jumps
- The shape of the body in the air while jumping and rolling
- Whether the jump involves a turn
- The direction of the rolling movements
- Where the hands and feet will be positioned in the two balance positions
- Where the start and the end of the sequence will be in the general space
- Whether the sequence travels a short or long distance
- Which type of upside-down position to use
- Whether the floor pattern/pathway is straight, curvy, zig-zag, or a combination

TEACHER'S DECISIONS
- The types of movements to be used (i.e., different jumps, rolls using different shapes, different balances on hands and feet, and an upside-down position)
- Must show starting and ending positions

FIGURE 5–9   Educational Gymnastics Challenge for Third Through Sixth Grades

The model (**Figure 5–10**) represents a continuum between total teacher direction and complete free choice for the children. Children experienced in Movement Discovery will need little teacher direction. The next six chapters include much suggested teaching material; use any of this material to practice the process of adding to and extending responses. You will soon find you can easily "think on your feet," which should give you the knowledge and security needed to enable children to learn and achieve more.

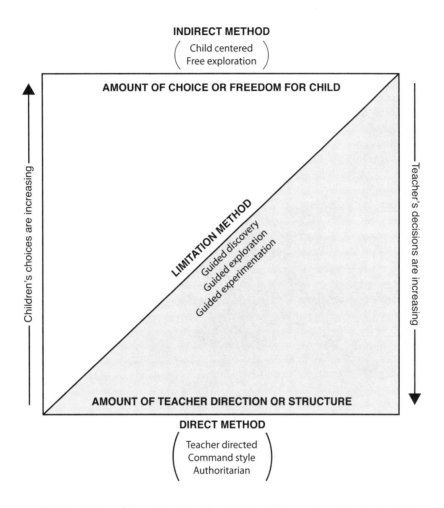

FIGURE 5–10   Methods of Teaching: Children's Choices Versus Teacher's Decisions

References

Arnett, C. (1979). *Project A.C.T.I.V.E.: Developing sex equity in elementary school Physical Education: Final report.* (Project No: 565AH700CB.) Washington, DC: U.S. Department of Health, Education and Welfare, Office of Education.

Oregon State Department of Education. (1988). *Legal liability in the gymnasium.* Salem, OR: Author. (ERIC Document Reproduction Service No. ERIC ED322607).

P.E. Association. (n.d.). Some aspects of the law relating to physical education teachers. *Information Notes, 1,* 9. Retrieved March 2009 from http://www.afpe.org.uk

Strain, P., & Hemmeter, M. (1999). Keys to being successful when confronted with challenging behaviors. In S. R. Sandall & M. Ostrosky, *Practical ideas for addressing challenging behaviors* (pp. 17–27). Longmont, CO: Sopris West.

U.S. Department of Education, Office for Civil Rights. (2002, May 8). Single-sex classes and schools: Guidelines on title IX requirements; notice. Part VI. *Federal Register, 67*(89).

U.S. Department of Education, Office for Civil Rights. (2006, October 25). Nondiscrimination on the basis of sex in education programs or activities receiving federal financial assistance: Final rule (Part III, 34 CFR Part 106.34). *Federal Register, 71*(206).

Discovering Developmental Games and Pre-sport Games

QUESTIONS TO DISCUSS

1. What does the phrase "team sports" mean to you? To your partner?

2. Discuss relay races with your partner. Describe your own experience or any observations of children playing them.

3. Mention any methods you have seen or experienced of picking teams. Try to imagine two new ways that could be used in an elementary school situation.

4. Discuss your experiences with large-group games (e.g., chasing, tagging, waiting for a turn, letting the team down, dropping the ball, being on a winning team). Describe both negative and positive experiences.

Sport is a rich part of many cultures. It is truly a basis for international encounters, and is one of the most important vehicles through which ordinary people communicate with one another. Historically the Iron Curtain was first breached by a soccer team, and the Bamboo Curtain by table tennis. In any community, but particularly in the United States, the fortunes, skills, and weaknesses of local sports teams and personalities are a basis for interaction at all levels of society. Many places of relaxation—restaurants, waiting rooms at bus stations, rail terminals and airports, even doctors' and dentists' offices—constantly depict sporting activity via a TV screen.

It is inconceivable that any attractive and purposeful Physical Education program for children would not include the major sports of any society. Nevertheless, children are not adults, and the complex nature of sports has put many of them beyond the attainment even of most adults. In today's world, interest in sport is too often reduced to the role of spectator or supporter.

In the past (1930s to 1960s), teachers and recreational leaders invented a large number of competitive group games for use at the elementary school level. Recreational organizations and such groups as Girl Scouts, YMCA youth groups, and summer camps found them very useful. Relay races, large-group games (e.g., Capture the Flag, Pirate's Treasure, Red Rover), and games such as kickball,

dodgeball, and softball, which required only one ball for a group of 20 youngsters, seemed to solve the problem of minimal equipment and time to spare. Unfortunately, with so many players inactive and arbitrarily included in a team, behavior is often noisy and partisan with these types of games. This places great pressure on children, especially if one fails or lets the team down in some way. When excited and cheered on by others, judgment and control are often impaired and accidents are more likely to occur.

In Chapters 2 and 3, we noted that an individualized program is inevitable if learning is to take place and enjoyment maintained. This chapter provides material that reflects the content of the major sports in our society and

Assignment 6–1

Record two accounts of games you have seen children playing when there were no adults present. Choose one with young children and one with older children. Describe the environment. Observe the children for at least 20 minutes and see how interest is sustained and the game developed or is abandoned. Is there any scoring? How successfully do the children cooperate or compete?

is suitable for children. Traditional large-group games will not be included in this book, for three reasons: There is little carry-over value from these games to major sports, they are difficult and time-consuming to organize with a large group of young children, and sometimes they are dangerous.

Traditionally, as teachers of preschool and kindergarten children sought to get individuals socially aware of their group, activities such as singing games, finger-plays, parachute activities, the Hokey-Pokey, Bunny Hop, Simon Says, What's the Time Mr. Wolf?, and various party mixers were used. Unfortunately for physical educators, these activities are often called "games." In fact, these activities should not be a substitute for developmental and pre-sport games; for this reason, they, too, will not be included in this book. They are simply not strenuous enough for inclusion in a physical education program.

Children can turn almost anything into a game. It is as if playing games is an attitude present when children are enjoying themselves. Your observations will have recorded children playing a game using the environment, other people, and various stimuli, even when confined to a car, a shopping cart, a church pew, a dining room table, a school desk, and so on. Your memories may also have recalled the trauma of many children involved in large competitive group games.

"I am playing tennis," said a 7-year-old boy playing a solo game of "keep-up" using a stocking bat and paper ball. "We're playing basketball," said a child bouncing a ball when his friend was trying to steal it; it was 1 v 1 game.

As children refine their early responses to sports equipment and explore the addition of more players and different configurations of space, they will play games that look more like recognized sports to an adult. To repeat, it is the process that is important, and it can only take place at the child's individual level.

This text speaks of "developmental games" and "pre-sport games"; in the following material, we use the word

"games" to mean these types of activity. The content material presented here focuses on actions and variations that are fun and may bear some resemblance to the skills used in major sports. The point is to give teachers possible cues, limitations, and realistic challenges to suggest to the children as needed. It is possible that the children will not need them, or at least only a few children will. Children need to *discover.* The teacher, in turn, needs to observe, understand, record, assess, and make suggestions only as necessary to promote further exploration and discovery by the children. After early exploration there will be a discernable progress toward the major sports.

The material here is divided into four levels:

- Level 1: the youngest children

- Level 2: children ready to work in twos or small groups

- Level 3: net, wall, court, and field pre-sport games for older children

- Level 4: linking material with recognized major sports

Assignment 6–2

Try to collect at least three brief descriptions of a major sport from children younger than age 12 years. For example:
  • Basketball is a game where . . .
  • In football, the players . . .
  • To win in a tennis match, you have to . . .
Try to get at least one statement from (1) a boy and (2) a girl younger than age 12 that include phrases like "The game I enjoy playing the most is . . . because . . ." This is a very important assignment and should help you begin to analyze the components of sport from a child's point of view.

Collect observations of parents or other adults trying to "teach" an immature child to "catch," "throw," "kick," or "hit with a bat." Assess the level of frustration in either the child or the adult.

Chapter 2, which focused on discovering differences, described how many physical factors contribute to individual differences in children. The same thing is true when we look at the behavior involved in playing games and sports. There are different shapes and weights of balls, different "bounce-ability," and different textures of the surfaces of the ball and of the floors and walls and outdoor areas that may be used. All of this variation provides different sensory input to the learners as they develop new motor skills. Repetition is needed as well as variety.

Simply put, if a child is given a ball, there are not only demands placed on the child as a physical body—the child moves—but also a host of things for the child to learn about balls and how they behave and what they can and cannot do. These demands from the ball, as it were, also require a variety of physical responses from the child, which must be learned. This is a difficult challenge, because the ball can also behave differently in different situations and particularly when another person uses it. To learn what another person's movement will mean when that individual hits or throws a large ball versus small ball, and so on, takes a long time to learn. To do so, the youngest children may need to work alone (Level 1) before working with another person (Level 2). To respond to another person requires new skills. The ability to anticipate what another player may do is crucial in later-learned sports.

In this sense, it is as if the complex neurophysiological maturation of the child is confronted with the realm of physics. Sir Isaac Newton stated his laws of motion in 1687, and these physics issues apply to bats, balls, hitting, catching, and a variety of other considerations—as well as to the human body. In fact, Margarete Streicher called gymnastics "games with gravity." The approach used in

this text in developmental and pre-sport games could be called "games with Newtonian physics" or "games with the laws of motion." To simplify matters, we will use the word "games" to describe these activities.

Although the material that follows involves a great deal of "applied Newtonian physics," experience tells us that children will discover most of what follows on their own if given enough time. This may take many months and many lessons.

Sometimes the material is presented here in something of a sequence. Always use this material in the light of student response, and *never* think that all of these "suggestions" must be covered. Just because there are 10 suggestions for an activity using bean bags does not mean that you should make all children do all of them. The various options are intended to give you confidence if the children should run out of ideas or lose interest. You may also find considerable overlap in the material. Make your own judgments.

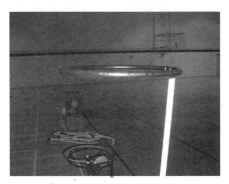

Level 1: The Youngest Children

Preschoolers and many first graders (even some children in second or third grade) will need no more prompting than simply making available a piece of equipment so that they can play a game with it. Have many different kinds of balls on hand. If necessary, make them yourself or get parents to help make them.

A young child just needs a piece of equipment and some of the challenges that follow—for example, encouragement to play with the object "up in the air," "along the ground," "against a wall," and so on. Vary the equipment so that children can discover the different properties of the objects they use. All children need to experiment with "all things," so stations, learning centers, or other demarcated areas may be needed (e.g., one area containing hoops, one area containing ropes, one area containing scoops and bean bags, one area with balls against a wall). This type of setup might use four corners of an area, and a simple rotation of groups would constitute a whole lesson. Perhaps children might do a running activity to begin and then play games with pieces of equipment in each corner of the room. The rotation of groups to four learning centers/stations may take longer than one lesson, however. Nevertheless, it is important to complete the rotation so that all children use all equipment.

CONTENT MATERIAL: ACTIONS TO USE IN GAMES

Here are some ideas you might start with either at the beginning level (young children) or at the beginning of a lesson with older children before they move into small groups. Following are some of the variations children can discover. With further experimentation, and with varied practice using different types and sizes of balls and other objects, the improvement in their object-control skills should lead to successful participation in these types of games and sports.

Bouncing

Freely
Using one hand
Using alternate hands
On the spot
On the move
A big ball
A small ball
At varying heights (e.g., high, low)
At different speeds
While moving in different directions
With body in different positions
With a bat, paddle, or other hitting implement
On different surfaces (e.g., walls, grass, blacktop)
With a friend
Make a pattern of bounces you can repeat
On the move; while remaining still
Around the body
Behind the body, in front of the body, at the side of the body
Between the legs

Running

Anywhere, anyhow
Backward and sideward
Using tiny steps and big steps
In different directions (Do not touch anyone.)
At different speeds
Around markers or other objects on the floor
Running and stopping on a signal
Change direction quickly
With a friend
Steady running for distance
Running combined with walking or slower jogging
Combined with jumps of different heights
Fast, over both short and longer distances

Throwing and Catching

Anywhere, anyhow
With one or two hands
High and low
On and off the ground
To the side of the body
In front of the body
With a friend
Against a wall
At a target, into a target, or over a target
Using balls or other objects of different textures
At different distances
Combined with hitting, pushing, and bouncing
While still; while moving
Different-shaped balls or objects (e.g., round, oval, birdie/shuttle, balloon, puck, ring)
Objects of different weights (light versus heavy)
Objects of different sizes (small versus large)
In the air (jump to catch or throw)
Outdoors: Throws very high above your head
Use different parts of the body

Striking (Hitting)

Objects on the ground
Objects off the ground
Stationary balls and other objects
Moving balls and other objects
Using bats of different weights
Using bats of different lengths
Using striking implements made of different materials
Pucks, balls, other objects of different weights and sizes
Using different body parts (e.g., hands, feet, head, forearm, fisted hands)
Over different heights (high, low)
From different distances (far, near)
Toward a wall
Into a goal area
At a target
Balls or other objects coming from different angles or distances in space
With a friend or small group

CONTENT MATERIAL: USING SMALL EQUIPMENT

The following lists of activities are in no way comprehensive. It is not especially important that all children experience all activities. Most teachers will feel confident that, given a piece of equipment, a child will quickly discover and invent activities to use it. Each young child should have a piece of apparatus. A few ideas have been included here that may act as a starting point for those who need them. As a physical educator, you should demonstrate your approval of success and hard work, and try to encourage children to make it more difficult for themselves.

Allow Children to Discover Activities Using a Variety of Small Equipment

1. Whatever the equipment, state, "You may have a _____. Play with it." This will probably stimulate activity (i.e., free play). Sometimes allow a free choice of equipment.
2. Whatever the equipment, stating, "Show me how many different things you can do with your _____," will result in prolonging activity.
3. Whatever the equipment, stating, "Put your equipment on the floor and see how many things you can do over or around or through it," will limit the movement around the room.
4. Whatever the equipment, stating, "Choose a position on the floor and make your equipment move around you," will probably result in good movement of the whole body.
5. "Play a game using two (or three) pieces of the same equipment."
6. "Make up a game using two (or three) pieces of different equipment."
7. "Make up an activity moving around the room with your equipment."
8. "Combine a jump in the air and another movement using your equipment."
9. "Make the equipment go above your head in some way. Choose two different ways of doing this."
10. "Use any part of your body except your hands to move the equipment."

Allow Children to Discover Activities Using Bean Bags

1. "Drop the bean bag. Try to catch it before it reaches the ground."
2. "Drop the bean bag a long way from your body. Try to pick it up with the other hand without changing your position. Experiment with different positions."

(continues)

3. "While on all fours, place a bean bag on your back. Wriggle to dislodge it. Try placing it on different parts of the back. Select the most difficult area and challenge yourself to dislodge the bean bag."

4. "Try any activity holding the bean bag between the feet."

5. "Place the bean bag on any part of the body. Try to throw it using that part."

6. "Send a bean bag into the air and change your position to catch it."

7. "Emphasize that catching involves going to meet the object and "giving" at the speed required. Try to catch a bean bag using different parts of the body—for example, the lap, back, feet, and chest. Throw the bean bag using different parts of the body."

8. "Combine a throw with one part of the body and catching with another."

9. "Find a way of making the bean bag go behind or underneath the body."

10. "Place the bean bag on the floor. Find ways of moving over or around the bean bag using your hands on the floor."

Many of these activities can be performed with a partner.

Allow Children to Discover Activities Using Hoops

1. "Bowl a hoop and run to keep close to it. While it moves, try to jump over it. Try scissors kick jumps, leaps, and turns. Try running a complete circle around the hoop while it is moving."

2. "Backspin a hoop. Jump over as it approaches, and run to catch it. This activity is also fun when a partner is involved."

3. "Skip using the hoop. Try holding it in both hands, holding it in one hand, and "half-skipping" or continuous jumping in and out of a swinging hoop."

4. "Try many ways of getting through a moving hoop without touching it. (Bowl slowly, backspin the hoop, or have the partner bowl it.)"

5. "Spin a hoop using your body. Try different parts of your body and try to spin the hoop while moving."

6. "See if you can move a hoop and get through it without using your hands."

7. "Hold a hoop in a wide grasp. See how many twisting movements and how many positions you can work in while maintaining your grasp."

8. "Support a hoop or hoops. (This can be done with a pile of bean bags, an individual mat, interlocking two hoops, or supporting the hoop by the use of skittles or blocks.) Make a pattern of movement including a jump, a roll, and a movement to get through the hoop."

9. "Combine taking your weight on your hands and a swing circle movement of the hoop."

10. "Jump in and out and over your hoop."

11. "Use hands only inside the hoop."

12. "What can you do with a partner using one or two hoops?"

In addition, hoops can be moved in the air, thrown and caught or spun, and used on the floor to mark an area (e.g., a "safe" area for a child with a disability, perhaps a mobility impairment).

Allow Children to Discover Activities Using Ropes

1. Show what you can do with your rope.
2. Place the rope on the floor. Discover many ways of arranging it to form shapes. Try a variety of jumping, hopping, and running patterns along it.
3. Walk along the rope using the sides of the feet or toes only. Pick up the rope using feet only. Rearrange the rope and repeat the activity.
4. Place the rope on the floor. Use hands on the floor to travel along the rope. Combine a movement taking the weight on the hands and skipping with the rope.
5. Hold one end of the rope in the hands and use another part of your body to try and tie a knot.
6. Place a doubled or folded rope in a circle underneath you and jump over the rope.
7. Try a variety of kneeling and sitting positions. Make a wide circle around the body so that one end of a folded rope is held in the hand and touches the floor at all times. Change hands.
8. Wriggle one end of a rope. Try to jump or step on the free end. (This is also fun as a partner activity.)
9. Make a rope swing. Try to jump forward and backward over a swinging rope.
10. Try skipping or "jumping rope." Children will discover many ways of skipping or jumping rope.

Young children need opportunities for free experimentation so that they can discover the many ways a rope can be used.

Allow Children to Discover Variations for Jumping/Skipping Activities Using Ropes

1. With two feet together.
2. Using alternate feet.
3. Hopping (same foot).
4. With bent knees, while low and near the ground (crouched).
5. With two turns of the rope to one jump (a "bump").
6. Jump and rebound rhythm.
7. Inventing patterns of jumping with a rope.
8. Showing a variety of steps (e.g., sideways, leg lifting, waltz step, "setting" or "pas-de-Basque" step, gallop step, step hop). Almost any dance step can be tried. A steady turning rhythm is important.
9. Moving and traveling around the room. Variations in moving forward but turning the rope backward, and the reverse, can be tried.
10. With crossed arms.
11. Including a free rope turn (no jump) to the side of the body to face the opposite direction.
12. Alternating double-speed skipping, even jumping, and jump and rebound rhythms.
13. Continuous rhythm allowing the rope to "check" so that backward turning can be combined with forward turning.
14. One hand high, one hand low. This is a kind of sideways skipping (one hand uses a "lassoing" movement overhead, while the other is held low "between the legs").
15. "Style" skipping showing neat footwork, arms held sideways, head lifted, and other positions.

(continues)

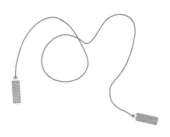

16. Skipping in twos. This can be very challenging when partners try to change turners while continuously skipping. Couples may each hold one end of the rope, or one may turn for the other. Practice in "running in" and "running out" rhythm should be tried both for backward and forward skipping.

17. Group skipping (no more than four children per group). This can involve many variations, including "Double Dutch" or using two ropes turning opposite ways at the same time. Change the "turners."

18. Keep the rope continually turning among groups of three or four children. One person takes a jump and then immediately goes to turn the rope. The one who jumps rope goes to the other end to turn the rope.

It is possible to turn and skip at the same time in group skipping, and no children should be left out of the activity because they are turning the rope.

Allow Children to Discover Activities Using Balls

Many of the activities suggested for bean bags, which generally are used more frequently by younger children, are made more difficult by using a ball.

1. Make the ball move by using your feet only. Try different directions and use different parts of your feet. Older children can try this activity while keeping the ball in the air.

2. Roll a ball around you using as many different parts of your body as you can.

3. Bounce a ball continuously. See if you can do it using the knees, feet, head, chest, and other body parts.

4. Try to get the ball from your feet to your hands in many different ways.

5. Bat or hit a ball so that it is not allowed to touch the ground. Can you change your position while you do this?

6. Drop a ball so that it is kept still on the floor by "trapping." Do this with a partner who sends the ball for you to "trap."

7. Place your feet apart. Try to bounce the ball in a large "figure eight" through and around the body.

8. Hold the ball between the legs with one hand in front, one hand behind. Change hands without letting the ball fall to the ground.

9. Let a ball roll across the body in some way (from one arm to the other), across the shoulders and so on. Try different positions such as kneeling. (Roll the ball from your neck to one foot.)

10. Try to move with the ball on the body while turning and rolling.

CONTENT MATERIAL: INVENTING AND PLAYING A VARIETY OF GAMES

In a seminal study in 1969, Iona and Peter Opie reported on children's games as they occur naturally. These researchers reported that children rarely keep score, seldom declare a winner or loser, do not need an umpire, and do not play for prizes. They appear to enjoy a large "luck" component so that direct comparisons between children are avoided (as cited in *Time* magazine in 1970). Mauldon

and Redfern (1969) reported similar findings in their classic text addressing a new way to teach games to elementary aged children. They were early proponents of the "creative games" movement.

In the 1970s, a shift became apparent, as Physical Education moved away from traditional sports in the elementary school and toward something more at the children's level. Phrases such as "creative games," "invent games," and "teacher/child-designed games" began to be used more often (AAHPERD, 1977).

A great deal of material has already been presented in terms of working with the youngest children: That may be sufficient for a short lesson with young children. However, to bring a focus to exploratory activity, the invention of games by the children offers exciting possibilities. If it inhibits the work children are doing, then they are probably not ready for this step. To determine their readiness, you might consider introducing the idea of "invent a game" and allow the children the choice of whether to try it.

The following list of suggestions can be used when working with a variety of age groups and different developmental levels. The games might be played either alone or cooperatively with a partner; they might also become competitive. Keep in mind when working with children in the lowest grades (PreK–1) that working with a partner or group is too difficult for children of this age. Perhaps a few children in first grade may be ready. In contrast, prekindergarten children can often work "alongside" but not "with" other children.

Invent and Play

1. Your own game
2. A game using (specify) a bean bag, a ball, a hoop, or another object
3. A "hit and run" game
4. A game "using the wall"
5. A nonstop moving game
6. An "under–over" game
7. A "change position of body" game
8. A "bounce and push" game
9. A two- or three-ball game
10. An "in and out" game
11. An "up in the air" game
12. An "on the floor" game
13. A game where you change places
14. A target game
15. A "carry it" game
16. A "jump to hit" game
17. A "rolling" game
18. A "rapid-fire" game
19. A "stealing" game
20. A game where you have to "lose"
21. A "freeze" game
22. A bat-and-ball game
23. A "keep it going" game
24. A game that uses two different pieces of apparatus
25. A circle game alone or with a partner
26. A lines game
27. A square game
28. A pattern game
29. A counting game
30. A sequence game (First this, then that . . .)
31. A color game
32. A "made-apparatus" game
33. An "exchange" game
34. An "upside-down" game
35. A nonrun tagging game
36. A "collision" game
37. An "opposites" game
38. A "beat your partner" game
39. A "hiding" game
40. A "one against great odds" game
41. A "throwing/catching" game
42. An "all active" game (Everybody on the move)
43. A "traveling" game
44. A "toss and hit" game
45. A "rhythm" game
46. A "back to front" game
47. A "surprise" game
48. A "pass your partner" game
49. A tag game
50. A bean bag game
51. A birdie game

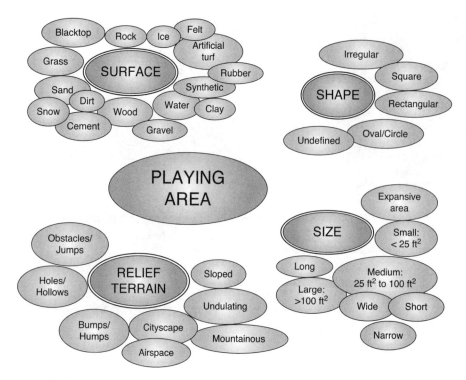

FIGURE 6–1 Playing Area

You might add some new variables to these suggestions as the maturity of the children allows (e.g., change only the surface of the playing area on which some of these games are played and observe what happens). **Figure 6–1** illustrates elements of the playing area that might be varied (i.e., the surface, the shape, the size, and the relief/terrain) to challenge and improve a game player's versatility.

The type of game can be printed and laminated on cards of various colors measuring approximately 4 inches by 4 inches. The style and size of the print (font) can be changed. On some cards, use all-capital letters; on others, use lowercase. You might also print the words on a curved or straight line. A card might also list the equipment to be used in the game. These game cards can be reproduced inexpensively and attractively on the computer using "WordArt" in a word processing or other graphics program. Google Images is an excellent source for clip art to add to the cards. The teacher can choose which cards to use and distribute them or the children might get to choose their own card.

Explanation of "Invent a Game" Figure

The five shapes in **Figure 6–2** contain content for assisting children in the creation of *new* games. The teacher can use this as a resource for ideas. The teacher or children can choose items from each of the "Actions," "People," "Things", "Places," and "Making It Harder" shapes.

When children can read and understand the vocabulary, these five shapes can be used in a variety of ways.

The sheet contains a lot of material for the invention of games. It can be used for many lessons and with varied grade levels. The sheet can be reproduced in color; it can be laminated; the sheet can be printed showing just the shapes with all the wording eliminated; the shapes can be cut out in cardboard and used as separate shapes rather than as a whole sheet. The shapes can be enlarged or reduced in size.

From one shape (e.g., "Things"), one or more items could be chosen as an element to be included in the game. "People," "Things," and "Places" might be combined in some lessons, whereas other lessons could focus on just "Actions" and "Things." Many combinations of the shapes and items within the shapes are possible.

Individual children or a group of children could pick three shapes from a basket, mixing and matching the shapes to give them some structure for the creation of their new game.

Some teachers have added color to the shapes.

One teacher had the shapes list only one item. She made 30 red circles, each with one "Place" on it; 5 green stars with "2" as the "Number of Players"; and so on.

Another teacher displayed on the walls of the gymnasium the large shapes that contained all the words. Different shapes were posted on different walls.

Children could be told to choose two shapes and a partner, and then asked to invent a game: "When you have your group, choose a place and two things to include in your game." Discover your own uses of this idea.

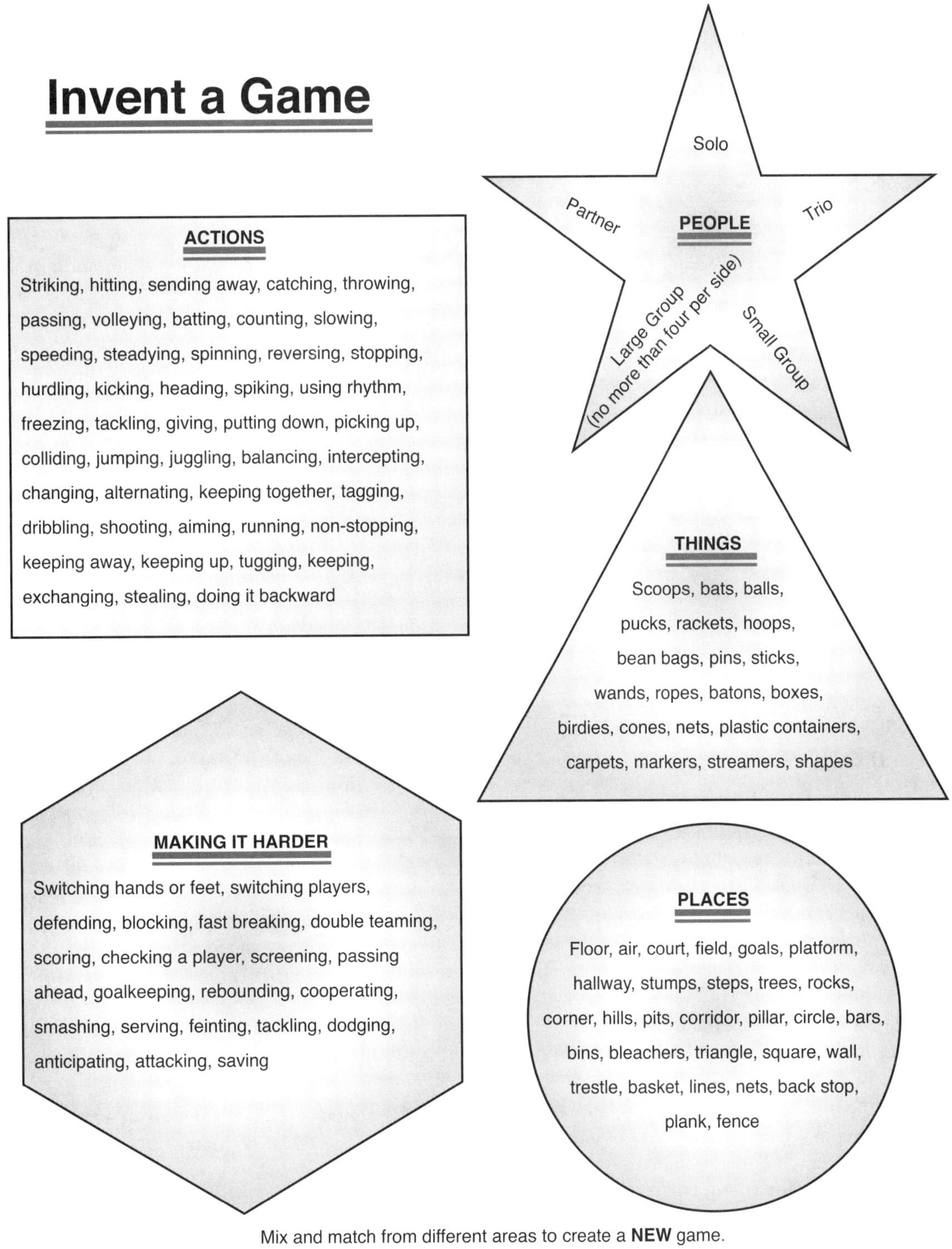

Invent a Game

ACTIONS

Striking, hitting, sending away, catching, throwing, passing, volleying, batting, counting, slowing, speeding, steadying, spinning, reversing, stopping, hurdling, kicking, heading, spiking, using rhythm, freezing, tackling, giving, putting down, picking up, colliding, jumping, juggling, balancing, intercepting, changing, alternating, keeping together, tagging, dribbling, shooting, aiming, running, non-stopping, keeping away, keeping up, tugging, keeping, exchanging, stealing, doing it backward

PEOPLE

Solo
Partner
Trio
Large Group (no more than four per side)
Small Group

THINGS

Scoops, bats, balls, pucks, rackets, hoops, bean bags, pins, sticks, wands, ropes, batons, boxes, birdies, cones, nets, plastic containers, carpets, markers, streamers, shapes

MAKING IT HARDER

Switching hands or feet, switching players, defending, blocking, fast breaking, double teaming, scoring, checking a player, screening, passing ahead, goalkeeping, rebounding, cooperating, smashing, serving, feinting, tackling, dodging, anticipating, attacking, saving

PLACES

Floor, air, court, field, goals, platform, hallway, stumps, steps, trees, rocks, corner, hills, pits, corridor, pillar, circle, bars, bins, bleachers, triangle, square, wall, trestle, basket, lines, nets, back stop, plank, fence

Mix and match from different areas to create a **NEW** game.

FIGURE 6–2   Invent a Game

A useful follow-up (and tool for assessment) might be to have children write a description of their game in the classroom. The children can make a numbered list of the instructions for playing the game, including the numbers of players, the equipment used, the rules, and a diagram of the layout of the playing space. They can also give their game an interesting name. The resulting sheets can be bound into an "Our Class's Book of Games" volume. This project can be used as both a literacy activity and a Physical Education assignment. Children love to read these books and then try out the games of other groups. These collections should not be used as a substitute for discovery, however.

Level 2: Children Who Are Ready to Work in Twos or Small Groups

A feature of Level 1 activities has been to allow young children to encounter and learn about the behavior of a wide variety of small apparatus (e.g., bean bags, ropes, hoops, scoops), some of which resembles adult sports equipment such as balls (hard and soft, large and small, round and oval), birdies, pucks, rackets, sticks, and bats (long and round). Next comes an essential part of most competitive sport—one or more other players. Some children will already have played with others; some will not.

Level 2 may look like a short section as far as content material goes. Remember, however, that almost all the material suggested in Level 1 should be repeated with another person, either as a teammate or as an opponent.

This level really marks a major shift in development and is very challenging for young children. Most major sports involve teams, and young children are egocentric. You will see how difficult and how fascinating it is for children to start thinking in relation to someone else. The physical skills involved are the very foundation of major sports. For this reason, this stage should not be hurried. Plenty of time will be needed, as one can progress only at the developmental level of the children.

Although some children may have already worked with a partner, it is recommended that you repeat Level 1 activities with the suggested additions that follow. This material, as before, is meant to be used on an as-needed basis. When children seek out another person to play with, they are usually ready both psychologically and physically for

the extra demands and challenges entailed by that kind of partnership. The previous activities should be tried with partners, sometimes cooperating, and sometimes playing against them. Working with different partners is important, because different people will provide different clues to a player and these all have to be learned. Adaptability, flexibility, and skill in reading "cues" as to likely outcomes are all essential in sport.

One top-level player once came off the center court at Wimbledon after having lost the championship, saying, "I don't know what went wrong; I played my usual game." One plays against people in sports, and there is much learning involved in completing the tasks of observation, assessment, and changing one's reactions to what another player does.

17. Working in twos, keep an action going.
18. Working in twos, use more than one piece of apparatus at the same time.
19. Pass a ball to your partner; make it hard for him or her to catch or retrieve the ball.
20. With a partner, practice some "fake" passing.
21. With a partner, move with your object, ball, or striking implement and set targets at which to aim. Bounce or hit the target as you also change speeds.
22. Try ways of throwing to your partner while stationary and while on the move.
23. Send a ball away using parts of your body other than your hands.
24. "Catch" a ball using different body parts.
25. Include in your practice the body actions of traveling, sliding, rolling, jumping, dodging, swerving, and changing direction quickly.
26. Try ways of hitting using a part of your body or a striking implement such as a bat or hockey stick.
27. Hit to your friend and then turn before getting ready to hit again.
28. With your partner, practice hits where you have to swing high and low.
29. With a racket of some kind, work on hits from the left side and then the right side of your body.
30. Hit a ball using one hand and then two hands. Experiment with open hands, fisted hands, and fingertips.
31. Try different grips with your hands while practicing hitting skills.
32. Discover what effect the different positions of hands, feet, knees (i.e., bent, straight) have on your hitting action, accuracy, and distance. Your partner can observe you and measure the distances.
33. Discover what effect the different positions of hands, feet, and knees (i.e., bent, straight) have on your throwing action, accuracy, and distance. Your partner can observe you and measure the distances.
34. Catch, trap, or field balls in a variety of positions and at different speeds and angles with a partner.
35. With a partner, do something in the air before the ball comes.
36. Try the following skill actions with a partner and with different apparatus (small balls, large balls, different-shaped balls, bean bags, birdies, pucks, rings, balloons): throwing, catching, kicking, hitting, swinging, hopping, keeping possession, dribbling, aiming, interfering, scoring, retrieving, tackling, passing, receiving, "faking," getting, feinting, deceiving. (These skills could be listed on a chart for easy reference.)
37. Try different skill actions with your partner where you either cooperate with each other or compete with each other.
38. Start beside your partner, who rolls the ball. Chase the ball, pick it up, and throw it back as quickly as you can.
39. Repeat activity 38, except this time kick, trap, and return the ball, instead of rolling it.

Small-Group Games Experiences

1. Try different skill actions with a threesome.
2. Try more than one action simultaneously.
3. Working in a group with three or four players, experiment with "rapid-fire" experiences.
4. Working in groups of four, invent a game and try scoring it in a variety of ways.
5. Play a game where you have a variety of targets, where you must also include both stationary or moving skills.
6. In a small group, practice throwing or hitting skills as you vary the height, distance, and speed of the throws.
7. Working in groups of three, focus on "off-the-ball skills": backing up, checking another player, anticipating the next play, "drawing" an opponent, keeping an opponent out of the scoring area, and so on.
8. Practice passing a puck to a player in your group at different distances.
9. Try "unusual" skills: backspin, use your nondominant hand or foot, and so on.
10. Combine and oppose one player, two players, three players, and so on.

(continues)

11. Develop sequences of play in your small group.
12. Invent pattern games.
13. Practice backhand actions with your striking implements.
14. Work on defending skills as well as attacking skills (offense/defense), and strategies in your game. Sometimes defend an "area," sometimes a player.
15. Include two to four rules in your game. Discuss the rules, decide which rules to use, and then use them in your game.

The teacher should ensure a variety of choices and assignments (stations, specific apparatus, specific actions, specific size of group, even specific individuals). Alternate between this kind of teacher direction and free choice for children.

It is possible that natural leaders may appear in a group. Allow this to happen and perhaps advise on leadership skills, but take care to ensure that many children get an opportunity to lead. Watch for gender equity in leadership. Also look for children who hang back and avoid getting involved. Use smaller groups and different kinds of games for any students who are afraid of a competitive group game.

Level 3: Net, Wall, Court, and Field Pre-sport Games for Older Children

The following suggestions are more sophisticated and should not be used until the children show signs of interest and readiness. Teachers must be ready to resist pressure from community coaches and impatient parents. Classroom teachers and Physical Education teachers know their children best. If playing areas or equipment are limited, it is possible to choose ideas from different categories (e.g., one group uses the wall, one group uses a net, and another uses the large areas as a "field," with all groups working at the same time). Allow children to work on their own or with a partner. Make sure they do not always work with the same partner.

Teachers can provide varying degrees of structure for the games experience, which in turn allows some freedom and choice for the learners. The teacher can decide on limitations with respect to the playing area, the equipment and skills to be used in the game, the number of players per group, direction with respect to scoring, and any rules to use. This section describes some sample variables that the teacher can manipulate over a long period

---

Pre-sport Games

"Net" games
"Wall" games
"Court" games
"Field" games

---

of time to facilitate the creation of interesting games, although the following lists are certainly not exhaustive. Each change made—whether it be the equipment used, the part of the body involved, the size of the playing area utilized, the scoring rubric for the game, the number and type of rules specified—means a new and different game experience for the learners. Allow children to impose these limitations on their own games.

"Net" Games

There is a temptation when playing net games to allow children to practice skills that send the birdie or ball to a player on the other side of the net. This is wrong. The skill that is actually needed is the ability to send the object over the net in such a way that the player on the other side of net cannot return it. It is far more important to learn how to exploit distance, direction, angle, and force to avoid players on the other side of the net and to find the spaces within the boundaries. Older children approaching volleyball-type games can learn to distinguish between helpful skills used with their own partner or a small team on their side of the net and ball skills designed to beat the opponents on the other side of the net. In badminton or tennis-type games, making life difficult for the opponent on the other side of the net is essential. Do not hit the object to a player.

Playing Area
- Either indoors or outdoors (sand, grass, blacktop, gym floor)
- Play in a large rectangular space
- Play in a small square

Equipment and Skills to Be Used and Varied
- Change the height of the net (low versus high)
- Use nets of different lengths (4–8 feet)
- Incorporate hoops, ropes, or spots as targets
- Send any object over the net
- Throw an object (e.g., ball, ring, bean bag)
- Strike an object (e.g., ball, birdie, puck)
- Strike a large ball

- Strike a small ball
- Strike with a poly-foam paddle
- Strike with a long-handled racket
- Strike with a short-handled implement (paddle, racket)
- Change the striking implement used
- Strike with any racket and ball
- Strike with a racket and birdie
- Strike the ball from above your head
- Strike the ball from the side of the body
- Strike the ball so it has spin on it (sidespin, topspin, backspin); watch the effects of these actions on bounce and flight in the air

Number of Players

- One to four players
- Change the number of players:
  2 = 1 v 1
  4 = 2 v 2, 3 v 1
  6 = 3 v 3, 4 v 2

Scoring

- Decide how you will score points.
- Decide how many points you need to finish the game.
- When the ball or birdie hits the ground, the other side scores one point.
- You can score points only if you are serving.
- You can score a point only if your opponent misses the ball.
- Invent your own scoring system.

Rules

Choose one or more:
- Start the game from anywhere in the playing area.
- The object must stay in the air, not hit the ground.
- When the ball, birdie, or puck goes out of bounds, decide what the consequences will be.
- All players must touch the ball at least once before it goes over the net.
- All players must use different implements; after several minutes, switch implements.
- The ball must bounce on the ground before going back over the net.
- Use only body parts to manipulate object—one hand, two hands, arms, feet, forearms.
- Use either an implement or a part of the body to send the object over, under, or through the holes in the net.

"Wall" Games

Squash, racquetball, and handball all utilize corners, which means a rebound shot can be discovered. Students can invent some kind of rebound game where the angle of shots and the rebound are important. Usually a hard hit is needed—for example, low and near a corner for the ball to rebound to the adjacent wall.

Playing Area

- Either indoors or outdoors (blacktop, gym floor, racket court)
- Use one wall or two, three, or four walls
- Specify how much of the wall will be used (low space versus high space)
- Play using a wall and a large rectangle
- Play using a wall and a small square

Equipment and Skill to Be Used and Varied

- Send any size of ball or puck toward the wall
- Incorporate markers, hoops, ropes, spots, or cones as targets
- Throw any type of ball that bounces
- Strike the ball from above your head or from the side of the body
- Try different wrist actions when you strike
- Strike a large ball
- Strike a small ball
- Strike with a poly-foam paddle
- Strike with a long-handled racket
- Strike with a short-handled implement
- Play shots close to a wall where the racket swings long and hard but does not touch the wall
- Swing the racket up or down close to the wall
- Change the striking implement used
- Strike with any racket and ball
- Strike with a racket and small ball
- Strike both forehand and backhand shots close to the wall
- Turn your body before you strike
- Strike the ball so it has spin on it (backspin, topspin, slice); use both forehand and backhand actions

Number of Players

- One to four players
- Vary the number of players

Scoring

- Invent your own scoring system.
- Decide how you will score points.

(continues)

- Decide how many points are needed to finish your game.
- When the ball hits the ground, the other player scores one point.
- You can score points only if you are serving.
- You can score a point only if your opponent misses the ball.

Rules

Choose/use one or more:
- Start the game from anywhere in the playing area.
- Try hitting the ball before it bounces. Try allowing one bounce on the floor before hitting the ball.
- Decide on boundaries. When the ball, birdie, or puck goes out of bounds, decide what the ruling will be.
- All players must use different striking implements.
- The ball must bounce on the ground before going back to the wall.
- Use only body parts to manipulate object—one hand, two hands, arms, feet, forearm.
- Use either an implement or a part of the body to send a ball.
- The ball must be caught by at least one person before it goes back to the wall.

"Court" Games

Young children can enjoy and learn a great variety of skills in different environments resembling a court. It is important especially as skills develop to challenge children with the contrast of performing skills that are helpful to another player and skills that make it impossible for a player on the other team to respond. Skills must be adaptable and performed differently in different contexts. Opposing teams must be clearly marked (use colored bibs).

Playing Area
- Either indoors or outdoors (blacktop, gym floor)
- Use a small "court"
- Use a large "court"
- Play using a large rectangular court
- Play using a small square court
- Specify how much of the court will be used by whom

Equipment and Skills to Be Used and Varied
- Use a court with goals or a ring (low or high)
- Use a court with a net
- Incorporate markers, hoops, ropes, spots, or cones in the game
- Use any size of ball, puck, or birdie
- Throw and/or kick any type of ball that bounces
- Strike and/or throw the ball from above your head or from the side of the body
- Strike a large ball
- Strike a small ball
- Strike with a poly-foam paddle
- Strike with a long-handled racket
- Strike with a short-handled implement
- Change striking implement used
- Strike with a hockey stick and puck
- Strike with a racket and small ball
- Send the ball so it has spin on it
- Send the ball into a goal ring from different distances and angles

Number of Players
- One to six players
- Vary the number of players:
  2 = 1 v 1
  3 = 1 v 2
  4 = 2 v 2, 3 v 1
  5 = 2 v 3, 1 v 4
  6 = 3 v 3, 4 v 2

Scoring
- Decide how you will score points.
- Decide how many points are needed to finish your game.
- To score points, the ball has to be thrown through the goal ring.
- You can score points only if you are serving.
- To score points, you need to kick or hit the ball into the goal.
- Invent your own scoring system.

Rules

Choose/use one or more:
- Start the game from anywhere in the playing area (e.g., the end, the middle).
- All players must use hockey sticks (or rackets, and so on).
- Decide on boundaries. When the ball, birdie, or puck goes out of bounds, decide what the consequences will be.

- All players must use different striking implements.
- The ball must be passed to at least two players before shooting for a goal.
- Use only body parts to manipulate the ball—one hand, two hands, arms, feet, forearms.
- Use either an implement or a part of the body to send a ball.

"Field" Games

The temptation when field games are developing is to spend too much time on dribbling-type skills and not enough on passing skills. Recall that good peripheral vision does not develop until shortly before adolescence. As a consequence, young children cannot appreciate some of the possibilities of working together as a team. It is essential to keep teams small and to give lots of challenges requiring judging distances, speeds, and avoidance tactics as well as tackling, intercepting, and blocking spaces. Upper-elementary-aged children can have fun creating spaces and moving so that another player can succeed. Younger children usually have a more immediate focus, but a slower reaction time. Allow much choice and variety of activity, and constantly observe the responses shown in any group of children. All children need to work at their own level.

Playing Area
- Grass surface, gymnasium
- Use a small square "field"
- Use a large rectangular "field"
- Play using an oval "field"
- Specify how much of the "field" will be used by whom
- If a full-size marked field exists, consider playing sideways on it (i.e., form two smaller "fields")

Equipment and Skills to Be Used and Varied
- Use a field with one or two goals
- Use both wide and narrow goals
- Incorporate markers, hoops, ropes, spots, or cones in the game
- Use any size of ball
- Throw and/or kick any type of ball
- Strike and/or throw the ball from above your head
- Strike and/or throw the ball from the side of the body

- Strike a large ball
- Strike a small ball
- Throw with a long-handled implement
- Strike with a short- or long-handled implement
- Change the striking implement used
- Strike with a hockey stick
- Send the ball so it has spin on it
- Send a ball into a goal from different distances and angles
- Send a ball over another person to a receiver

Number of Players
- One to six players
- Change the number of players:
  2 = 1 v 1
  3 = 1 v 2
  4 = 2 v 2, 3 v 1
  5 = 2 v 3, 1 v 4
  6 = 3 v 3, 4 v 2

Scoring
- Decide how you will score points.
- Decide how many points are needed to finish your game.
- You can score points only if you are serving.
- To score points, you need to kick, hit, or throw the ball into the goal.
- Run the ball over a boundary line to score points.
- Invent your own scoring system.

Rules
Choose/use one or more:
- Start the game from anywhere in the playing area (e.g., the end, the middle, the side).
- Only feet can be used for passing the ball—no hands.
- All players must use hockey sticks or lacrosse sticks.
- Decide on boundaries. When the ball goes out of bounds, decide what the consequences will be.
- All players must use different striking and throwing implements.
- The ball must be passed to at least two players before shooting for a goal.
- Use body parts to move the ball—one hand, two hands, arms, feet, forearms, head.
- Use either an implement or a part of the body to send a ball.

GAMES TASK CARDS

The use of task cards (see sample in **Figure 6–3**) helps to save time and get an experienced class to start more quickly. These cards are prepared ahead of the lesson and can be reused. Children could also prepare them. If you have seen a particularly successful game being played, get the children to write it down and create a task card like it for another group. Encourage children to give their game a name.

Figure 6–4 displays a variety of surfaces where children should play some of their games. Balls behave differently on blacktop and grass!

Assignment 6–4

Using the samples given in this section, design 10 additional games task cards for fourth- or fifth-grade children.

Here are three examples of games task cards (see **Figure 6–5**, **Figure 6–6**, and **Figure 6–8**). You can create many more of your own, of course.

Figure 6–7 displays a variety of shapes for the playing area where children can play some of their games. Games played in oval areas have different characteristics than games played in square playing areas. Playing areas can also be a variety of sizes. **Figure 6–9** presents a few ideas for the size of the playing area.

Level 3 task cards really begin to limit children and can focus on specific sports as the real rules are incorporated; a real court, field, and marked areas begin to be used. However, even when a task card is quite specific, children can still create something new and different. This is good. After all, even established sports change. Perhaps the children you teach will produce new sports in the future.

Level 3 includes a great deal of sports-like activities. Progression is evident when more players are added and children in third through sixth grades focus on the more recognizable sports skills. Tried-and-true and successful ideas have been presented throughout this section to help you maintain quality and interest in your program.

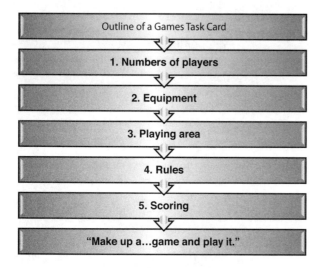

FIGURE 6–3   Games Task Card

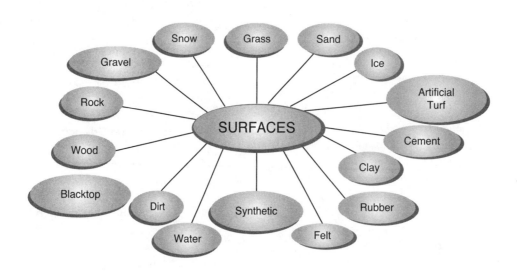

FIGURE 6–4   Surfaces

Sample Games Task Card

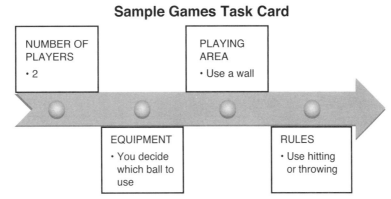

FIGURE 6–5   Sample Games Task Card

Sample Games Task Card

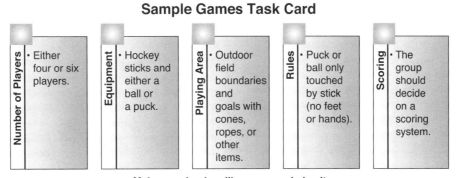

FIGURE 6–6   Hockey-Like Games Task Card

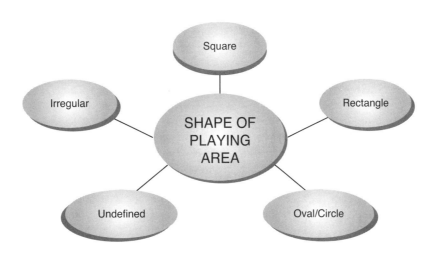

FIGURE 6–7   Shape of Playing Area

SAMPLE GAMES TASK CARD

1. Number of Players	• Two players.
2. Equipment	• Small net of any height, rackets or paddles, birdie or foam ball.
3. Playing Area	• Small, square indoor area
4. Rules	• Object must be hit, not thrown. The object should not hit the ground.
5. Scoring	• Score 1 point every time the birdie or ball touches the floor on your opponent's side of the net.

Invent a "striking" game. Give it an interesting name.

FIGURE 6-8   Striking Games Task Card

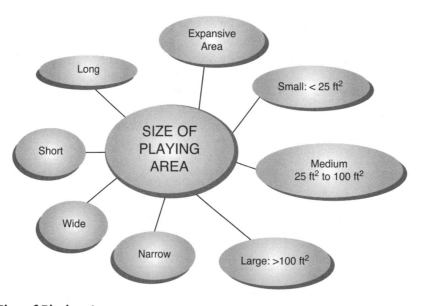

FIGURE 6-9   Size of Playing Area

Level 4: Linking Material with Recognized Major Sports

The following material is intended for teachers to use in the same way as the previous material; that is, these tasks should not be imposed on all children, even if they are older. The teacher suggests, observes, and challenges as needed. This material is intended to direct your attention to specific factors that may apply only to some sports. If children are experienced and their interests become focused on the traditional sports, there are many more guidelines and suggestions to use that relate to the major sports. Rules and team positions with special functions can develop.

Approaching the major sports in an elementary school with all children presents problems with equipment. Most regulation-size courts and fields are too large, the basketball hoop is too high, and nets placed at regulation

Assignment 6-5

Go to a friend who is a good active player of a major sport (or use your own expertise). Identify the essential skills of a good player, and develop 10 challenges to give children approaching Level 4 based on the information you have been given. Try to find different ways to experiment with and refine these skills. If possible, try your challenges out on children.

height are often too high relative to the size of youngsters. At this level, some children are ready for real badminton rackets, real tennis rackets, real field hockey sticks (flat on one side only), regulation balls specific to the sport, and so on. Some sporting bodies do provide junior-sized equipment, however. In particular, it is important that junior-sized basketball hoops with backboards be provided and a smaller court used.

It is possible that local clubs and sports associations might be asked to help. When such bodies see the quality of work and the skill level of some younger children, they may become interested in tapping into this source of talent. A word of caution is in order, though: It is the educational process for *all* children that is important. Classroom and elementary Physical Education teachers know the children best and are sensitive to their developmental needs. The skill development and physical well-being of all children are paramount concerns, but the gap between star players and professional sports and the local children does not need to exist. Teachers should be prepared to tap into local resources to develop their programs.

When teachers begin to be more involved in the "invent" games situation at the higher grade levels, more discussion may result. Although any arguments should not be allowed to take up too much time, the teacher should not jump in too quickly with the answers. If arguments become a problem, making the group smaller or splitting one game into two different ones with different rules might be useful. Even so, it is a good idea for children to be involved in the process; such discussion can give insight into how a game is played.

Some children may be involved in sports outside school time and bring their superior knowledge with them. The super-organized teacher may be tempted to step in too soon and take over the organization and decision making. The value, however, does not lie only in the end product. Instead, the process by which the problems encountered are recognized, and the solutions and agreements reached, are themselves important outcomes and should not be provided as ready-made solutions by the teacher. The process of discovery can allow children to understand the nature of a team game, the need for spe-

cific functions of certain players, and the purpose of rules and penalties for infringement.

Many sports require totally different behavior and skills to be combined in the same "game." This complexity is difficult for children to master; they will need lots of practice. A player also needs to learn skills that relate to teammates. All on-the-ball skills are used sometimes to help someone and to make it easy for them to respond (and what is "easy" is different for different players and cannot jeopardize the overall purpose of the team). At other times, on-the-ball skills relate to defeating opponents, avoiding them or putting the ball, birdie, or puck into a goal or onto the floor. This is a major difference, and cues should be varied to produce "cooperative" skills versus "antagonistic" skills.

Competition will be evident at the upper grade levels among some children. Observation shows that some children never develop a competitive nature, whereas others do so early on. When team sports are involved, cooperation is just as important as competition. If children treat all others as competitors, they are not ready for teams. If team players "hog the ball," they probably need more on-the-ball experience.

Remember that peripheral vision may not be developed in children of this age. One often sees a child in a team situation competing to "have a turn" with the ball. The child may be looking anxiously for someone to send the ball to and by the time he or she makes a decision it is "too late." This is common when the team situation is presented too soon.

In general, as children gain experience, cues will need to reflect the speed objectives of the particular sport, and maybe some rules will need to be implemented (e.g., "no hands" in soccer, flat side of field hockey stick only). Research suggests there is little, if any, transfer of training between skills performed slowly and those performed quickly. When children are approaching major sports in their invented games, it is time to give cues, which should focus on the difficulties. A player in possession of the ball will be challenged or tackled, so one-on-one games where the objective is to "spoil," "steal," and "prevent" are needed. They require fast reactions, "faking," and reading signs that are minimal and momentary. At the same time, they are lots of fun and usually provide strenuous activity.

Assignment 6-6

Try to observe a local game involving preadolescent children that is connected to a major sport, (e.g., Little League baseball, youth soccer, junior basketball, junior tennis, coach-pitch baseball, football club game). Pick out 10 specific examples of immaturity interfering with performance.

It will be important not to play with or against the same person all the time. Teachers may also begin to question children more about what they are doing.

Following are some suggestions for particular sports. As before, these challenges are intended for a teacher to use only on an as-needed basis. There are inherent limitations in major sports based on specific rules. These sports also require a more intense focus on those skills that are allowed. For example, a field hockey stick can be used on only one side of the stick; no hands may be used in soccer except by a goalkeeper.

Children should still be allowed choices, and it is unlikely that all children will become skillful at all sports. Elementary school is the time to explore all sports, but preferences may start to appear in the upper grade levels. Ultimately, by the time they become adults, all individuals should have had successful, enjoyable experiences in many sports activities, even though only few adults play top-level sports.

Soccer

Soccer is an Olympic sport for both men and women. This zigzag passing game is played on a rectangular field with net goals at either end. Players move the ball into the opponent's goal to score; they may advance the ball by kicking, heading, or using any part of the body except the arms and hands. A large ball is moved forward, backward, and sideways to players on the move. The goalie is the only player who may touch or move the ball with the arms or hands.

Soccer is one of the major sports that school Physical Education programs can address. Much of this material can be used with or against a partner. No team should be larger than four on a side.

Following are some sample challenges:

1. Strike the ball with different parts of the feet.
2. Strike the ball far and close distances, long and hard, short and quick.
3. Pass the ball to a player in front of you. Where does the player want it?
4. Make the ball spin when you kick it.
5. Kick the ball "high" over others to a particular player.
6. Make a player run fast to get to your pass.
7. Put a pass close to another player.
8. Have a partner send you the ball at different heights, different speeds, and to the side, high or low. No hands are allowed, so stop or "trap" the ball using your body (chest, lap, stomach) or using feet only.
9. Stop the ball and send it away quickly.
10. Send the ball away to a target (or another player) using your head (forehead) only.
11. Jump to "head" a ball at a target.
12. After a partner sends you a ball, have the partner "rush" you so that you have to get the ball away before the other person reaches you.
13. Pit one player against another. Try to take the ball away from the player who has it using feet only. Kick or stop only the ball—that is, without kicking the player.
14. Repeat activity 13 and add another player.
15. Play a 2 v 1 game. (This leads to realistic games. It allows cooperation between two players to defeat or block one opponent.)
16. Extend the game to 2 v 4.
17. Practice falling on a ball to smother it (goalkeeping skills).
18. Bat or punch a high ball away at an angle (goalkeeping skills).
19. Get behind the direction of a hard kick to catch it. Try it with the ball coming hard on the ground and in the air (goalkeeping skills).
20. Using a 2 v 1 group game, practice moving sideways a yard ahead of the goal mouth to cover an approaching ball (goalkeeping skills).
21. Get behind the direction of a hard kick and catch it using your arms or your body. Try stopping shots in the air or on the ground (goalkeeping skills).

Basketball

Basketball is an Olympic sport played by both men and women. This game is played between two teams, with the objective being to score by throwing a ball through an elevated basket on the opponent's side of a rectangular court. Players can move the ball by dribbling (a slower game) or by passing (a faster game) with the hands.

Following are some sample challenges:

1. Dribble a ball while on the move, using both left and right hands.
2. Dribble a ball while constantly changing direction.
3. Dribble a ball while traveling at different speeds. Be sure to try getting faster, slowing down, and stopping abruptly.
4. As you dribble, change the pathway on the floor that you are following.
5. Repeat activity 4 against opposition.
6. Working in pairs, send the ball to your partner at different distances. Practice really long throws to both the left and right of your partner.
7. Dribble the ball and pass it to a partner on your left, your right, and ahead of the moving player.
8. While dribbling with a partner, have him or her try to take the ball away or steal it from you. Score points for every steal. Start side-by-side or face-to-face.
9. Working in pairs, throw the ball to your partner with and without a bounce.
10. Repeat activity 9 at different distances.
11. Have a 2 v 1 game where one player will try to intercept the pass to your partner. What do you have to do to successfully intercept the ball?
12. Play a 2 v 2 game where passing the ball in different ways is refined.
13. Play a 3 v 3 passing/intercepting game. Try to anticipate the angle of the pass.
14. Practice catches where you are high off the ground when you catch the ball.
15. Practice catches where you are running either forward, sideways, or backward to catch the ball.
16. Using appropriate height goals with backboards, practice moving toward a goal and shooting from different distances and different angles.
17. Repeat activity 16 but add another player who will try to interfere with your successful shooting of a goal.
18. Free throw shooting: Practice this shot directly in front of the goal at an appropriate distance for the age of the children. Experiment with both the arc/trajectory through the air and the spin on the ball.

Field Hockey

Field hockey is an Olympic sport for both men and women. This game is played on grass. Two opposing teams of players, using curved sticks, try to advance a small ball down the field into the opponents' net-type goal.

Have a hockey stick and ball available for each child. If plastic sticks are used, it is essential to have one side of the stick marked clearly in a different color or with tape. Mark the left side of a stick when the stick is held in front with the curve of the blade facing forward. Have at least one real field hockey stick available to show that only one side of the blade is flat. Although there are no left-handed hockey sticks, "reverse" stick work can be included from the outset and left-handers will probably excel at this skill.

A lighter ball should be used with plastic sticks (such as old tennis balls—try your local tennis club for discarded balls).

Following are some sample challenges:

1. Run with your stick while keeping the ball moving ahead of you but close to you.
2. Run faster; try to hit the ball less often but still just ahead of you.
3. Repeat activities 1 and 2 while trying different positions of the hands on the stick. Discover which position gives you the best control.
4. Repeat activities 1 and 2 while using the flat (or colored) side of the stick only, but hitting the ball a little way from side to side, but still just ahead of you.
5. Travel as fast as you can without losing control of the ball.
6. Repeat traveling as fast as you can while trying to turn the stick over the ball to hit it (flat or colored side only touching the ball, but with the stick over the top of the ball). This is called using "reverse sticks."
7. Repeat as quickly as you can. Switch to the reverse stick side as fast as you can.
8. Hit to a partner using the reverse stick action (stick over the top of the ball). Try to be quick in turning your stick over.
9. Repeat this dribbling action when someone is trying to take the ball away. The opponent may use only the flat or colored side of the stick and must contact the ball.
10. Switch the roles of tackler and dribbler. Score points for a successful tackle or successfully keeping possession. Find out what is the best time to make a tackle.
11. Hit a moving ball at the wall and receive the rebound. Sometimes use a reverse stick action.
12. Hit a moving ball at an angle to the wall.
13. Scoop a ball to hit the wall. Try a gentle and slow motion, and then a hard and quick motion.
14. Try a flicking action to lift a ball or deflect it suddenly.
15. Run with the ball and hit it to a partner on your left, to a partner on your right, ahead of the moving player, and at the stick of a moving player.
16. Repeat activity 15 using a reverse stick action. Notice the differences and effects of your action.
17. Repeat activity, and try to use a swing before you hit. Notice how the angle of the swing affects the direction of the ball. Try different positions of the feet and hands when you hit.
18. Have a 2 v 1 team where partners try to pass successfully to each other while player 3 tries to intercept or tackle.
19. Run beside a player who is dribbling the ball and swing your stick into the player so that only the correct side of your stick contacts the ball.
20. Repeat trying to jab the ball away from the dribbler.
21. Set up two targets or goals and play a 1 v 1 game. Each player tries to pass the opponent and score, or score before the opponent can tackle you.
22. Repeat the game with 2 v 2 or possibly 3 v 3 formations (no larger groups).
23. Goalkeeping can be taught, but keepers must wear pads on the legs and feet. Teach goalkeepers to stop a shot with the feet or legs and to kick the ball. Use the hands to strike down a lifted ball and to clear the ball by kicking to the sides of the goal.
24. Teach goalkeepers to move sideways to cover the angles of shots.
25. Floor hockey in a gym can substitute for field hockey outdoors. Pucks or rubber rings can be used.

Volleyball

Volleyball became an Olympic sport in 1964, with beach volleyball being approved as an Olympic sport in 1996. Volleyball is a game played by two teams on a rectangular court divided by a high net. Teams use a maximum of three hits on their side of the net before sending the ball across the net to score a point if possible (i.e., ball touches the floor or sand). Hands or arms may be used to bat the ball, but players may not catch or carry it.

Following are some sample challenges:

1. Without a net, hit the ball accurately to a teammate to the side, in front, or behind you without the ball touching the ground. Practice high and low hits in all directions. These are hits to practice to your teammates, not to your opponents.
2. Strike the ball with one hand or both hands to a partner or a wall.
3. Bump the ball high to a partner using two hands with thumbs parallel. Use wrists, thumbs, and forearms. The partner then tries to spike (smash—hard hit) the ball to the side. Do this activity with and without a net.
4. Try hits to the floor on the other side of the net.
5. Using a net, practice serving the ball over the net into the court on the other side.
6. Using a net, try hits that are directed downward as well as hits that are directed upward.
7. Practice hits with varying degrees of force and at different angles over a net.
8. Vertically jump high to spike the ball over a net.
9. Dive to hit a ball that has been sent over a net.
10. Serve. Try to be accurate for distance and angle.
11. Hit the ball into spaces between players on the other side of the net.
12. Try hits to the floor on the other side of the net where there is a space.
13. Play a 2 v 2 game with a net of appropriate height. Start with a serve over the net.

Tennis

Tennis is a game played with rackets and a light ball by two players, or two pairs of players, on a rectangular court of grass, clay, or a hard surface that is divided by a net. The objective is to hit the ball over the net and into the opponent's half of the court in such a way as to defeat the opponent's attempt to reach and return the ball. The serve puts the ball in play, and players can hit the ball into any part of the opponent's court until a point is scored. Rallies are won when either player scores a point.

Following are some sample challenges:

1. With a racket, hit the ball so that it goes straight, to the right, and to the left. Hit a ball that comes to your right or left side.
2. Hit a ball that bounces high, low, or somewhere in between these extremes.
3. As you practice hitting, try different body positions relative to the net or line or a wall.
4. Hit a ball from "underneath" (to put topspin on the ball). Try to "backspin" the ball (i.e., create downward action).
5. Hit a ball that is overhead. Hit hard and "down."

6. Experiment with hitting a ball when it is at your side or "before" it gets to you. Lean into the hit. Try two hands on the racket, and then one hand.

7. Practice a "drop shot" so it lands just over the net.

8. "Volley" a ball with a partner. The ball should be delivered without a bounce. Do not do this over a net. Make the hit hard to return.

9. "Serve" a ball into the service box from both the right and left sides (i.e., at different angles). Aim for the corners and the centerline.

10. Try many long forehand and backhand hits that are fast and skim the net and that land close to the backline just inside the court.

Badminton

Badminton is an Olympic sport. This "up in the air" game is suited to an indoor court with a high ceiling. Learning focuses on the variety of strokes and the placement of shots. Although badminton is often called a "racket" game, it really involves unique skills because the aerodynamics of a shuttlecock (birdie) are quite different from those of a ball. It will be essential when children's sports activity begins to resemble badminton to have birdies with which to play. The timing of strokes (hits) is specific. Also, because a birdie is light and loses speed in flight, all kinds of wrist action need to be explored and developed. A "snap" of the wrist, a sideways flick, a scoop, a gentle hit just strong enough to skim the net, a serve (placement is crucial), and the fun of the smash and the "deep high clear" are unique to this sport. One can explore all kinds of rotation of the body and limbs, which contribute to an "explosion" of power at the point of impact.

A light net and plenty of space overhead will be needed when badminton is taught. Following are some sample challenges:

1. Play "keep-up," mixing gentle hits and strong ones. Watch how the birdie behaves with each hit.

2. Practice getting under a falling birdie to hit it even higher. Try both an underhand action and an overhead one.

3. Try to avoid a player on the other side of the net and make the player move sideways, backward, and forward to return your hit.

4. Repeat trying not to let your opponent have time to reach your shot. Experiment with the force of your hit, the angle, backhand and forehand hits, overhead shots, and turning your body to mask your intentions.

5. Practice serving for accuracy while disguising your shots.

6. Practice "deep high clear" shots from different parts of the court to ensure the birdie falls inside the boundaries.

7. Vary the angle at which your racket hits the birdie and notice the effects.

8. With an opponent, practice moving quickly and taking a shot in mid-air.

9. With an opponent, quickly disguise a forehand shot and turn it into a backhand at the last minute.

10. Try to make the birdie hit the ground on the other side of the net.

11. Try to make it hard for the other player to return the birdie.

12. With an opponent, hesitate or spurt in your approach to a return. Use your feet in different steps.

13. Play a game in threes, with two players both sending birdies over the net to one side of the court at a space near the third player. The single player has to move rapidly from side to side and play good returns. Have several birdies available and speed up the game so that the single player has a "rapid-fire" experience. The two players should alternate the height and depth of their hits as well. Rotate players, perhaps keeping a personal individual "score of successes."

Baseball/Softball

Baseball and softball are games played with a bat and ball (either a small, hard ball or a softball) by two opposing teams. Each team plays alternately in the field and at bat. The players at bat have to run to four bases laid out in a diamond pattern to score. A larger, softer ball is pitched underhand in softball.

Following are some sample challenges:

1. Fielding practices: In groups of three or four, using 10 small balls, have a student hit balls to players in the field for them to stop or catch in some way. Field balls rolling on the ground at different speeds and in the air.

2. Batting practices: Using an appropriate length and weight of baseball bat, hit small balls thrown to you by a partner to different distances and different angles as well as to the right and the left. Where a wall space is available, hit toward a wall to save time in retrieving the balls, or use fielders.

3. Pitching practices: Practice pitching at a target to contact it as many times as possible.

4. Catching practices: Have a player pitch a ball directly to you to catch. Catch in front of the body, to the right and left sides of the body, and very close to the ground. Bend the knees to field low balls. Avoid other runners.

5. A simple foursome game: One player is a fielder, one is on a base, and two batters with several balls (10). Players can keep individual scores. The fielder must stop the ball and throw immediately to the base. The person on the base can field or receive the throws from the fielder and roll them back to the batters. Batters toss a ball and hit it hard in different directions, either as a fly ball or low out into the field.

Make the fielder move to field the ball, and time your hits with the other batter so that the fielder has a "rapid-fire" experience.

6. When a softball game is played, it is possible to reduce the number of inactive children by reducing the number of bases and scoring on an individual basis so that only one batter is up and only one batter is waiting. The children rotate into the field (back-catcher, base, three fielders, and batter). Have several balls available and reduce any nonplaying time as much as possible. (Allow only one strike?)

7. If a game is attempted during class time, have a strenuous running activity before starting the game that should be preorganized and use the game as one of four group activities. Choice can be given, but note that many track and field activities combine well with softball (e.g., one group at a long jump pit, one high jumping, one group at a double or triple flight of hurdles, and the reduced softball game).

Track and Field

Track and field sports are the origin of Olympic competition. This important—but much neglected—area of activities suits young children extremely well. It is natural to compete with oneself to improve performance. Many children are more interested in improving their personal best performance than in competing with other children. An elementary school playing area can easily be adapted to include jumping pits, a sprinting track, and a peripheral running course. Material for track and field is included in the sample lessons for games presented in this book.

Assignment 6–7

Choose a major sport mentioned here and identify at least six key actions. Present three challenges for each action that might guide students to discover the action.

Lifetime Pursuits

Competitive sports include a large number of activities in which the aim is to prove oneself or one's team better than an opponent or an opposing team. These pursuits include many pair games such as badminton or tennis, the individual activities of track and field athletics, and the more familiar team games. Combat activities also include an element of personal contact, such as fencing, wrestling, and judo. Conquest activities use the environment as the source of challenge—"Can I do it?" The obvious sports in this last category are outdoor activities like mountaineering, skiing, hiking, and sailing.

The early attempts of the child to demonstrate almost any skill have an element of "conquest" activity. A balance must be arrived at between the demands of the environment or situation and the ability of the participant. Although an all-out effort may be called for, the interaction centers largely on how the individual can change the situation so that he or she can succeed and how the individual adapts to that which cannot be changed. Mastery is very satisfying and will lead to repetition and tackling increasingly more difficult situations.

Physical contact with another human being also seems to be important at a stage in children's development. Many teachers are aware of the fighting, wrestling, clinging, and holding behaviors that occur somewhere in mid-childhood.

Basically, all sport is competitive, although the ability to indulge actively in a civilized manner probably represents a highly sophisticated and educated achievement. Writing on aggression, Lorenz (1969) states:

> The value of sport, however, is much greater than that of a simple outlet of aggression in its coarser and more individualistic behavior patterns, such as pummeling a punch-ball. It educates man to a conscious and responsible control of his own fighting behavior. . . . More valuable still is the educational value of the restrictions imposed by the demands for fairness and chivalry which must be respected even in the face of the strongest aggression-eliciting stimuli. (pp. 271–272)

This notion may sound idealistic in contemporary society. After all, when observing much competitive professional sport, one rarely sees "chivalry." As opportunities for international competition increase, however, perhaps attention can be paid to the wonderful opportunity for sports to inspire goodwill between nations. Sports are one of the few activities that are truly international. Perhaps peacekeeping forces in the future should be equipped with soccer balls or sports equipment appropriate to the country where they serve. Teachers may like to be reminded that the "aggression-eliciting stimuli" are inherent in most games and activities, and that fairness and good conduct will largely need to be provided or developed by the teachers and children themselves. If games behavior is disruptive or too "emotional," a teacher can suggest that the activity be dropped altogether. We have also found that if two children fight over equipment a simple statement—"If you can't agree who will have it, then neither of you will"—usually solves the dispute.

Writing on aggression, Lorenz (1969) states there is no sport in which serious contests are not held, even when the main enjoyment of the activity is in performing skilled movements for their own sake. He continues:

> Sporting contests between nations are beneficial not only because they provide an outlet for the collective militant enthusiasm of nations, but also because they have two other effects that counter the danger of war: they promote personal acquaintance between people of different nations or parties and they unite, in enthusiasm for a common

cause, people who otherwise would have little in common. (Lorenz, 1969, p. 273)

This unification will not happen automatically. Teachers will need to make a deliberate effort to encourage this kind of cooperation.

The teaching of games in schools is a worthwhile and important educational activity. Within the range of competitive activities, children need to experience both small one-to-one situations as well as "small team" experiences. In education, teachers of competitive activity will need to develop what is, perhaps, a release of aggressive behavior into a collective effort that becomes restricted by mutually agreed regulation and that ventures into relationships with unknown groups.

Crucial to the current social situation (i.e., our increasingly sedentary lifestyle), sport can provide a means for adults to continue strenuous physical activity. Whether they do so will depend on how motivated they were, how successful they were, and how enjoyable their early experiences were, in addition to how confident and skillful they become and if participatory opportunities exist in the community. It might be preferable, for example, to focus on lifetime sports such as tennis and swimming instead of football and basketball. With a couple of hours to spare on a weekend, an adult is more likely to seek out a friend for a game of handball, squash, tennis, badminton, or a swim than try to find a team and a facility for basketball and football. Even so, it is hoped that more facilities and club organizations will continue to be developed. If enough people care strongly enough, it can happen. Certainly sport can provide strenuous activity for adult participation, but the facts indicate that few adults participate in team sports. Individual activity or family activities such as hiking, swimming, skiing, and biking are more popular. Perhaps we should plan to adapt our high school and college curricula to include lifetime strenuous sports. We know children will readily move and create activity.

Although overt behavior may give the impression of highly competitive sport activities, we do not always know the basis of satisfaction and enjoyment that children experience. Some children get sensual pleasure in activity: It feels good! There are many popular sports where "combat" seems to be the purpose. Wrestling, judo, Tai Kwan do, fencing, and boxing have many devotees and, in fact, are Olympic sports. Playground supervisors in the elementary school often approach children involved in what looks like mortal combat to be told, "We're only playing."

Many individuals like to "conquer" the environment or their bodies, and enjoy sports such as rock climbing, swimming, sailing, hiking, snowboarding, downhill skiing, surfing, canoeing, kayaking, whitewater rafting, golf, or ice skating. Team games are often attractive not just to show superior skill physically, but as a battle of wits. Sport in society has many functions.

A Model for Pre-sport Games

INNER CIRCLE

The inner circle of the diagram in **Figure 6–10** indicates the early, basic games skills that teachers need to encourage children to discover, practice, and refine. These will form the core of the program. Throwing, catching, kicking, striking, running, jumping, and propelling objects are the skills to focus upon. Children should be free to discover as much as possible about how these skills can be performed, improved, and perfected. Very young children should not be overwhelmed with teacher direction, however. Children may be absorbed and busy, in which case the best advice is "Leave them alone." Some children may need encouragement, and some "help" might be needed to find a space or get a piece of apparatus.

The role of the teacher once activity has begun is very much like a ringmaster in a circus. One watches, notices, and is ready to help, smile, and encourage as needed. Teachers are trying to develop responsibility in children. Noise level need not be unduly high. Children should develop an understanding that they look after themselves, do not interfere with others, and simply get on with their "work" (which in this case is "play"). It is important to spend plenty of time in this process. Skill development takes time and lots of practice. All children learn motor skills at different rates, starting from birth, and these differences persist into the elementary school level and beyond.

Model for Designing Developmental Games and Pre-sport Experiences

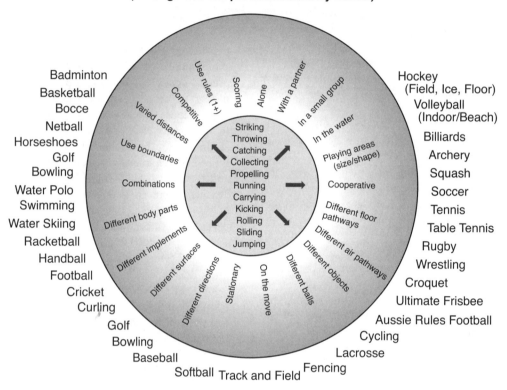

Creative Games
(other games not predetermined by adults)

Badminton
Basketball
Bocce
Netball
Horseshoes
Golf
Bowling
Water Polo
Swimming
Water Skiing
Racketball
Handball
Football
Cricket
Curling
Golf
Bowling
Baseball
Softball   Track and Field   Fencing

Hockey
(Field, Ice, Floor)
Volleyball
(Indoor/Beach)
Billiards
Archery
Squash
Soccer
Tennis
Table Tennis
Rugby
Wrestling
Croquet
Ultimate Frisbee
Aussie Rules Football
Cycling
Lacrosse

Inner circle: Striking, Throwing, Catching, Collecting, Propelling, Running, Carrying, Kicking, Rolling, Sliding, Jumping

Middle circle: Use rules (1+), Competitive, Varied distances, Use boundaries, Combinations, Different body parts, Different implements, Different surfaces, Different directions, Stationary, On the move, Different balls, Different objects, Different air pathways, Different floor pathways, Cooperative, Playing areas (size/shape), In the water, In a small group, With a partner, Alone, Scoring

FIGURE 6–10   Model for Designing Developmental Games and Pre-sport Experiences

MIDDLE CIRCLE

Variations of the core skills listed in the inner circle of the model are found in the middle circle. Children will perform these variations at different ages and stages in their motor development. If such variety does not emerge, then the teacher should suggest activities that focus the children's attention on the variations listed. There are many variations that children should incorporate over time into their ever-expanding movement vocabularies.

Assignment 6–8

Choose two skills from the inner circle. List five movement activities or tasks for each skill. Write the tasks exactly as you might present them to a class.

OUTER CIRCLE

Material in the outer circle is appropriate for older children. It will look more like pre-major sports material. Listed on the outer circle of the diagram are recognizable sports. Younger children may already have used the names of these sports. A first grader pushing a rubber ring with a stick said, "I'm playing hockey." He worked up speed and took the stick out of the ring so that it slid against the wall, as in ice hockey.

Most of the sports listed on the outer circle have been played for many years in different parts of the world; they

Assignment 6–9

Choose four skills from the inner circle. For each skill, list two movement activities or tasks that incorporate variables from the middle circle.

are highly sophisticated adult activities. All of the elements of these sports are well known by those teenagers and adults who play them. Over the years, there have been some minor changes to rules; the equipment used; the size, shape, and surface of the playing field; and the method of scoring. Nevertheless, these sports are fairly stable.

Some of children's games may look like recognized sports and can be called pre-sports. Children at the elementary school level will gradually become familiar with many of the elements of these major sports and will often create and play games that are "like" the sports listed in the outer circle. Large teams, adult equipment, and adult-sized playing fields are not recommended for children in elementary school. Instead, children should create a "volleyball-like" game or a "hockey-like" game with a team of four players as a maximum size.

Remember to use *small* teams; two people are a team. Adapt the sport to child-sized equipment and small playing areas, although in the upper elementary grades games will often need to be played outdoors in a larger area. Remember to have many markers to delineate the playing area.

Mitchell et al. (2006), in what they describe as a tactical approach to teaching games, outline lesson material for teaching sports skills and games in middle schools and high schools. Some of this material may be suitable for students in the upper grades of an elementary school.

Different cultures play different games and sports, so the model includes many sports played in a variety of cultures. Within the United States, schools include children with highly diverse cultural backgrounds: Native Americans, children from Latin American countries, Europe, Asia, and so on. In today's world, there is massive media coverage of sports from all over the world, and this factor will affect the "games" children develop.

The short time available for lessons in schools must be used to the full and augmented by before- and after-school and recess activities. Look at your school environment and organization to assess the possibilities for recess and before- and after-school use; see if improvements could be made.

The overall guidelines for games lessons in an elementary school are to encourage strenuous activity and enjoyment for all children. These two factors must always be present when you use the material presented in this chapter. Games lessons must mean fun, satisfaction, growth in skill, and strenuous activity for all children. When they are allowed choice and given responsibility, the program can almost run itself.

References

American Alliance for Health, Physical Education, Recreation and Dance (AAHPERD). (1977, September). *Games teaching.* Reston, VA: Author.

Lorenz, K. (1969). *On aggression.* New York: Bantam Books.

Mauldon, E., & Refern, H. (1969). *Games teaching: A new approach for the primary school.* London: MacDonald & Evans.

Mitchell, S. A., Oslin, J. L., & Griffin, L. L. (2006). *Teaching sport concepts and skills: A tactical games approach.* Champaign, IL: Human Kinetics.

Opie, I. A., & Opie, P. (1969). *Children's games in street and playground. Chasing, catching, seeking, hunting, racing, duelling, exerting, daring, guessing, acting, pretending.* Oxford, UK: Clarendon Press.

Sample Developmental Games and Sports Lessons Using the Discovery Approach

The NASPE Standards referenced by number in the lessons in this chapter can be found listed in Appendix 3 of the text. Many states have their own interpretation of these Standards and you should check those that apply in your state.

LESSON 1

MANIPULATION OF BALLS AND BEAN BAGS

LEVEL 1

Appropriate grade level: Preschool through second grade

Lesson length: Approximately 30 minutes

NASPE Standards: 1, 2, 5, 6

State Standards: _____

OBJECTIVES

The learner will:

- Experiment with balls, bean bags, and hoops to discover what can be done with these items.
- Practice throwing and catching moving balls and bean bags in different ways.
- Make up a game alone or with a partner using the available equipment.

LESSON MATERIALS

Balls of all kinds, bean bags, hoops, scoops, ropes, targets, markers

ACTIVITIES

Free Practice

- If appropriate to the teaching situation and children have done this before, provide for free practice. If not, go straight to the introductory activity.
- Suggest that when the students are ready, they can choose a piece of apparatus and find out what it will do.
- The teacher encourages the activity, sorts out any disputes, and so on.

Introductory Activity

Consists of simple running while changing directions until breathlessness is reached.

- "Pick up your apparatus and see if you can run with it." Repeat, stressing safety and staying spread out. Establish a "stop" response.
- "In a space, bounce and catch your ball. Those who do not have a ball, put your apparatus away and get a ball." Stop and check spacing; repeat. Repeat running holding the apparatus. Stop in a space.
- "Bounce the ball, or bounce and catch the ball all around you in a space."
- "Try to jump and bounce at the same time." Allow for a variety of continuous bouncing, bounce and catch, big jumps, jumping crouched, and other skills.

- "Stop. Hold the ball high above your head. Put it on the floor and run around it." It is likely that the balls will roll, so much practice will be needed trying to watch the ball, run in a circle, and not bump into anyone else. Stress looking out for other balls as well as other people.

- "Sit on the floor, roll the ball around yourself in a complete circle, also with straight legs."

- "Move around the room taking the ball with you." Many children will bounce or roll the ball, and some will use the feet to guide the ball.

- "Walk, run, or jump with your ball." Emphasize keeping the ball close to oneself unless you are working outdoors when more freedom and speed can be encouraged.

- The teacher collects the box of bean bags for the next activity while the children are busy.

Individual Skill Activity

- "When you put your ball away, take a bean bag into a space and do this." The teacher shows a simple catch and throw. Point out the "gathering" nature of catching. As children begin, encourage "one-handed" (left and right) as well as two-handed skills.

- "Stop. Put your bean bag on any part of your body where it will stay. Now try to throw it using that part of your body." Encourage use of a variety of body parts. Possibly suggest different positions (e.g., kneeling, lying on the tummy). Continue until all children have tried a good range of activity. "Now use a different part of your body to throw the bean bag."

Individual/Partner Skill Activity

- "Make up a game using a bean bag." Most children will continue to "play" with the bean bag. Some will run. Allow playing with a friend, and using more than one bean bag if plenty are available.

Learning Centers

Hoop Area

Scoops/Bean Bag Area

Rope Area

Wall/Large Ball Area

FIGURE 7–1   Learning Centers

Group Activity

- *Learning Center 1:* Hoops.
- *Learning Center 2:* Ropes.
- *Learning Center 3:* Scoops/bean bags.
- *Learning Center 4:* Wall space/large balls for throwing against a wall. This group will need the most space and, if possible, should be positioned where stray balls will not interfere too much with the other groups. If the lesson is taking place outdoors, have some targets or markers to use for aiming (**Figure 7–1**).

- "When you get to your corner (or learning center, station, or group), use the equipment that is there, immediately." Equipment can be put into learning centers prior to class. The teacher will send learners to the learning centers/stations. An easy way to get four equal groups is to ask children to sit with a partner. "With your partner, both of you stand, and both sit quickly." Repeat it. Then join up with another group of two to make a small group of four. One child in each group stands up and is sent to one of the learning centers. A second child from each group stands and is sent to another learning center. Repeat for the third and fourth child. If

learning centers have not been set up prior to the beginning of the class, send the standing child to collect a specified piece of equipment and go to the appropriate area and begin work immediately. The teacher circulates a minimum of once to each group.

- "Stop! Put your apparatus on the floor or in the containers." Children point to the next learning center and make one change. If there is time, move to more than one center in the lesson.

Final Activity

- Put all apparatus away neatly.
- Walk in a space. Cover all the space and walk to the door.

LESSON 2

HANDBALL-RELATED SKILLS

LEVEL 1

Appropriate grade level: First through third grades

Lesson length: Approximately 30 minutes

NASPE Standards: 1, 2, 5, 6

State Standards: _____

OBJECTIVES

The children will:

- Practice different ways of using hands to hit paper balls and other small balls.
- Demonstrate hits in different directions, at different levels, and different angles toward a wall.
- Create a game resembling handball with a partner using either one or two walls and hands only for hitting the ball.

LESSON MATERIALS

A variety of small balls (yarn balls, newspaper balls, Ping-Pong balls, tennis balls, racket and squash balls, small playground balls)

ACTIVITIES

Individual Activities

- Show how you can move a crumpled piece of notebook paper (i.e., a paper ball) around the general space. Make the "ball" and tape it into a "round" shape.

- Spread sheets of paper on the floor. Try a variety of locomotor movements around the pieces of paper. Move quickly and lightly around the gym as you move from paper to paper and freeze for one second in a low position at each paper.
- Keep the paper in the air by using different parts of your body to propel it. How lightly can you hit the paper with your hand and keep it in the air? How high can you hit it?
- Change directions while you are hitting the paper. Change levels while hitting the paper.
- Can you hit the paper first with one hand and then with the other hand?
- Find the best way of shaping the hand for hitting the paper ball.
- Choose any kind of small ball and show how to hit the ball against a wall using the hand as a hitting object.
- Choose from any of the balls that are in the containers. Hit the ball at different angles against the wall. Hit the ball against the wall; let it bounce once before hitting it again.

Partner Activities

- How straight can you hit the paper ball back and forth using your hand with a partner?
- With a friend, can you hit the paper ball first with one hand and then with the other hand?
- With your partner, change directions while you are hitting the paper ball. Also change levels while hitting the paper ball.
- Working in groups of two, invent a game using a ball, the wall, and your hand as a hitting object.

Assessment/Reflection Activities

- Show and discuss the games.
- Discuss the rules used in the games the children invented and played.

Conclusion

- Children hold their balls and run anywhere in the space. Put your ball in the container as you pass it. Include a change of direction when you run. Stop. Commend games that started quickly, with minimum of talking and without arguments.
- Commend games that showed good cooperation, discussion, and decision making.

LESSON 3

SKILLS WITH BALLS AND JUMP ROPES

LEVEL 2

Appropriate grade level: Third through fourth grades

Lesson length: Approximately 30 minutes

NASPE Standards: 1, 2, 5, 6

State Standards: _____

OBJECTIVES

The learner will:

- Practice moving balls in different directions using right and left hands or feet.
- Try patterns and increases of speed with balls.
- Use jump ropes for jumping or skipping alone or with a partner.
- Make up a "threesome" game using the apparatus provided.

LESSON MATERIALS

Balls of different sizes, weights, and textures; jump ropes

ACTIVITIES

Free Practice

- Practice things from your last lesson.
- Alternatively, choose a ball or a rope and do *two* different things with it.

This section of a lesson can be very instructive for the teacher who observes.

Introductory Activity

- "If you have a rope, put it away and get a ball. Make continuous movements with your feet or hands to keep the ball with you. Stop."

- "Vary the direction in which you travel and use both the right and left sides of your body. Stop."
- "Make a pattern of one right, one left, and change direction. Increase the speed. Stop. Repeat. Exchange your ball with somebody near you and repeat."

Individual Skill Activity

- "Put the balls away. Collect and place a jump rope on the floor. Do any movement from side to side along the rope."
- "Choose two different movements and show one as you go from one end of the rope to the other. Then show the other movement as you return backward." Encourage the use of hands on the floor as well as different kinds of jumps.

Partner Activity

- "Show any kind of skipping or jumping using your rope."
- "Find a partner and make up any kind of skipping or jumping game." Pairs can use two ropes, or one. Many will simply skip individually but try and go faster or longer than the other. If a few couples are really skilled, then suggestions of variations in turning, rhythm, and changing ends can be made. Put the apparatus away and make a group of three people.

Group Activity

- "Plan a game that does not travel. Get the apparatus and start." (Apparatus can be restricted, or free choice can be allowed. Limits of one or two items can be imposed. If space is very limited, you can use a threesome game on the floor i.e., not on the feet or half the class can use the floor only while the rest may travel.)
- After a considerable period of activity, the class can be "pulled together" either by all having one last turn or by half the class observing the other half. Switch.

Assessment/Reflection Activities

- Discuss and demonstrate some of the skipping games and the threesome game elements.

Conclusion

- Put apparatus away neatly. Slow jogging, slow down to a walk, and stop.
- Apparatus should always be checked so that children learn to take pride in a neat, well-organized storage space.

LESSON 4

BALL AND OBJECT CONTROL SKILLS

LEVEL 2

Appropriate grade level: Preschool through fourth grade

Lesson length: Approximately 30 minutes

NASPE Standards: 1, 2, 5, 6

State Standards: _____

OBJECTIVES

The learner will:

- Discover a wide variety of manipulative activities with balls of different sizes, weights, and textures.
- Make up a game either alone, with a partner, or in a small group using the available lesson materials.

LESSON MATERIALS

Plastic, rubber, leather, yarn, foam, or vinyl balls; beach balls, balloons, "Nerf" balls, playground balls, SloMo balls, GatorSkin balls, softballs, racket balls, tennis balls, sock balls, newspaper balls, scoops, bats, paddles, rackets, stocking bats, markers

ACTIVITIES

Introductory Activities

- Running, dodging, swerving, and steps sideways, backward, and forward.
- Run and stop.
- Jump and leap and land quickly.
- Fix the feet, stretch the body, and then twist your body. Move one leg and foot to repeat. Switch legs. Let your arms swing and make you jump or stretch. Move in different directions.
- Arch your back in as many ways as possible.

Individual Activities

Require the children to get their play apparatus quickly and efficiently from the available containers. The teacher circulates, observes, and makes suggestions. The following challenges can be offered:

- Practice any skills of your choice for a few minutes.
- Travel with a ball in the air, on the floor, bouncing, and so on.
- Kick the ball. Stop the ball with your foot, use your head, or use other parts of your body and perhaps your knees.
- Bounce and catch your ball in a variety of positions.
- Pass the ball around your body, through your legs, and so on.
- Roll the ball with different parts of your hand or body. Try different speeds and directions.
- Bounce the ball off the wall (or ceiling).
- Bounce the ball hard or soft, quick or slow.
- Hit or smack the ball on ground and into the air. Use different parts of your hand (fist cupped, flat, heel of palm, fingers, wrist, and side).
- Throw the ball in many different ways—for example, using two hands, one hand up, under, over, and sidearm.
- Try to flip, spin, and rotate the ball. Do a trick before the ball returns.
- Use your feet, then your head to strike the ball. Try different parts of your foot to move the ball.
- Develop a pattern with your ball.
- Make up an interesting game with a ball by yourself.

Partner/Group Activities

- Work with a partner, or as maturity allows, have children work in small groups. The same games task will produce very different games when played by two children than when played by a small group of children.
- Play in different environments and on different surfaces, both indoor and outside. Playing on a grass field is very different from playing on a blacktop area or on a wooden gym floor.
- Allow teams of two or three.
- Use a wide variety of "sports environments" (targets, nets, walls, lines, circles, baskets, and obstacles).
- Choose one or two of the following activities. *Repeat these activities in several lessons.* Keep the

ball moving with your partner. You could invent a game where you cooperate with your partner rather than compete with him or her.

Allow children to discover:

- A game with a partner. Use any of the equipment in containers in the gym or outside.
- A game using the floor (or a wall, a line, or a hoop).
- A traveling game.
- A "net" game.
- A "striking" game.
- A "change places" game.
- An "up in the air" game.
- A "roll and run" game, a kicking game, or a leading game.

The teacher circulates, observes, and challenges while children are playing these games.

Conclusion

- Put apparatus away. Children use all the space and run using sideways and backward steps.
- Review the consistent procedures you use for dispersal and collection of apparatus.

LESSON 5

TENNIS-RELATED SKILLS

LEVEL 2

Appropriate grade level: Third through fifth grades

Lesson length: Approximately 30 minutes

NASPE Standards: 1, 2, 5, 6

State Standards: _____

OBJECTIVES

The learner will:

- Practice different ways of striking a ball of any size over short distances, with force, using a racket or paddle, and using backhand and forehand actions.

- Discover different ways to strike a ball to a partner, with and without the ball touching the ground.
- Experiment with different activities at eight stations designed by the teacher.

LESSON MATERIALS

Flat wall space, tape, paddles and rackets, tennis and other small balls, beach balls, and hoops

ACTIVITIES

Individual Activities

- Collect a paddle. Balance the ball on the face of your paddle. Can you move quickly through general space (about the room) while maintaining this balance?
- With your paddle and a ball, practice striking the ball above the 3-foot line on the wall. (Use tape.) How many times can you strike it in 30 seconds? Go! Face the wall and use short hits, sideways-to-the-wall hits (backhand and forehand hits), and hard hits.
- Practice striking your ball upward. How many times can you keep the ball bouncing before it stops? Switch hands.

Partner Activities

- With a partner, practice striking any kind of ball, back and forth, with and without a bounce. Try to hit the ball to your partner so he or she has to move to hit the ball back. Use a paddle or a racket.
- Choose a partner for a "cooperative lob" game. Place a hoop between the partners. See how many times the two of you can strike a high ball so that it drops into the hoop. The partners choose the distance between the hoops.

Group Activities

Divide students (three to four) per station and rotate every 1 to 3 minutes. Use task cards.

Station 1: Create a "help your partner" game. (Equipment: hoop, beach ball, and paddle.)

Station 2: How many times can you keep a ball up? (Equipment: paddles and balls.)

Station 3: Can you alternate hits off opposite sides of a paddle using a ball?

Station 4: Create a "one bounce" game with your partner. (Equipment: paddles and balls.)

Station 5: Is anyone able to keep two balls going off a wall? (Hint: Start the second ball as the first hits the wall.) Can you use backhand and forehand hits so that the ball bounces in a hoop? Hold the paddle and "reach out." (Practice for quick volley: Children need to know this.)

Station 6: Place a hoop next to the wall. Can you strike a ball off the wall? (Equipment: paddles, balls, and hoops.)

Station 7: Can you play a ball off the wall with your opposite hand? Switch hands quickly.

Conclusion/Assessment/Reflection Activities

- Put apparatus away neatly and gather around the teacher. Be seated.
- What new things did you learn today about "striking" a ball?
- Which station was your favorite? Why?
- At which station did you play your most interesting game?

LESSON 6

TENNIS-RELATED SKILLS

LEVEL 2

Appropriate grade level: Third and fourth grades

Lesson length: Approximately 30 minutes

NASPE Standards: 1, 2, 5, 6

State Standards: _____

OBJECTIVES

The learner will:

- Choose an appropriate ball and hitting implement to perform different kinds of hits.
- Demonstrate different types of hits that go varied distances (approximately 10 to 30 feet).
- Practice hits toward a wall, to a partner, or over a "net" of 3 feet high at an angle.

LESSON MATERIALS

A variety of small balls; a variety of hitting implements including lightweight rackets, racquetball rackets, and wooden/plastic paddles; suspended balls, cones, markers, jump ropes, and wall space

ACTIVITIES

Individual Activities

- Running, jogging, and leaving the floor with low jumps every so often. Repeat with a sudden spurt. Try sideways and backward steps.
- Choose any kind of bat or racket that feels comfortable for you to hold. Also choose any kind of small ball. In a free space, try just hitting the ball so it gets to your friend or a wall. See if you can do many hits. Balls suspended on elastic cords can be made available for students needing stationary balls to hit or stationary balls can be hit off cones or tees.

Partner Activities

- Continue practicing hitting against the wall or with a partner from a sideways position. Use backhand and forehand strokes.
- Try hits that go over a "net" or obstacle approximately 3 feet high with a partner.
- In the play space, set up jump ropes, bean bags, or markers of some kind that are different distances from the hitting area. Try hits that land on the markers. The hitting for different distances can be done over a net or without a net. Have a partner retrieve the balls and then switch roles. Include an overhead hit. Sometimes deliberately make it difficult for your partner to return the ball.

Conclusion/Assessment/Reflection Activities

- Put apparatus away.
- Briefly discuss hitting from different distances and hitting over an obstacle.

LESSON 7

BASKETBALL-RELATED SKILLS

LEVEL 2

Appropriate grade level: Third through fifth grades

Lesson length: Approximately 30 minutes

NASPE Standards: 1, 2, 5, 6

State Standards: _____

OBJECTIVES

The learner will:

- Experience and practice a variety of activities used in basketball (e.g., dribbling, passing, stealing the ball, etc.).

- Experience playing against an opposing player.

- Manipulate a medium- to large-size round ball in a variety of ways, both alone and with a partner.

- Make up a dribbling/passing basketball-like game in a small group.

- Make up a game where there are opponents.

LESSON MATERIALS

A variety of balls, cones, chairs, and hoops; colored team bibs or sashes

ACTIVITIES

Individual Activities

Everyone has a ball.

- Find different ways of moving the ball around the gym (e.g., bouncing, running and tossing the ball in the air to catch, rolling, and kicking).

- Using hoops, cones, chairs, or other obstacles, move the ball in and around the items. Dodge and change directions quickly. Trade balls. Notice the different behavior of different balls. Have a few players who are "stealers on the prowl." If someone steals your ball, go and steal someone else's ball.

- Find a place across from a wall. Catch the ball as it rebounds off the wall. Jump high to catch the ball.

- Pretend that the ball is a yo-yo; that is, the ball goes to the floor and comes back to you. On command, dribble forward, backward, and sideways. Do the same thing around obstacles. Bounce the ball through your legs and behind your body. Use both hands. Get down on the floor and up again while still bouncing the ball.

Partner Activities

- With a partner, dribble the ball high, now low, now halfway in between. Which way would avoid a "steal"? One person dribbles the ball while the other tries to take it away. Stress limited body contact and good dodging and faking. Switch roles. Continue for several minutes.

- Move around the gym passing the ball back and forth. Bounce a pass, and throw a high

pass to make your partner jump. Pass hard and straight ahead of a moving player.

- Find different ways of passing the ball back and forth (e.g., under the leg, over the head, one-handed, bounce pass, concealed pass where players cross over, etc.). Pass quickly. Learn and apply the "no traveling" rule.

Group Activities

- Working in a group of three or four, make up a game involving dribbling and passing. Cones, chairs, or other items could be used as obstacles or boundaries. It is important to include interception. In basketball, one rarely has a free player to pass to. Try to get free in order to receive a pass. Have a group show their game while the rest of the class watches. Follow up with questions related to the observation. Continue game playing until the end of class.

Conclusion/Activities

- Put apparatus away.

- Review the no traveling rule.

LESSON 8

STRIKING SKILLS USING DIFFERENT IMPLEMENTS

LEVEL 3

Appropriate grade level: Fifth and sixth grades

Lesson length: Approximately 30 minutes

NASPE Standards: 1, 2, 5, 6

State Standards: _____

OBJECTIVES

The learners will practice a variety of striking skills:

- Use different body parts, and hands in particular, to keep a ball in the air.

- Send a ball to a wall from different distances and at different speeds.

- Serve a ball or birdie in different ways over a net to a partner who evaluates where it hits the floor.
- Make up a game using a net of any height, where the players score points.

LESSON MATERIALS

Paddles (short handled: wooden or polyethylene/plastic), badminton rackets, hockey sticks, pucks, birdies, small balls, jump ropes, cones, Polyspots, or markers

ACTIVITIES

Individual Activities

- Free practice: Move around using bat or stick and ball, birdie, or puck.
- Choose a striking implement and a ball, and strike the ball to the wall. Try lots of different things. Select a sensible space on the wall for your practice.
- Pick a spot on the wall and try to hit it. Count how many times you hit the target. You choose your distance from the wall when you are striking. Try to improve your own score.
- Strike the ball when you are close to the wall and then when you are far from the wall.
- Practice striking your ball to the wall without a bounce.

Paired/Group Activities

- With a partner, use a different striking implement and a birdie, and practice different ways to strike it. Include hard and soft hits as well as high and low hits.
- Work in groups of three. Each group member collects the same kind of hockey stick. Choose either a puck or ball as the object to strike. Try to get the puck or ball past the person in the middle. Try different ways to do it. (Teacher's

follow-up question: What did you do to get the puck successfully past the person in the middle? What did the person in the middle do to make it harder for you to pass?)
- Work in groups of two, three, or four. Students can choose the size of group for their game invention. All groups have the same task card, which should have been previously prepared by the teacher for quick distribution.

Striking Game Task Card

Numbers of players: 2, 3, or 4
Equipment to be used: Must use a wall space. All or some players must use striking implements. Use any type of ball or puck.
Playing area: Square area of any size, wood floor. Mark the boundaries.
Rules to be used: You must invent a scoring system and any rules related to the striking equipment you use.
Skills to be used: Striking with or without a striking implement.

Invent and play a STRIKING GAME. Give your game an interesting name.

LESSON 9

PASSING/INTERCEPTING

LEVEL 3

Appropriate grade level: Fifth and sixth grades

Lesson length: Approximately 30 minutes

NASPE Standards: 1, 2, 5, 6

State Standards: _____

OBJECTIVES

The learner will:

- Practice passing skills and the receiving of passes using basketballs, soccer balls, volleyballs, and a hockey stick and ball/puck.
- Play three-a-side games using interception.

LESSON MATERIALS

A variety of 8-inch-diameter balls, volleyball trainer balls, hockey sticks, small balls or pucks

ACTIVITIES

Individual Practice Time

- Using a ball or a puck, show continuous possession of some kind. Show an increase in speed (while bouncing a basketball, dribbling a soccer ball, hockey dribbling, volleying, heading a soccer ball).

Partner Activities

- Find a partner and decide which kind of "possession" you wish to use. One child puts the ball away and tries to take the ball or duck away from his or her partner. Emphasize no personal contact; beat the opponent by skill or "legal" trickery. Switch roles. The teacher observes and gives feedback, watching for the point of least control and a sudden tackle rather than "brute force" or continuous tackling. Repeat. If possible or relevant, suggest a change in direction when possession has been gained. (In sports, you gain possession of the ball so as to do something with it.)

- Keep the same pairs with the same apparatus; establish a "receiver" and a "feeder." The feeder has to send a pass of some kind, which the receiver must move to receive and get rid of as soon as possible. Try receiving at different speeds, from different directions. Encourage the receivers to give exact instructions to the feeders of where and how they want the pass. Switch roles. Repeat and encourage greater speed for the reception and greater accuracy for the "get rid of" step. Allow feeders to make it harder for the receivers.

- Encourage the "feeder" from the previous activity to move in to tackle or intercept the receiver and "get rid of" the apparatus.

Group Activity

- Children choose or are sent to certain areas to play the game suitable for that area. (Over a series of lessons, the groups can be rotated.) In a large gym, several mid-air passing and scoring games (three-a-side) can go across a basketball court. (Score a basket by throwing the ball to hit a target on the wall.) The corners of the room are useful for couples to play "squash" or "handball." A "high net game" should be set up in an adjacent area, hallway, or stage. A "field" area will be needed for a moving team game of football, hockey, or soccer.

- If this kind of group work is not possible, then as many children who can play comfortably in the available space should be allowed to play; the rest should be sent jogging or cross-country running. Groups will rotate in subsequent lessons. (Give the opportunity to all, but allow choice.) Use all areas, perhaps devoting a small area to individual practice.

Conclusion/Reflective/Assessment/Planning Activity

- Describe weaknesses in tactics and strategy related to your own play.

- What were some of the weaknesses of your opponent's play?

- Discuss ways of scoring successfully.

LESSON 10

VOLLEYBALL-RELATED SKILLS

LEVEL 3

Appropriate grade level: Fourth through sixth grades

Lesson length: Approximately 30 minutes

NASPE Standards: 1, 2, 5, 6

State Standards: _____

OBJECTIVES

The learners will practice a variety of volleyball-related skills:

- Use different body parts, and hands in particular, to keep a ball in the air.

- Hit a ball to a wall from different distances and at different speeds.

- Volley and serve balls in different ways against the wall or over a net to hit a target.

- Volley to a partner so they can spike the ball over the net.

- Practice blocking a spike.

- Make up a game using a net of any height, where the players score points.

LESSON MATERIALS

Beach balls, balloons, light balls, volleyballs, nets, stretch ropes, cones, and Polyspots/markers are in containers around the perimeter of the room.

ACTIVITIES
Individual Activities

- Run, skip, slide, or hop around the Polyspots/markers on the floor, going in different directions and not bumping into anyone. Run and jump over spots. See how many spots you can jump over in 30 seconds. (Repeat until children are breathless. Encourage good spacing.)

- Everyone collect a ball. Practice keeping the ball up in the air using different body parts. Use finger tips, flat hand, wrist, and forearm. See how long you can keep the ball going without allowing it to touch the floor.

- Using just your hands, try batting the ball against the wall as many times as you can. Stand close to the wall, then farther away. Which was easier? When sending your ball against the wall, try to anticipate how far back you need to be and how fast you need to send the ball to the wall. Try underhand hits and overhead hits.

Partner Activities

- Volley to a partner so that your partner can "spike" the ball over the net.

Group Activities

Set up seven volleyball-related stations or learning centers. Use groups of matched ability.

Station 1: Wall volley. Everyone has his or her own ball and sends it to the wall practicing the "volley." Numbers or targets are put on the wall to try and aim for, so as to improve accuracy.

Station 2: Practice a "set," a "bump," and a "spike" with a partner.

Station 3: Serving. With a partner, serve back and forth over the "net." Practice any overhand, underhand, or sidearm serve. Have the partner evaluate where the serve lands.

Station 4: Mats on floor near the wall. Kneel and practice bumping against the wall. All children should have a ball. Try to accurately hit a target on the wall.

Station 5: With a partner, see how long you can keep the ball up before it touches the ground. Make your partner look good. Make your partner move to return the ball. (Accurate passing *to* a teammate on your side of the net is important.)

Station 6: Game station. Make up a game using a net of any height. Try to score points.

Station 7: Using a net and four players to each side of the net, practice a "set" and "spike" where the opposing players jump close to the net with flat hands to block the spike.

Conclusion/Assessment/Reflection Activities

- Have a group show the game its members made up. Observers should try to observe how the position of the body affects the action.

- Discuss how it is easier to make the ball go higher from underneath.

- Discuss the importance of moving the body to get to the ball and under it.

- Which skills do you use if the ball comes below your waist?

- Discuss the rule of not touching the net when performing a "block."

- Discuss "getting along" and cooperating with members of your groups.

LESSON 11

VOLLEYBALL-RELATED SKILLS

LEVEL 3

Appropriate grade level: Third through fifth grades

Lesson length: Approximately 30 minutes

NASPE Standards: 1, 2, 5, 6

State Standards: _____

OBJECTIVES

The learners will practice a variety of volleyball-related skills:

- Use your hands to send the ball in the air, to a wall with different parts of the hand, and using different balls.

- Volley balls to a partner on the same side of the net.

- Serve balls over a net where the partner evaluates the serve.

- Invent a volleyball-like game involving volleying and serving, where players score points; the game should use a net and include boundaries and spiking and blocking if possible.

LESSON MATERIALS

Containers spread around the perimeter of the gymnasium containing a variety of large beach balls, balloons, light balls including practice volleyballs, small improvised nets, chairs, cones, markers, domes, and stretch ropes.

ACTIVITIES

Individual Activities

- Run and jump high. Use a jump to change direction. Continue until you are breathing heavily.
- Every child has a ball. Using just the hands, find ways of keeping your ball in the air for as long as you can without allowing it to touch the floor.
- Using just the hands, try hitting the ball against a wall as many times as you can. Try two hands and then just one hand. Try to send the ball to different heights on the wall.
- Everyone has a ball. Find a space opposite a wall and try sending the ball to the wall using different parts of your hand. Use the palm of the hand, the heel of the hand, or a fist. Some children may use a cupped hand.
- Trade balls and repeat the preceding activities.

Partner Activities

- Volley the ball back and forth to a partner. See how long you can keep it going.
- Try an underhand serve from the back line of a court over the net using the palm, heel, or fist of the hand. Your partner will evaluate where the serve lands.
- Use a cupped hand, the heel of the hand, or a fist to do an overhead or sidearm serve over a net from the back line. Have several children (1) show how the hands can be used for hitting and (2) demonstrate serving against a wall.
- Try setting, bumping, and volleying to your partner who is close to an obstacle, a net, chairs, cones, rope, or stretch rope.
- With a partner, serve the ball back over a net so your partner has trouble getting to it.

Group Activities

- Working in groups of three or four, invent a game involving volleying and serving, in which players score points. The net, ropes, chairs, cones, and other items could be used as obstacles or boundaries. Make sure children do not send the ball over the net to a person but rather to a space.
- Play a "volleyball"-like game that includes spiking and blocking using three or four per side.
- Stop play and show two good examples. Return to your game and use some of the ideas you just saw.

Conclusion/Assessment/Reflection Activities

- Check which children could beat their own scores for numbers of continuous hits.
- Have a group show the game they made up. Discuss the good/effective plays in the game.

LESSON 12
TENNIS-RELATED SKILLS
LEVEL 3

Appropriate grade level: Fourth through sixth grades

Lesson length: Approximately 30 minutes

NASPE Standards: 1, 2, 5, 6

State Standards: _____

OBJECTIVES

The learner will:

- Practice and demonstrate the lob, volley, drop shot, smash, topspin/backspin, forehand, and backhand drive in tennis.

LESSON MATERIALS

A variety of small balls; a variety of hitting implements including lightweight improvised rackets, racquetball rackets, and wooden/plastic paddles; suspended balls, cones, markers, jump ropes, wall space, small improvised nets (6 to 8 feet long)

ACTIVITIES

Individual Activities

- Stretch with arms up and down. Circle the arms forward and backward. Swing from side to side. Add a body stretch to the arm action.
- Get a hitting implement of your choice and a ball. Freely practice hitting against a wall. Use the body and arm swing. Try hitting a ball that is beside you and a ball that is in front of you. Try hitting forehand and backhand shots. If wall space is restricted, allow some lob and smash activity in the center of the room.

Partner Activities

- Practice serving a ball over a "net" into the corners of the service box from the base line. Work on a serve over a long distance.
- Experiment with hits that go very high in the air (lobs) and hits that stay low. Find out how you must hit the ball differently for each kind of hit. Hit hard and low to skim the net. Try spinning (topspin/backspin/slice) and chopping the ball in addition to the drop shot.
- With your partner practice volleys where the ball doesn't hit the ground.
- Have one person hit or throw the ball high so that your partner can smash it. Switch roles.
- Try hitting a ball that comes on the right side (forehand, for a right-handed person) and one that comes on the left side (backhand, for a right-handed person) of your body. Go to meet ball or move backward to hit ball. Invent a "score."

Conclusion/Assessment/Reflection Activities

- Name terms used in tennis (e.g., serve, lob, volley, smash, drop shot, forehand and backhand drive, and topspin/backspin/slice).

LESSON 13

FOOTBALL-RELATED SKILLS

LEVEL 3

Appropriate grade level: Third through sixth grades

Lesson length: Approximately 30 minutes

NASPE Standards: 1, 2, 5, 6

State Standards: _____

OBJECTIVES

The learner will:

- Practice throwing and aiming using different throws and at different distances.
- Practice lateral and forward passes to a partner while stationary and then on the move.
- Experiment with and then describe where to place a pass to a moving player.
- Make up a passing game while working in groups of four.

LESSON MATERIALS

Balls: One ball per person. Oval balls, footballs, Frisbees, cones, or markers.

ACTIVITIES

Individual Activities

- Provide one ball per person. Pass the ball ahead and run to catch. Try to keep your ball in the air while you are moving about the field.
- Include throwing and aiming at something on the field—see how close you can send the ball to the target.
- Vary your distance from the target.
- Vary the way of throwing. Throw high; throw low. Throw the ball with curve, with spin, or in a spiral. How does the ball behave in the air?

Partner Activities

- With a partner, use one ball to practice lateral and forward passes. Think about where you want to place the ball. Make your partner move to catch the ball.
- What can your arms and shoulder do to direct the ball?
- How can you shift your body weight to add force?
- Try twisting your body.
- Try the right and left hands. Which works best?
- With your partner, see how you can use forward and lateral passes while moving about the field. Vary the length of your throws.
  - What do you need to think about when throwing a ball to a player at different distances?
  - Where should your ball be placed?

Group Activities

- Working in groups of four, use one ball and four cones or markers. Make up a game using boundaries where the ball is moved by passing. Invent two rules.
- Think about what you can do to give everyone in your group a chance to pass.
- Can you move to the open spaces?
- How can you work with teammates?
- Can you intercept a pass?
- How could you improve your game?
- Continue playing your game.

Conclusion/Assessment/Reflection Activities

- Put the apparatus away neatly.
- Which changes would you make to your game next time? Why?

RACKET SPORTS AND HANDBALL-RELATED SKILLS

LEVEL 3

Appropriate grade level: Fourth through sixth grades

Lesson length: Approximately 30 minutes

NASPE Standards: 1, 2, 5, 6

State Standards: _____

OBJECTIVES

The learner will demonstrate:

- The ability to manipulate paddles, bats, or rackets in a variety of ways (e.g., overhead, backhand, below waist, etc.).
- The skill to manipulate birdies and balls of different sizes and weights.
- The skill to make the balls change speeds and rebound at different angles.
- Accuracy while sending balls at targets and over nets of different heights.
- The ability to design a game using a wall, a net, and a partner.

LESSON MATERIALS

A variety of sized, weighted, short-handled, and long-handled paddles, bats, and rackets (scoops, Ping-Pong bats, stocking bats, wooden paddles, tennis rackets, or badminton-type rackets).

A variety of small balls (yarn balls, newspaper balls, Ping-Pong balls, tennis balls, racket and squash balls, small play balls, and birdies).

Use the hand as racket.

ACTIVITIES

Introductory Activities

- Run, jump, and turn, with feet wide apart. Shift your weight. Use small steps. Hop, and stretch high or wide in mid-air.
- Do sudden movements, practice quick change of direction, and twist the body quickly while the feet are stationary.
- Run forward, backward, and sideways; switch directions quickly.
- Shadow a partner; try to follow the partner's quick changes in direction. Anticipate a change.

Individual Skill Activities

- Fix the feet, and twist the body in a variety of directions. (Allow the children to discover ways when their feet are fixed.)
- Stretch wide, with feet wide. Twist or rotate the body. Pivot on one foot.
- Let the arms swing, with first the body following, and then the feet. Reverse the action (feet move, then body, then arms). Use a variety of levels and speeds. Add a crescendo of movement.
- Jump, turn, and reach. Alternate high and low movements.
- Bounce and hit your ball with a striking implement.
- Practice hitting a ball or a birdie in different positions relative to the body (behind, under, over at side, far away, or close).
- Move around and rebound a ball from the wall or floor, or a birdie hit to the ceiling. Change hands, levels, and directions. Vary the speed, strength of hit, and body positions. Notice the angle of rebound or flight of the birdie.
- Run and repeat hitting against a wall or corner. Try different angles of hitting, receiving, or volleying after the ball bounces once.
- Alternate sides; alternate hands. Try overhead shots, hit low, hit close to the wall, hit far away, and so on. Hit "up" the wall. Hit "down" the wall. Hit hard; hit soft and quick. Flick the wrist to hit. Make up a pattern of hits. Switch equipment or birdies.

Partner/Group Activities

- Try ways of sending a ball to your partner with or without a striking implement. Make your partner move by hitting to a space.
- Vary the hitting speed, level, direction, and force. Hit the ball with your partner facing you, your partner behind you, your partner beside you, and so on.
- Experiment with hitting a birdie or a ball just over the net (skim the net). You and your partner can choose the height of the net. Challenge your partner by making him or her move to hit the ball or birdie back to you to a space.
- Send a ball to your partner on the move and while stationary. Try to beat your partner by "faking" and deceiving him or her using a backhand hit and a forehand hit.

- Make up a game that uses a wall or a net and a partner. Include a bounce, a volley, and a "serve." Try both cooperative and competitive games. Decide how you are going to start the game. Discuss the different ways the students decided to *start* their game. Discuss the rules they devised and the reasons for the rules. Do this while students are working.

Conclusion/Assessment/Reflection Activities

- Record and show some of the interesting games the children design during the lesson.
- Commend safe use of striking implements and cooperative behavior.
- While listening to the discussion, rotate children's wrists, and press their hands against each other to extend the range of movement at the wrist.

LESSON 15

FIELD SPORTS SKILLS

LEVEL 4

Appropriate grade level: Fifth and sixth grades

Lesson length: Approximately 30 minutes

NASPE Standards: 1, 2, 5, 6

State Standards: _____

OBJECTIVES

Students will:

- Manipulate footballs, soccer balls, hockey balls, rugby balls, and pucks in different ways.
- Demonstrate an awareness of spatial factors relevant to field space and moving players.
- Gain knowledge of the skills of field sports games and demonstrate this knowledge in the playing of a variety of field games
- State major rules of field sports, including soccer, football, field hockey, and rugby.

LESSON MATERIALS

Footballs, soccer balls, hockey balls, rugby balls, hockey pucks, goals (including relevant/regulation goals of appropriate size and height, if possible), a variety of lightweight balls, markers, cones, Polyspots

ACTIVITIES

Introductory Activities

- Practice stopping, starting, and showing zigzag floor patterns when running. Use all available space. (Set the boundaries beforehand if you are working outdoors.)
- Run sideways, backward, and forward. Have the feet meet as well as cross over. Watch out and avoid others. Move the feet quickly. Try to see "out of the corners of your eyes." Try not to "advertise" when you make a switch. Turn, and vary your speed.
- Working in twos, have one partner lead the other, who acts as a "shadow." Beat or lose your shadow. Fake a switch. Include a sudden stop. Repeat, including a stick and ball or puck, using one ball or puck between two people. (Use one side—the flat side of a field hockey stick.)

Partner Activities

- Play 1 v 1 with a round ball. The player in possession will start away from the partner and approach. The waiting partner performs a "legal" tackle to gain possession. Switch partners. When is the best time to tackle? Surprise your partner by stepping back or stepping forward and lunging with outstretched stick in one hand only. "Jab" the ball, but do not touch the stick. Use a similar "disguise tackle" for soccer.
- Place partners at a distance. One kicks an oval ball to bounce in front of the opponent. The opponent catches the bounce or picks it up and prepares to run before the kicker can get there. Wait, fake, and dodge. Switch partners. Practice a swerve before being "tagged."
- Partners (oval ball): One partner feeds the other with a high pass to the side or over the partner's head. The receiver has to jump, leap, or run backward to catch the ball. Switch roles.
- Partners (round balls): One partner kicks a pass waist high. The other partner stops the ball using his or her chest, stomach, or hips (no hands!) and attempts to kick it back immediately when it drops. Switch roles.
- Repeat the previous activity with pass a bit lower or bouncing. The receiver should use the feet as well as the body to bring the ball to ground. Rush the recipient and encourage a "dodge."
- The previous activities can be repeated with hockey sticks (use the flat side only to touch the ball).

Group Activities

- Use "learning centers" where small group games can be played.
- Invent (for those who choose) hockey, soccer, or football.
- Have a variety of goals available. No body contact should be allowed. Be clever!
- Play a "football-like," "hockey-like," or "soccer-like" game in threes.
- Play a 2 v 2 game where goals can be scored and prevented.
- Invent a 2 v 2 game that has boundaries (a penalty is incurred if boundaries are crossed) and two rules.
- Invent a 3 v 3 game that includes a change of position.
- Invent a 3 v 3 game in which all players must have possession of the ball at some time.
- Invent a 4 v 4 game where players on the team have different tasks to do. Rotate players.
- Play a 4 v 4 game and take time to plan a strategy. Plan the timing of certain actions.

Conclusion/Assessment/Reflection Activities

- Before the group activity ends, ask the class to prepare a comment for the reflection/assessment activity to follow. Do they have any questions? Remember what was successful. Would you revise a rule? What worked best in your game?
- Stop and retrieve all apparatus and jog with it in the total space. Put the apparatus neatly away and assemble around the teacher.

A SERIES OF 10 PROGRESSIVE SOCCER LESSONS

SOCCER LESSON 1

Appropriate grade level: Third through sixth grades

Lesson length: 30 minutes

NASPE Standards: 1, 2, 3

State Standards: _____

OBJECTIVES

All children will:

- Show kicking and dodging while trying to keep a ball away from your opponent.
- Play some kind of "soccer-like" game with three and four players in the group.
- Explain the "no hands" rule of soccer.

LESSON MATERIALS

Round balls of 8-inch diameter, at least one per student. Check that all balls are in good condition.

ACTIVITIES

Individual Activities

- Walk while dodging in and out of everyone else. Jog, stop, and change directions. (Stress good spacing and keeping spread out.)
- Run and kick a foot to the side but continue running. Include a sudden switch in direction. (Emphasize the quick switch. Use the feet to push off in a new direction. Use the arms to balance your body.)
- When you have a ball, run to a space and start to travel, keeping the ball close to you. Use different parts of your foot or feet, and different speeds and directions. (Stress control. Use the heel, inside of the foot, and outside of the foot. Pull the ball toward you, using the bottom of the foot, toes, or instep.)
- Can you lift the ball with your foot as you travel? Can you stop the ball quickly? Change direction, then stop, lift the ball, start, and so on. Try using the heel, toes, sole of the foot, knee, shin, and chest.
- Trade balls and see how a different ball behaves.
- Can you move the ball around the area without touching anyone else and switch direction eight times? Repeat with a different ball.

Partner/Group Activities

- With a partner, have a "keep up" contest using head, feet, but no hands or arms. Teacher can quickly introduce the "no-hands" rule in soccer.
- With a partner, try playing one-on-one. Keep possession or try to steal the ball. No contact is allowed. Switch partners if the contest is uneven.
- Working in groups of four, make up a game using one ball and your feet.
- Working in groups of three and using two balls, make up a game.

Conclusion/Assessment/Reflection Activities

- Practice sideways running in the large space. Stop and sit.
- Remember for next time: (1) What works best to stop the ball? (2) What happens if hands are used?
- Children will place balls neatly in container.

SOCCER LESSON 2

Appropriate grade level: Third through sixth grades

Lesson length: 30 minutes

NASPE Standards: 1, 2, 3

State Standards: _____

OBJECTIVES

The learners will:

- Show dribbling with speed and changes of direction.
- Explore and practice dropping, trapping, kicking, and stopping balls with their feet.
- Make up a game with a group of four players.
- Explain the "out-of-bounds" and "no-hands" rules of soccer.

LESSON MATERIALS

Balls of soccer size, spaced out in a gym or playing field in containers. Spots, markers, and cones should also be available.

ACTIVITIES

Individual Activities

- Skip, while dodging in and out. See how many spots you can *jump over* before the teacher claps. Jog in and out of spots. See how many spots you can touch using a different part of your body or foot, and "freeze" when the teacher calls. (Encourage students to get breathless and stress spreading out so there are no collisions.)
- Each student should collect a ball and begin by dropping and trapping it quickly with his or her feet. Review manipulation of balls. Review stopping the ball.
- Review dribbling and changing directions. Vary the speed of dribbling; include a sudden spurt. If the class is ready, allow use of a wall—kicking and stopping the rebound—as they dribble.
- Trade balls and repeat.

Partner/Group Activities

- Choose a partner who has the same kind of ball as you do. Put one ball away and find a space. Kick the ball back and forth as many times as possible without losing it. Make your partner move to get the ball.
- How many ways can you kick and how many ways can your partner stop the kicked ball? Make your partner look good. Stand facing your partner, sideways to your partner, and on the opposite side of your partner. Use different parts of the body to stop the ball. (No hands!) Stress control.
- Try the same thing moving around the field. Change direction on a clap. Boy couples should find a girl couple, and vice versa; mixed couples should then find another mixed couple and make up a game in fours. (Cones are available to include in your game.)

Conclusion/Assessment/Reflection Activities

- Put the apparatus away and come and sit down.
- Did you have a procedure to follow if the ball went "out of bounds"? Mention the "throw-in."
- Discuss who can use hands in soccer. Mention goal-keeping.

SOCCER LESSON 3

Appropriate grade level: Third through sixth grades

Lesson length: 30 minutes

NASPE Standards: 1, 2, 3

State Standards: _____

OBJECTIVES

The learners will:

- Explore and practice sending/passing a ball by heading and kicking it.
- Make up a game with both a partner and a group of four players that uses heading and kicking and a scoring system.
- Include the "throw-in" and some "goal-keeping" skills in their games.

LESSON MATERIALS

Enough balls for half the class; cones, hoops, inner tubes, stretch rope, "goal posts"

ACTIVITIES

Individual Activities

- Run in and out without touching anyone.

- Move in and out as if you were dribbling a ball. Dodge another person. On a clap, jump high to "score" a goal. Stretch your arms high.

- See how high you can jump in the air. Now try jumping while reaching high or diving to save a goal.

- Run and on a clap, jump to "head" an imaginary ball. Head to "flick" the ball. Jump to touch a stretch rope with your head.

Partner/Group Activities

- With a partner you have never worked with before, send a ball back and forth using your head. Vary the distance between partners. Help your partner to do it well. Which part of the head works best? (Use the forehead, not the top of the head.) Deliberately head a ball to go down or up or to the side.

- Try to keep the ball in the air using alternate feet and passing to your partner.

- Try picking a ball up with your feet and sending it to your partner. Get under the ball.

- One partner tosses the ball so that the other person stops it or heads it back to the first person. Use the body, legs, and feet to stop the ball. For the skillful, extend this activity by including a jump to head the ball.

- Make up a game with your partner using a hoop or the wall where you head the ball or make it bounce from a header or a kick.

- In a group of four (not all boys or all girls), play a game where heading is involved. You can include a "throw-in" and use cones, goal posts, inner tubes, or hula-hoops. Invent a way to score. (If groups of four work well, ask children to remember who is in their group and use the same groups in the next lesson.) The teacher should circulate, helping with any problems and giving encouragement.

Conclusion/Assessment/Reflection Activities

- Put the apparatus away, and come and sit down. Circle the feet in the air, stretch the ankles, and flex the feet. Turn the feet to both sides.

- What happens if your hands touch the ball?

- What does the goal-keeper do?

- Which part of the head is best for heading the ball? (The answer is the strongest bone in the body—the forehead!)

- Commend good cooperation, efficient organization, and other appropriate behavior.

- Observe and discuss effective scoring.

- Children can continue exercising their feet and ankles during the discussion.

SOCCER LESSON 4

Appropriate grade level: Third through sixth grades

Lesson length: 30 minutes

NASPE Standards: 1, 2, 3, 5, 6

State Standards: _____

OBJECTIVES

The learners will:

- Explore and practice dribbling with changes of direction.

- Perform a "throw-in."

- Shoot at a goal-keeper defending a "goal."

- Kick or head the ball into the goal at different angles.

- Practice intercepting passes.

- Play a game with three people, using their feet; include heading and a goal-keeper.

LESSON MATERIALS

Balls for everyone, cones, goal posts

ACTIVITIES

Individual Activities

- As you enter, get a ball and dribble in a space. Weave in and out. Use ankle movements to flick the ball a short way sideways. Use both feet. Keep control of your ball. Switch directions. (Commend quick starters who do not fuss.)

- Perform a "throw-in" to the wall. Control your ball with your feet only. Go on dribbling and cross to another wall. Repeat. (Emphasize "no hands" to stop the ball and aiming for a target on the throw-in.)

Partner/Group Activities

- Choose a friend and set up a goal (e.g., cones, space on wall, posts). Kick the ball to your partner into the goal. Aim for distance or accurately shoot at the corners inside the goal; try a "fake" shot. How far back can you shoot and score?

- Find ways of passing to a partner who shoots on goal. Commend good work, control, and accuracy.
- Kick or head the ball into the goal at different angles.
- Pass the ball four times before shooting.
- Have one partner play goal-keeper and save shots. Switch roles. How many goals can you make out of 10 shots? Switch roles.
- One player should approach the goal and the partner should "tackle" before the shot. Switch role.
- Working in groups of three, try intercepting passes.
- Use the same groups as in Lesson 3. Play a game using your feet; include heading and a goal-keeper. Encourage the goal-keeper to smother the ball on the ground with their body; catch and clutch the ball to the body using both arms; jump to retrieve a shot; jump to deflect a high shot over the top bar of the goal; move sideways to cover an approaching player who has the ball. Check that everyone in the group gets lots of practice. Everyone should practice goal-keeping. Invent a penalty for a foul if needed. Point out good "spread" of players if possible (not everyone chases the ball). Encourage players to position themselves to receive a pass that they shoot at goal. Mark boundaries so that a throw-in can be practiced when the ball goes out-of-bounds.

Conclusion/Assessment/Reflection Activities

- Put the apparatus away. Sit in a group.
- How does a soccer game start?
- Describe a corner kick (when the ball goes out-of-bounds over the back line).
- Commend cooperation and lack of disputes.

SOCCER LESSONS 5 AND 6

Appropriate grade level: Third through sixth grades
Lesson length: 30 minutes
NASPE Standards: 1, 2, 3, 5, 6
State Standards: _____

OBJECTIVES

The learners will:

- Explore and practice heading, shooting to score, goal-keeping, corner kicks, and passing in small groups.
- Invent and play small group games using the skills of heading, keep-away, corner kicks, and passing.
- Explain checking a player and checking a space.
- Practice corner kicks.

LESSON MATERIALS

Balls, hoops, cones, chairs, posts, possibly areas previously designated or set up

ACTIVITIES

Individual Activities

- Run all over the area, dodging quickly, but not touching any apparatus or people. Freeze. With the person nearest you, see if one can do what the other one does and move wherever the leader moves. Switch roles. Include a sudden stop.
- Collect a ball and practice kicking a corner shot high and hard against the wall putting spin on the ball if possible.

Partner/Group Activities

Everyone sits in the center of the playing area. Point to the station where you would like to go to first. (The teacher arbitrates if choices very uneven, and ensures a gender mix at stations.) Explain the stations.

Station 1: Heading. Contains four hoops and two to four balls. Make up a heading game using the equipment.

Station 2: Invent and play a soccer-like game using four cones and one ball.

Station 3: Shooting on goal/saving shots on goal. Allow penalty kicks on goal from approximately 12 yards. . . . Contains four cones and two to four balls. Set up goals and take turns being the goal-keeper. Try to disguise your intentions. Encourage goal-keeper to dive and save.

Station 4: Set up a limited area and play one-on-one inside that area using only feet.

Station 5: Balls. In groups of three, play "keep away" by heading or kicking the ball across the area. (The person in the middle should try to intercept the ball.) Switch players.

Station 6: Balls. Play two-on-two, trying to score the highest number of consecutive passes. Speed up the game and focus on passing ahead of a moving player.

Conclusion/Assessment/Reflection Activities

- Put equipment away neatly. Commend cooperative and skillful play in games.
- Discuss checking a player versus checking a space. How does this affect your passing?

SOCCER LESSON 7

Appropriate grade level: Third through sixth grades

Lesson length: 30 minutes

NASPE Standards: 1, 2, 3, 5, 6

State Standards: _____

OBJECTIVES

The learners will:

- Play a three versus three soccer-like game.
- Explain the following rules: how to begin a game of soccer; the throw-in rule; rules for goal-keeper; corner kick, penalty kick, and rough play.

LESSON MATERIALS

Balls, cones, goal posts, colored bibs

ACTIVITIES

Introductory Activity

- Free choice of activity. Practice your weakest skill. Get a friend to help you. Switch roles. Put the balls away, jog around the soccer field, and come to center and sit.

Group Activities

- Review the way to begin the game: throw-in, rules, simple rules for the goal-keeper (use hands in circle only), corner kick, penalty kick, and good tackling (tackler contacts the ball only. Do not trip or push another player).
- Create mixed teams of three children. (Assign colored bibs to one team per game. Assign an area for play of each team.) Children can set up the goals, choose ends, and begin to play. Everyone on the team must touch the ball before you can shoot a goal. Play a 3 on 3 game.

- Stop the class and mention one thing (e.g., the need to keep spread out, the need to check or look for space, or the need to pass before you are tackled) and then resume play trying to remember that one thing.
- If there is time and some games are not going well, switch and play with different groups of three.

Conclusion/Assessment/Reflection Activities

- Put the apparatus away, and then come and sit in the center of the playing area.
- Discuss incidents of good play, ways to make a space and moving to create a space, helping others, and good sportsmanship.

SOCCER LESSON 8

Appropriate grade level: Third through sixth grades

Lesson length: 30 minutes

NASPE Standards: 1, 2, 3, 5, 6

State Standards: _____

OBJECTIVES

The learners will:

- Explore and practice kicking skills to put spin on the ball.
- Practice heading, throw-ins, corner kicks, passing, and tackling with a partner and in a small game situation of 4 versus 4.
- Explain good plays and good tackles.
- Review selected soccer rules.

LESSON MATERIALS

Balls, cones, goal posts, colored bibs

ACTIVITIES

Introductory Activity

- Free fast running until breathless.

Partner Activities

- Work with a partner. Review and practice heading, throw-ins, passing, and tackling. When you kick a stationary ball, try to put spin on it and make it curve in the air. Use different parts of the foot. Put the balls away. Jog with your partner in and out. Try to sprint and beat your partner, slow to a jog, and repeat.

Group Activities

- Gather as a group and sit. Review the rules briefly. *Prearranged teams* can go to the assigned area with their bibs. (By now, the teacher should be able to preplan teams of four or five who are well matched.) Set up the game and begin play. After 10 minutes, have groups switch to play a different team. Try to rotate the goalie if there is one; also assign a defensive role to some players and the function of a "striker." Comment on any kicks that spin or curve the ball.

Conclusion/Assessment/Reflection Activities

- Put the apparatus away. Gather and sit.
- What were some good plays? Was a defensive player helpful in checking/stopping a "striker"?
- What were some good tackles?

SOCCER LESSON 9

Appropriate grade level: Third through sixth grades

Lesson length: 30 minutes

NASPE Standards: 1, 2, 3, 5, 6

State Standards: _____

OBJECTIVES

The learners will:

- Play a four-a-side soccer game with a new group of players or invent another type of game.
- Try to fake and deceive an opponent.
- Explain ways to set up opportunities for a team to score.

LESSON MATERIALS

Balls, colored bibs, cones, and goal posts

ACTIVITIES

Introductory Activity

- Engage in free practice, either individually or with a partner. Try to put the ball where your partner wants it. (Commend good "feeding" by your partner.) Be a good tackler.

Partner/Group Activities

- Continue working in teams and play a new group. Allow individuals to practice alone if they are very uncomfortable in a team and fill

in or adapt teams as necessary. If by now there are a few children who dislike soccer, offer an alternative. Create a station where another game is possible—perhaps an "invent" game. Allow a four-a-side game and possibly smaller games at the same time.

- Try to set up spaces and ways for someone else to score.
- Because attention is usually on the ball, try to fake and deceive your opponent; make the person in possession of the ball take his or her eye off the ball. (Create an opportunity for a teammate to "steal" the ball.)

Conclusion/Assessment/Reflection Activities

- Put the apparatus away.
- Did you learn anything new in this lesson? Discuss ways to set up situations for your *team* to score. How were goals scored? Which kinds of play led to a goal? Preplan for final lesson and possibly arrange tournament matches against another class.

SOCCER LESSON 10

Appropriate grade level: Third through sixth grades

Lesson length: 30 minutes

NASPE Standards: 1, 2, 3, 5, 6

State Standards: _____

OBJECTIVES

The learners will:

- Practice various "tricks" with the feet and a ball.
- Play a soccer or soccer-like game in groups of six or eight players.

LESSON MATERIALS

Balls, colored bibs, cones, goal posts

ACTIVITIES

Introductory Activity

- Move anywhere with a ball. Show clever "tricks." Run. Stop and show another trick.

Group Activities

Children will enjoy playing "soccer." Preplanned groups are used. Everyone plays soccer or a soccer-like game. Everyone tries to "get it together" whether you play four-a-side or three-a-side. (NEVER 11-a-side!) Repeat what you enjoyed doing most in this series of soccer lessons. Allow choices.

Conclusion

- The teacher should be able to see greater skill in the performance of the team sport of soccer.
- Children record two written comments about their experience in soccer.

Track and Field

Track and field is a much neglected sport, even though these activities have an immediate appeal to elementary-school-aged children. Running for speed or for distance, jumping for height or for distance, throwing a long or round object as far as possible, heaving a heavy weight, and pulling oneself up and over an obstacle using a rope or pole are fun. There is another very attractive aspect to most track and field activities: Individuals can compete without necessarily other people being involved. Many individuals will enjoy competition if it is personal; to compete with oneself can be very satisfying. To set oneself a target for greater achievement does appeal to some children who would not be comfortable in a team situation.

The hurdling, running, jumping, and throwing skills emphasized in track and field can be used in Physical Education lessons from preschool to fifth or sixth grade levels.

It is also comparatively easy and inexpensive to provide a sand-filled jumping pit with an approach and take-off board at the side or end of a playing area, a large foam-filled net for landing on from a height (and a bar and stands for high jumping), and a mini-track around the circumference of a field or playground. Hurdles can be simply improvised; only two "flights" are needed. (It is important to have a flight of hurdles.) Hurdling is a continuous smooth action over several low obstacles, and the "style" used to go over one is far less important than the ability to run through several flights and keep going. Hurdling is *not* jumping.

When space is available, pie plates (weighted and sealed) and canes or long rolled newspaper "spears" allow the spinning action and straight throw of the discus and the javelin, respectively.

After enjoying experimenting with a variety of this equipment, one can focus on some of the limitations required by the actual sport. For example, a "spear" may not be thrown with a spinning action—to throw a javelin in the manner of a discus would require new stadiums to be built.

Young children should not be asked to specialize too soon. They should be encouraged to simply explore the options available and to enjoy and become familiar with all equipment. Very often the children themselves will add the "farther," "faster," and "for longer" challenges.

One of the reasons track and field is included in Physical Education is because, although the spring season often allows outdoor activity and softball is popular, basically softball is an inactive game. If teachers wish to include softball at the elementary school level (upper grades only), it is recommended that when a softball game is played (after much activity with all children using bats and balls and running), there should be only one game, which is a "group" activity. Other "group" activities going on at the same time could use a long jump pit, a high jump area, two flights of hurdles, and a "safe" area where objects can be thrown. Switch players in a subsequent lesson or halfway through. Think of these activities as mimicking an Olympic Stadium with many activities going on at the same time and a "modified" softball game going on in the center.

Some sample lesson material with a "track and field" focus (Olympic games) for those who would like to use them is included here. Track and field activities are, of course, ultimately competitive, but it is also possible to enjoy the process of discovering personal efficiency and then simply to compete with oneself. Many children who react negatively in the face of competition may feel comfortable when there is no audience and when the means of scoring or measuring is in their own hands.

TRACK AND FIELD LESSON 1

HURDLING

Appropriate grade level: Kindergarten through fifth grade

Lesson length: Approximately 30 minutes

State Standards: _____

OBJECTIVES

The learners will:

- Explore and practice rhythmic repeated running patterns as used in hurdling.

LESSON MATERIALS

Sticks, wands, hockey sticks, and plastic bats spread in a scattered formation on the ground, with large spaces in between the obstacles. A light stick can be made with a tightly rolled newspaper bound with masking tape. The flight of hurdles should be placed at a constant distance, and spaces between the hurdles should always be the same.

ACTIVITIES

Individual Activities

- Run anywhere in the area, trying to cross over the obstacles on the ground as you run. Do not break your rhythm as you go over the sticks. Try a different pace—slow, steady, and very fast.

- Try to approach obstacles at different angles. Repeat, try a big stride, and use your arms to help you go fast.

- Try to make an even pattern and discover which leg you like to lead with. Use the same leg first each time you go over an obstacle. Try the same number of strides between the hurdles.

- Stretch your legs and sit. Change positions and ways to stretch your legs. Encourage slow twisting, rotating, and increase distance between the legs. Try one leg tucked, and one leg straight. Switch.

- Keep the legs stretched and still, and move your upper body. Try many different positions. Bend low over your legs. Reach with the arms, do back twists, and so on.

- Sticks are raised a few inches from the ground (set them up on low cones, bleach containers, or blocks, or held by children if no alternative is available). Run evenly; try making shapes in the air as you run, but do not alter your rhythm. Go as fast as possible, and go over several sticks in a row. Allow lots of space between sticks. Encourage long and wide stretch shapes. Try to keep your body low and near the ground while still stretching your legs. Can you skim the stick? Can you always lead with the same leg?

Group Activities

- ***Stations:*** long jump, high jump, softball throw for distance, track or baton changing area, hurdles.

- Try different angles of approach, and turn as you roll or jump over the bar. Keep the high jump bar at a low position and add a well-dug pit or foam pad to land on.

- Try running for the long jump and using the take-off board. Make your body move or change position while in the air. Fall forward after landing in a well-dug pit.

- Throw a ball. Throw a "stick" like a spear. It will be important to establish one direction only for throwing from behind a line out into a space. You might perhaps want to specify that children are not allowed to collect their implements until all have thrown—this is important for safety.

- Try to keep the baton moving at full speed even though you have to hand it to someone else. Approach from the side, not from directly behind. You need to keep running and pass the baton while both partners are moving. The receiver starts to run just before the baton holder arrives.

- Sprint from the start to finish line, leaning forward and running over hurdles as you go. Don't slow down or jump over the hurdles. Hurdles should be in the "proper" position (several are an even distance apart in two or three lanes). It is important early on to set up a flight of hurdles (keep them low) and encourage an even, fast pace of repetitive running.

Conclusion/Assessment/Reflection Activities

- Jog slowly in and around the area, without touching any apparatus.

- Collect and return all equipment.

- Discuss each of the stations and the skills involved at each.

This sample lesson can be repeated over several weeks as *all* children use *all* apparatus and rotate between different stations. A child needs more experience at each activity in each station.

Progress in track and field skills in the later stages depends on use of a consistent environment. Ultimately, the environment is fixed in these sports. Discuss how the shot, javelin, hammer, hurdles, and batons are standardized, as are distances for running. Although children and "juniors" can compete without adult equipment, the improvised apparatus to be used in elementary schools for all children will need to be replaced when children develop higher skill levels.

Both the high jump and the long jump (with take-off board), pole vaulting, and even a "triple jump" station can easily be created in an elementary school environment.

For jumping events, it will be necessary to provide large, safe landing pits.

TRACK AND FIELD LESSON 2

ACTIVITIES FOR OLDER CHILDREN

Appropriate grade level: Fourth through sixth grades

State Standards: _____

OBJECTIVES

The students will:

- Discover the most efficient ways to move their bodies as they perform high and long jumps.
- Perform a variety of running and throwing track and field events.
- Confront the discipline and limitations of measurement of physical performance by measuring jumps and timing runs.

LESSON MATERIALS

The environment is crucial. Consider creating or implementing the following items:

- Landing materials for high/long jumping. It is essential to have deep foam pads, deep sand pits, and sawdust piles. Large resilient areas are required to enable landing in a variety of ways on different parts of the body without injury.
- Take-off markings or boards, high jump stands and poles or metal bars that are easily dislodged, measuring tapes or sticks, circle areas, long run-up areas, restraining lines or curbs, pole-vault slots, track markings for straight and curved lanes, "take-over" boxes, and hurdle markings.
- Low obstacles (hurdles that tip or canes, sticks, rolled newspapers, cones, supports, and frames).
- Long "sticks" (javelins), short "sticks" (batons made from paper towel centers).
- Heavy round things (overstuffed bean bags and sand-filled rubber balls).
- Stout jumping poles with rubber tips, lightly weighted rope, and stretch rope.
- Round heavy discs (rubber and filled paper plates), frisbees, rings, heavy ball on string (ball in sock), wands, fence or solid "gate" (to be stepped on), uphill or sand areas for running, obstacle or a "steeplechase" course.
- Stopwatches on cords to be hung around the neck.

ACTIVITIES

Introductory Activities

- Children should practice timing and measuring using "buddy" checking.

- Set up areas and apparatus safely and quickly. A rule might be that no apparatus should be used until all is ready and the teacher gives permission. The original purpose of most track and field apparatus was use as a lethal weapon—children may need much teaching about awareness of environment, movement, and safety before free practice can take place.

Individual Skill Activities

Choose a variety from the following:

- Running: steady slow, short sprints, chasing, jogging alongside, and vary pace.
- Run to break tape at speed. Use a very light wool thread that is easily broken. Emphasize being at top speed when you break the tape.
- Practice an explosive start and a crouch start. Emphasize a long low trajectory of the body, not a sudden "upright" position.
- Run to "slow down," sudden stop, and check speed.
- Run low, while high stepping, at a very even pace, and with an even pattern of different steps and shapes.
- Try a combined step, hop, and leap evenly. Try the pattern of a hop, a step (leap), and a jump off one foot. Hop, stride, and jump off one foot to land on both feet.
- Move arms more quickly than legs.
- Run in lanes.
- Run sideways with crossover steps. Try different feet to cross.
- Use bouncy steps, quick steps, and a long stride. Walk with hip rotation.
- Use steps to spin and turn, hop and slide steps, stop suddenly, and find your balance.
- Practice rhythmic running through hoops, over obstacles, uphill, and downhill.
- Practice "strength" running with low knee bending, foot extension.
- Stretch the whole body and parts of the body.
- Try hopping, jumping, leaping, slide steps, and crossover steps.
- Turn, spin on one foot, and take off. Try a two-foot take-off.
- Run and carry a long stick. Try different positions, and carry the baton in different ways.
- Make your body tuck in mid-air, run in mid-air, arch your body, stretch and turn your body in

mid-air, spread your legs and turn, and tuck and turn.

- Try landing on foam or in a pit in different ways. Try to position the upper body in a different way than the lower body. Make shapes in mid-air.
- Keep your stepping or running pattern even and make shapes in mid-stride.
- Try throwing the "shot-put." Try the pushing action with different parts of the body. Emphasize different parts of the action and different parts of the body. A push or putt is not a throw.
- Spin and throw, slide and toss, bend and push, twist and release, develop a crescendo action, and come to a sudden stop. Heave your body up quickly on a stick or rope. "Kip" on a bar quickly. Get your legs high and twist to land.
- Try variations of movement and timing of effort in every action.
- Link different actions into a smooth whole.

Use appropriate apparatus, either improvised or real. Allow measures and markings of height, speed, distance, direction, and power. Try to keep key concepts simple:

- Run and throw a long stick while running. Stop suddenly after you throw. Crescendo or get faster before you throw.
- Spin once and let the discus go in a forward direction. Crescendo with the discus before you release from the back of hand.
- Run evenly over hurdles and keep running. Use the same leg to lead.
- Bounce and spring high before you roll or arch over the bar. Use your arms to help you go high.
- Get your whole body under the heavy bean bag (shot) before you push. Rotate your shoulders. Bend your body and extend it suddenly to make the shot go farther.

Partner Activities

- Race a partner, group running, team running (relay). Run and twist the upper body, with arms crossed, legs straight, legs crossed, arms straight, and so on. Run, stop, and run again.
- With a partner, exchange the baton in different ways (the baton should travel quickly). Practice different ways of handing and receiving the baton, run and reach behind, look forward, look back, practice with the same person, and use

lanes and "boxes." Increase your speed during the exchange.

Group Activities

- Divide the class so that small groups get to use the proper apparatus in the "correct" environment.
- Engage in team running (aggregate scores on relays).
- Develop team events (aggregate scores or throws).

Conclusion/Assessment/Reflection Activities

- Collect all of the apparatus.
- Discuss any difficulties with using the stopwatches or measuring tapes.
- Scores should be recorded by children with an emphasis on "beating your own record."
- Discuss how the different throwing, jumping, and running skills can be improved.
- Discuss visual images of athletes in action. Children can download images from the Web and bring them to school to add to the teacher's collection.

Draw attention to the Olympic games, the Paralympics, the Special Olympics, or any other competition held locally. Keep the focus on competition on beating your own individual record. Have measuring tapes and stopwatches available. Older children love the mechanics of measuring and it can make a fun application of mathematics.

This chapter has presented only a few sample lessons that might be used to demonstrate the discovery approach to games and pre-sport experiences for children. Plan and implement lessons that are developmentally appropriate for the students whom you teach.

The NASPE (2004) National Standards for Physical Education referred to in each of these sample lesson plans are to be found in Appendix 3 of this text. In addition, most states have their own Physical Education Standards. Readers who wish to examine the NASPE Initial PETE Standards can find the list of six Standards also in Appendix 3 but are directed to the NASPE (2009) publication, *National Standards and Guidelines for Physical Education Teacher Education* (3rd edition) for a more detailed study.

References

1. National Association for Sport and Physical Education. (2004). *Moving into the future: National standards for physical education* (2nd ed.). Reston, VA: Author.
2. National Association for Sport and Physical Education. (2009). *National standards and guidelines for physical education teacher education* (3rd ed.). Reston, VA: Author.

Discovering Creative Dance and Expressive Movement

8

The imagination is the faculty which bridges, co-presents and co-articulates the visible and the invisible.
—J. O'Donohue (1997)

QUESTIONS TO DISCUSS

1. What is your experience of dance? Negative? Positive?

2. Was dance ever included in your school education? How? When?

3. Describe your opinion of dance as a means of developing physical fitness. (Think about muscular strength, flexibility, and cardiovascular endurance.)

4. In your own experience describe ways in which you think your imagination was developed.

5. Did you ever as a child have a conscious inner world that you kept private? Describe it.

6. Have you ever seen dance used in other cultures by aboriginal people? Describe characteristics of that use of dancing. Mention the participation of children if relevant.

Observe children as they use their bodies expressively. This will prepare you for the contents of this chapter.

Assignment 8–1

Observe young children moving when there is no apparent reason for doing so. You will have seen children moving for a purpose, to do something, to achieve an obvious goal, or in interaction with other children. Try to find a child, probably alone or just near others, who is moving without a purpose, possibly fidgeting or moving rhythmically, or expressing an obvious feeling (e.g., impatience, anger, frustration, annoyance, excitement, daydreaming, curiosity, boredom). Perhaps the child is responding to a stimulus not obvious to the observer—space, weather, sound, or music. This is referred to as subjective movement, as opposed to objective movement, although there is often an overlap between the two. Does a child jumping up and down with excitement qualify as moving without a purpose? Strong feelings in a child often produce physical expression—perhaps a release? Observing any individual showing even small inconsequential movements can betray a state of mind. We often call this *body language* and the acting profession uses skills this way to communicate a great deal. Posture often communicates emotion as well.

Try to see evidence of spontaneous movement that appears to have no obvious cause. Do children sometimes move just for the sake of moving? Do you ever see movement in children that says something to them, but not necessarily to

(continues)

others? Look for a child moving even briefly who seems totally absorbed in the feel of it. Such a child is being, not doing.

Record your observations and describe at least three of them to a friend. Do you notice any differences in boys' and girls' responses? Record any interaction with adults if this occurs.

Anecdote 8-1

A male college preservice student was most skeptical that creative dance could be used with preteen boys. As a compromise, he agreed to call it "fitness training" and try it out on his Boy Scouts troop. He came back the next day thrilled. "They love it," he said. The children asked if they could do it again. When this young man was in his first elementary school teaching position, he was appointed as a music teacher. He had the whole school moving throughout the building to music going up and down staircases, along corridors, out into the playground, and into a hall—a regular symphony of activity. The principal was thrilled (no reports from other teachers!).

We must allow all children to participate in the dance of life. To live is to dance; to dance is to live. All young children need an acceptable medium in which they can be themselves. The child is not yet an adult, and does not think and feel in the way that adults do. To some extent, a child inhabits a child's world. Although one learns more and more to conform to reality (an adult world) and behave the way others want, one also needs a private world to try out parts of oneself that one is not sure about and that one may feel are unacceptable to others. Children also need freedom to interpret facts in their own way and to gain pleasure in beauty untrammeled by others' opinions.

Piaget has spoken of assimilation and accommodation. It may be that creative activities in which the child becomes absorbed offer an occasion for assimilation, integration, and self-knowledge. Much of our school program is fragmented, however, and parts of it are meant only to involve the child intellectually. Children cannot really operate in parts. Creative activities offer a milieu in which the blending of the various facets of children's awareness achieves greatest balance and, for once, the whole child is involved. Certainly, when one sees children doing creative dance, one cannot help but feel that the absorption they demonstrate is profound and serving some useful purpose. Perhaps in the future, schools will give more emphasis to activities that serve to educate the emotions.

Movement is very readily available to children and, among all the creative arts, is perhaps the easiest for a teacher to evoke. All that is needed is space. In our society, older children may have acquired inhibitions about revealing themselves in creative activity, which may make it more difficult for a teacher if the children are unfamiliar with dance. The very term "dance" may have to be avoided in mixed classes with older children, although it is often the boys who respond more readily to the activity. Perhaps care should be taken to include vigorous movement if boys are involved. At the same time, boys often enjoy delicate and gentle movement and many girls enjoy being energetic.

Educators often debate about using the word "dance" because for many it conjures up images of performing to an audience, a purely social activity, or an absent or unpopular part of a former Physical Education curriculum. Should we just call it P.E.? Fitness? Drama? Creative Physical Education? Creative movement?

One advantage that movement has over the plastic arts is its ephemeral nature. For this reason, it often makes a good beginning for creative activity that may flourish later in other media. Children are not constantly faced with the results of their creativity in movement and, therefore, feel free to make mistakes and try out only half-realized ideas and feelings. Thus creative movement in its earliest forms can serve as a basis for other art forms. It can also develop into dance—either more traditional forms or contemporary dance. This subject can be a medium for emotional control. Later, disciplined technique can serve to refine the early unformed reactions. Creative movement can also offer a therapeutic benefit where the child can become immersed in a world of his or her own and avoid or act out anything that is disturbing. In today's mechanized and industrialized world, it may be that "immersion into the flow of movement . . . is like a refreshing swim of two-fold importance; it cleanses and it is enjoyable" (Laban, 1948, p. 20).

It is important to remember that the basis of true expression comes from within. Every effort must be made by teachers to avoid imposing artificial ideas or modes of expression onto children. We must allow children to be themselves! Also, we should not feel disappointed if sometimes what appears does not seem to us to be very

Nicholas, age 6 years, had been a page at a family wedding celebrated in a garden. He was still dressed in white shirt and kilt. Now evening had come, and many of the guests were dancing to a band. Nicholas found a corner where he could not be seen and proceeded to dance using all kinds of gestures and unstructured body movements. He stayed mostly in one place. Some of his movements seemed designed to make his kilt flare out and twirl. He was totally absorbed in his own world.

meaningful. Creative movement must first have meaning for the child; only later will this activity parallel adult performance. It is possible that teachers do not know enough about children's creative work to be able to interpret it properly. Dance communicates, but the adult may not be able to receive a child's communication.

There is a sequence of development in art, and it is probable that similar sequences exist in movement. Laban (1948) suggested that simple reactions to various stimuli are the first stage. Laban also felt that attention to formations is too restrictive in the early stages and that using space imaginatively precedes directional movements and floor patterns. Laban movement will be described and developed later in this chapter.

Many teachers feel more comfortable using dramatic material as part of the educational experience. Even when dramatic material is used, it is often suggested that teachers include "free dance" (Joyce, 1994), "culminating dance" (Cone & Cone, 2005), or "improvisation" (Mettler, 1989), where children can take more control of what they do. Readers are reminded to revisit their observation journals and realize that children may not need to be taught to dance. As in so many applications of Movement Discovery, teachers capitalize on children's natural tendencies, provide structure, and develop interest, skill, and progression in basic urges to move that are already present in young children.

Teachers can choose a variety of stimuli: Words, sounds, music, dramatic ideas, and imaginative situations may all evoke movement of the whole body freely in a space. Strong, direct, and quick actions can be asked for or simply allowed to appear in response to stimuli that are likely to evoke them. It should perhaps be emphasized at the outset that the dramatic ideas and the imaginative situations mentioned previously do not mean presenting the child with instructions such as "Pretend to be . . ." . Skill is required by a teacher to deal with dramatic material in such a way that literal representations do not seem obvious, and so that the child's attention is caught by qualities that do not restrict movement to a performance of a stereotyped

action. "Pretend to be a bird" can lead to running around the room flapping the arms. In contrast, if ideas of soaring, swooping, diving, gliding, fluttering, flying, riding the wind currents, fighting against a wind, floating, and hovering were suggested, and the whole body was then used to experience these movements, the results may or may not be birdlike—but they would at least be childlike and the child's interpretation of birdlike qualities. Unfortunately, much of the material suggested by teachers for young children's imaginative movement, such as mimetics and story/finger plays, is quite restrictive. It attempts to impose adult ideas on children for them to imitate rather than stimulate the children to be creative.

"It is the author's experience that far better and more varied movement is obtained without imagery than with and that this movement is much more free in that the children are less likely to imitate each other" (Bruce, 1965, p. 3). This quotation is based on experience gained from Listen and Move, a longlasting series of radio programs used widely by teachers in Great Britain in the 1960s. Creative movement essentially comes from the child. Ideas are seen from the child's point of view—a perspective that may be difficult for adults to appreciate. When questioned, a child may well say, "I'm a bird," or something equally imitative, but it is likely that the teacher could never have guessed it from the movements the child was making. The teacher should attempt to create a state of feeling in the child that will then naturally cause expressive movement. This need not be an emotional performance and can often be evoked quite simply by asking the child to perform different qualities of movement.

Implementing an Expressive Movement Program

The simplest feeling to evoke is one of contrast. By choosing contrasting extremes of movement, children can feel simple differences and use them as they wish.

Examples of Contrasting Movements

Jerky . . . . Smooth
Curved . . . . Straight
High . . . . Low
Wide . . . . Narrow
Quick . . . . Slow
Gathering . . . . . Scattering
Soft . . . . Loud
Still . . . . Traveling
Gentle . . . . Strong
Stiff . . . . Wiggly

Any others you can think of

The efforts suggested by Laban offer good material for teachers and will be developed later in this chapter. A contrast between moving/traveling and being still might help to establish control and teach children to listen for the teacher's voice, drumbeat, or clap. When using music, percussion, or dramatic ideas, it will serve to clarify children's responses if a contrast is emphasized. The teacher will need to praise or appreciate different responses. Children have often been restricted in movement even in the home and in infancy.

Locomotor action words will be most suitable to start the lesson in the *introductory/instant activity*. Try to use some form of locomotion that uses space and is continued until the children are breathless. Usually this activity can also be linked with the theme.

Locomotor Action Tasks

- Run.
- Skip.
- Hop.
- Jump.
- Leap.
- Run and turn.
- Run in different directions.
- Run in and out of everyone else.
- Run so that you cover all the space.
- Run so that you make a curved pathway.
- Run low and jump high in the air.
- Run slowly and then jump quickly.
- Show different ways of jumping.
- Run straight and do a jump that turns you around.
- Spread wide in the air when you jump.
- Run fast and stop quickly.
- Jump to make a ball in the air.
- Try your own ideas!

When a child is asked to move in a certain way, there is a tendency to use only the immediate space in front of the body and to use the hands or arms. For example, "show a darting movement" would probably result in the fingers and hands being flicked in front of the face. One of the purposes of creative movement is to use the whole body as a means of expression and to move sensitively in a space. Thus teachers are immediately presented with two ways of extending children's experience. Whatever the theme or movement planned later, ask the children to move other parts of their bodies (can you make your feet dart, your middle, your head?). Then the child can use space other than in front of the body (e.g., Can you do a darting movement above you? Behind you? To the side? High in the air above you? Below your body or near the floor? and so on). One can then use the space in the room. Later (albeit probably not until ages 8 or 9 years), when children are familiar with the content of the dance, they will become interested in perfecting their movements and extending patterns into sequences.

Using space means not only moving around in a space at different levels and in different directions, but also following curved, undulating, or twisting pathways either as gesture or as a floor pattern. As a consequence, we have three immediate ways to stimulate initial movement responses: (1) use other parts of the body, (2) use the space around the body, and (3) use the space in the room.

This kind of training and activity suits the beginning section of the lesson. In dance, it will often help to develop the right atmosphere in a lesson if different movements are not too isolated. It is usually possible to combine the introductory activity and the *individual activity* into a smoother phrase. It is very strenuous to combine movements of locomotion with jumping, and to combine gesture and movements on or near the floor.

It is possible that a theme would already have been introduced at this point, and an attempt made to interpret and try out a great many movements in the early parts of the lesson. If it has not, then a theme can be introduced in the *skill focus* section of the lesson. If progression is important, then repetition will be required. The precise type of repetition will depend on the theme or any limitation that the teacher wishes to set. Remember that in creative dance, the skill in question is that of expressive and communicative bodily movement, rather than prowess in manipulating the body, although that may be relevant. Therefore, rather than techniques of physical performance, teachers should attempt to improve the significance and meaning of movement. Sincerity and integrity of performance are required, which may prove difficult to achieve.

The purpose of the skill focus section of the lesson is to build some kind of statement or integrated experience that has meaning, at least to the performer. The performer will have consciously selected movements for a purpose related to the theme. Obviously, with young children, this should be interpreted loosely. Sometimes a piece of music to dance to, a pattern of drumbeats and sounds, or a vague dramatic idea (e.g., "under the sea," "a fire burning," "water boiling") is sufficient to give some unity to individual activity. *Children should work alone at first* and only later attempt to combine their movements with the dances created by others. Young children, in particular, need to work alone in expressive activities.

Fitting a specific movement to a rhythm or accompaniment is very difficult for many children, especially for those in the younger age groups. It places great demands on neuromuscular coordination. However, a teacher can try to elicit repetition of movement at appropriate times. Accuracy, quality, and appropriate conscious responses are emphasized. Older children can work with partners and small groups, although this should not always mean unison activity. "Make up your own pattern and see if you can fit it to the sound" is often a sufficiently demanding challenge. Later, more limitations can be established so that the process of selection becomes more precise and greater accuracy and variety can be obtained. Too few limitations from a teacher can mean vague and unsatisfying movements, and children doing something different each time. Conversely, too many limitations, or limitations before the children are ready for them, can mean that spontaneity and joy are squelched and the inspiration behind what children do becomes stifled and stereotyped. A teacher will need careful observation and must be prepared to adapt or even abandon a planned approach. A simple "Let's just finish with a dance all on your own" may be enough for young children; likewise, "Repeat what you have done while I beat the drum or play some music" can elicit the desired responses.

The *group activity* section of the creative dance lesson for older elementary school children involves some kind of performance or dancing and should represent a climax. This does not mean that the results of the selection and practice that have gone on will necessarily be brought to perfection in one lesson. Nor does it mean an audience will watch the performance. Rather, the group activity is simply an attempt to bring some kind of conclusion to the previous work, an attempt to give of one's best at least once, to forget the details of technique or repetition at least momentarily in an effort to recapture some joy or spontaneity and make the composition communicate. The activity may consist of an interim performance of part of a pattern, or an attempt to show what has been achieved, or an attempt to clarify what is beginning to appear. Young children, of course, will need the satisfaction of performance frequently and quickly. Older children can work for longer—sometimes several lessons—before completing a pattern. In the early stages, do several short patterns; later, children can attempt longer, more complicated patterns. The lesson should finish with something approaching dance if possible. Satisfying free movement can be performed to music or the simple introductory activity can be repeated just for fun if the group-work section of the lesson did not produce suitable results for performance.

As needed, a *final activity*, relaxation, or gentle unison movement or an assessment activity can be used to draw the class together and prepare for the next lesson. Remembering, reflecting, thinking, and planning all serve as "quieteners," though this phase should be brief.

Suggested Outline for a Creative Movement Lesson

For teachers who like structure, the following outline could be used for a single lesson.

1. *Introductory Activity/Instant Activity.* The purpose of this activity is to counteract previous sedentary activity and to allow a quick experience of free movement. Some form of locomotion can be used. Run; spread out all over the space to jump in different ways; travel into every part of the room; try different directions, different levels, and different actions. Much other suitable material follows.

2. *Individual Activity.* The purpose of this activity is to focus on using different parts of the body in a variety of ways, including gestures; encourage children to use the floor and the space above, below, to the side, and behind them.

3. *Skill Focus.* The purpose of this part of the lesson is to introduce a theme (if not already introduced previously). Learners will be engaged in selection, repetition, and composition with the material. This can be done individually, in pairs, in small groups, or as a whole class.

4. *Group Activity.* The purpose of this activity is to refine and perform and to allow the children to experience a sense of satisfaction and achievement.

5. *Final Activity.* The purpose of this phase is to slow children down to transition to their next class, relax them, and allow them to think about what they've done. In addition, the teacher can engage in assessment and planning for future work.

Movement Content

LABAN MOVEMENT

Historically, both Isadora Duncan (1878–1927) and Rudolf Von Laban de Varalja (1879–1958) have been major influences in the development of children's dance in an educational setting. Interestingly, both had more influence on women physical educators and both reflected a shift in understanding the educational process. Both emphasized the importance of learner activity and the creativity within individuals.

Laban was a very creative and artistic person but did not usually work with children. As a refugee in Great Britain, however, he was dependent upon the support offered by the educational establishment.

When Laban worked with adults, his "movement themes" were usually heroic: war and peace, reconciliation between conflict and harmony, natural cycles of birth, growth and death, emotional states of anxiety expressed in movement leading to calm, peaceful resolution and so on.

Teachers may like to present such ideas even to young children—for example, "Curl up on the floor in a small space. Grow—but it is very hard to grow. Something always seems to be stopping you. There is a heavy burden on any part of your body that you must push away. Slowly you do and you overcome. You get rid of what is stopping you. The force against you is lighter. Now move more freely. Enjoy the feeling. Dance anywhere in the room and show how lovely it is to be free."

Obviously, such a theme has emotional content, and there may well be situations where emotionally disturbed children would overreact. There are therapeutic needs in many children, and expressive movement—dance—can be very beneficial for all (as well as for adults!).

Using the theme of "freedom" and the joy of being "free" is not the same as a license to do anything. It does not mean a lack of opposition, oppression, or restriction to abandon self-control and consideration of others.

A similar "feeling/emotional" theme for a lesson even with young children might use an initial idea of anger—strong, sharp, quick movements to express the feeling in activity. Then ask the children to show how anger can change, fade away, or simply get less active or less strong. Show calm, happy, peaceful moving. This kind of movement can still be quick and strong, but it feels different. Move about the room among other people using this kind of action.

When working with such themes and groups of people, Laban never prescribed or described the actual movement and activities to be used. Instead, individuals were expected to respond in their own way and all responses were accepted. Sometimes general directions like asking the "strong" group to move from this part of the space over to a specific place were used to give shape to what was happening. How participants responded came from within each person. There is much specific material suggested in this chapter, however, and later content material may seem quite restrictive. It is included for those teachers who feel the need for it.

It cannot be emphasized too strongly that dance should be allowed to come from within. Dance is an expressive art form, and the ability and need to express oneself is present from birth in the human being. When teaching, offer a free response and add direction and suggestions as needed.

Laban also included celebration, worship, comedy, and story dramas in his work, which many people found very satisfying. For teachers working with young children, it is easy to provoke satisfying responses from children.

A brief description of the content of Laban movement is included here, as many teachers have found it to be a readily accessible framework that can be used in almost any situation to extend and develop children's dance. You may find this material elsewhere called Laban's Analysis of Movement; remember, however, that it is descriptive and not scientific.

Laban was not particularly interested in schools and children, but he loved to work in industry and with large populations of movers. Movement choirs were his true avocation, and he believed that wars would cease if all people had an opportunity to dance. His original observations and inspiration were taken from the world in which he lived. Notably, Laban observed a quality that he called *free flow*. In nature, this type of movement usually resulted from an operating force, which dominated the mover. It was unpredictable, much like the branches of a tree tossed in a hurricane; the branches have no control over their movement in this setting. Most human movement is controlled and, therefore, bound. Indeed, we would go further and not include free flow movement in a school environment. Perhaps it can be included in therapy, but we believe safety in schools requires controlled movement at all times (which need not preclude using the words "free" and "freely" to encourage confident activity). In fact, Laban phraseology does not need to be used at all with children; use words that they can understand more easily. Laban's framework, however, is an excellent tool for teachers and one that is easily remembered.

Laban noticed that when any movement took place, it was observable and it used *space*. In addition, it required energy, whether a great deal or a little; Laban called this factor *weight*. Finally, the movement either lasted a long time or was brief, which Laban called the *time* factor. Thus the basic three elements of movement are as follows:

Laban's Elements of Movement

Space

Weight

Time

Laban further noticed a quality that applied to all movement and characterized the nature of it. He called this factor *flow*. It was either free, uncontrolled, and unfocused or bound (i.e., inhibited, purposeful, skilled, controlled).

In summary, he postulated the existence of three elements—space, weight, and time—which were combined with the overall characteristic of flow. Extremes within each element were experienced. Space was used with either a direct pathway or an indirect one. Weight was either strong or light. Time was either quick or slow. One can combine three elements in eight different ways if one uses the contrasts within each element. Thus Laban labeled eight basic actions that he called *efforts*.

As more teachers experimented with Laban's techniques, some of the original effort words were changed or

Laban's Efforts

Slashing
Thrusting
Flicking
Dabbing
Wringing
Pressing
Floating
Gliding

Efforts	Time Element	Weight Element	Space Element
Slashing	Quick	Strong	Indirect
Thrusting	Quick	Strong	Direct
Flicking	Quick	Light	Indirect
Dabbing	Quick	Light	Direct
Wringing	Slow	Strong	Indirect
Pressing	Slow	Strong	Direct
Floating	Slow	Light	Indirect
Gliding	Slow	Light	Direct

amplified (recall that Laban's first language was not English). "Indirect" was often called "roundabout," "quick" was sometimes changed to "sudden," "strong" became "heavy," "slow" became "sustained," and so on.

It is generally inappropriate for children to be taught or presented with any of this material. Rather, this content is intended to inform the teacher. Laban's framework is very simple, and the three basic elements can be remembered easily. When one realizes that space, weight, and time apply to all activity and can be varied, then a wealth of teaching material becomes available. Use your own words or words that children know or invent. When one varies the focus to what the body does, focuses on different parts of the body, and uses space in different ways, then an extensive amount of teaching material becomes self-evident. Classroom teachers or Physical Education specialists can easily think on their feet and be confident that teaching material will arise naturally out of

the children's activity. Remember a naive response that would use the hands only and the space in front of the face (e.g. "a darting movement").

Extend the Variety of Children's Creative Responses

As you develop creative movement activities, keep in mind the many movement concepts that can easily be used to extend the variety of children's creative work.

Ways to Extend Creative Responses

- Size of the movement
- Speed of the movement
- Body part(s) used
- Direction of the movement, including up, down, and around
- Pathway(s) to follow (air/floor)
- Stationary or on the move
- Different levels
- Using a little bit of space or a lot of space
- Add more strength/force or lightness to the movement
- Add more smoothness or jerkiness to the movement
- Make the movement continuous, ongoing
- Make the movement with stops and starts or as broken-up patterns
- Gradually increase the size and/or speed of the movement
- Gradually decrease the size and/or speed of the movement
- Change the shape of the body as it moves
- Do it alone, with a partner, or in a small group
- Combine movements into different patterns and formations

Assignment 8–2

Find a willing friend and ask him or her to move. Notice what your friend is *not* doing and suggest it is a way to extend their response. Think of the elements of movement and remember to use different parts of the body. You will soon find it is easy to build on their responses.

Choosing Themes for Creative Dance Lessons

Many themes can be taken from the regular classroom curriculum. Children learn through movement, and we need to exploit that fact in both the gymnasium and the classroom. Moving to make shapes of letters and numbers can provide powerful multisensory input and enhance learning. If these themes are used in the Physical Education program, the normal requirements of purposeful, strenuous activity should still apply. The ideas included here are meant to get the novice teacher started in creative movement. Teachers will develop many more ideas on their own, of course, and will discover ways of developing them in all parts of a curriculum.

Wherever possible, choose a *contrast* in movement. Some teachers refer to these activities as choosing opposites. Themes can focus on such things as body actions, gestures, sounds, shapes, and a variety of dramatic ideas.

BODY ACTIONS

The content material for expressive movement and creative dance is centered in the children themselves. The human body is capable of a great variety of movements. Encourage children to discover some of them by using any action words that the children will understand.

> The body will curve, jump, run, hop, skip, twist, bend, corkscrew or spiral, spring, spin, slide, roll, bounce, spread out, gather, and tuck in. It will change from a line to a bridge, a star, a ball, a wheel, an arrow, an arch, and even new ways that your students discover.

Gestures

The following action words describe gestures of limbs and hands:

> thrust, float, stamp, glide, press, point, poke, pat, squirm, wriggle, stiffen, flop, swing, flick, pull, push, slash, jog, jerk, twitch, flutter, ripple, melt, freeze, tap, stop

Teachers and children can easily extend these lists of suitable words. Some movements can be experienced that scarcely fit any known words; sounds or nonsense words can be used to evoke them.

SOUNDS

Discover the variety of sounds that can be made by the voice, body, and percussion instruments. Explore the vast array of recorded sounds and music, including such sounds as those made by whales or dolphins.

Many musical terms—for example, staccato, legato, crescendo, diminuendo, glissando, and allegro—have an obvious interpretation, and different sounds will provoke a variety of responses. Children can show the sound in movement or vocalize a sound to match their movement. Movement sounds are fun. If instruments are used, there should be enough for each child to have one, and exchanges of instruments can prolong the activity. Percussion instruments can be used to *stimulate* or *accompany* movement. Even a percussion instrument can be used to provide *continuous* or *interrupted* sound.

Instruments are easily made, possibly in conjunction with art, music, or science lessons. Any kind of solid metal that can be suspended makes a gong or continuous sounding instrument. Bells, shakers, maracas, scraper boards, clicking sticks, tin drums, rattles, tambourines, tambours, and triangles are all useful. Many sensitive sounds are produced with wind chimes or by shaking and scraping sheets of cardboard or tin foil. Finger cymbals, bongo drums, and soft maracas all allow sensitive and varied movement.

Rhythm and meter have a place with older children, as does music proper. In the early stages, however, it will probably be easier to provoke a freer response without sound, although music can be very helpful in setting a mood. Atmosphere music and much contemporary classical music falls into this category. Some electronic or digital sounds usually enhance a response. At the same time, pronounced galloping music, waltz time, and similar rhythms should be avoided because they are too restrictive, as are those recordings that tell children what to do.

CDs and recorded music work well for dance classes. Most teachers will want to make their own recordings of

Assignment 8-3

List letters of the alphabet that suggest sharpness and smoothness. Repeat this exercise using numbers.

suitable music phrases using appropriate breaks for ease of use. Usually short excerpts are most useful. Specially recorded music for creative dance is also available. With the recording technology in use today, teachers and children can easily and inexpensively prepare their own sounds or music on DVDs or CDs for creative dance lessons. There are also many wonderful recordings of the classics that can and should be used in the elementary school. When selecting music, it is a good idea to collaborate with the music teacher because recordings used in musical appreciation sessions can often be explored in creative dance lessons.

The use of instruments should not inhibit movement. It must be possible to move and play at the same time or to listen briefly and then move extensively.

Vocal sounds and body sounds are all useful. Phonics sounds (ch . . . ch . . . t . . . t . . . tttt . . . sssssss . . .) and simple chords are also interesting for young children. Young children often spontaneously initiate both voice and body sounds as they move. Teachers should capitalize on those inventions. Encourage children of all ages to experiment with different sounds they can make with their voices.

Allow children time to discover the sounds that parts of their body can make and use those sounds in their dance experiences.

Sounds

- High sounds
- Low sounds
- Sounds that go up and then down
- Sounds that start high and then go down
- Fast and slow sounds
- Strong and light sounds
- Sharp and smooth sounds
- Loud sounds
- Soft sounds
- Sounds that start softly and gradually get louder
- Sounds that start loudly and gradually get softer
- Humming sounds
- Hissing sounds
- Whistling sounds
- Clicking sounds
- Phonetic sounds

Body Sounds

- Clapping hands
- Clicking/snapping fingers
- Slapping legs
- Tapping on the floor with toes and/or fingers
- Rubbing hands together
- Popping lips/mouth
- Stamping feet

Children can actually dance to the sound of whole words and manipulate the rhythm of them. For young children, this activity may be easier if the teacher directs the contrast; older children can make their own accompaniment and work in pairs or groups. Single words or poems and sentences can stimulate movement. At the same time, it is important to distinguish between sound used as an accompaniment and sound used as a stimulus. Movement can interpret and enliven sound, but sometimes the movement should come first, with accompaniment being added later.

Bruce (1965) writes:

When a dancer moves without sound it is as if the sound were within, emerging with the flow of the movement, the rhythm and phrasing appearing in space. It is essential, too, that movers have an opportunity to develop their own rhythms, and an external accompaniment often prevents this. (p. 10)

Teachers must also remember that music is complex and may be a too complicated structure for young children. Atmosphere sounds and much of modern classical music (such as Peart and Tavener) are useful in this regard. Let the children suggest good music for their movement lessons.

SHAPES

The theme of *shape* has many possibilities. Children can be guided to discover how the body bends, stretches, and twists or to use combinations of these movements to make many different shapes. There are round, angular, and

twisted shapes, and pin-like, ball-like, and screw-like shapes. With young children, many words can be used to suggest and describe the body's shape—for example, wide, narrow, long, twisted, rounded, curved, angular, big, small, stretched, curled, symmetrical, asymmetrical, and lopsided. Movement tasks can focus on the body taking on different shapes while standing, kneeling, sitting, and lying down. Transitions between these different positions and shapes can be introduced early so that dance work does not deteriorate into making a series of static poses. Instead, phrases of shapes should be encouraged.

Sample Learning Experiences Using Shape

- Be still in a curved shape, and then change slowly into an angular shape.

- Begin in a long shape, and move to a low, rounded shape.

- Make a wide shape as your starting position. Quickly change into a narrow shape.

- Change your group's shapes at different levels (this activity can help to train sensitivity and group awareness in children ages 8–9 years and older).

- Make or use the shapes of various letters as you move or dance. (Use the whole body and gestures of the limbs; follow different pathways in space; make the shapes at different levels and as floor patterns.) Do it when part of you is touching the floor.

- Make the shape of the number 1 (or 2, or 3, and so on). (Younger children often enjoy making the shapes of various letters and numbers.) Do it all over the floor.

- Try to show the letter M (or any other letter or number) in movement. Add both speed and force variations. (These movement variables and concepts can add interest to expressive movement.) Do it partly as a floor pattern and partly in the air.

- Contrast curving letters or figures with angular ones.

- Contrast cursive script with capital letters.

- Contrast Arabic with Roman numerals.

The basis of dance performance is fluid and changing. Design, as well as differences in tension and timing, can be applied to bodies, spaces, and patterns.

Group shapes, floor patterns, and different levels are interesting for older children. The inclusion of relationships with another person, stairs or blocks, blank walls, curtains, sheets of plastic, rope, bamboo poles, pillars, or platforms can also add variety. Flight through the air incorporates a difficult and challenging medium for shape and design; likewise, the use of the floor with a variety of body support can give interesting effects. Remember many children watch DVDs and a whole variety of visuals on the Web. Some modern movement and design is very inventive and innovative.

If used too soon with children, themes emphasizing shape tend to make them too self-conscious and show the overweight or awkward child to disadvantage. Teachers can incorporate the tracing of shapes of letters, numbers, or words in these activities—either in cursive or as printed letters. Both uppercase and lowercase can be explored. Different parts of the body, including the fingers and hands, can be used to trace different shapes. Tracing can be done on the floor, in the air, or on the wall. Children can experience movement along different floor pathways and patterns and use different air pathways while doing this activity. By changing the size of the letter shape, children experience big movements and smaller movements.

Geometric shapes are more difficult for children to learn than typographical ones. Use the shapes of numbers and letters, and dance to the phonic sounds. Use differences in sound—the soft "ch" in German as opposed to the hard "ch" in English, for example. This type of expressive movement links very naturally with learning in other areas of the curriculum.

DRAMATIC IDEAS

Dramatic ideas are best taken from the child's experience and offer an excellent link with content and subject matter in other areas of the preschool and elementary school curriculum. Remember, however, that dramatic ideas can be quite restrictive, especially if a teacher imposes a preconceived interpretation. Always elicit movements; do not impose them. A dominant teacher can restrict responses, whereas an enthusiastic committed teacher can inspire them. Be guided by the responses of the children you teach. Much of the content related to literature, poetry, science, art, music, and environmental social studies can provide excellent themes for an alert teacher. Teachers should constantly be alive to the possibility that movement would enhance any material being presented.

Often dramatic themes produce an eager response and, unless carefully chosen, can overexcite a group. Also, they must not be used too often. Children need to concentrate on the significance of different movement qualities, and some children are easily carried away by a dramatic situation.

Themes from the science curriculum and nature work well for a variety of age groups and can usually provide a contrast for emphasis. Children can collect photographs or pictures to bring from home to illustrate some of the themes listed in **Table 8–1**. Teachers can also utilize appropriate visual images from their own collections. These images can be used as a basis for discussion about the shapes, sights, sounds, and movement possibilities of the dramatic idea. Eliciting *descriptive vocabulary* during the discussion is also an excellent literacy activity.

Teachers and children can collect and use different objects from nature as stimuli (e.g., rocks of different sizes and shapes, different-shaped leaves, sticks of different shapes, snow, icicles, hailstones).

Dramatic ideas and other themes and ideas from the general early childhood and elementary curriculum can be used in Physical Education to extend understanding in these subject areas. Rich movement material can be found in **Table 8–2**.

Think about which objects could be used as a stimulus for creative movement, based on any of the themes and ideas in Table 8–2. Such objects might include simple costumes, streamers, scarves, hats, canes, puppets, flags, popcorn, bubbles, mechanical objects, toys, yarn, bells, and springs, among many other possibilities.

Assignment 8–4

From the list of dramatic ideas in Table 8–2, select five that you could use with a third-grade class (or another grade class). List the movement content that you might explore with each idea. Try to find visual images, videos, short poems, or stories that could be used in an interdisciplinary experience using the idea.

LINKS WITH LITERACY

Early childhood and elementary classroom teachers have many opportunities every day to link expressive movement and literacy. Physical educators can collaborate with classroom teachers to explore appropriate grade-level content for dance movement. This section highlights three sample areas to explore: expressive action words, poems, and stories.

TABLE 8–1 Themes from the Science Curriculum

Plants	Insects
Bubbles	Food
Snow storm	Forest fire
Plant life	Space
Hurricanes and tornadoes	Hail stones
Water falls	Volcanoes
Whirlpools	Farms
Waves on rocks	Rainforests
Animals	Animal life
Weather	Surf and tides
Frost and sunshine	Mud pools and geysers
Lightning and thunder	Dust storms
Oceans	Cloud burst
Tsunami	Forces of nature

TABLE 8–2 Dramatic Ideas and Other Themes

Astronauts	Halloween
Mirrors	Characters
Robots	A toy shop
Aliens	Leaves
Traffic	Inventors/inventions
Balloons/blimps	Kites
Magicians	Magnets
Monsters	Historical events
Imaginary . . . ?	Sounds
Puppets/puppeteers	Mechanical objects
Imaginary vegetables	Special days
Skeletons	Seasons
Food	Emotions
Superheroes	Daily activities
Growing plants	Hunters (e.g., sharks, cats)
Machines (parts turn, go up and down, back and forth, lift, and so on)	

Expressive Action Words

Word selection will depend on the age group and developmental level of the learners. Here are some examples of useful action words:

- **Stomp:** It's strong; it emphasizes the legs and feet or lower body; it can follow any pathway and can occur at a slower speed.
- **Tip-toe:** It's light/soft; it emphasizes the feet and being up on the toes; traveling can occur along any pathway and at different speeds.
- **Whirl:** It's circular and goes round; it can change height (high to low; low to high) and size (big movement to small movement); it can be strong or light.
- **Tap:** It's light; it can be done with the fingers or feet; it can be both fast and slow; it's a direct movement that goes mostly up and down.
- **Melt:** It's a continuous, ongoing movement that starts with a solid shape (i.e., ice); fast or slower movement occurs in different directions.
- **Creep:** It can be done on feet or all fours; it's low; it's light; the body can move at different speeds, directions, and pathways.
- **Explode:** It consists of strong movements that can go in different directions and levels in space; any parts of the body can be used or the whole body; an explosion can be any size.
- **Floppy:** It's loose; it goes in all directions; it can be done with any part of the body; it can occur at any level; the speed and size can change.
- **Collapse:** It goes downward; it can be a whole-body movement or just a part of the body can be used; it can be very fast or quite slow; it starts high and ends low; it drops in different directions; the shape of the body changes.
- **Rise:** This movement goes up; its speed can be varied; single body parts can show it or it can be a whole-body movement; it can go in different directions and to different levels in space; it can be a small or big movement; it can travel a short or long distance; it might be a jerky or smooth movement.
- **Fall:** It can bend, twist, or stretch as it goes down (body shapes can change); it can occur at different speeds and in different directions; it can include big and small falls, straight or bending pathways in the air, and falling a bit at a time or all at once.
- **Bend:** It can be done with any joints in the body or the whole body; it can be fast or slow; it can occur in any direction; it can be a big movement or a small movement; it can take a lot of time or a little bit of time; it follows a direct pathway.
- **Slither:** It follows a curving pathway; it's continuous, smooth, ongoing, and twisting; it often takes place at a low level; it is a whole-body movement.

Assignment 8–5

On the computer, create a table in a word processing program using three columns (see **Table 8–3**). In column 1, make a list of at least 30 expressive action words of your own. "Run," "jump," "hop," and "skip" should not be used. In column 2, list beside each of the action words the movement qualities and variations that could be discovered and practiced by the children. In column 3, design a creative dance movement task using the word and one or two of the variations you've listed.

TABLE 8–3	Example Table for Assignment 8–5	
Expressive Action Word	Movement Qualities/ Variations	Creative Dance Task
1.		
2.		
3.		
4.		

Ideas for Use of Expressive Action Words

Teachers can prepare these words on word cards made from different-colored cardboard or paper, using different fonts. Font characteristics to change might include the size; color; use of italic, bold, and underlining; sloping letters versus vertical letters; and mixture of lowercase

Assignment 8-6

Create a list of expressive actions that young children could practice in combinations of two. Contrasting movements or opposites work well.

Try to:
> *Creep* and *pounce*
> *Shake* and *freeze*
> *Freeze* and *melt*
> *Twirl* and *collapse*
> *Rise* and *fall*
> *Drop* and *explode*

Try movements which are:
> *Rigid* and *loose*
> *Jerky* and *smooth*
> *Stiff* and *flexible*
> *Restricted* and *free*
> *Straight* and *bent*

and uppercase letters, among other things. (WordArt works well within the Microsoft Word program.) This visual distinction helps children generalize their ability to recognize words under many changing conditions, and the different shapes can elicit different ways of moving—curvy, straight, continuous, broken, up and down.

The teacher can write the word on one side of the card; on the back of the card, he or she can write some qualities of movement and variations for the children to practice. When introducing an expressive action, both the teacher and the child can use this visual. These ideas will help the teacher reinforce the true meaning of the word. Children can *see* the word, *say* it, *hear* it, *write* it in the air or on the floor, and use movement or the kinesthetic sense to *show* the meaning of the word. This type of activity represents a multisensory approach to learning new words as well as a creative movement experience.

Word cards can be attractively displayed as *word walls* on the gymnasium or classroom wall as they are used.

Assignment 8-7

For older children, create a list of three or more action words that can be explored as a *sequence* of movement or as a *movement sentence*. Consider these examples:

> Rise, turn, collapse
> Tip-toe, crouch, hide
> Stiff, loose, stiff, loose, crash
> Up, down, up, down, swivel, stop
> Roll, twist, slide, stop

Sometimes a picture of an object, which suggests the action, might accompany the word. These lesson aids can be used as a summative assessment activity at the end of the lesson. Several children could be selected to point to different words used in the lesson and show their meaning in movement.

A natural progression for using expressive action words is to combine them in a movement task. Start with two words. Then, as children gain more experience, they will be able to combine them into longer movement sentences or dance sequences.

Poems and Stories

Use the poems and stories that children write as well as the published works of other authors. Poems can provide structure to the dance experience. As a part of the literacy program in all preschool and elementary schools, teachers read poetry and stories to children frequently. In addition, children read and write their own stories and poetry. Stories and poems should be carefully selected for their creative movement potential. They should also be developmentally and age appropriate. It is helpful to collaborate with classroom teachers to see which material children are using that might be useful for the content of a creative dance lesson. Some will not be appropriate.

The process can also be reversed. A satisfying dance experience can be preserved by turning it into a poem. Allow children to do this in a literacy lesson.

Poems serve as stimuli, can help generate an idea or ideas, and can be an accompaniment or used as a culminating activity. When using poems and stories, formulate questions of the *what, how, where,* and *why* type. These questions can be used to elicit specific movement ideas. They can also be used to clarify the movement experience that will be used to write a poem or story. Nevertheless, it is important for children to remain physically active and keep talking to a minimum.

Examples of *What, How, Where,* and *Why* Questions

- What does the character/thing look like? Describe its color, shape, size.
- How would you describe the movement of the machine or . . . ?
- Is there strength in the movement or is it a very light movement?
- Where does the animal live? Or travel? Or sleep? Or play?
- Why do you think . . . ?

To be successful using the discovery method of teaching, and in particular when teaching creative dance, teachers must develop and practice their ability to formulate varied and stimulating questions.

A poem can provide a predetermined sequence and structure to a part of the lesson or to the lesson as a whole. The lesson's movement content can follow the actions in the poem. Sometimes just the titles might be useful as a stimulus; the poem itself might not be used. Often a teacher might choose to select only a few actions from the poem. With older children, the action words can be explored singly and then joined in sequences to create a dance composition. The dance sequence may or may not follow the original poem. It is better to avoid miming the poem because that tends to limit children's creativity and can lead to stilted movement.

Sometimes *selected phrases* from poems and stories might suggest creative movement ideas. Poems and stories that suggest a lot of physical action can often be read to children as they move (i.e., as an *accompaniment* to their movement). A story or poem might be used at the beginning of a lesson to set the stage for the material to follow. Both types of material can also be used to conclude a lesson as a culminating or even assessment activity, to pull the lesson material together and evaluate what

Assignment 8-8

Collect the titles of 10 poems or stories that you could use as creative dance material. Create a two-column table in Word or another word processing program. Column 1 should list the titles of the poems and stories; column 2 should identify ideas about how the title could be used in creative dance lessons.

Titles of Poems/ Stories	Ideas for How the Title Could Be Used in Creative Dance Lessons
1.	
2.	
3.	

happened during the class. Children can write their own story to end a creative dance lesson—for example, what happened next?

LINKS WITH THE ART CURRICULUM

Preschool children especially are very interested in painting. They paint with different colors using different line widths, pathways, and directions. They discover they can make blobs and smooth, squiggly, straight, and crooked lines. The products can be interesting to explore in creative movement. Alternating the movement patterns and qualities and contrasts can be turned into a painting—a visual representation of a physical experience. Teachers can also create simple line designs for children to dance. **Figure 8–1** is one such example.

Using Poems and Stories: A Summary

1. Choose poems that have lots of movement possibilities. Those with many movement or action words or action ideas will work best.

2. Choose the most appropriate action words and, through skillful questioning, elicit and explore the movement qualities of each in terms of creative movement.

3. Select the most appropriate actions and words (invent new words) that have been explored, and practice combinations and sequences of these movements, words, and phrases.

4. Incorporate the actions with a variety of relationships to invent/compose a dance or poem or story.

5. Refine and practice the invention/ composition and perform it or write it down. Performance or a poem can be just for peers.

6. Allow performance to lead straight to the verbalization of a poem or story to be written later in the classroom.

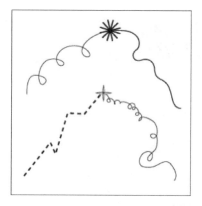

FIGURE 8-1   Line Design to Dance

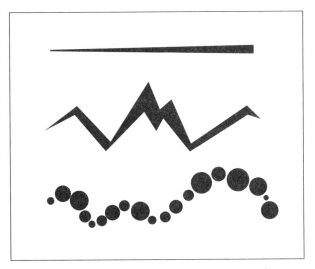

FIGURE 8–2   Possible Pathways to Follow

The design shown as **Figure 8–2** could be used to emphasize different kinds of pathways, both in the air and on the floor, that the whole body or parts of the body can follow. The thickness of the lines could be used to show more or less force in the movement. Try creating some designs of your own. Both the teacher and children can create interesting designs that can be used as stimuli in expressive movement.

Early attempts at painting by very young children are quite abstract and do not look like anything to the untrained observer, but they may stimulate the child. Children's paintings and drawings change as they mature.

Children like to create shapes with play dough, modeling clay, wet sand, and building blocks and construction materials of all shapes and sizes. The teacher can use art products as a stimulus for creative dance activities. Conversely, creative dance can provide a stimulus for art activities.

Here are some examples:

Clay: Using clay, an art task may be to take a chunk of clay and work with it. Find out what it's like, what it feels like, and how it behaves. This type of task can be pursued for quite a long time. The teacher could describe what the children are doing as they experiment with their clay by saying such things as, "I see some of you are poking holes in your clay; many of you are squeezing and rolling it into different shapes. Try shaping your clay some other way. Take some time as you work to turn your piece around so that you can see it from different vantage points. You should begin to see its three-dimensional solid form." Other variations can be introduced like this: "Try curving the clay. Stretch it long or high. Change it to a broken or jagged shape or sculpture piece." These same shaping experiments can then be performed with the body! Alternatively, experimenting with different shapes,

efforts, textures, and actions of the body can be used on the clay.

Wire: Line and shape experiments are possible with wire lengths. Fine copper wire (30–36 inches long) is best for small, individual constructions, while 6- to 8-foot lengths of thin aluminum wire (diameter ⅛ or 3⁄16 inch) allow for work on a larger, whole-body scale. Predrilled wooden blocks, clay, Styrofoam, or cardboard bases are desirable for such sculpture pieces. The wire can be shaped to show straight, curving, zigzags, turning, and upward and downward movement. Such sculpture work can be then used as a stimulus for a creative dance based on the theme "Shapes in Flight." Sculptures should be viewed from all perspectives. Make a model of a dance you created.

Paper: Shape paper of different colors, textures, and thicknesses by cutting, tearing, and curling it. These shapes can be used to make collages and pictures of all kinds utilizing either two- or three-dimensional effects. These two-dimensional or three-dimensional designs of paper, cardboard, clay, or wire can be of different sizes. Such art products can easily be used to stimulate new movement sequences or creative movement sentences and dances. The lines and shapes can act as a manuscript or score for the creation. Let children discover which lines and shapes can be created with yarn, string, thin wire, cotton balls, buttons, toothpicks, bottle tops, straws, corrugated cardboard, colored paper, and other materials.

Multiple media: A variety of art materials and found objects can be used to construct all kinds of structures. Readily available items include 1-liter and 2-liter plastic bottles, egg cartons (1 dozen and ½ dozen sizes), cardboard boxes of all shapes and sizes, cardboard toilet paper or paper towel rolls, wire coat hangers, and plastic half-gallon or gallon milk jugs, plus many other possibilities. Encourage children to invent and discover different uses for these materials. The following assignment would work well with students in third through sixth grades.

Assignment 8–9

Create a two- or three-dimensional design, and draw and/or construct it on a sheet of cardboard. This could also be done on a whiteboard in a virtual classroom. List the types of movements your design suggests. Design a creative dance task that could be used with children working alone in first grade and for a small group of children at the fourth-grade level.

Invent, design, and build something new and futuristic, using any combination of the items listed below. Try to make something that no one else will think of. In addition to the items listed here, use tape, glue, string, paint, paper clips, and pins in the construction of your project. Items you may use include these:

- Plastic bottles
- Egg cartons
- Cardboard rolls
- Wire or wire coat hangers
- Plastic milk jugs

Design a creative dance lesson plan with the theme of "Inventions." Include a short discussion of inventors and inventions. Use short demonstrations to show the materials students are to use and encourage them to discover and explore the different and unusual ways materials can be used either alone or in combination. (Tear apart the cardboard rolls, bend the wire hanger, and so on.) Students could work in groups of two or three.

MUSICAL SCORES: AN IDEA FOR INTEGRATING MUSIC, ART, AND MOVEMENT

Children can design musical compositions or musical scores using a variety of graphic means. Musical scores can be invented without relying on traditional notation—the composers and choreographers can experiment with colored paper of different thicknesses and shapes, strips of paper (which may be curled), paint, straws, chalk, and other media. There are many ways to represent pitch, loudness, softness, speed, smoothness, sharpness, space, rhythm, pathway, and amount of force, effort, or energy to be expended. Large sheets of paper secured to the wall or placed on the floor can be used for this activity. This is an excellent small-group task, with limitless possibilities. Percussion instruments can be used in combination with both voice and body sounds. The teacher might ask for certain types of sounds or movements to be included. The creative dance tasks can be open-ended, allowing students freedom and choice, together with scope for individual inventiveness. This one assignment integrates naturally the art, music, and movement areas of the curriculum.

Classroom teachers have a real advantage in teaching creative movement. They know the stuff of life that the children are already involved in. A multisensory approach will facilitate learning for more learners.

Exploring Relationships in Dance Movement Lessons

Young children will enjoy working on their own. When children begin to want to work with a friend it is possible to make use of a variety of relationships with another person. The following relationships can be explored as appropriate to the developmental level of your learners:

1. **Number:** The number of children relating to each other can vary.
   - Individual
   - Partners
   - Small groups
   - Whole class
   - One group may relate to another group
   - The teacher or an individual may relate to the group
2. **Identical:** Children can do the same actions as the other person, either successively or simultaneously.
   - Matching
   - Echoing
   - Mirroring
   - Shadowing
3. **Contrasts:** Children can use opposite shapes, actions, effort qualities, or amounts of space.
   - High/low
   - Stretched/curled
   - Forward/backward
   - Big/little
4. **Interactions:** The way children can move together.
   - Lead and follow
   - Meet
   - Meeting and parting
   - Actions and reactions
   - Relationship with an object
5. **Contact:** Touching, connecting, or supporting another person.
   - Connecting
   - Supporting
6. **Formations:** Ways in which the group can be arranged.
   - Circles
   - Lines
   - Squares
   - Group shapes (irregular, long, narrow, wedge, arrow)
   - Scattered

The natural progression in dancing is from creative work to more limited and structured work. Different formations such as circles, squares, and lines feature prominently in folk, square, and line dances, in addition to creative dance. Children in elementary school are not really ready for formal rhythmic dances to music until grade 5 or 6, and then it is usually the girls—and not the boys—who are mature enough for these activities. Just before adolescence is a good time to experience rhythmic moving to music. Many teachers also feel that introducing social dancing before adolescence makes it easier for the children later. Elementary school is really too early to learn sophisticated social dance that can be used in later life. It has, however, a wonderful carry-over value and should be included in middle and high schools.

For those students who choose to develop their creative dance experiences in the future there is a possibility of participating in a modern contemporary dance group. Some fitness groups are beginning to explore the use of creative dance movement for their classes. Various forms of more formal, structured dancing, such as on ice, line dancing, and folk dancing, are available in some communities. Social dancing can be very satisfying and when pursued competitively often gives rise to creative adaptations. Creative movement in the elementary school not only aids in all-round education but can provide a basis for many forms of movement activity in later life.

References

Bruce, V. (1965). *Dance and dance drama in education.* London: Commonwealth & International Library Series, Pergamon Press.

Cone, T., & Cone, S. (2005). *Teaching creative dance.* Champaign, IL: Human Kinetics.

Joyce, M. (1994). *First steps in teaching creative dance to children* (3rd ed.). Palo Alto, CA: Mayfield.

Laban, R. (1948). *Modern educational dance.* London: Macdonald & Evans.

Mettler, B. (1989). *Materials of dance: As a creative art activity.* Tucson, AZ: Mettler Studios.

O'Donohue, J. (1997). *Anam cara: A book of celtic wisdom.* New York: Cliff Street Books.

Sample Creative Dance/
Expressive Movement Lessons

This chapter includes sample lessons that have worked well for others and can serve as a starting point for the teacher who is new to the teaching of creative dance. Your own ideas will be the best choices, however, because they reflect your knowledge of the children in your class. At any time you should feel free to abandon planned activities to repeat activities that get a good response and to allow the children to enjoy any activity that particularly interests them. A good expressive movement/dance lesson often "takes off" as children become absorbed in what they are doing. Follow this interest and do not be too ready to interrupt and to push a lesson toward your preplanned objective. Repeat a lesson if you like, and pick things up where you left off rather than present a totally new lesson.

A matter-of-fact approach rather than an emotional one will probably work best with a new class. Joining in with the children can be an advantage and a confident manner can work wonders. The inclusion of slow-motion moving, some running and jumping, and some collaps-ing and falling are popular activities. Dance can be very strenuous. Sometimes teachers have found that a request to try a new type of lesson as an experiment has produced a good response. The important thing is to try several lessons before attempting any judgment.

You will notice that the early lessons give maximum opportunity for children to be creative. Try at least one of these lessons before proceeding to the more structured lessons suggested for grades 3, 4, 5, and 6 where there are fewer choices for the learners. If you have not taught dance before, you may feel more comfortable with the more structured lessons. The time allocation listed in the lesson plans is an approximation. Be flexible and base your judgment on the children's responses.

The NASPE Standards referenced by number in the lessons in this chapter can be found listed in Appendix 3 of the text. Many states have their own interpretation of these Standards and you should check those that apply in your state.

SMOOTH AND SHARP, SOFT AND HARD MOVEMENTS

Suggested grade levels: Kindergarten through third grade

Lesson length: 20–30 minutes

NASPE Standards: 1, 2, 4, 6

State Standards: _____

LESSON MATERIALS

Visuals of letter C

OBJECTIVES The learner will:

Psychomotor
1. Contrast smooth shapes of the body and soft sounds of the letter "C" with the sharp shapes and hard "C" (cat, can, Cathy) sounds.
2. Use the soft "C": (ceiling, cent, Cindy) or hissing sound as an accompaniment for movements.
3. Shape different parts of the body.

Cognitive
1. Create a dance using sharp and smooth movements along with soft and hard sounds (voice or percussion).

Minutes (Approximately)	Scripted Movement Tasks	Cues/Things to Stress
3	**Introductory/Individual Activity** 1. Run. Try to cover all the space. Stop. Run. This time try to run on a smooth, curving, or circular pathway. Stop. Run and try to let your whole body curve as you go. Stop. Let your arms swing to turn you around on the spot. Now run and try to let your body or arms curve to help you turn. Try to use different levels, near the floor, in the middle, and high in the air.	Emphasize: ■ Spreading out to use the whole room space ■ Fast stopping ■ Curving pathways ■ Smoothness as children travel
3	2. Lie on your side curved into a ball. (If the floor cannot be used to lie on, crouch in a ball near the floor and stretch up to the ceiling.) Stay on your side and open out to arch your back. Repeat. Try to make a smooth curve from your fingers to your feet. Let your head join in. Curl. Open out to a letter C (use a visual of the letter C). Try jumping to arch the body in the air. Make a C in the air.	Try a variety of C shapes (side, back). Pick out an interesting C shape and show it to the others and then invite all children to improve their shapes. With some classes this amount of direction would not be necessary and the initial instruction could be "Make your body curve or arch to show a C shape," and then as necessary specific suggestions could be added to ensure variety and encourage use of back muscles. Allow choice.

Minutes (Approximately)	Scripted Movement Tasks	Cues/Things to Stress
3	3. Try to "open out" to show a curve in a different part of your body. Use your side, legs, and arms. Try *small shapes* as well as *large* ones. Try rolling over so that the weight is supported on different body parts. Repeat several times—keep moving. Move from a small c to a large C. Move on a curve from a back C to a side C, and so on. Try to make a variation between a slow curl before each quick opening or a quick curl-up and slow stretching and arching. Vary the speed!	Suggest use of one hand, one foot, shoulders, and knees. Suggest making the shape diagonally across the body or with a twist. Remind learners that the C can be horizontal or vertical or diagonal. Stress the *size* of the C. Stress variations of speed because that adds challenge and interest to expressive movement.
6	4. Join the running activity on a curved pathway by showing three different C shapes on the floor. Spend time improving the response. Possibly include rolls and jumps. Use cursive writing shapes, not printing. Use the three C positions to get you up on your feet again ready to repeat the running.	Work for smooth transitions between the running and floor work. Repetition of the phrases will improve the quality. Allow time for that repetition.
12	5. Try to repeat the same pattern. Clarify what you do. Make a soft "c" or hissing sound to accompany the smooth movements, and the hard "k" sound three times to show the shapes. Change from the continuous hissing and moving to three sharp, quick c shapes at the beat of a drum (teacher) or clap. Spend time to refine the pattern.	

Performance

| | Repeat the pattern, trying to make the dance of the C's.
You might want to finish the dance of the C's possibly to a bouncy drum beat or by making soft and hard "c" sounds to accompany your own movement. (The teacher should use a drum only if needed, because it forces conformity.) Try to let everyone "dance" their pattern before finishing (all at the same time). | Repetition can be done individually with the children taking their own time.
Encourage the children to capture the smoothness of the hissing sound in body movement, locomotion, and transition.
Stress that the difference between the smooth and sharp movement should be very obvious.
Refining the pattern involves repeating it over and over.
Make a possible link with classroom work in printing, writing, reading, or phonics.
The dance of the C's can be worked on in a future lesson. |

Minutes (Approximately)	Scripted Movement Tasks	Cues/Things to Stress
3	**Final Activity/Assessment/Reflection** 6. Name the types of movements we worked on today. Walk smoothly in and out of everyone tracing a C pattern. Use your arms and head to show curves in the air and around your body. Continue moving smoothly to the door as you get ready to leave class today.	

Similar lessons could use other letters and numbers. For the letter "M," for example, a teacher could almost repeat the lesson using zigzag pathways, sharp turning of "corners," and a continuous "MMMmmmm" humming sound for "smooth" and "soft" sounds.

LESSON 2

FLOOR AND AIR PATTERNS WITH SPEED VARIATIONS

Suggested grade levels: Prekindergarten through third grade

Lesson length: 25–30 minutes

NASPE Standards: 1, 2, 4, 6

State Standards: _____

LESSON MATERIALS

Visuals—line designs prepared by the teacher or children displayed on sheets of colored paper

OBJECTIVES The learner will:

Psychomotor
1. Demonstrate fast and slow movements with the whole body and at least four parts of the body.
2. Move using a variety of pathways in the air and on the floor (e.g., straight, curved, zigzag, wide, thin lines, scribbling).

Cognitive
1. Show the difference between very slow movements and very fast movements while painting pictures with different parts of the body.

Minutes (Approximately)	Scripted Movement Tasks	Cues/Things to Stress
3	**Introduction/Individual Activity** 1. We're going to work on very fast and very slow movements using different parts of our body today. Find a space. Move your whole body as fast as you can and stop when I say stop. Ready . . . go . . . stop. Do it again, but this time move just one part of your body fast . . . like your hands, hips, back, head. Ready . . . go . . . stop.	Word cards with the vocabulary "fast" and "slow" can be posted on the wall. Describe/name the body parts you see children using to move fast. Encourage immediate stops.

Minutes (Approximately)	Scripted Movement Tasks	Cues/Things to Stress
3	2. Move around the room as slowly as you possibly can. Keep the slow moving going without stopping. Can you sometimes move down low? How slowly can you roll? Crawl slowly? Can you try very slow turns? Skip slowly? Collapse slowly? Shake?	To capture very slow movement, the teacher might say, "I should hardly be able to tell that you're moving because you're going so slowly!" Refer to a slow-motion film.
3	3. Let me see you do your own very fast movements and then change to very slow movements. Change from fast to slow whenever you want to. Run quickly. Switch to slow moving on the floor.	Emphasize that the movements should look and feel very different because of the speed change. It's harder to control a slow roll or change of position.
6	4. We are going to paint with our bodies. Look at this design. (Show a visual.) With red paint on your fingers, scribble everywhere as fast as you can. Put green paint on your head and scribble very slowly everywhere in space. Remember high and low. Paint with a different color on your feet and stamp the paint all over the floor. Make an interesting pattern. Put another color paint on your back and make big, wide bands of color. (Show a visual.) Use black or purple or yellow and paint thin, slow, careful lines using any part of your body. (Show a visual.) The lines might be straight or curved or zigzagged. You can paint on the floor or in the air or both.	At first the teacher designates the body parts and speed of the painting. The variable of different thicknesses is then introduced (i.e., wide and narrow) as well as the level of painting. Finally, the pathway variable is added. Allow children time to discover the curved, straight, and zigzag patterns.
10	**Culminating Activity** 5. To finish, we are going to paint a huge picture. Let me see your beginning position. Start painting your picture slowly, close to the ground. As you paint up higher, make your painting faster. Be sure to paint with different parts of your body. Travel across the floor. This is a very big picture. Finish your painting with slow lines and dots/spots. End in a low shape on the floor. Choose three parts and repeat. Do your painting again (three parts).	Encourage children to use the space of the gym/classroom sensibly as they paint their *big* picture. Check that all children have selected a stationary beginning position. Remind children to paint high, with different parts of the body, and to include a traveling movement. Suggest children watch a partner and identify the three different parts in the dance, and then switch roles.

Minutes (Approximately)	Scripted Movement Tasks	Cues/Things to Stress
5	**Conclusion/Reflection/Assessment Activity**	Select several individuals to show their dances or ask for volunteers.
	6. Let's have half the class show the other half of the class their fast/slow painting dance:	
	■ Which part of David's dance was very fast?	
	■ Which body part did Katie use for the slow part of her dance?	
	■ Did Lyn use slow straight, slow curvy, or slow zigzag lines in her dance?	

LESSON 3

MOVING TO SOUND (PERCUSSION INSTRUMENT) AND MOVING SILENTLY

Suggested grade levels: Any grade level

Lesson length: 20–30 minutes

NASPE Standards: 1, 2, 4, 5, 6

State Standards: _____

LESSON MATERIALS

A variety of percussion instruments

OBJECTIVES		The learner will:
Psychomotor	1.	Play different percussive instruments and create different types of sound with each.
	2.	Contrast soft continuous sounds with sudden, sharp, loud sounds using jumps, a variety of gestures, rising, falling, turning, and spinning movements.
	3.	Perform a sound–silence dance with a partner.
Cognitive	1.	Create a sound–silence dance.
Affective	1.	Work cooperatively with a partner to create a sound–silence dance.

Minutes (Approximately)	Scripted Movement Tasks	Cues/Things to Stress
4	**Introductory/Instant Activity**	Have instruments (both home-made and commercially bought) spread out at the edges of the room.
	1. Pick up any percussion instrument and run with it.	
	Stop.	Include enough instruments for one each. If noise level might be a problem, omit tambourines and drums and substitute home-made maracas.
	Run and jump and bang, shake, or play your instrument when you are in the air only.	
	Try not to let the instrument sound as you run in and out of everyone, and then make a big jump and a clear sound.	Allow a trade of instruments between children and repeat the activity with the new instrument.
	Repeat until quite a lot of vigorous activity has occurred.	
	Stop and put your instrument on the floor.	
	See how high you can jump. Jump quickly. Repeat this jump several times. Exchange your instrument for another.	

Minutes (Approximately)	Scripted Movement Tasks	Cues/Things to Stress
3	2. Crouch over the instrument and play very softly, trying to make a continuous sound. Stop. Then try jumping over the top. Repeat the soft, continuous playing, trying to get movement as well. A simple turning around in a crouched position or on the floor works well as a good contrast.	The teacher may also encourage rolling or changing position smoothly with no break in the sound.
4	3. **Working individually.** Show the contrast between *soft continuous sound* with some kind of appropriate movement (allow gesture of arms and legs, rising and falling, turning, slow spinning, and so on) and a *sudden, sharp, loud sound* (probably a jump or a freeze). If the noise level is high, stop, repeat the movement without the instrument, showing "sound" by the way the learner moves.	If children are young, the teacher can specify the timing (e.g., three jumps and bangs and then everyone move smoothly to a stop). If children are older, they can be encouraged to make up their own pattern and show clearly that their movements fit the sound. If the noise level is too high, teachers can include a phrase of silence. Silence becomes very significant when contrasted with percussion. To improve sensitivity, include a crescendo or decrescendo and avoid steady loud banging or shaking. Simply for a rest, the movement can be repeated while imagining the sound. Sometimes this results in improved and more sensitive movement. (Put the instrument on the floor while you practice your pattern.)
11	4. With a **partner** and only one instrument between you, create a sound–silence dance. **or** Start silently and then discover the sounds. Each partner should make a different sound while the other moves to it. Finish silently. **or** The sound wakes you up and makes you move, but then you find you don't need it anymore and your movement overcomes the sound.	This dance can be freely composed by the children, or the teacher can set limitations if children need them. For example, the order can be set. The contrast could be specified of *level* (pitch), low or high, or of moving around the room and on the spot around each other. Couples could *start apart* and *come together*, or the reverse. There could be a suggestion of *cooperation* or *conflict*. Older children could work in larger groups. Subsequent lessons could repeat similar ideas but include voice sounds or musical phrases. Both children could play the instrument, or alternate.

Minutes (Approximately)	Scripted Movement Tasks	Cues/Things to Stress
6	**Performance/Assessment Activity** 5. Would any of you like to volunteer to share your sound–silence dance? Now everyone perform your dance and sit when you are finished. Name some of the percussion instruments used and describe some of the types of movement that the sounds suggested.	Observers should watch for contrast and see whether the movement is appropriate to the kind of sound. Follow up in the classroom by creating wall charts or a personal worksheet. Depict the percussive instruments and have children write beside each instrument the types of movements for which each might be used.

LESSON 4

FIRECRACKERS

Suggested grade levels: Any elementary grade level

Lesson length: 20–30 minutes

NASPE Standards: 1, 2, 4, 5, 6

State Standards: _____

OBJECTIVES The learner will:

Psychomotor
1. Contrast explosive actions with smooth continuous movements while exploring the dramatic idea of firecrackers.
2. Perform a firecracker dance.

Cognitive
1. Create a firecracker dance.

LESSON MATERIALS

None

Minutes (Approximately)	Scripted Movement Tasks	Cues/Things to Stress
3	**Introductory/Instant Activity** 1. Run and jump. Try to zigzag across the room and jump and turn. Try as many different jumps as you can think of. Include an explosion or a bursting out action when you jump.	If the class is experienced at spacing themselves, extend this activity by asking them to "Run quickly and jump high." If not, stress running to find a space and then jumping high in the air. The teacher can specify jumps off two feet, leaps from one foot to the other, hops from one foot to the same, or making different shapes in the air (e.g., stars, curve, twist, turn).
3	2. Get on the floor in any position, and then roll or move near the floor in a smooth, slow action. Try every possible way of transferring your weight to different parts of the body with slow control. Take a small jump to land deep onto the floor. Try collapsing into the floor. Practice a landing and collapse or a roll that is smooth and safe.	Try to transfer weight ■ Gently or lightly ■ By going slower and smoother ■ By using hands to help a smooth transition. ■ By standing Emphasize a controlled, safe landing, while bending knees and hips.

Minutes (Approximately)	Scripted Movement Tasks	Cues/Things to Stress
4	3. Join together the two previous activities. Practice and repeat them until there is a clear difference in quality between the sharp, strong, explosive run and jump and the dying away into the floor. The movement can start suddenly or slowly, gathering momentum into the explosion. Do one or a series of jumps, and then either collapse or slowly die away. Now we will use these movements in a group.	Depending on the age level and the response, emphasis can be given to showing the quality with the whole body, with fingers, feet, and head included. The more delicate, lighter movement may need practice. Challenge students to extend the phrase, take longer, and show a gradual transition as well as a quick one.
10	**Group Activity** 4. **Older Children** We're going to use firecrackers as our theme today for our dance. Describe some of the firecrackers you have seen. What colors do they show? What air patterns do they make? What sounds do they make? Each group should choose one kind of firecracker and try out your ideas in movement and sound. Choose a beginning and ending position. Remember to try it out. You can always change it later. **or** **Younger Children** (up to second grade— no groups) Each of you choose one kind of firecracker and show how it might perform. Repeat the pattern and clarify it.	Divide the class into small groups containing no more than six children. Introduce the theme of firecrackers and relate movements showing explosiveness and dying away to drifting smoke and ashes. Allow an unstructured trying out of ideas in the group. Keep an eye on the general atmosphere and level of noise and response. Be quick to help those groups who need suggestions or approval. Encourage movement first and thinking or talking about it later. Sometimes stopping the whole class and directing attention to ways of beginning the phrase, different starting positions, and different shapes of the group can be helpful. An effective contrast to explore in the group might be movement on the spot and movement that travels. Depending on the maturity of the group, appropriate sounds could be allowed (e.g., hissing, popping, "whoosh" as a rocket).
3	5. Choose different starting positions and turn the whole room into a **fireworks display**. "I'm going to light the display. I hope to see firecrackers that fizzle, jump, sparkle, explode, and erupt until all the force is spent and they stop or die away and fill the room with drifting, curling smoke."	With groups, watch the initial response. If necessary, make specific suggestions— rocket, pinwheel, sparkler, Roman candle, jumping cracker, squib—and even allocate these types of fireworks to different groups as a variation/extension.
2	6. Create completely new firecrackers never before known.	

Minutes (Approximately)	Scripted Movement Tasks	Cues/Things to Stress
5	**Final Activity/ Performance/ Assessment Activity** 7. Let's do the firecracker dance/display one last time as best we can. I'm going to fill the room with drifting smoke so you can die away. The rain is going to fall and extinguish all activity. Does any group that has worked out a pattern want to show the rest of the class? Describe the actions of the new firecrackers, never before known, that you created.	Half the class can watch; the other half of the class can perform. The teacher can watch the whole class. Use a slow shake on a tambourine and drums or a hissing sound as an accompaniment. Some groups may prefer no sound accompaniment. Do not require children to show their dance if they are unwilling. The descriptions of the new firecrackers could be extended into the classroom as an art and literacy activity. Draw and write about your creation! What a variety.

LESSON 5

PATHWAYS: STRAIGHT AND CURVED

Suggested grade levels: Second through fifth grades
Lesson length: 20–30 minutes
NASPE Standards: 1, 2, 4, 5, 6
State Standards: _____

LESSON MATERIALS

Visuals of different pathways (lines on cards)

OBJECTIVES The learner will:

Psychomotor
1. Contrast straight-line pathways with circular, spiraling, or curved pathways at different levels and using different parts of the body.
2. Practice sudden, sharp, light, fast, and slow movements.
3. Perform an individual dance and a group dance.

Cognitive
1. Create a dance alone or in a group with contrasts of spirals, curves, straight lines, and circles with or without the choice of sound accompaniment.

Affective
1. Work cooperatively with a small group of peers to create a group pattern.

Minutes (Approximately)	Scripted Movement Tasks	Cues/Things to Stress
2	**Introductory/Instant Activity** 1. Run in all directions. Stop. Look at these line drawings. With your hand and arm, quickly draw a straight line anywhere around you. Next quickly draw circles—first a big one, then a small one—with your fingers and hands. Look at this spiral drawing. Draw a spiral with your arms and hands. Let it start down low and gradually spiral upward. Do the same movement using a different part of the body.	Encourage sensible use of general space while running. Praise fast stopping. Be sure all children can see the visuals of different pathways on the wall. Drawing in the air while stationary allows the teacher to see that all children understand the contrasts of straight and curved. Observe that the children use parts of the body other than just hands and arms.

Minutes (Approximately)	Scripted Movement Tasks	Cues/Things to Stress
1	**Individual Activity**	
	2. Run sometimes in straight lines and then contrast with running in circles, in spirals, and on a curved pathway. Now show what your hands can do as you travel in the room.	The teacher will observe some children using short straight lines while others use long straight lines. Encourage these differences. Comment on those children who use large versus small circles and spirals. Curved pathways can take on a variety of floor patterns. Look for different levels. Have some children quickly demonstrate their different curved pathways. Look for variety of body parts.
1	3. Choose a starting position and move your body to show a straight pathway, a curved pathway, a spiral, and a circle without traveling.	
2	4. Show slow-motion, curved moving near the floor. Go down on the floor, keep moving, and get up again. Repeat this several times.	Emphasize controlled slow motion with curves. Stress that different body parts can make the curves.
2	5. Alternate running straight with a high springy jump into the air, and then come down low to end with slow twisting. Start over.	Stress linking the straight running with the high jump into the air, followed by the low, slow twisting. Repeating these movements improves children's mastery of the short sequence and clarity of action.
2	6. Repeat step 5, but this time put an emphasis on your jump by exaggerating the sharp, sudden, quick, jagged explosiveness of the jumps.	Praise the sudden, sharp jumps you observe.
2	7. Repeat step 6, but this time think of a light movement down to the floor.	As children repeat these steps, encourage a greater variety of jumps and include all parts of the body and all directions of movement.
12	**Group Activity**	
	8. You have a choice to work in group of, say, four or six children. Work out a pattern in your group that has spirals, curves, straight lines, and circles not necessarily using unison movements.	As groups design/create their dances, remind them of the variety of their previous activity and particularly their pathways! Sounds to accompany the dance might include vocal sounds (like hissing or popping or clicking), body sounds made by jumps, claps, stamps, and so on.
	9. Now add sound effects to accompany some of the movement. Have a clear beginning and a clear finish to your dance.	
6	**Assessment Activity**	
	10. Let's see some of the group dances you created today. Let's finish by filling the room with curving floor patterns. Slow down until you are stationary.	After each group demonstration, ask children questions about what made the dances interesting to watch, which qualities of movement were used by the group, how shapes were created, how the members of the group related to one another, and so on.

AN AQUARIUM

Suggested grade levels: Third through sixth grades

Lesson length: 20–30 minutes

NASPE Standards: 1, 2, 4, 6

State Standards: _____

LESSON MATERIALS

Music: "The Aquarium" (by Saint-Saens from "The Carnival of the Animals")

TEACHER PREPARATION

- Listen to the music selection several times so that you are familiar with it.
- Use short pieces at the beginning of the selection. Include the "ripple" (high to low part).

	OBJECTIVES	The learner will:
Psychomotor	1.	Demonstrate smooth, continuous actions at different speeds, with turns, at different levels and along different pathways.
	2.	Use different parts of the body to show ripples, bubbles, swirls, and calm movements.
	3.	Show movements of creatures found on the ocean floor, either real or imaginary.
Cognitive	1.	Create a dance of movements in an aquarium either alone or with a partner to "The Aquarium" music by Saint-Saens.
	2.	Match the movement to the music.
Affective	1.	Work cooperatively either with a partner or a whole group to create the aquarium dance.

Minutes (Approximately)	Scripted Movement Tasks	Cues/Things to Stress
5	**Introductory Activity**	Emphasize:
	1. Children enter the activity area and are asked to cover all the space, moving in and around others without touching. Now vary the height of where your body goes, low near the floor, then medium level, and sometimes high if you jump. Stop. Add a turn or a curved pathway. Keep changing the height. Stop. Make all that you do part of a smooth, liquid, continuous action. Vary the speed. Show by the way you move what a wave, a ripple, a bubble, a swirl, a strong current, or a calm patch might look like. (Keep this going until at least some children get breathless.) Repeat.	■ Spreading out to use the whole room space ■ Smoothness as children travel with changes of speed ■ Change of level/height ■ Turns and curving pathways ■ Waves, ripples, bubbles, swirls, strong movements, and calm movements Emphasize continuous participation to ensure children get some cardiovascular benefits.

Minutes (Approximately)	Scripted Movement Tasks	Cues/Things to Stress
5	2. Find a space on the floor where no one can touch you and curl up. When I say, "Begin," start to stretch out your arms, legs, neck, toes, and fingers. Try stretching one part, more than one part, or all of you at different speeds to the music. Begin. Stop.	The teacher should observe, encourage, and move around the group. While this happens, the teacher lets a short piece of the music begin. Watch what happens, and sometimes suggest variations. Encourage and make comments such as, "I saw someone move sideways like a crab" or "There are some pretty weird creatures here with all kinds of horns and feelers."
	Imagine you are some kind of creature on the ocean floor. You might like to "wake up" more quickly and begin to move across the floor. Perhaps you get frightened or see danger and curl up quickly. You might find the water, or maybe a wave makes you move and carries you or part of you. Begin. Stop. You might want to hide from some of the other "creatures."	
	We'll do that again, but this time listen for a ripple or a change in the music. The first part sets the scene—all liquid in our aquarium—but there is also a "ripple" where the music starts high and goes low and then goes back to the beginning. Show that "ripple" when you move. Stop. Sit. Repeat. The first time, warn the children when the "ripple" is coming. Later, just watch.	
3	3. You can choose which part of the aquarium to be. Perhaps you want to be the water itself; you can show how the water moves. Perhaps you want to be a "creature." You might like to think of something else you would see in an aquarium—bubbles or weeds or grains of sand. Think about it and choose a starting position to show what you are going to be. Ready?	Allow some time for children to think about the way the water moves, creatures in the water, bubbles, and so on. Stress that children should find a starting position and that they should hold it still. Remind children to move when the music begins. Approve of ideas and variety. "Do it again the same way. Repeat."
	The music begins and children move. The teacher may say, "Here comes the ripple!" just before the appropriate piece of music. Stop. Sometimes don't warn about the "ripple" and see if children can recognize it.	

Minutes (Approximately)	Scripted Movement Tasks	Cues/Things to Stress
6	4. If children are older, suggest they might like to combine with someone and together show their idea; otherwise, they can continue on their own. Allow some rehearsal and planning (without music). Younger children or beginners can simply be asked to choose a starting position, move when the music begins, show a way to let it all "die away" at the end, and hold the finishing position. Observe. Repeat with a few suggestions of how to "improve" and make the dance clearer or allow "any way of moving to show an aquarium." The whole room is filled from ceiling to floor and all the corners. "This will be the last time."	Repetition can be done individually with the children taking their own time. Suggest ways to improve their work or to make the movements clearer. Stress/remind children that they are finding ways of moving to show an aquarium. Repetition will improve the quality. Allow time for that repetition. Doing movements the "last time" gives children an opportunity to do it "really well" and provides a sense of climax.
3	**Final Activity/Assessment/Reflection** 5. Good. Hold your last position and imagine the water evaporating or drying out in the sun, draining the tank. Slowly move to the floor and flatten yourself. Make your body quite limp—it isn't there anymore. **Assessment** Make some sort of identification of the music. Older children can state the title and composer of the music used. Link what has happened to "an aquarium."	Finishing positions will be different. Encourage these differences. Help children experience the limpness and stillness. Do not spend too much time on this point. Suggest future observation of an aquarium. Some children may have an aquarium, or they may have seen one in a pet shop or another place. Link this activity with a future art lesson.

Additional Material

1. Plan a lesson where water moves in nature. Think about rain, a cloudburst, or hail (hail forms when water goes up and down in the atmosphere, freezes, grows, thaws, and refreezes—it is strong but melts). Other types of water may include rivers (a trickling stream or raging torrent), tsunamis, waterfalls, rapids, calm meandering of a large river near the sea, and so on.

2. Plan another lesson where water and machines move (e.g., washing machines, showers, toilets, pumps).

3. Plan a similar lesson where water is used in "sprinklers." There are all kinds of sprinklers. Think how they make water move. Create a group sprinkler.

4. Plan a lesson around the theme of household appliances. Use groups, and encourage students to move in "jerky" and "smooth" ways.

Creative Folk, Square, and Social Dance

An easy way to approach some kind of free dance for children who are used to structured responses is to parallel lessons in folk, square, or social dancing. Many schools already have recordings of suitable music. The teacher needs to select a musical piece ahead of time. The music should have a clear rhythm of moderate speed; good choices include polka and square dance tunes, which have two phrases. A clear change from part A to part B will be helpful.

LESSON 1

FOLK, SQUARE, AND SOCIAL DANCE INVENTIONS

Suggested grade levels: Third through sixth grades

Lesson length: 30 minutes

NASPE Standards: 1, 2, 4, 5, 6

State Standards: _____

LESSON MATERIALS

Folk/square dance music with regular, rhythmic beat

OBJECTIVES The learner will:

Psychomotor
1. Perform different stepping patterns, in different directions and at different speeds, to music.
2. Experiment with different body positions/relationships and traveling around a partner.

Cognitive
1. Create a part A/part B step dance to folk dance or square dance music.

Affective
1. Work cooperatively with a partner to perform a dance.

Minutes (Approximately)	Scripted Movement Tasks	Cues/Things to Stress
4	**Introductory Activity** 1. Dance freely anywhere in the room to the music. Try to change direction and move forward, backward, and sideways. Try to vary your speed, and take whole steps, half-steps, and two-beat slow steps. Alternate patterns of timing: 2 steps per beat, 3 steps per beat, or 4 steps per beat.	If the class is mature, suggest syncopated steps as well.
3	**Individual Activity** 2. Repeat free dancing but try to make variations of steps *on the spot*. Try heel clicks, stamps, knee bends, jumps, turns, heel–toe patterns, hop steps, pas-de-bas, grapevine, and so on.	Encourage a real variety of every known and unknown step.

5	**Partner Activity**	
	3. Repeat the variety of steps with a partner. Copy some of the partner's steps. Experiment with different ways of holding your partner: waist, shoulder, hands crossed, straight, one hand, elbows bent, ballroom hold. Try facing, back-to-back, sideways facing, and sideways side-by-side. Try different ways of traveling and going around your partner. Try to vary the levels.	Allow dancing with a partner using no touching.
16	4. Listen to phrase A-B in the music. Decide on a starting position and make up a dance where part A is on the spot and part B is traveling (or the reverse or allow choice). Repeat and polish the dance. (One of the pair will travel while the other will stay on the spot, then roles will be reversed.) Listen to this folk dance music. In pairs, invent a dance where you begin alone, meet a partner, and then travel together.	Listening is an important part of the activity. Children should be still during that time so that they can focus just on the music and its beat and speed. This is how they become familiar with the music for their dance. Emphasize the two parts: stationary and traveling. For some students, a small amount of structure might be helpful.
2	**Final Activity** 5. Let's dance freely to this different tune. **or** With a partner, copy one type of dance step from your peer and repeat it.	

LESSON 2

USING MUSIC AND VARIED SMALL APPARATUS

Suggested grade levels: Third through sixth grades

Lesson length: Approximately 30 minutes

NASPE Standards: 1, 2, 5, 6

State Standards: _____

LESSON MATERIALS

Balls, beanbags, small hoops, ropes, rhythm sticks, scarves, streamers, CD/DVD player; music—lively music with a pronounced rhythm

OBJECTIVES The learner will:

Psychomotor 1. Demonstrate moving selected pieces of small apparatus rhythmically at both low and high levels.

2. Perform three different ways of traveling with the equipment and repeat the sequence accurately to the music.

Cognitive 1. Create different movements in time with the music in both "slow time" and "double time."

Affective 1. Work cooperatively with a partner.

Minutes (Approximately)	Scripted Movement Activities	Cues/Things to Stress
1	**Introductory/Instant Activity**	
	1. Use a part of the lively music. Move to the music in your own space showing the rhythm of the music.	Check for keeping a rhythm.
1	2. Move in general space, combining running, jumps, turns, and skipping. Change directions.	
1	**Individual Skill Activities**	
	3. Select a piece of equipment (e.g., ball, beanbags, rhythm sticks, streamers, scarves). Move your equipment in time with the music. Move your body as well as the equipment.	Encourage a variety of movement and good control of the equipment. This could be varied, with some part of the movement done with equipment and another part done without equipment.
1	4. Try different activities with the equipment. Try activities in "double time" and in "slow time."	
1	5. Change equipment with someone else. Try new activities.	
1	6. Alternate two activities to fit the rhythm	
1	7. Can you move and keep the equipment moving?	Encourage children to keep a rhythm.
1	8. Can you start at a low level, such as sitting, with the equipment moving up to high level and then down again slowly?	
3	**Partner/Group Activity**	
	9. Find three ways to use the equipment with this task. Share your ideas with a partner when you have yours completed.	Observe and listen to the ideas being shared. Occasionally comment on interesting ideas that emerge with the small equipment.
3	10. Change your equipment with another person. Repeat the previous challenges.	Try to suggest challenges that lead to more skillful activity such as rising and falling, traveling, and changing direction with no break.
2	11. Keep the equipment moving while you are traveling. Develop a sequence and repeat it.	Challenge the children to add speed and level changes.
3	12. Devise three different ways to keep the apparatus moving while you are traveling. Do the first way, then the second way, and finally the third way; then repeat the sequence over again. Be as accurate as possible.	Comment on accuracy of sequences invented.

Minutes (Approximately)	Scripted Movement Activities	Cues/Things to Stress
4	**Conclusion/Assessment/Reflection Activity**	
	13. Show the sequences. Observe half the class first, then change to observe the other half of the class. Discuss originality in the sequences or what caught your attention. Did you see any surprises during someone's pattern—such as an unexpected change of pace, rhythm, or level?	Observe to see that the movements change to fit the rhythm. Commend accuracy when repeating the sequence of three parts.

LESSON 3

A LINE DANCE USING MUSIC AND VARIED SMALL APPARATUS

Suggested grade levels: Fourth through sixth grades

Lesson length: Approximately 30 minutes

NASPE Standards: 1, 2, 5, 6

State Standards: _____

LESSON MATERIALS

Balls, beanbags, small hoops, ropes, scarves, streamers, CD player, lively music with a pronounced rhythm

OBJECTIVES The learner will:

Psychomotor	1. Perform a sequence of movements in a circle, using small equipment.
	2. Perform a line dance in a group.
Cognitive	1. Create a movement sequence using a circular formation.
	2. Design a group line dance to music.
Affective	1. Work cooperatively with a partner and in a group to create sequences of movement to music, using varied small apparatus.

Minutes (Approximately)	Scripted Movement Tasks	Cues/Things to Stress
1	**Introductory Activity**	
	1. Skip or hop around the room and find a partner in the process.	Ensure that the dividing of the class into partners is done quickly.
3	**Partner Activity**	
	2. Partners: Select one or two pieces of equipment. Find four activities to do with the equipment and keep time with the music while moving around the room.	Encourage movement around the room keeping time to the music.

Minutes (Approximately)	Scripted Movement Tasks	Cues/Things to Stress
8	**Group Activity**	
	3. Divide into groups of three to six people. The group decides on what equipment to use and designates a student to go and collect it. Choose from ropes, balls, hoops, beanbags, or scarves/streamers. Create an activity where all of the group members are moving and doing the *same* thing with the equipment *in a circle*. Complete the movement with each person making up their own activity to fit the music. Practice and refine the sequence.	Supervise the collection of props. Stress that movement should be in a circle. Most children will not need directions, but if they can't agree, the teacher can help. Consider different ways of making the circle move.
10	4. Keep the same groups. Start an activity with everyone *in a line*. Invent a line dance. How can you vary the line? A line can move! Listen and move to the music.	Stress that a line formation is to be used rather than a circle. Consider these suggestions: Move backward or forward or sideways, or up or down. Consider marking a change of direction with a clap or a stomp.
8	**Conclusion/Assessment/Reflection Activity**	
	5. Show a "line or circle dance" that groups felt that they did best.	Use volunteers, or have half of the class watch the other half of the class. Comment on other ideas and skills that could be included in the dance to make it more interesting (i.e., jumps, turns, change of direction).
	6. Everyone dance around the room individually showing one idea you saw and liked.	

There is no substitute for sensitive observation in teaching dance. A teacher must also remember that mood is very important and can be largely created by the teacher. If children are completely inexperienced in dance, try repeating several lessons with perhaps one variation. In the early stages, be fairly free with approval and try to give the impression that the teacher, at least, is enjoying the activity. There should be a balance between freedom and choice for the children and incorporating the teacher's suggestions. It is important that if the children show signs of creativity, it should be encouraged and allowed to develop.

Teaching Specific Dances

Even if a specific folk, square, or social dance is taught in the elementary school, it will still probably be most helpful for children to *dance freely* to the music at the beginning of the lesson as an introductory activity. Very young children are not ready to learn specific dances. A lesson sequence might be structured as follows:

- Dance freely to the music. Children can include some of the correct steps as they dance, copied from either the teacher or anyone who happens to be doing those steps.

- Make an attempt to link the steps with the correct music.

- While they are still dancing freely, allow children to do the steps to the music as it occurs and dance with a partner if this is part of the dance.

- Last, deal with formation (walk it through to the music if necessary). Above all, *dance*. Too frequently teachers are in a hurry to teach, only to go on to a new dance as soon as one is learned.

- Spend time refining and polishing a dance so that it can be performed really well.

Teachers need not feel guilty about using traditional music for creative folk dancing. Frequently the traditional dances are no longer authentic but have been lovingly preserved by Physical Education teachers. Many were invented especially for Physical Education lessons.

Teachers should not assume that boys would not enjoy traditional dancing. In many schools, children come from cultural backgrounds where dancing is regarded as a male prerogative and is still actively pursued.

Music for Creative Dance

- Bartok: *Mikrokosmos*, 6 volumes for piano. A true musical microcosmos, from the child-like simple to the sublime—a tremendous variety of rhythms, moods, and contrasts.

- Britten: *A Young Person's Guide to the Orchestra*. Short variations, based on a single effect of great variety and contrasting moods.

- Grofe: *Grand Canyon Suite* (includes *Cloudburst*).

- Khatchaturian: *Gayne Suite* (Boston Pops) excerpts.

- Kodaly: Children's dances: *Harry Janos Suite*, excerpts.

- Lully: Marches, fanfares.

- Milhaud: *Le Boeuf sur le toit; Scaramouche Suite*.

- Mussorgsky: *Pictures at an Exhibition*. Some very powerful pieces to generate creative movement.

- Orff: *Music for Children*—a must!

- Prokofiev: *Grand March* from *Peter and the Wolf*; Suite from *Love of the Three Oranges; Scythian Suite*—powerful, barbarian, evocative!

- Peart: A modern Danish composer. Atmosphere music.

- Saint-Saens: *Carnival of the Animals*. Excellent contrasts and mood music; an underwater dance to the aquarium (include the "ripple").

- Shostakovich: *Symphony #1, Scherzo, #10 Scherzo*.

- In a short piece, a maximum of change in pace, mood texture. Shostakovich: *Age of Gold: Polka*.

- Stravinsky: *Danses Conertantes;* Dumbarton Oaks, Concerto in D for Strings; *L' Histoire du soldat*, Suite.

- Copland: *Rodeo—Billy the Kid:* Celebration dance.

- Weinberger: *Schwanda the Bagpiper* polka.

- Smetana: *Golliwog's Cakewalk*.

These suggestions are in addition to obviously suitable music like ballet music, Spanish guitar music, and music written to dance rhythms (e.g., Prokofiev's *Waltzes*, Suite 110). Sometimes early music, recorders, and medieval instruments with percussion are very exciting for children. Modern electronic music also produces good results. Popular rhythms of jazz, calypso, and rock music can also be used.

Film soundtracks (e.g., *Lawrence of Arabia, West Side Story, The Titanic, Harry Potter* films, *Lord of the Rings*) often include good music and have lots of atmosphere.

Even the inept and beginner can sometimes produce good sound on the piano by using the contrasting efforts of the theme.

Ask the children to listen and bring good moving music to school.

Sources for Creative Dance Material

Excellent material for creative dance can be found in the following publications:

Boucher, A. (1988). Early childhood physical education. *Journal of Physical Education, Recreation and Dance, 59(7)*, 42–72.

Boucher, A. (1994). Dance: Its interdisciplinary potential in the elementary school. In *ECHOES II*, Reston, VA: American Alliance of Health, Physical Education, Recreation and Dance.

Joyce, M. (1993). *First steps in teaching creative dance to children* (3rd ed.). McGraw-Hill Humanities/Social Sciences/Languages.

Overby, L., Post, B., & Newman, D. (2005). *Interdisciplinary learning through Dance 101 MOVEntures*. Champaign, IL: Human Kinetics.

Purcell-Cone, T., & Cone, S. (2005). *Teaching children dance* (2nd ed.). Champaign, IL: Human Kinetics.

Purcell, T. (2001). *Becoming a master teacher in dance*. Champaign, IL: Human Kinetics.

Russell, J. (1965). *Creative dance in the primary school*. London: MacDonald & Evans.

Stinson, S. (1990). *Dance for young children: Finding the magic in movement*. Reston, VA: AAHPERD.

Wiseman, E. (1978). Process not product: Guidelines for adding creative dance to the elementary school curriculum. *Journal of Physical Education and Recreation, 50(9)*, 50–52.

Many physical education and education journals and Web sites also contain creative dance and expressive movement material.

Discovering Educational Gymnastics

10

QUESTIONS TO DISCUSS

1. Do you feel comfortable with the appearance and present capacity of your body? Discuss this issue with your partner and describe any changes you would wish to make.

2. Recall any experience you may have had with family or friends admiring the appearance or physical capacity of others. (Beauty contests? Bodybuilding competitions? Acrobats?) Discuss any comments particularly relating to children or yourself as a child.

3. Much art or sculpture depicts the human body naked or in action. Do you admire some physiques more than others? Discuss any "memorable" comments made about particular strength or fat or flexibility in others.

4. Did you climb as a child? (Perhaps ask your parents?) Discuss the use of trees, fences, railings, gates, walls, ladders, counters, bars, rocks, ropes, or any favorite climbing place based on your observation of children and the experience of your partner.

5. Did you (or your partner or any of the children you observed) try to stand on your head or your hands, or do back-bends, "splits," walkovers, cartwheels, and so on? Did you ever practice hard to master gymnastic skills? Discuss your own and your partner's experience of any gymnastics class or "display" you encountered as a child.

6. Have you experienced or seen others use special gymnastic apparatus (e.g., bars, rings, trampoline, vaulting horse or box, trapeze, or swings)? Discuss this issue with your partner.

7. Can you explain how you became as strong or as flexible as you are? Share information with your partner.

8. Recall and describe any fear or discomfort with activities like rolling, using the hands alone to support the body weight, hanging from a height, and sliding and agility activities such as hand springs, back springs, and going head over heels. Did you or your partner ever have or observe an accident in gymnastic activity?

9. Describe any previous program that you experienced that was called "Gymnastics." Can you remember watching any performance or display called "gymnastics"? (Include group activities and any repeated activity to music called "gymnastics.")

10. Other countries or cultures use "gymnastics." Share with your partner anything similar you have seen or watched. Would you apply the word "gymnastics" to any cheerleading routines? Circus acts?

11. Have you ever participated in or observed a "fitness center" (often called a gym)? In these locations, physical fitness is sought by using machines (e.g., stair-master, treadmill, rowing machine). Discuss what you consider to be the benefits and inadequacies of such centers with your partner and comment on the educational value of participation. Consider what may be motivating the participants.

The word "gymnastics" is often used to refer to systems of exercise designed to produce specific effects on the human body; historically they were used to counteract the effects of sedentary living. These systems have also been called "drills" and "calisthenics." Usually large groups of people performed the same exercises in unison—the same amount for all.

"Gymnastics," as used in this chapter, refers to individual activity that uses the human body as a piece of apparatus—with learners exploring its capabilities, discovering its versatility, increasing awareness, and developing potential. Previous chapters have emphasized the ways in which physical objectives such as strength and flexibility can be achieved (Chapter 2) and the demands that a wide variety of gross motor movement can place on the developing sensory, neurological, kinesthetic, proprioceptive, and vestibular organization of the brain (Chapter 3).

Some people believe that, given a body, there is a moral imperative to use it to achieve its greatest well-being, health, and potential for skills. Interesting scientific material (albeit outside the scope of this text) suggests the growth process may include critical periods that favor specific physical development. Benefits will be longer last-

ing if enjoyment of gymnastics is acquired during childhood. Certainly one can observe the excitement and pleasure children show when discovering ways to manage their bodies as they bend, stretch, curl, roll, rotate, twist, bounce, swing, balance, climb, hang, and turn upside down. "Look at me . . . I can . . . " Activities involving diagonal movements across the mid-line of the body, lateral and cross-lateral movement, taking the weight on different parts of the body, and hanging from a bar high enough to allow the body to swing (from knees, arms, or hands only) all extend the range of sensory input and neurological stimulation beyond the everyday. Gross motor activity precedes finer neurological organization.

Streicher (see Appendix 1, Additional Historical Roots) called gymnastics "games with gravity." Indeed, the application of Newtonian physics is experienced by the body as it rotates, swings, slides, spins, pulls, pushes, and invents the "new" and the "different."

All of these kinds of activities simply require a body, space, and a floor. (Padded gym mats will encourage many children to join in.) If one adds walls, climbing ropes, bars, benches, balance beams, ladders, trestles, slides, trapezes, rope ladders, cargo nets, vertical poles, boxes, platforms, and heavy objects for pulling or pushing (e.g., a heavy ball), then there is a basis for needed strenuous activity and the development of gymnastic skills.

Assignment 10–1

Observe children of various ages playing on and around climbing equipment at a community playground. Try to observe a play space that has bars, ladders, slides, and ropes of all kinds, where the children can hang, climb, swing, slide, invert, and go up high. Record the types of equipment and describe how the children use this equipment.

Anecdote 10–1

Keith, a second-grade student, was in danger of failing his year and having to repeat grade 2 because of poor written work and manual dexterity. His classroom teacher reported that his handwriting was atrocious. In a week of Movement Discovery body management activities in the gym, Keith used his shoulders and arms to support his body weight and climbed on large apparatus. His improvement in classroom work was so dramatic that he passed his year (demonstrating proximodistal neurological development).

The term "gymnastics" is also used to refer to competitive gymnastics, like those seen in the Olympic Games and rhythmic gymnastics (see Appendix 1, Additional Historical Roots). Should individuals wish to acquire skills in these areas, the content material in this chapter should help them develop confidence and will be good experience for developing such specific skills later. If one begins to include large apparatus as mentioned previously, however, some very important safety and educational factors must be considered; theses issues were addressed in Chapters 4 and 5.

As a preparation for learning the content of this chapter, it will be essential that you observe children climbing, hanging, swinging, jumping, and sliding. An understanding of the way children naturally behave and move provides teachers with a sound foundation for the development of the Physical Education curriculum in body management. In your journal of observations of children, you will have noted incidents where you saw children climbing trees and using gates, bars, ditches, fences, a slope (both up and down), and other "invented" obstacles consisting of everyday objects used to challenge body management. (A kitchen counter? A drinking fountain? An adult's body?)

In a school situation, these opportunities will inevitably be diminished. Nevertheless, there is still space, a floor, walls, and perhaps a platform or stage. Some schools may have large apparatus such as climbing equipment (e.g., Whittle equipment) available. Explore the Web site for Gerstung's Children's Movement & Fitness Equipment. Gerstung Intersport (Baltimore, Maryland) is a major U.S. supplier of quality, versatile climbing, hanging, sliding, and swinging equipment suitable for young children. Siegfried Gerstung has been in the Movement Education equipment business for more 40 years. Gerstung manufac-

tures GymThing and other equipment similar to the Whittle equipment, which originated in the United Kingdom.

Wedges, foam rolls, foam shapes, tunnels, bridges, large building blocks, big balls, push/pull toys, low slides, trestles, planks, sliding boards with hooks, rings, trapezes and ropes, bars of different heights and combinations, ladders, benches, beams, mats, curved bridges, low gymnastic stools, and boxes can all be used in different combinations for a variety of learning centers. Some can be set up very easily in the early childhood classroom for daily use by prekindergarten-age children. Allow children time to explore and discover what they can do at the learning centers by using such phrases as "Show me what interesting things you can do." "Try lots of different things with your body." "Do two different things on the apparatus." Simple large apparatus can be built or improvised (a bench, a balance beam, a padded box, an inclined surface, a padded floor mat, climbing ropes, a vertical pole).

All schools can easily acquire a plentiful supply of small equipment. (See the section in Chapter 12 on improvising and adapting apparatus/equipment.) This kind of equipment can also stimulate gymnastic activity, and its use can extend each child's vocabulary of movement or physical literacy at all levels.

Children have been observed "walking" on the shoulders, forearms, and knees; with a rocking movement on the tummy and back; rolling; and using a sequence of body parts. One can turn in a circle or change between two-sided and one-sided uses of the body. Sometimes children use both hands and feet. Take time to think and discuss the process of "walking" with your partner.

One child with a disability, who could not walk normally, "walked" across the floor using elbows and a wriggle from his very long body. Later he added a push from the inside of his knees. When he could support some of his

With your partner as a teacher (to observe, record, comment, encourage, and challenge), walk. Just take a few steps. Is this gymnastics? Can you find a different way to walk? Walk on one leg. (Partner/ teacher: Do not accept a hop—walking involves continuous contact with the floor.) Is this activity body management? Is it boring? Challenging? On one foot, evert or turn the foot sideways and take the weight on the ball of the foot. Move the heel in the same direction. Take the weight on the heel and move the ball of the foot in the same direction; now repeat. You will be "walking" on one foot. Vary the speed of your action. Both of you record your reactions. Switch partners and repeat.

Vary how this activity is done. Change the speed of the action. Try bigger "steps." Notice how both of these variables change the demands made on your body. Switch partners. Change the shape of your body over the weight-bearing foot. What makes it harder or easier to control? Try a crouch position. The feet contain both small joints and muscles. How are they challenged? Have you been using the same foot for this activity? If so, change feet and record your reactions. Are you improving your skill on one leg?

Think what you have discovered. Think of the different physical demands made on your sensory coordination and brain.

Switch partners and try to discover another way of "walking" using another part of the body. (For example, sit on the floor and "hip walk.") Try the same variations with this body part. Are there more directions possible than with the feet? Hip walk, while leaving the leg on the floor; then try it with legs held in the air. Notice the different demands on the body.

body weight using his hands, he did a double push and a hip movement on the floor to go forward. No one thought to challenge his efforts. Could he have traveled backward and sideways? "Find another way" is a phrase you will find very useful to extend learning experiences for children.

As you use the content material that follows in this chapter, remember the process in Assignment 10–2. It takes time to think through all the implications of a challenge. "Walk on one leg" was the original challenge; perhaps it was rejected as stupid. Many people will have said, "I can't." We have two legs for walking, not one—and yet the task led to a great variety of responses using the whole body and possibly extending the range of motion in some small joints and strengthening less used muscle groups.

Progression

LEVEL 1: YOUNGEST CHILDREN

Exploration

When the focus is on body management, the first level tries to extend the existing use of the human body. Young children enjoy moving the body as a whole but can also focus on different parts of the body, different ways of using the space, and apparatus and actions that are commonly used in gymnastics (balancing, rolling, turning, twisting, swinging, inverting the body, and getting weight onto the hands/arms).

It is most important that young children be allowed early experimentation with taking their body weight on arms and hands and in finding different ways of being upside-down. Inversion and the demands that taking weight on the hands place on children need time to develop and should be included at the earliest opportunity. Just "pushing" the walls or the floor is a basic action to develop gymnastic skill and can be tried in many different positions using different parts of the body. Many children will have "crawled" as infants and even climbed and pulled themselves up or along furniture. This experience needs to be extended and the children's capacity increased.

Working at Level 1 for the youngest children is also important in any new environment. For example, even if children are considerably older, the first time they are asked to use climbing equipment, they should be allowed time for exploration. Faced with a totally new challenge to body management, an individual needs to focus on the equipment, the "external" factor. Children need to have plenty of unhurried time to explore and relate and discover their existing capacity in the new situation.

Repetition

Children need adequate time in the exploration stage to produce confidence and self-awareness, and for these learnings to become established. Repetition is essential, not boring. Both brain and body need repeated stimulation. Confidence and familiarity require repetition. The performers will move on when they are ready. Teachers need to *observe* (and record if necessary).

Extensions

After young children have gained confidence and experience from exploration and repetition, they are ready to extend their capacity and experience. This is where a teacher proves invaluable. Teachers can challenge even young children to try new ideas and to become more aware of themselves, of others, and of the "physics" of movement. Figure 10–1 shows "Content Material" to be added to the children's (and teachers!) own ideas. They should provide plenty of material for many lessons.

Gymnastics provides the kind of activity that should overload the various muscle groups in the body and extend the range of movement possible at joint complexes. Gymnastics can teach children how to manage themselves and their bodies in many forms of traveling in space and to be aware of others. Body control can lead to self-management at all times and in different situations—a valuable life skill. Apparatus should be used as part of the work of extension. Large apparatus extends experience dramatically, but even small equipment can be useful for similar purposes.

In summary, Level 1 includes a process of exploration, repetition, and extension on an individual basis. These processes are used in an attempt to focus on the content of space, including the floor, walls, and different pathways; levels; traveling; and jumping. In addition, many activities focus on the body itself and its capabilities. All attempts are made to extend and increase those capacities, again on an individual basis. Apparatus is used, both large and small. Various management and "gymnastic" type actions are suggested and children allowed to develop skill and confidence in their performance. Individuals in a group setting can also learn responsible self-management and awareness and care for others. Controlled and versatile self-management is the basis of safety in physical activity.

Some young children may start to link different movements together, and this practice should be allowed. Such children are moving into Level 2.

LEVEL 2: MORE EXPERIENCED CHILDREN (GRADES 2 THROUGH 4)

Level 1 allows a great deal of exploration on an individual basis. It should be used whenever large apparatus is used for the first time, regardless of the children's age. Most children will develop confidence, versatility, and body awareness, as well as good body management, when exposed to a wide range of activities.

Even the youngest children can support their body weight on their arms and hands, and all enjoy turning upside down. If large apparatus has been used, the children will have developed strength and flexibility, and possibly cardiovascular endurance if lessons have been strenuous enough.

In Level 2, children progress so that they can cooperate with one another or even just work alongside another person. This can stimulate great interest and extend the range of material that children will invent.

Extension of Phrases and Sequences

It is possible for a more mature child to sustain longer movement phrases and to combine different kinds of movement. A teacher can use the same ideas and content material as before, but should expect to see different responses combining different content material into a pattern. Longer sequences of movement are a feature of Level 2 work. The following pages suggest many ways of extending phrases and sequences.

Limitations

Level 2 is characterized by a more proactive approach to skills. Even the youngest children respond to a stimulus, but with experience comes more deliberate, intentional activity. Children will have become aware of a much bigger range of possibilities, so there are many opportunities to combine and recombine different material in a satisfying way.

Experienced children enjoy the challenge of limitations and requirements that force them to select and choose only some responses. These constraints should not be too specific, but rather should allow a variety of responses. Children can observe and assess one another to see that tasks and limitations are fulfilled. Responding to limitations suggested either by a teacher, another child, or themselves requires discipline and is an integral part of the problem-solving process.

Working with Another Person

It can be very satisfying to work together with another person to devise a sequence or pattern. There will be much repetition without realizing it as the partners share, rearrange, practice, and perfect their routine. But this kind of repetition does *not* mean that some children make others copy their skills. Unity does not mean uniformity; a pleasing "whole" does not have to have identical components. Unison can mean two people moving at the same time but not necessarily doing the same thing. In fact, contrasts, opposites, alternating speeds or shapes, and relationships within the phrase can be very pleasing. Both children do not have to use apparatus at the same time, if at all. Similar or related movements can be included, using different situations or even different parts of the body. The overall principle of Movement Discovery is a child working at his or her own level—and it must not be compromised. Children can learn inclusion and tolerance of differences at an early age. Children must not feel that they have to attempt something they do not wish to do simply because they work with a partner. At the same time, it is also true that working with another person can sometimes stimulate a child to try something new.

If large apparatus is available, the children themselves should be allowed to plan simple arrangements and variations of the setup. The addition of a mat to a particular piece of equipment, for example, will suggest all kinds of additions before or after an activity on the equipment.

It is also possible to use another person as a piece of apparatus—perhaps for support, as a counterbalance, to assist flight, or to add extensions to a phrase. In fact, if no large apparatus is available, another body can offer resistance or an increased challenge to strength and control. Care will be needed to ensure good matching of partners for size, weight, strength, and skill. Some classroom teachers may feel that the hazards of such activities are beyond their level of expertise. Historically, many partner activities were strenuous and fun and will exist where a "gymnastics" curriculum includes "stunts" and "tumbling." It is suggested here that if competent children include them, such activities should be allowed. If older children attempt them, they can be allowed with sensible and well-behaved classes but should never be required or imposed by a teacher.

When working with a partner, it is possible to show a *contrast*, moving in opposite ways (opposite directions when traveling, starting close and ending far apart, and starting far apart and meeting). Include opposites with levels and body shapes; move with contrasting speeds or continuous and stopping. Start at opposite ends of the apparatus and pass in the middle. The *relationship* to a partner may include facing, back-to-back, or side-by-side positions. A partner can be used as *apparatus*—that is, as a piece of equipment to get through, over, or around. Because the human "apparatus" can also move, this creates many possible ways to contrast or combine different actions to form a sequence. These actions do not require contact between partners. Working alongside a partner can be allowed for children who are not yet ready to relate to another person.

Older children can be required to "polish" their work and try to do it as well as possible. A "stretch" in a sequence should be to the limits, transitions between actions should be smooth and controlled, some "quick" actions can be made more precise, and so on. Children enjoy "practicing" and trying to improve to the best of their ability, and a teacher can expect responses to body management challenges to look more like "gymnastics."

The level of difficulty can rise for all children during such activities; the process of improving variety, versatility, accuracy, control, and "good form" is a key part of gymnastics. Some children may already participate in gymnastic classes or clubs outside of school hours, and many children use trampolines and swinging apparatus at home. Movement Discovery allows those children to include their skills as a response to the many challenges and tasks a teacher gives. Nevertheless, it is important that highly skilled children do not dominate the activity and that less skilled children also receive approval and praise when they respond to limitations and suggestions at a simpler level.

LEVEL 3: EXPERIENCED CHILDREN (GRADES 5–6)

Gymnastics in later life is not widely practiced among the general population. It is developed more by an elite who link their activity with competition. The public is often mesmerized by gymnastic performance during the Olympic Games but rarely sees it at other times. There is a wider participation in simpler group gymnastics movement in some forms of recreation, but few men participate in this kind of activity (see Appendix 1, Additional Historical Roots).

The use of large apparatus provides for strengthening and improving flexibility in ways that few other sports do. If these benefits are to accrue, then schools will be faced with making the necessary expenditures on suitable apparatus.

Perhaps in the future teachers using a Movement Discovery approach can devise new apparatus areas. Apparatus must be strong but need not be expensive.

Level of Difficulty

Older and experienced children will wish to combine more difficult actions, use the apparatus in more complicated ways, and probably develop longer sequences. Children should never be required to work on large apparatus if they are unwilling, but suitable alternatives can nevertheless challenge them and provide for the development of skill, strength, and flexibility. It is very enjoyable to move continuously from one skill to another, and the presence of large apparatus greatly increases the variety of options available. Even without large apparatus, teachers can impose limitations that allow individual choice of activity at the student's own level.

Level 3 does expect that students will develop sequences that have a definite beginning, middle or main focus, and an ending. Sometimes, for fun, students will mimic the triumphant arms up and "stationary" posture of Olympic gymnasts.

1. *The approach.* This may consist of a movement on the floor and a "take-off." Specifications can be made regarding the angle or direction of the approach, perhaps based on the floor pattern or in relation to the body. ("Sideways," for example, can mean from the side of the apparatus or with the body sideways to the apparatus.) Challenges can limit the speed or number of steps; specify using certain parts of the body or certain actions such as rolling. Very often actions on the floor can be used when the body is partly supported on the equipment.

2. *The mount (getting on the apparatus).* This assumes that the performer will land on the equipment in some way, although the landing may also be a second "take-off" (as in vaulting), when the apparatus is used only momentarily. Limitations can describe the landing exactly or specify the part of the body to be used (e.g., "upside-down," "in a crouch position," "feet first," "with one knee on the apparatus," "hands only"). The performer can be asked to make certain

shapes of the body in the action of mounting (e.g., "legs straight," "body tucked," "body asymmetric") or use certain actions such as a jump, roll, twist, swing, turn, stretch (extension), or balance.

It is sometimes very difficult to control the speed and timing of a vault; this issue needs to be related to the strength and size of the learner. Children need to experience a variety of "mounting" situations. Oblique approaches often combine easily with a turn to mount. Mounting apparatus that is located overhead presents different problems. *Do not lift or support children and do not let them help one another; it is an unsafe practice.*

3. *Moving on the apparatus.* Sometimes teachers should require children to invent movements and activities to be performed on the equipment; at other times the equipment should be used merely to assist the already moving body. Climbing apparatus obviously is very suitable for linking a number of different actions together, but care must be taken that moving on the equipment is related to gymnastic movement and makes use of the apparatus in some way. Posing, unless it is part of balancing, and extra movements of arms and legs that do not assist the action should not be used too frequently. Sometimes, however, teachers may require a sequence of movement to be performed on the apparatus.

Again, the obvious limitations of direction, relationship, types of actions, use of the body, variation in speed and level, and the inclusion of "held" balance positions could be used. Perhaps the limitations may relate to the equipment itself. Certain parts of the apparatus can be used in specified ways and various patterns of over, around, through, and under can be required. Ropes can be used as both moving and still equipment. Using the apparatus in a pattern of movement can also include several mounts done similarly or in different ways.

Repeated movements of limbs or the whole body that increase acceleration and work up enough speed to dismount the apparatus are demanding and can also be used to travel from one part of the apparatus to another. When children are skilled, tasks involving "continuous" movement on apparatus can be given. Changes in direction or in the use of different parts of the body when movement is continuous are very difficult and need sensitive timing. The "dead" point of a swinging movement will need to be realized. Using part of the body or the limbs to act as levers provides for many different experiences. If rotation, spinning, turning, and circling are possible on the equipment, then a rich variety of sensory experiences are readily available to children. Subtle variations in compression, weightlessness, angular momentum, increased weight due to acceleration, and experience of

control in the air will all extend the variety of movement experience.

If "figure eight" patterns and tasks of traveling where the floor is not used are explored, much strengthening activity is likely to ensue. Strengthening also occurs when swinging movements are used and the body moves with speed. Relaxed hanging can also have effects on both strength and flexibility.

4. *Dismount (getting off of the apparatus).* The dismount is part of the sequence of activity and the usual limitations can be set. The "take-off" from the apparatus is separate from the landing, and the ability to land safely and with control will limit the types of dismounts that can be performed. A variety of landings should be experienced, with the learner gradually absorbing momentum by further movement and using his or her strength to stop quickly. The take-off from the equipment is often the most exhilarating part, but the challenges posed to learners should not be too demanding until teachers are sure of a mature response. The actual timing of the "push" or release of grip is highly specific to an individual performer in a take-off where the body is already moving. If a teacher is to give advice, accurate observation will be needed.

As with other activities, variety in using large apparatus can be obtained by allowing children to work with a partner or in a small group. Be aware, however, that too much combining with others can prevent highly skilled individuals from extending the upper limits of their capacity, because a group performance tends to demand a unity or cohesion of individuals. For this reason, some poorly skilled children thoroughly enjoy group work and find confidence and support by working with others.

By this stage, lessons should almost run themselves, with students selecting and choosing to add to familiar and established skills. Teachers can have cards and wall charts and allow students to plan their own components for a sequence.

At Level 3, students will likely be able to add more activities in mid-air. "Flight" can include using hands and arms as a second take-off (e.g., in vaulting). Simple tasks to encourage turns or changes of direction, a sudden "stop," or a held position also place great demands on control and offer new sensory stimulation. These experiences are available to less skilled children.

Progression in gymnastics also relates to the way activities are performed. Level 2 and 3 activities are intended to help students develop control and skill because there are components that can be improved. The combining of different moves is, in itself, a challenge. Principles of inertia and angular momentum, velocity, and weight-related speed will be experienced as children are challenged and limitations imposed.

The instruction "Include a balance and a roll before you finish," for example, will make it more difficult to link movements and requires great control to accomplish. Precision, accuracy, and the ability to repeat the activity are all signs of progression, and all will need to be learned. This book contains many suggestions on ways to construct these kinds of lessons, and teachers must realize that the content is both challenging and time-consuming. Never attempt to have all children try all challenges. The children themselves may get involved in working out a particular sequence or routine; this kind of self-direction provides for excellent motivation. Allow this kind of creative control to happen. During body management/gymnastic lessons with older children, a teacher can often give "free time"—particularly before a lesson begins—for children to practice or repeat something they have been working on. Too often, faced with lists of content material and suggested challenges, teachers feel they must include "fresh" or "new" material in each lesson. It is part of the character of Movement Discovery lessons that the inclusion of new and fresh content comes largely from the children and is "built into" the process. Teachers affirm children when they trust them to work at the upper limits of capacity. Experience will prove the point that leaving the initiative for improvement to the children really does work.

Level 3 work can also extend the development of routines to include more people. Even so, the groups should probably not be larger than four. Three people working together offers interesting possibilities for different pathways on apparatus and different floor patterns. If the teacher and children are confident with children supporting and using one another as apparatus, much variety and interesting results will likely emerge.

Composition, Smooth Transitions, Timing, Good Form

At the highest level of gymnastics, much value is attached to the composition of routines. The degree of difficulty attached to the skills involved, linking movements, precision and accuracy of execution, variety, quality and good form, and style, among other things, all matter. For youngsters in school, teachers can certainly emphasize form: "Do it the best way you can." This kind of encouragement is important, and some children will have out-of-school experiences that support this approach. A smooth transition between actions shows control and intention and is as important as the skills themselves at higher levels. Timing is integral to successful performance, especially if more advanced skills include aerial action. This type of movement is not suggested in our content material, but some students experienced in using trampolines or in gymnastic clubs may include it.

The position of the child's center of gravity relative to take-offs and landings is highly significant when it comes to gymnastics. Angular momentum is slower for a "spread" body than for a body in the "tucked" position. Vaulting includes a second take-off when hands and arms are used. Flips, hand-springs, back-springs, and knee-springs also require precise timing and management of the body's speed.

Performance

Performance in Movement Discovery is used to provide satisfaction and a sense of achievement. It does not require an audience and, if used, should demonstrate modest and low levels of skill as well as advanced skills. Often a general suggestion of "Does anyone have anything they would like to show?" works well, but this invitation should not prompt the same children to perform too often. A better choice of wording is "This time, show me the best you can do," with only the teacher watching the performance. Alternatively, the teacher might say, "Before we finish, everyone show as much as you have done and do it the best you can." This invitation allows for different responses at different levels but reminds students that the skills of body management and gymnastics have progression and that they are expected to show good form.

Good work will need attention and approval from a teacher. As stated earlier, in Movement Discovery, progression is built into the process and can apply at low levels of skill.

Visuals in the area used for Movement Discovery will be particularly valuable at Level 3 as the activity begins to resemble gymnastics.

Suggested Content Material for Educational Gymnastics

Gymnastics involves developing a strong upper body, a strong and flexible spine, and, perhaps most important, the ability to use the arms and shoulder girdle to take the total body weight. It is essential that teachers help children to develop this capacity early so that wider ranges of body management skills become possible. Most gymnastic skills involve taking the body weight on both arms or one arm alone; a whole range of exciting skills becomes available when this capacity develops. Such progression will happen naturally if large apparatus can be used and if challenges include inverting the body and requiring weight-bearing activities using the arms and hands on the floor, even from the youngest children. To strengthen muscles requires an "overload." The weight of the body provides an overload in gymnastics using large apparatus; also flexibility is improved when the body weight causes the stretching of ligaments and tendons. Using momentum, as in swinging, can considerably increase this overload.

The "Content Material: Body Management and Gymnastics," **Figure 10–1**, offers some ideas that children and teachers can use to stimulate body management activities and the development of gymnastic skills. This material is certainly sufficient to initiate a program and allow the teacher to start slowly; he or she can pick content to match the level of the particular children involved. It is important to understand and apply information included in Chapters 4 and 5.

The following pages describe a variety of activities, challenges, limitations, and suggestions that have been used successfully in a variety of situations by different teachers. Do *not* use them just because they are here. Your ideas and the children's ideas may work much better! Select, adapt, ignore, and use this material as you wish. No

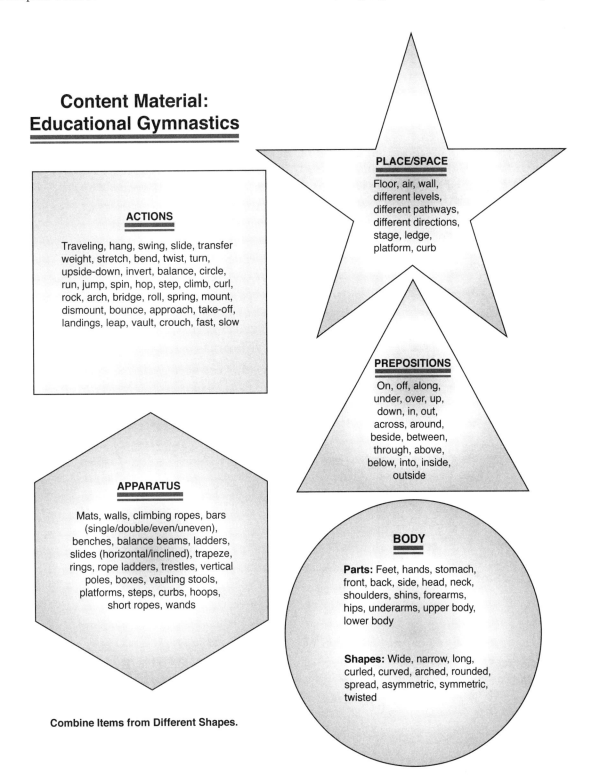

Content Material: Educational Gymnastics

ACTIONS

Traveling, hang, swing, slide, transfer weight, stretch, bend, twist, turn, upside-down, invert, balance, circle, run, jump, spin, hop, step, climb, curl, rock, arch, bridge, roll, spring, mount, dismount, bounce, approach, take-off, landings, leap, vault, crouch, fast, slow

PLACE/SPACE

Floor, air, wall, different levels, different pathways, different directions, stage, ledge, platform, curb

PREPOSITIONS

On, off, along, under, over, up, down, in, out, across, around, beside, between, through, above, below, into, inside, outside

APPARATUS

Mats, walls, climbing ropes, bars (single/double/even/uneven), benches, balance beams, ladders, slides (horizontal/inclined), trapeze, rings, rope ladders, trestles, vertical poles, boxes, vaulting stools, platforms, steps, curbs, hoops, short ropes, wands

BODY

Parts: Feet, hands, stomach, front, back, side, head, neck, shoulders, shins, forearms, hips, underarms, upper body, lower body

Shapes: Wide, narrow, long, curled, curved, arched, rounded, spread, asymmetric, symmetric, twisted

Combine Items from Different Shapes.

FIGURE 10-1   Content Material: Educational Gymnastics

attempt has been made to apply a grade level to any of the sample tasks. The trained teacher can select and extend those ideas that are appropriate for the different developmental levels of children in the class. The tasks are *not* presented here in order of difficulty, and they should not be used as a progression. This is *not* a curriculum.

Teachers do have the responsibility to present suitable material to children, so observation and assessment by a teacher will be crucial to progress.

Content Material: Actions

Following are some suggested variations for some body management actions. These suggestions should *not* be taught or presented as a series of lessons, one after the other. The teacher should select and use only one or two ideas per lesson. A Physical Education teacher or classroom teacher should have this content knowledge.

Some Suggestions to Extend Traveling

- On different parts of the body
- On hands and feet only
- On the front of the body
- On the back of the body
- With hands close to feet
- With hands far from feet
- On three different body parts
- Using turning movements
- Along different pathways
- At different levels
- In different directions
- In contact with the floor
- On and off the floor
- With feet together
- With feet spread apart
- With feet going first/leading
- With head going first/leading
- With hands leading
- With feet leading
- By sliding
- By rolling
- By stepping
- By jumping
- Using patterns of traveling (e.g., jump, step, slide)
- For short distances/long distances
- Around objects
- On the ground
- Off the ground

Some Suggestions to Extend Swinging

- With a long body shape
- While gripping with different parts of the body
- Followed by jumping and landing
- With the body in different shapes
- Combined with twisting, turning, and circling
- On bars
- On ladders
- On ropes/rope ladders
- On poles/trapezes

Some Suggestions to Extend Hanging

- By gripping with different body parts
- By hands
- By backs of knees
- By hands and feet
- With the body stretched out
- With a twist
- With the body curled up tightly
- With a curve in the body
- Combined with traveling
- Combined with circling
- On apparatus of different heights

Some Suggestions to Extend Sliding

- On different parts of the body
- On just feet
- On the stomach/front of the body
- Using a turning movement while sliding
- Fast/slow speeds
- With small parts of the body touching the sliding surface
- With the head going first
- Changing directions
- With the arms in different positions
- Making different body shapes
- Down an inclined bench
- Along or down a pole/bar

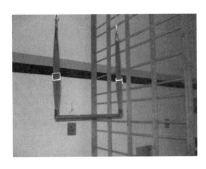

Some Suggestions to Extend Stretching

- While rolling
- While traveling
- While hanging on different pieces of apparatus
- On different body parts
- While balancing
- With the feet together
- With the feet apart
- With crossed legs
- While jumping on the floor
- While jumping off a piece of apparatus
- To get onto a piece of apparatus
- In different balance positions
- While swinging
- With the body's weight on the hands

Some Suggestions to Extend Rolling

- With the body in different shapes
- In a stretched position
- In a tight, curled position
- In different directions (sideways, backward, forward)
- From different starting positions
- With the feet together
- With the feet apart
- With crossed legs
- Using consecutive rolls
- Around bars
- To get onto a piece of apparatus
- While getting off a piece of apparatus
- At different speeds
- Out of different balance positions

Some Suggestions to Extend Jumping

- While stationary
- While traveling in general space
- Following different pathways on the floor (e.g., zigzag, curved, straight)
- In different directions (forward, backward, sideways)
- While changing directions constantly
- With turns (90 degrees/180 degrees)
- Continuously
- For extended periods of time (1–3+ minutes)
- Over different distances
- With stops and starts
- Making a jumping pattern
- While high off the ground
- While keeping low to the ground
- From different heights
- Using different take-offs
- Using different landings
- With feet apart
- With feet together
- With legs crossed
- With legs bent
- With legs straight
- With one leg bent and one leg straight
- With arms apart
- With arms together
- With arms crossed
- With arms bent
- With arms straight
- Making different shapes with the body (e.g., long, wide, twisted)
- With the body fully stretched from fingertips to toes
- Down off
- Up onto
- Over objects
- Along lines/ropes
- In combination with other movements (e.g., jump, then roll)
- Using different rhythmic patterns (e.g., different sound patterns)

Some Suggestions to Extend Balancing

- On one or two feet
- On hands and feet
- On two hands
- On the front of the body
- On the back of the body
- On large surfaces of the body
- On small surfaces of the body
- With the back facing up
- With the stomach facing up
- With one side of the body facing up
- On four parts of the body (e.g., two hands/two shins; two forearms/two feet)
- On three parts of the body (e.g., one hand/one forearm/one foot)
- On two body parts
- On the same two body parts
- On two different body parts
- On two body parts on the same side of the body (right or left)
- On two body parts from the opposite sides of the body
- With the body stretched
- With one part of the body stretched/straight
- With the body bent/curled/rounded
- With one part of the body bent
- Showing a twist in the body
- Where one part of the body is the highest point (e.g., a knee)
- Using a small base of support
- Using a large base of support
- To be held for 3–5+ seconds (for increasing periods of time)
- A sequence of different balance positions
- A balance followed by another movement (e.g., a roll)
- On the ground
- Off the ground on equipment

Actions children can explore and practice in an educational gymnastic program are illustrated in **Figure 10–2**.

ACTIONS

Traveling, hang, swing, slide, transfer weight, stretch, bend, twist, turn, upside-down, invert, balance, circle, run, jump, spin, hop, step, climb, curl, rock, arch, bridge, roll, spring, mount, dismount, bounce, approach, take-off, landings, leap, vault, crouch, fast, slow

FIGURE 10–2 Actions

Allow Children to Discover Activities Using Different Body Actions

1. Practice high jumps.

2. Roll over on the mat in different ways.

3. Run around all the spots or markers on the floor.

4. Move along the floor first with your body very small, then change to move with it very big.

5. Discover some way of spinning round on the floor. Try a variety of positions (e.g., on your knees, one foot, tummy). Sliding may also be possible.

6. Find places on the equipment where you can safely jump down.

7. Can you find four places on the equipment where you can get upside-down or where your feet are higher than your head?

8. Stretch out and bend while you're moving on the equipment.

9. Try ways to twist and turn as you move on the equipment.

Allow Children to Discover Traveling Actions

1. Travel in different ways around the general space.

2. Using a hoop, travel "around" your hoop three times, then finish with six jumps in the "middle" of your hoop.

3. Stretch your own jump rope on the floor. Travel "along" it from one end to the other or "over" or "across" it.

4. In pairs, collect six spots and two jump ropes. Travel "between" and "around" the spots and "along" the ropes.

5. Use two traffic cones to support a PVC or wooden dowel on top. Go "over" and "under" the pole.

6. Find different ways to get "on" and "off" benches, ladders, or the gym stage.

Allow Children to Discover Stretching and Bending Actions

1. Stretch your body out to become "big," and bend or curl it to become "small."

2. Balance on part of your back and stretch both of your legs very straight in the air. Stretch your legs four different ways.

3. Bend your body tightly and roll across the mat or floor.

4. On the large equipment, create a sequence that has two bending movements and two stretching movements.

5. Using four hoops placed in some formation on the floor, travel to each hoop. When you get there, show either a bent balance or a stretched balance in each hoop. Repeat the traveling movements and four balances until you have smooth transitions in the sequence.

Allow Children to Discover Twisting, Turning, and Circling Actions

1. Experiment with spinning or turning on your stomach, buttocks, or one foot.

2. Find five places on the large equipment where you can twist, turn, and circle over or around. Bars of different heights are good places to try this movement.

3. Rotate or turn your body in the air as you jump. Keep your body under control when you land softly.

Allow Children to Discover Moving and Stopping Actions (Motion and Stillness)

1. Move around the general space. When I say, "Stop," I want you to "freeze" where you are. Stay very still.

2. Hop, jump, slide, or run without bumping into anyone until I clap my hands; then "stop" immediately.

3. Run and stop, and run and stop, but change directions each time you stop.

4. Move to any of the spots on the floor. When you get there, stop and balance on one foot. Count to 3 and then move on and stop at another spot.

Allow Children to Discover Actions Using Bridges

1. Using one foot and two hands, make a bridge on the mat. Have a partner travel over, under, and around the bridge.

2. Make a bridge where your right foot is the highest point of the bridge. Have your partner *match* the bridge shape you've made. Experiment with two other bridge shapes for your partner to match. Switch so that the other person makes the bridge shape to match.

3. Using any of the pieces of the large equipment, make a bridge with your feet above your hands. You must touch the equipment with a part of your body. Try to make different-shaped bridges on each piece of equipment.

4. Demonstrate three different types of bridge shapes. (This is a good assessment activity.)

5. Everyone find a partner who is similar in size. One person should make any type of low bridge on the floor while the other person travels "over" the bridge. Suggestions: Try to use jumping and stepping-type movements.

Allow Children to Discover Actions Using Different Speeds

1. When rolling along the mat, try some rolls that are performed slowly and others that are performed more quickly.

2. Slowly and carefully travel along the bars as you twist your body.

3. Move along the balance beam and the bench showing some slow movements and some fast movements.

4. Practice fast spins on your feet or your hips on the floor, bench, or balance beams.

5. Roll across the mat very slowly and smoothly. You choose the shape of your body.

6. Make two quick jumps followed by two slow rolling movements.

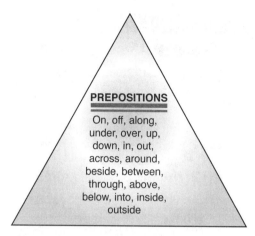

FIGURE 10-3   Prepositions

PREPOSITIONS

On, off, along, under, over, up, down, in, out, across, around, beside, between, through, above, below, into, inside, outside

Content Material: Prepositions

There is much activity to discover when focusing on ways to use the large apparatus. **Figure 10–3** contains simple prepositions that will stimulate children.

Allow Children to Discover Activities Focusing on the Spatial Concepts

1. Find ways to travel "along" and/or "across" the ladder or bench or rope on the ground.

2. Practice jumps that go "up," "down," and "around."

3. Try gripping and hanging in different ways "under" the ladder or bars.

4. Get "on" and "off" the climbing equipment in different places.

5. Get "on" and "off" any piece of equipment at different heights.

6. Get "on" all the different pieces of equipment in different places.

7. Focus on different ways to get "off" five pieces of equipment.

8. As you move about the obstacle course, go "up" and "down."

9. Find many "holes" or square spaces in the climbing frame or Whittle equipment that you can go "through."

10. Find a way to go "through" a hoop.

11. Travel using different kinds of jumps to go "in" and "out" of the hoop on the ground.

12. Go "around" your hoop on your hands and your feet.

13. Find ways to go "over" and "under" the equipment.

Content Material: Place/Space

Expand on the items in **Figure 10–4**. For example, a pathway can be straight, curved, zigzag, or round. Think of different ways to use directions: forward, backward, sideways, up, and down. Also consider that there are three levels: high, low, and middle.

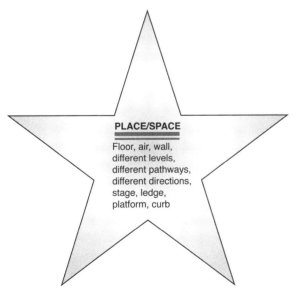

FIGURE 10-4   Place/Space

Allow Children to Discover Activities Using Different Pathways

1. Travel around the general space making curving pathways.
2. Find many places where you can move in straight lines on the large apparatus.
3. Jump and hop along this zigzag line. (Use visuals to illustrate the pathway.)
4. Use the lines on the gym floor that are straight and curved and run and jump along them. Keep going for 3 minutes.
5. Design a floor pattern with your partner using hoops, ropes, and spots. Include a zigzag line, a straight line, and a curved line in your pattern. Travel along the pathway, being sure to include some movement where you get your body weight onto your hands.

Allow Children to Discover Activities Using Different Directions

1. Try different movements as you travel around the general space in the forward direction.
2. Find ways to move sideways on your hands and feet.
3. Practice jumps that go up and down—high ones and low ones.
4. Move backward along the bench, ladder, bars, or ropes on the floor.
5. In general space, travel forward on your feet, then travel sideways and backward. You decide when to change your direction. Avoid other students when you come close to them.
6. Find three different ways to travel sideways along your jump rope that is stretched out on the floor.

BODY
=====

Parts: Feet, hands, stomach, front, back, side, head, neck, shoulders, shins, forearms, hips, underarms, upper body, lower body

Shapes: Wide, narrow, long, curled, curved, arched, rounded, spread, asymmetric, symmetric, twisted

FIGURE 10–5 Body

Allow Children to Discover Activities Using Different Levels

1. Experiment with movements at low levels and high levels on the large apparatus.

2. Make up a sequence that includes some movements close to the floor and some movements high in the air.

3. Put your hands on the floor and lift or kick your legs up higher than your hands. Be sure your feet land quietly and under control.

4. Practice movements where your body is at a low level. Do a low roll, spin, and slide. Next, try some movements on the opposite level (i.e., high). Try very high jumps.

5. Combine a high jump with a low roll, and finish with a low spinning/turning movement.

6. Climb on the large equipment up "high," then climb to where you are down "low" on the equipment near the floor. Repeat the sequence of "going high" followed by "coming down low."

Allow Children to Discover Activities Using Body Parts

1. Move on your feet and go jumping all around.

2. Put your hands on the floor. Now you have your hands and feet on the floor. Move all about on your hands and your feet.

3. Touch your stomach or the front of your body. Move on your stomach with your hands or feet or both to help you.

4. Balance on your two shins. Try it with shins together, then a little apart.

5. Balance on your two forearms and two shins. Change the position of these four body parts.

6. Hang on to the bars or ladders by your elbows, knees, or underarms.

7. Choose two parts of your body on opposite sides. Try to make one touch the other, and then stretch them far apart. Change the position of your body and try again.

8. Travel around the general space where your feet lead the way, or where your feet go first; then change to having your hands lead the way. Try different body positions as your feet lead the way.

Content Material: Body Parts and Body Shapes

Expand on the items in **Figure 10–5**. Try to invent your own challenges involving different parts of the body and the shapes the body can make.

9. Try moving around the general space where your hands go first or they lead you about.

10. Let your hands lead the way to pull you along the bench.

11. Keep your feet fairly still while you move your hands so that they come together and then they go apart from each other. Do this three times.

12. Experiment with hanging on the large equipment where your hands are close together, then slightly apart, and finally far apart.

13. Try to spin around on your shins using your hands. Spin in both directions.

14. Start with both hands and shins on the floor. How many different ways can you travel where you use your shins, along with some other parts of your body?

15. Combine three different balances that use shins.

16. Using your forearms, travel along the floor and slide your body behind. Try moving in different directions.

17. Use one or both forearms, and other parts of the body, to balance yourself. Try several combinations using your forearms.

18. Find a position near the large equipment where your forearms are on the floor and other parts of your body are on the equipment. Join three of these positions into a movement sequence.

19. Find different ways to travel with your hands and feet both touching the floor. Travel quickly but under control.

20. Find different ways of jumping using both hands and feet.

21. With two hands on the floor, find different ways to make your body move. Put your hands underneath, to the side, and in front of your body.

22. Find three different ways of hanging on the large apparatus while using your hands and/or parts of your feet and legs to grip the apparatus.

23. How many different ways can you travel on the large apparatus (around or in and out) where you use your hands and feet to support yourself?

24. Find three different ways of putting your hand on one piece of apparatus while having your feet on another piece of apparatus.

25. Working in twos, set up your own hoops course using six hoops. Travel the course using hands and feet in two different ways.

26. Use your hands to push the body into different shapes.

27. Lie on the floor (side, back, front). Use your hands to move your body.

28. Spread your body out as far as you can while balancing on your hips.

29. Balance on your hips. Try moving the rest of your body.

30. Balance on one hip and repeat.

31. Can you "walk" on your hips alone in different directions?

32. Try a shoulder support. Twist your body while balancing. Find other ways to use your body with shoulder support only.

33. Lie on the stomach only and move the rest of your body. Can you touch your head with your toes?

34. Try rocking on the front of your body. Keep your hands still in one place on the floor and move your feet all around on the floor.

35. Let your feet come close to your hands, go to the side of your hands, and go behind your hands.

36. Try putting your hands on the floor while your feet or some other part of your body rests higher on some piece of apparatus like a bench or bar.

Allow Children to Discover Activities Using Different Body Shapes

1. Jump in the air and demonstrate any shape with your body. Land safely and softly.

2. Try making different shapes with each jump (e.g., curved, wide, long, triangle, circle, square, spiky, symmetrical, asymmetrical).

3. With both hands and feet on the floor, create different shapes with your body while you remain stationary.

4. Experiment with placing your hands and feet in different positions on the floor to change your body shape. Move through four different positions. Hold each position for about 3 seconds.

5. Try lifting either one foot or one arm, and explore the different shapes you can make while balancing (use hand/foot symbols in different positions).

6. While moving along the equipment, stop and hold three different shapes for about 4 seconds each. Include some stops where you have to hang and hold a shape with your body.

7. Show me some shapes where your feet are over/above your head. Try different pieces of equipment to do this.

8. Make part of your body curved, or choose a round part and rock back and forth on it. Try to increase the rocking movement from small to large; also try from large to small.

9. While moving along the equipment, make your shape grow from a small shape to the larger version of that shape.

10. Experiment with balances where both sides of the body look the same (i.e., use a symmetrical shape). Find three ways to do this.

11. Asymmetrical balances are positions you can hold where each side of the body looks different. Find three ways to balance where both sides of your body do not look the same.

12. Design a symmetrical and asymmetrical movement sequence on any piece of large apparatus. The sequence should include balances as well as traveling movements.

Content Material: Apparatus

Almost all of the previously described challenges can be used again in relation to a piece of small equipment. Expand on the items in **Figure 10–6**, which uses both small equipment and large apparatus. If large apparatus is in short supply, then use small equipment so that no child is waiting for a turn to use the large apparatus. As a future teacher, you should now be ready to invent your own challenges.

APPARATUS

Mats, walls, climbing ropes, bars (single/double/even/uneven), benches, balance beams, ladders, slides (horizontal/inclined), trapeze, rings, rope ladders, trestles, vertical poles, boxes, vaulting stools, platforms, steps, curbs, hoops, short ropes, wands

FIGURE 10–6 Apparatus

Allow Children to Discover Activities Using a Variety of Small Equipment

1. Using whatever small equipment you have available, tell students, "You may have a [certain item]. Move your body around, over, or through it in different ways."

2. Do two different things using a piece of small equipment.

3. Hold a wand vertically on the floor with one hand. Go under your arm without moving the wand.

4. Hold both ends of a wand and climb through your hands. Reverse the movement.

5. Support a wand on traffic cones or blocks and move from side-to-side using your hands on the floor.

6. Show what you can do with your rope, wand, or hoop and your body.

7. There is a variety of small equipment spread on the floor. Use each piece a different way.

8. I have lots of beanbags spread all around the room. Move around these beanbags using all different kinds of pathways—some straight, some zigzag, some curved.

9. Place your rope on the floor. Discover many ways of arranging it to form different shapes. Then try a variety of jumping and hopping patterns along the rope.

10. Walk along the rope using the sides of the feet or toes only. Pick up the rope using only your feet. Rearrange the design of your rope on the floor and repeat.

11. Place your rope on the floor. Travel with your hands and feet on the floor along the rope from one end of the rope to the other. Try some sideways and backward movements as well as forward movements.

12. With your rope on the floor in a straight line, travel with your hands on one side of the rope and your feet on the other side, from end to end.

13. Place two beanbags some distance apart, and find different ways to travel from one to the other. Include a movement where your body turns over if you can.

14. Make a pattern with three beanbags. Find a fast movement to travel from beanbag 1 to 2, a slow movement from beanbag 2 to 3, and a different action from beanbag 3 back to 1.

15. Make a circle with your rope or use a hoop. Put your hands in the middle of the circle and move your feet in different ways around the outside of the circle.

Remember that when children use large apparatus for the first time, they should be left to explore it. Also offer an alternative activity. Almost all of the previously described challenges can be used again in relation to large apparatus. Invent your own challenges using this material. When the children are ready, exploration on the large apparatus can be expanded by making small changes in the setup and arrangement of the apparatus. This can result in new movement possibilities for the children. The body will be used in new ways when the angles, slopes, and height of equipment are changed. Different muscle groups will also be challenged. Changing combinations and arrangements of large apparatus are particularly appropriate for children of prekindergarten age.

It is the teacher's responsibility to plan interesting changes in the height, angle, slope, and variety of combinations and placement of the large apparatus. This variation presents new challenges to body control.

Varying the Use of Large Apparatus

Try these changes with the large apparatus and observe the children's responses.

- Change the degree of slope of an inclined sliding board.
- Change the setup from two even horizontal bars to two single horizontal bars.
- Change two even horizontal bars to one horizontal bar high and one bar lower.
- Change a ladder from lying flat on the floor to a sloped/inclined ladder that is hooked onto a bar on a wall frame, vaulting stool, or trestle.
- Use a 10- or 12-foot balance bench by itself, and then change the formation by adding mats either at the end or either side, or one mat at the end and one mat at the side.
- Place two 10-foot benches end to end, and then change them to a side-by-side configuration so that they are approximately 12 inches apart.
- Change the position of two trestles (wooden or metal) from side-by-side to one trestle in front of the other to form a type of tunnel.
- Raise or lower the height of the ladder or horizontal bar by 6 to 12 inches.
- Design a physical arrangement to include small items combined with larger items (e.g., hoops, cardboard boxes, jump ropes, foam shapes, sturdy building blocks, markers, spots).

Expand on the items in the hexagon that use large apparatus. You can also use much of the previous material in the other shapes (circle, square, triangle, and star) with large apparatus.

Allow Children to Discover Activities Using Bars/Trestles

1. Show me what you can do on the bars and trestles.

2. What different movements can you do on the bars?

3. Can you hang using different parts of your body on any of the bars?

4. Swing on the bars. Use the momentum to let go and land safely.

5. Travel underneath the bars from one end to the other.

6. Try making your body into different shapes while you're on the bars.

7. Sometimes change the direction of your movement from forward to backward.

Allow Children to Discover Activities Using Ladders, Benches, and Slides

1. Get from one end of the bench or ladder to the other.
2. Change the way you move as you travel on the ladder, bench, or slide.
3. On the bench, pull or push yourself from one end to the other.
4. Move along the bench or ladder on your hands and feet.
5. Slide on different parts of your body. Try the front of your body and the back of your body.
6. Hang and swing under the ladders.

Allow Children to Discover Activities Using Vaulting Stools and Mats

1. Climb onto the vaulting stool and find a way to get back down.
2. Jump down and land safely from the vaulting stool.
3. Try some turning movements as you come down from the vaulting stool.
4. I'm going to hook a sliding board to the vaulting stool. Now find some interesting ways to get on, go along, and get off these pieces of apparatus.

Allow Children to Discover Activities Using Climbing Ropes, Poles, Rings, and Trapezes

1. Swing on a climbing rope, wooden pole, rings, and trapeze. See what different kinds of swinging you can do on each.

2. Change your body shape as you swing.

3. Find ways to swing, circle, and change direction on the rope, pole, rings, or trapeze.

4. Experiment with your hands in different positions as you grip the climbing rope, climbing pole, rings, or trapeze to practice swinging.

5. Grip or hold on for as long as you can. Try to increase the time you can do this for!

More Advanced Content Material: Sequences and Linked Patterns

This is more advanced work that can be developed when children have had plenty of experience working alone. Children need to be confident enough in their own abilities before being asking to perform another person's composition. We need to teach the acceptance of individual differences to the children. Inventing a sequence or pattern with a partner does not necessarily require performing the identical movement.

Allow Children to Discover Sequences Alone and/or with a Partner

1. Choose three of your best balances and link them together smoothly. Add a beginning and an end.

2. Repeat challenge 1 with a partner. You do not have to do the same balances as each other, but you should begin and end at the same time.

3. Take part of your partner's weight in as many different balances as you can. Try the balances on different levels.

4. Make up a sequence that has two quick and two slow actions. Match the speed, not the actions.

5. Show movement in a circle and movement along a straight line. Match or alternate the pathway, but move differently on the pathways.

6. How many ways can you find of meeting and parting using all of your apparatus?

7. Show a sequence involving putting your weight on your hands, moving over the apparatus with feet together, and finishing with a jump that turns.

8. Make a sequence with your partner where you include a movement along the floor with two different body actions; the sequence should end with the two of you in a wide shape.

9. With a partner, choose a piece of large apparatus and make a pattern of "on" and "off." Use your hands on the floor to finish.

10. Invent a sequence that includes a roll, hands on the floor, and a jump.

11. Compose a sequence with your partner that shows one upside-down position, one balance on hands and feet, and a way of traveling on the floor.

12. Start with a roll, which brings you to a standing position, and then add two different kinds of jumps.

13. With a partner, use a sequence of "over," "under," and "through" actions on the floor.

14. Repeat challenge 13 using the large apparatus.

15. On the large apparatus, find a place to hang in two different shapes and add a way to get down.

16. Travel on the floor using your stomach, and find a way to lift yourself up onto the large apparatus.

17. Join together a curled shape on the apparatus, a dismount, and a stretch position on the floor.

18. With a partner, develop a pattern that shows a bridge, a jump, and a roll.

19. Do two different actions on the large apparatus and use a swing to dismount.

20. With a partner, start at opposite ends of a piece of apparatus and invent a sequence where you approach and pass each other before dismounting.

Educational Gymnastic Task Cards

The use of task cards (see **Figures 10–7, 10–8, 10–9**, and **10–10**) can save time and get an experienced class to start more quickly. These cards are prepared ahead of the lesson, can be laminated, and can be used and then reused. See how a simple rearrangement of the same apparatus will produce different responses.

Outline of an Educational Gymnastic Task Card

1. Apparatus to use (type/setup)
2. Movement task

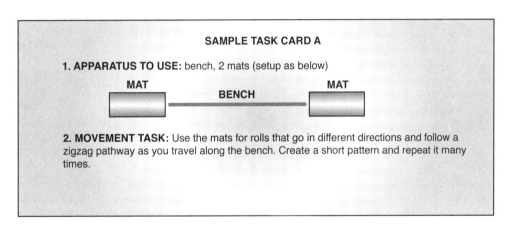

FIGURE 10-7 Sample Task Card A

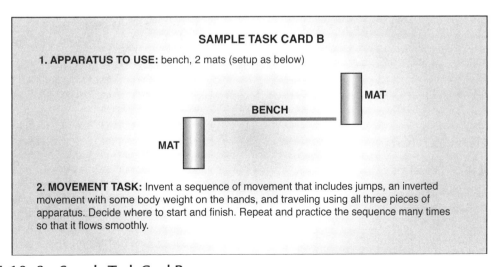

FIGURE 10-8 Sample Task Card B

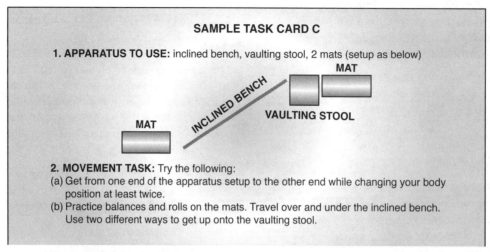

FIGURE 10-9   Sample Task Card C

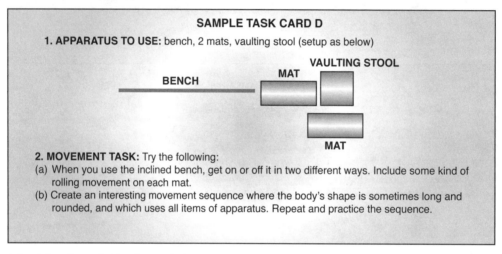

FIGURE 10-10   Sample Task Card D

Assignment 10-3

Using Figures 10-7, 10-8, 10-9, and 10-10 as samples for guidance, design 10 additional "Educational Gymnastic Task Cards" for fourth-, fifth-, or sixth-grade children.

Sources for Educational Gymnastics Material

Excellent material for educational gymnastics can be found in the following publications:

1. Bilbrough, A., & Jones, P. (1964). *Physical education in the primary school.* London: University of London Press.
2. Boucher, A. (1978). Educational gymnastics is for everyone. *Journal of Physical Education and Recreation, 49(7),* 48–50.
3. Boucher, A. (Ed). (1988). Early childhood physical education. *Journal of Physical Education, Recreation and Dance, 59(7),* 42–72.
4. Boucher, A. (1990). Developmentally appropriate movement activities for young children. In W. J. Stinson, (Ed.), *Moving and learning for the young child.* Reston, VA: NDA/ NASPE/AAHPERD.
5. Cameron, W., & Pleasance, P. (1971). *Education in movement—gymnastics.* Oxford, England: Basil Blackwell.
6. London County Council. (1962). *Educational gymnastics, A guide for teachers.*
7. London County Council. (1964). *Movement education for infants.*
8. Mauldon, E., & Layson, J. (1965). *Teaching gymnastics.* London: MacDonald & Evans.
9. Parent, S. (Ed.). (1978). Educational gymnastics. *Journal of Physical Education and Recreation, 49(7),* 31–50.
10. Werner, P. (2004). *Teaching children gymnastics* (2nd ed.). Champaign, IL: Human Kinetics.
11. Wiseman, E. (1978). The process of learning in gymnastics. *Journal of Physical Education and Recreation, 49(7),* 44–47.

11

Sample Lessons and Short Unit Plans in Educational Gymnastics

The following material, which contains sample lesson plans, should be used at the discretion of the teacher. As indicated in Chapter 5, there is no substitute for the care and knowledge of a wise and prudent teacher. Other teachers in different situations have used this material successfully, but *how* the material is used is crucial. The lessons are meant as examples only; they should not be taught in sequence. Choosing developmentally appropriate material is important at all levels, whether at preK through the end of the elementary school. The NASPE Standards that are listed in both the lesson and unit plans can be expanded by student teachers. This will depend on the requirements of the different school systems where preservice teachers do internships or student teaching.

Movement Discovery is a teaching method where self-knowledge, motivation, safe use of an individual body in a variety of situations, and the development of individual capacity are paramount. It is a new process for each child. Traditionally, teachers of gymnastics, stunts, tumbling, agilities, and more general body management skills obtained material from the previous generations of children and adults. These activities were then taught to the children.

In contrast, the Movement Discovery approach suggests a revolutionary idea: *Teaching all children the skills that result from one person's experimentation and refinement is wrong.* Educational gymnastics does not mean teaching a log roll or an egg roll or any specific skill that a child has developed, giving it a name, and then using this as content material for others. This process is even more undesirable when large apparatus is used. Just because one child goes

from one end of the parallel bars taking the body weight on the arms alone, it does not mean that other children should copy that behavior unless they choose to do so. Likewise, the teacher should not admire a movement and then require all other children to do the same. If there is only one response possible, then the activity does not qualify as educational gymnastics. Learning self-body management and discovery capacity in a gymnastic environment is the aim.

The implementation of lessons in Movement Discovery will obviously present children with a great variety of choices. Using the body to discover what it can do safely and discovering which scientific principles of physics apply when the body is active on large apparatus are interesting and challenging to young children. Such activity simply extends and builds upon earlier experience. It has been stressed previously that such activity will need to be pushed to the limits of present capacity to increase range of motion in joint complexes, endurance, and muscular strength. If this is done, fitness will improve.

Safety using the Movement Discovery approach has been discussed previously in this book (Chapters 1, 4, and 5). The use of the following lessons *must* involve the teacher's observation and assessment of the readiness of the children. To repeat, it might be wise to try the method using the body, the floor, the walls, and the small equipment (e.g., hoops, mats, and benches, as in Lessons 1 and 2) before allowing children to use larger, higher, moving apparatus.

Teachers should also understand the simple laws of motion. For example, to balance the body, the center of gravity needs to be over the base of support. The center of gravity in a human body will vary within children based on their weight distribution, body type, and pattern of growth. It also changes as a body matures and develops. Even a subtle change in the center of gravity requires new learning. Standing on one foot is easier with an upright body over the foot. If the body is spread wide, bent forward, or twisted, this type of body position becomes more difficult. If the size of the base is decreased (e.g., if the heel is raised or only the ball of the foot is used), it becomes even more difficult. A rolling action of the body increases momentum when the body is curled into a smaller shape. When the same action involves a stretched body, it is harder to initiate. In mid-air, momentum is greatly affected by body shape. Action and reaction are equal and opposite. For example, jumping straight into the air and turning to the right to land would require an action to the left of the arms and head. If you try this, ensure the turn is not initiated at take-off.

Knowledge of these principles of movement is fun for children to discover and should *not* be presented as theory. Children can naturally learn safe body management in a wide variety of situations while they also increase their physical literacy. As teachers ask children to try different body shapes, different manipulation of the body as apparatus, different ways of jumping, different means of traveling, different body actions in different situations, and so on, a wide range of sensory input results. Stability of cognitive processes is learned.

Many of the sample lessons that follow will have movement tasks that can be explored on a variety of items of large apparatus. Photos are in this text to illustrate some of these items. Bars: single, double, triple-use at different heights for hanging and swinging; Whittle apparatus; climbing/swinging poles, ropes, and trapezes; sliding

surfaces (sliding boards); ladders with hooks (horizontal/ inclined); curved ladders; benches with hooks (horizontal/ inclined); solid foam shapes; A-frames/three-sided frames; vaulting stools of different heights; small vaulting boxes; trestles (wooden and metal) of different heights (3 feet to 6 feet); rope ladders; horizontal ropes; balance beams (wooden/foam); climbing wall frames (6 to 8 feet in height); tumbling mats; individual mats. Where lesson materials are not specifically listed teachers should use whatever items of large apparatus that are available in their schools.

BODY MANAGEMENT EXPERIENCES USING HOOPS AND/OR ROPES

Appropriate grade levels: Second through fourth grades

Lesson length: Approximately 30 minutes

NASPE Standards: 1, 2, 5, 6

State Standards: _____

OBJECTIVES

The learner will:

1. Discover a variety of ways to use ropes and hoops.
2. Jump and travel while experimenting with using different parts of the body, ropes, and hoops.
3. Devise a pattern or sequence alone or with a partner that incorporates ropes and/or hoops.

LESSON MATERIALS

Single jumping ropes of different lengths (one for each child); hoops of different diameters (one for each child)

Minutes (Approximately)	Scripted Movement Tasks	Cues/Things to Stress
	Individual Activities	
1	Hop or skip anywhere in the room. Continue until you are breathless.	Work for some cardiovascular endurance effects.
2	Get a rope or a hoop. Discover what you can do with it. Work in your own space.	Have children choose equipment quickly and in an orderly fashion (e.g., by the color of the shirt they are wearing, hair color, month of birthday).
2	Place the rope or hoop on the floor and make a shape with the rope. Jump over the shape. Show another kind of jump. Show three different jumps.	Encourage a variety of shapes and jumps.
2	Switch ropes and hoops. Travel around the shape in different ways.	Encourage a variety of ways of traveling.
2	Travel in and out of all the rope shapes or hoops in the room.	Traveling longer distances using the general space should be encouraged.
2	Combine two favorite jumps over the rope or hoop and two different ways to travel around it.	Repeating combinations of jumps and traveling will enable children to refine their movement.
2	Show a stretch position over the rope or hoop; use two different body parts. Use another set of two different body parts.	Stretching activities encourage body extension and full range of motion of the joints involved.

Minutes (Approximately)	Scripted Movement Tasks	Cues/Things to Stress
2	Support your weight on a large part of your body inside the shape. Place one body part inside the shape, and travel around the shape by changing body parts and ways to travel.	A short demonstration by a child with an idea of what he or she can do might be helpful to stimulate thinking on the part of some students.
3	Show a way to jump with the hoop or rope; one foot or two feet. Can you find three ways to jump with the hoop/rope? Try to do consecutive jumps. Change direction.	Consecutive jumping requires practice and is more difficult than single jumps. Changing direction adds to the difficulty.

Partner/Group Activities

3	Devise a pattern using jumps and a change of direction with your rope or hoop. Both use both pieces.	This more complex combination will be appropriate only for older students.
5	Invent a partner sequence with your rope and hoop on the floor. Show a sequence of movements that adds balances.	Encourage older students to practice their ideas so that their movements are varied, interesting, and well controlled.

Conclusion/Assessment/Reflection Activities

2	Have the children show their three jumps. Select three or four couples who volunteer to show their pattern.	Comment on the different shapes of the body used in the jumping patterns and balances.
2	Discuss with children how one can make a higher jump and a quieter, more controlled jump. Allow observers to describe the parts of the body used for balances. Is it hard? Easy?	Allow several children to offer ideas.

BODY MANAGEMENT EXPERIENCES USING ROPES

Appropriate grade levels: Second through fifth grades

Lesson length: Approximately 30 minutes

NASPE Standards: 1, 2, 5, 6

State Standards: _____

OBJECTIVES

The learner will:

1. Discover ways to transfer body weight while using a stationary jump rope on the floor.
2. Invent ways to balance on different body parts inside a rope shape on the floor.
3. Creative a sequence of traveling, placing weight on hands, and finishing with a balance using a rope as the focus.
4. Experiment with a variety of single and consecutive jumps using a turning rope.

LESSON MATERIALS

Single jump ropes of different lengths and weights

Minutes (Approximately)	Scripted Movement Activities	Cues/Comments for Teachers
	Individual Activities	
3	Get a rope. Experiment with it or try some activities you've learned in a previous lesson.	Observe and comment on the different uses of the rope and the skills being used.
1	Place your rope on the floor in any shape Run, skip, and hop in and out of all the ropes. Change direction on signal.	Encourage safe traveling in general space. Describe the direction changes the children use.
2	Go *across* each rope shape using a different jump.	Describe jumps with legs apart, crossed, with turns, and so on. Use several short demonstrations of the ideas produced by the children.
3	With your own rope in your own personal space, show a wide, stretched shape over the rope. Change position to another wide, stretched shape. Discover five of these shapes in your own time. Try tummy up and back uppermost.	Explain that wide stretches help keep the body flexible. Balance is also involved. When the balance is held for a period of time, the children should understand that muscular endurance is improved.
3	Shape your rope into a circle. Place your weight on your hands in the center of the rope and get your feet to the opposite sides; try it in different ways. Let your feet come down to the floor without a bang!	Practicing putting weight on the hands in every lesson helps strengthen the upper body. This value can be quickly addressed as children are working.

Minutes (Approximately)	Scripted Movement Activities	Cues/Comments for Teachers
4	Show a sequence with the rope in a shape on the floor; travel around the rope; place your weight on your hands to get across; finish with a balance.	The teacher should observe children performing many different sequences. Stress that they include all the items listed.
3	Hold the rope using one hand or two hands. Turn the rope. Can you jump over it? How many times? How many consecutive jumps?	Reinforce quiet, controlled jumps. Skilled children will do many consecutive jumps showing great variety in the types of jumps attempted.
4	Use your rope to skip or jump. Can you show three different ways to skip/jump the rope?	Encourage variety—double jumps, turn the rope forward, turn the rope backward, rock step, and jump on one foot.

Partner/Group Activities

4	Choose a friend to work with you. Use one rope to develop a pattern where you both skip and change the turner as part of the pattern **or** work on your own and change the direction of the rope as part of the pattern.	The teacher can circulate to observe the different patterns students create.

Conclusion/Assessment/Reflection Activities

3	Check who can skip/jump a rope. Choose children to show their individual, creative ideas involving *any* of the lesson material. Skip rope as you travel around the room. Stop. Put the ropes away.	A quick survey of the attempts will allow the teacher to assess the skills of jumping or skipping rope. Choose different ideas that have evolved. Comment on the quality of the performance, while giving hints for improving the skills.

EXPLORING PERSONAL AND GENERAL SPACE

Suggested age levels: 3- to 5-year-olds

Lesson length: Approximately 10–15 minutes focusing on body management.

OBJECTIVES

The learner will:

1. Demonstrate body control when moving among others in general space by responding quickly to starting and stopping signals.
2. Discover ways of safely managing the body and many body parts on large apparatus.
3. Demonstrate increased confidence by showing less muscular tension, confident body language, relaxed activity, less tentative movement, no indecision, greater variety, smoothness, height, and speed of movement.

LESSON MATERIALS

PolySpots, markers of all kinds, mats, a variety of slides, ladders, bars, trestles

Minutes (Approximately)	Scripted Movement Tasks	Cues/Comments for Teachers/ Things to Stress
2	Can you spread out and use up all the space in our room by finding your own space? Let me see you run. When I say, "Stop," stop as quickly as you can. Let's do it again. Run . . . Stop. David stopped *so fast*! I'm watching to see who else can stop really quickly.	Use a scattered formation. Establish "start" and "stop" routines. For good class control, it is important to have the children listening and responding very quickly. Once this pattern is established, it helps reduce downtime or unwanted inactivity.
2	Run and jump. Do it lots of times, and then stop.	Encourage the children to keep going. This should be a vigorous activity that increases their heart rate. Getting airborne challenges balance both in the air and on landing.
3	Move from one spot to another spot on the floor on your hands and your feet.	PolySpots or cardboard markers are spread at varied distances all around the working space. Approximately 8 to 15 feet apart works well. These items are concrete aids to help young children spread out. Hands and feet are also known body parts. Teacher can *describe* the ways the children move or travel on hands and feet (e.g., Sara has her tummy facing up; Andre has his hands moving in front of his feet; Jo is moving in a circle by going around and around; Ann moves and lifts her feet off the floor sometimes; Heather is traveling very slowly from spot to spot).

Minutes (Approximately)	Scripted Movement Tasks	Cues/Comments for Teachers/ Things to Stress
2	On the mats, or on the grass outside, can you roll over? Roll any way you want to.	Small individual mats (2 feet by 4–5 feet) are lightweight and easy for young children to manage and move around. If mats are not available, go outside and roll on the grass. Rolling over sideways is easiest. Some children may try rolling forward or backward. Let them experiment and practice their ideas.
4–6	There are many places where you can use the apparatus. The rule is that you don't touch or help anyone on the apparatus. Let me see all the different places you can go and use the apparatus. Try some things at one place and then move on to another place if there is space or use learning centers with small equipment and free choice.	The space might consist of a gym or outside playground equipment. Note the suggested list of developmentally appropriate large apparatus to use. Repeat the rule of "not touching" *many* times in the first few lessons. Also repeat the word "safe" *many* times as young children are working. Compliment children on their safe behaviors: "I like how you're keeping yourself safe. You controlled yourself very well as you were sliding down the sliding board." Describe *actions* and *body parts* children are using: "I see Pat hanging on the bars. He's using his hands and feet to hold on or grip." "Dante is sliding on his tummy." "Robin can jump off and turn in the air!"

LESSON 4

EXPLORING MANY ACTIONS

Suggested age levels: 3- to 5-year-olds

Lesson length: Approximately 10–15 minutes focusing on body management

OBJECTIVES

The learner will:

1. Demonstrate steps and jumps using hoops.

2. Travel on large apparatus, finding different ways to move on, off, and along the apparatus.

3. Explore a variety of actions on the large apparatus (e.g., hanging, sliding, climbing, traveling).

LESSON MATERIALS

PolySpots, markers of all kinds, mats, a variety of slides, ladders, bars, trestles

Minutes (Approximately)	Scripted Movement Tasks	Cues/Comments for Teachers/ Things to Stress
4	Go to the hoops and go from hoop to hoop any way you can. Try two different ways. ■ You might practice some different steps and jumps! ■ Perhaps you could do some sideways moving! ■ You could go *around* the hoops as you go to each one!	Place groupings of seven or eight hoops (small/large) in different formations about the working space. Plan enough groupings that there is no waiting for a turn. The bulleted items are variations that the teacher might suggest for the children to try if they are so inclined. When stating the possible variation, the teacher might "step" and "jump" to serve as an example as the suggestion is verbalized. For instance, when stating the possible variation of "sideways," the teacher might demonstrate sideways moving to accompany the statement. The teacher could use a hand gesture to draw a circle to indicate going "around" the hoop. Words alone do not always communicate.
4	Get your own hoop and see what you can do with it.	Encourage children to discover what they can do with the hoop (e.g., roll it, spin it, jump in and out of it, walk around its rim). The teacher can describe what the children are doing so all in the group can hear the comments. The teacher's feedback is helpful in facilitating new ideas.

Minutes (Approximately)	Scripted Movement Tasks	Cues/Comments for Teachers/ Things to Stress
4	A variety of climbing/sliding/hanging apparatus: Go and use the apparatus where there is a space. If you do not want to use large apparatus, use mats in a corner or hoops supported off the ground.	Very young children should be free to choose which pieces of apparatus they want to work on and for how long they want to stay on the same piece. This task can be used for *many* lessons with very young children. All children may look busy, but one child may not do many things. The teacher should be on the move around the large apparatus, observing everyone. With new groups of children, the teacher should: ■ Constantly praise safe behavior. ■ Emphasize not touching others. ■ Describe the way children are moving to encourage new ideas. ■ Make constant *individual* comments: "I like the way your legs are crossed when you're hanging on the bars." "Nice sliding on your shins." "What an interesting way to travel *along* the bars." "Can you tell me which parts of your body you're using to push yourself along the bench?" "What a good jump with a turn!" "What can you do when you get to the end?" "Your body is making a long, thin shape." "I see you're traveling backward some times and then you go forward." Many of these comments and questions help children generate new ideas as they are freely working on the apparatus. The teacher is describing what different children are doing. The language used refers to the content of the Physical Education curriculum.
3–5	Find some places to practice jumping down or dropping off.	Emphasize controlled jumping, with knees slightly bending when landing. Later encourage different kinds of jumps. Comments like the following are helpful to facilitate this movement: "I see jumps with straight legs and jumps with turns—also low jumps and some high jumps!" "Jill is hanging by her hands and then jumping down."

Minutes (Approximately)	Scripted Movement Tasks	Cues/Comments for Teachers/ Things to Stress
3	Try getting upside-down in lots of places.	Suggest to children that they try to get their feet higher than their head to get upside-down. This activity is an excellent way to encourage changing the position of the head in space. Get one foot high.
5	Find a place to get on, move about, and then find a different place to get off.	The sequence of "on–travel–off" can be explored over many lessons. Encourage different ways to get "on," "travel," and get "off." Children can discover many combinations of body parts, many types of movements to use, many pathways to travel, many directions to use, a variety of levels, different speeds, different body positions, and so on. The teacher will be very busy establishing good behavior. If children get overexcited or aggressive toward others, they may not use large apparatus but be asked to watch first (with teacher guidance).
5	Find some good places where you can practice hanging and swinging your body. You could try hanging and swinging on the bars, the ladder, the trapeze, and the hanging ropes.	Encourage children to try different heights of apparatus to hang and swing. Describe the different ways children grip the apparatus with different parts of the body: "David is gripping the bars with one hand facing out and the other hand facing in." "Eli is gripping or holding on under his armpits." "Sandra is using the back of both her knees and her elbow joints to hold on with." "Lyn is swinging along the ladder using just her hands and arms." Allow young children to decide when to move on to the next piece of apparatus. Over time, they will usually try all pieces. Some items may interest them more than others at particular points in their development. Repetition is very necessary if they are to become more skillful; this means using the apparatus for many weeks.

BODY MANAGEMENT USING LARGE APPARATUS

Appropriate grade levels: Kindergarten or first grade

Lesson length: Approximately 30 minutes

NASPE Standards: 1, 2, 5

State Standards: _____

OBJECTIVES

The learner will:

1. Demonstrate curling and stretching actions.
2. Travel on large apparatus finding different ways to use each piece.
3. Explore safe rolling, jumping, traveling, climbing, and balancing on the floor and large apparatus.

LESSON MATERIALS

Large apparatus as available

Minutes (Approximately)	Scripted Movement Tasks	Cues/Comments for Teachers/ Things to Stress
2	**Introductory Activity** On the spot, jump up and down. Push very hard with your legs and feet so that you go high in the air. Repeat. This time, jump so that you slightly bend your knees when you come down. Repeat. Repeat running and leaping. Get your hands as high as you can. Repeat.	Repetition and prolonging the activity are important to increase cardiovascular endurance. Good resilience at the hips, knees, and ankles is required for controlled landings.
3	**Individual Activity** Curl up into a little ball on the floor. Stay curled and see if you can rock or roll around in a circle. Stretch out as far as possible. Curl up again. See if you can stretch out again, but this time in a different way. Curl up into a different position. When you can't stretch any further, curl up and do it again. Go on working in your own time while I watch.	Emphasize care of the head and "no bumps or stops." Work for smooth, continuous movement. Encourage children to repeat the curling and stretching using a variety of curled and stretched positions—possibly only curling or stretching one part or side of the body, and so on. Try to get children to change from curling to stretching without waiting for the teacher's instruction so that movement is continuous.
3	**Skill Activity** Place your hands on the floor. See how many ways you can move your legs. While lying on the floor, use your hands to push one part of your body away from the floor.	Encourage a variety of ways and "hands only" on the floor for at least a few seconds if possible. Overweight children or those lacking arm/shoulder strength may find this activity difficult but should at least "lean on" their hands.

Minutes (Approximately)	Scripted Movement Tasks	Cues/Comments for Teachers/ Things to Stress
20	**Group Activity** Go to your group space. Remember: No one may touch anyone else. The rule is "You look after yourself."	Send prearranged groups to prepared corners or learning stations. Try to arrange a different learning experience in adjacent corners. Children should work on their own as soon as they are ready.
	Group 1 Some kind of *climbing* where the weight can be taken on the arms. Benches/ sliding boards can be used to pull, slide, or push along; a steady box-top or table that is high can be used; vaulting stools, climbing ladders, bars, climbing ropes, platforms, and stages all are suitable.	There must be enough benches or fewer children so that there is no waiting for turns and no overcrowding.
	Group 2 *Rolling.* Mats should be used as a piece of apparatus, and any kind of rolling movement is encouraged.	Stress variety and smoothness as children roll. There should be no bumps or erratic movements as in the earlier part of the lesson.
	Group 3 *Jumping and landing.* Use any situation, steps, stage, box, or benches where a vigorous jump can be taken. Remember—no waiting for a turn.	Children choose the height they wish to use. Use a mat if available.
	Group 4 *Some kind of crawling through or getting under.* Sticks can be placed on supports or traffic cones; hoops can be used; benches may be useful if available. If there is enough apparatus, allow jumping over and running around, as well as crawling through.	Encourage children to discover different ideas.
	Group 5 *Free activity.* Use car tires or hoops (enough for one per child if possible).	Describe and praise the varied ideas the children discover.

Minutes (Approximately)	Scripted Movement Tasks	Cues/Comments for Teachers/ Things to Stress

Group 6

Free activity in some kind of situation where *balance* is difficult, such as stepping on blocks or logs, moving along a narrow beam (using hands, feet, going backward, crawling, and so on), or trying to keep to a restricted surface (even just a painted line or a stretched-out jump rope). Lightweight solid foam beams could be used.

The groups will rotate completely in a series of lessons (with perhaps one or two changes in any one lesson).

If there really is no means of arranging for these kinds of experiences with large apparatus, then make use of small equipment. Group 1 could use hoops, Group 2 could use balls, and so on.

2

Final Activity

All apparatus to be put carefully and neatly away. "Stand in a space. Go up on your tip-toes. Stretch your feet as hard as you can. Stand. Bend your knees and keep your feet flat on the floor. Repeat standing on your tip-toes."

Establish a routine for collecting and storing all the apparatus used.

Children should be taught how apparatus is assembled properly. The teacher must check the condition of large apparatus (e.g., for any loose fastenings, splinters).

LESSON 6

JOINING MOVEMENTS INTO SEQUENCES

Appropriate grade levels: Third through fifth grades

Lesson length: Approximately 30 minutes

NASPE Standards: 1, 2, 5

State Standards: _____

OBJECTIVES

The learner will:

1. Practice different kinds of jumps and turning movements.

2. Invent ways to pass a partner on pieces of large apparatus.

3. Creative a sequence of three movements on the floor and/or the apparatus.

LESSON MATERIALS

Selection of large apparatus as available

Minutes (Approximately)	Scripted Movement Tasks	Cues/Comments for Teachers
3	**Individual Activity**	
	Run and jump. Show as many different kinds of jumping as you can. Repeat. Show a jump or leap that turns you around. Repeat. Show different movements of your legs while you're in the air. Repeat.	Encourage and describe a variety of jumps and different leg movements.
2	Lying on your side, show as many movements of the legs as possible. Change the support, and continue to show different leg movements that help you change your position on the floor.	Choose several children to demonstrate their different leg movements. Ask questions regarding the differences.
5	Select one running and jumping movement and two movements on the floor that you have just tried. Repeat a sequence joining the three movements together. End the sequence back on your feet.	Children should work at producing a smooth, continuous flow of movement rather than isolated actions. Insist on clarification and an exact repetition so that children could teach someone else the sequence.
18–20	**Partner/Group Activity**	
	If large apparatus is available, set up a variety at each station and either establish specific challenges at each station or else ask for a *common* challenge such as these: ■ "Show an activity where your feet are higher than your head." ■ "Develop a sequence where you pass a *partner* on the apparatus without touching." This activity can be attempted regardless of which kind of apparatus is available. If no large apparatus is available, work on the sequence in the prior activity only with a partner where both children do not have to do the same movements.	If interest is sustained, time allows, and large apparatus is not available, let the children choose a partner to teach and ask for one sequence between them where one part is in unison or "matches."
1–2	**Final/Assessment Activity**	
	Select a few good sequences on apparatus to observe or allow a few "volunteers" to show their creations. Put apparatus away, and have children walk in and out of everyone without touching. Increase speed and deliberately "dodge" in and out. Slow down again to walk. Stop.	Do not feature only the very skilled children to demonstrate their work. Show more moderate achievers and check for gender mix.

BODY PARTS AND BODY ACTIONS

Appropriate grade levels: Second through fifth grades

Lesson length: Approximately 30 minutes

NASPE Standards: 1, 2, 5

State Standards: _____

OBJECTIVES

The learner will:

1. Practice different kinds of high jumps, both on the floor and on the large apparatus.

2. Travel on many different body parts, using different actions on the floor and apparatus.

3. Experiment with different balances on the floor and/or the apparatus.

LESSON MATERIALS

Selection of large apparatus as available

Minutes (Approximately)	Scripted Movement Tasks	Cues/Points to Emphasize
	Introductory/Individual Activities	
2	Find your own space in the room so that you are not too close to anyone else. Show me how you can jump. Go as high as you can. What do you have to do to get your body high in the air? Do different kinds of jumps. Run to a space. Repeat.	Children should be in a scattered formation. For height, stress "spring," "push" from the feet and legs, and use of arms to help with the "lift." Observe and describe the variety of movements: shapes, feet apart, with turns, and so on.
2	Travel on different parts of your body. What were some of the body parts you found you could travel on? Try on your stomach and your back.	Mention the different parts of the body on which the children move. Ask children to name the body parts. Include some specific suggestions.
2	Find as many ways as you can to move about on your hands and feet. Let's take a look at some of the ideas you found. Now that you've seen some of your classmates' ideas you might like to try some of those!	Observe ideas. Have children demonstrate some interesting or skillful ideas. Suggest trying hands first, feet first, stomach up, back up, movement in different directions, use of one hand, or use of one foot.

Minutes (Approximately)	Scripted Movement Tasks	Cues/Points to Emphasize
4	Experiment with balancing, or being still, with your hands and feet in different positions. I'm going to choose four children to show their different balance positions. How are they different?	Static balance activity: Encourage children to hold the balance for increasingly longer periods of time to increase muscular endurance and balance. Encourage children to discover that hands and feet can be close together, far apart, one foot or one hand can be in front of the other, legs can be crossed, and so on.
2	Balance on just your seat with no other parts of your body on the floor, and tilt or tip your body as far as you can without losing your balance.	Tilting challenges children's balance. Encourage children to spread their body position over their base.
1	Rest on your tummy and make your body twist. Now twist a different way.	Twisting movements produce flexibility effects in the body.
2	Put your hands on the floor and move your feet all about. Sometimes let your feet (one or two feet) leave the floor. Practice your ideas.	Keep the head up when supporting weight on hands. Arms and shoulders are strengthened as children do these movements on hands.

Tasks Using Large Apparatus

3	Use your body in lots of different ways on all the pieces of apparatus. Do not touch anybody else.	Stress/praise safe working on apparatus.
3	Find some places where you can jump down to land on your feet.	Stress controlled landings.
3	Try to get your body upside-down while you are on different pieces of apparatus.	Good stimulation for the vestibular system. Encourage at least one foot higher than the head.
6	Travel on only your hands and feet as you move on the bars, ladders, trestles, and mats.	Choices have been narrowed to just hands and feet.

Suggested Summative Assessment Activity

Place a worksheet or chart of body parts on the gymnasium wall. Name or circle four parts of the body that you used today. Finish with brief running and jumping high.

FEET TOGETHER, FEET APART

Appropriate grade levels: Second through fifth grades

Lesson length: Approximately 30 minutes

NASPE Standards: 1, 2, 5

State Standards: _____

OBJECTIVES

The learner will:

1. Experiment with balances on different body parts where feet are together and apart.

2. Travel and jump while keeping feet together and apart.

3. Demonstrate a variety of body actions on large apparatus while the feet are kept together or placed far apart.

LESSON MATERIALS

Large apparatus as available

Minutes (Approximately)	Scripted Movement Tasks	Cues/Points to Emphasize
	Introductory/Individual Activities	
2	Stand with your feet together somehow. Stand with feet apart as wide as you can. Make your feet wide apart in a different position.	Quick introduction to together/apart idea. Stress "wide" apart to increase flexibility of the hips.
3	Experiment with different jumps where you get your feet far apart from each other. Land with control.	Expect asymmetrical/symmetrical body shapes and, therefore, subtle balance adjustments in the air.
3	Move about with hands and feet on the floor. Try this with your feet sometimes together and sometimes apart.	Traveling just on hands and feet is different when the feet are either together or far apart. A change of direction can be suggested.
2	Balance with your shoulders and some other parts of your body on the ground. Try this with your feet sometimes together and sometimes apart. Be really stretched out.	Static balance on the shoulders helps children manage their bodies in different positions.
2	Balance on your bottom—no hands or legs on the floor. Tip yourself backward, forward, and side-to-side without falling. Keep your legs stretched out.	Tipping of the body helps strengthen children's balance reactions when sitting.
2	Balance using your forearms and shins as a base. Can you get one foot far away from the other foot sometimes by stretching? Then lift one arm. Keep still. Start again on two shins and two forearms, and lift one at a time off the floor.	Decreasing the size of the base of support makes keeping one's balance harder. Spreading the body over base makes keeping one's balance harder.

Minutes (Approximately)	Scripted Movement Tasks	Cues/Points to Emphasize
3	Rest your weight on your hands, or on your head and hands, and then jump with one foot or two feet off the floor. Let your feet land in a new place, like to the side, behind, or in front of your hands. See if you can keep your feet in the air for a longer and longer period of time.	Stress keeping hands flat. Begin with small jumps of the feet to ensure children can hold their body weight on their hands. Tell children the goal is to improve the strength of their upper body and arms.

Assessment Activity

	In pairs: Have a peer check the following: ■ Demonstrate two balances with feet apart. ■ Demonstrate two balances with feet together. ■ Demonstrate a jump with feet apart. ■ Demonstrate a jump with feet together.	A written peer checklist could be used for this assessment.

Tasks Using Large Apparatus

8	Have a turn on all pieces of apparatus, being sure to keep yourself safe. No touching is allowed. If a space isn't available on the apparatus, use the floor space.	Interact with all children to ensure there are no lines and that they try *all* pieces of available apparatus.
5	Where can you hang by different parts of your body and have your feet far apart from each other? Try some other places where your feet are close together.	Describe the different places children have chosen to practice "hanging" skills. Point out individuals with feet far apart and feet close together. Use children to demonstrate these ideas.

Final Activity

Walk covering all floor space. Do not touch large apparatus, but move in and around it.

TWISTING AND TURNING ACTIONS

Appropriate grade levels: Second through fifth grades

Lesson length: Approximately 30 minutes

NASPE Standards: 1, 2, 5

State Standards: _____

OBJECTIVES

The learner will:

1. Experiment with twisting and turning movements on different body parts on the floor.

2. Travel over, under, and around a partner bridge-shape.

3. Demonstrate a variety of twisting and turning actions on large apparatus.

LESSON MATERIALS

Large apparatus as available

Minutes (Approximately)	Scripted Movement Tasks	Cues/Points to Emphasize
	Introductory/Individual Activities	
2	In your personal space, jump and turn in the air so that you land facing different directions. Jump up straight. Turn a quarter to the left by swinging arms to right. (Action and reaction are equal and opposite!)	Have children engage in instant, vigorous activity. Get the class started quickly. Suggest small turns in the air at first to ensure all children have control of their landings. More advanced children can show 90°, 180°, and 360° turns in the air
1	Balance on your side and find different places where you could move your big toe in the space around you.	Encourage stillness on the side of the body. This involves twisting and turning the body.
2	Make your body turn around or turn over. Practice turning your body over or around in different ways. Change position during a side roll.	Turns should be tried on different body parts Spinning is a fast turning movement to try. Rolling sideways is the easiest roll to try. A twisting movement initiates a roll to the side.
1	Balance on your knees and shins. Lift one knee up for as long as you can. Next, lift the other knee up for as long as you can.	This activity helps refine balance on knees and shins, which is an asymmetrical, more difficult balance position.
3	Practice bringing one foot down at a time while your weight is on your hands. Where might you try to bring your foot down?	Small twisting movements are often involved in this action, particularly if the foot comes down to either side of the body rather than directly behind the hands. Keep the head up when supporting weight on hands. Arms and shoulders are strengthened as children do these movements on hands.

Minutes (Approximately)	Scripted Movement Tasks	Cues/Points to Emphasize
5	Working in groups of two or three, one person can make some kind of a solid bridge so that the other person(s) can find interesting ways to go over you, under you, and around you.	Check for appropriate pairs/groups, based on body size/strength and personality. Hands and shins make a solid bridge. Flat on stomach or back is another solid position. A solid support has body over base (e.g., when on all fours, solid support is over arms or hips, not the waist).

Tasks Using Large Apparatus

6	Select any piece of apparatus and practice some movements you like to do there. After a while, change and have a turn at a different piece of apparatus. You decide when to make the change and work on the floor if no space is available on large apparatus.	Observe and interact with all children to ensure that there are no lines and that children try more than one piece of the available apparatus. Compliment safe movement from piece to piece of the apparatus.
2	Find a comfortable height and practice jumping down. Then try turning in the air to land smoothly on your feet.	Stress that there are many ways to jump and turn, and that children should discover those movements. One characteristic of good gymnastic movement is to land smoothly and with control.
1	As you are moving on the apparatus, try to include twisting and turning movements.	Emphasize that twisting movements involve one part of the body facing one way while another part faces a different way.
4	Find ways to hang and swing on the apparatus, but try to include a twist or a turn as you do that.	Encourage children to discover hanging from hands only, from hands, from parts of the leg, and so on, so they can show a twisted shape or a twisting movement. Twisting the spinal column may increase flexibility in that area of the body if a full ROM (Range of Motion) is stressed.
3	It is free practice time on the apparatus. You choose some things to practice safely without interfering with anyone else.	This is an excellent time to assess improvement in skills being worked on, strength and flexibility, and children's interests. Praise safe, considerate behavior constantly. Praise "hard work" where children go to their limits.

Suggested Summative Assessment Activity

Create a checklist with two columns, with "Yes" and "No" at the top of the columns. Each child will be quickly checked off as demonstrating the following by a partner:

- Jumping off the apparatus from two feet, with a turn.
- Hanging with a twist.

MOVEMENT IN DIFFERENT DIRECTIONS

Appropriate grade levels: Second through fifth grades

Lesson length: Approximately 30 minutes

NASPE Standards: 1, 2, 5

State Standards: _____

OBJECTIVES

The learner will:

1. Practice short and long jumps in different directions.

2. Travel on hands and feet while moving in different directions.

3. Demonstrate forward, sideways, and backward actions on the floor and large apparatus.

LESSON MATERIALS

Selection of large apparatus as available

Minutes (Approximately)	Scripted Movement Tasks	Cues/Points to Emphasize
	Introductory/Individual Activities	
2	Jump forward, sideways, or backward with some turns. Sometimes use little or short jumps and sometimes long jumps. Use one-foot take-offs. Take off from both feet.	Look for the difference in the length of the jumps children make (short/long) and skill in one- and two-foot take-offs. State that you are looking for controlled turning movements in the air.
2	Move in different directions on your hands and feet. Try to include turning movements.	Emphasize that only hands and feet should be on the floor. Describe the directions children are using: "I see Sally is moving backward."
4	Using a 12-foot ladder laid on the floor, get onto your hands and feet and move forward along the spaces of the ladder without touching the ladder's bars. (Assessment: Note the children who touch the bars and count the number of "touches." Repeat this task in several weeks to see if body control has improved as evidenced by a reduction in the number of "touches.")	Avoiding the bars requires precise movements of the hands and feet and increased body control. Children can count "touches": This is a simple pre-/post-test assessment of body control in a forward direction.

Minutes (Approximately)	Scripted Movement Tasks	Cues/Points to Emphasize
2	Rest on your back and hold your head up off the floor. Count. Now lift your feet with knees bent. Hold them up and count. See if you can beat your own score.	Share with children that this movement may strengthen muscles on the front of the body if worked hard (abdominals). Self-evaluation should be encouraged.
1	In a half-kneeling balance position on one shin and the opposite foot, tip yourself forward, to the side, and then backward. Try to do this movement while keeping your hands far from the floor.	Tilting challenges children's balance. This type of movement improves equilibrium/balance reactions in the half-kneeling position.
1	Cross your legs as you move. You can use different types of steps and jumps.	Encourage vigorous traveling in general space.
1	Practice some of the turning movements you tried yesterday.	Revisit ideas from preceding lessons often.
4	Get together with the person you worked with in the last class and experiment with some more ways of going under, over, and around the "bridge" that person has made with the body.	Check for appropriate pairs/groups. A variety of traveling movements can be used with these prepositions.

Tasks Using Large Apparatus

6	Have free practice time on any of the pieces of apparatus.	Excellent time to assess improvement in skills being worked on. Praise safe, considerate behavior constantly.
4	Using several 12-foot ladders laid on the floor, get onto hands and feet and move along the ladder, supporting yourself on parts of the ladder without touching the floor.	The narrower surfaces and slight increase in height off the floor make this activity more challenging for some children. Emphasize NOT touching the floor!
3	Can you move sideways or backward on the different pieces of apparatus?	Allow individual children to choose when and where they will use these two directions for safety reasons.

Suggested Assessment Activity

Demonstrate any traveling movement that goes in a "backward" direction on any piece of apparatus. It can be a slow movement.

MOVEMENT USING A LOT OF SPACE OR A LITTLE BIT OF SPACE

Appropriate grade levels: Second through fifth grades

Lesson length: Approximately 30 minutes

NASPE Standards: 1, 2, 5

State Standards: _____

OBJECTIVES

The learner will:

1. Demonstrate actions that use a little bit of space, contrasted with actions that use a lot of space (e.g., short and long jumps in different directions).

2. Travel on hands and feet while moving in different directions.

3. Demonstrate forward, sideways, and backward actions on the floor and large apparatus.

LESSON MATERIALS

Selection of large apparatus as available

Minutes (Approximately)	Scripted Movement Tasks	Cues/Points to Emphasize
	Introductory/Individual Activities	
1	Start on your stomach. Get up slowly and end on your feet. Do it several different ways. Use momentum to help.	Problem solving is involved as well as rising up against gravity in different ways and with control using a small amount of space.
1	Start on your back and get up to your knees somehow. Try it again, but do it in a different way.	Some twisting movements will be used to perform this task, which challenges balance and may improve flexibility.
3	Practice jumps on one foot and two feet. Try little and big jumps as you travel around the gymnasium using a lot of space.	Performing little jumps and big jumps involves using different amounts of force in the body, which is important for improving body control.
3	Rest on your back. Work at holding your head up approximately 6 inches off the floor and count until your head wants to go down. Keep your knees bent. Try it again and beat your score.	This activity may strengthen the abdominal muscles. Uses only a little bit of space.
2	Travel on your hands and feet while turning your body over.	Encourage slow turning at first so that the body is kept under control.
6	**Partner Activity**	
	Choose a partner your size. Make a bridge. Balance with some or all of your body on the person who is the bridge. Be sensible and safe when working with your partner. Switch the balancer and support roles.	Check for appropriate pairs. A variety of body parts can be used "on" the bridge. The rest of the body will be supported on the floor. Strength is likely to be improved when children work against resistance.

Minutes (Approximately)	Scripted Movement Tasks	Cues/Points to Emphasize
	Tasks Using Large Apparatus	
4	Using a 10- to 12-foot ladder laid flat on the floor, move along on only hands and feet, using only the little spaces. Try to challenge yourself by missing some of the rungs and using a bigger stepping movement.	This activity calls for precise movement of hands and feet and, therefore, greater body control.
4	Practice swinging and hanging using different parts of your body to hold on. Try some swinging and hanging movements that use a little bit of space and some that use a lot of space.	Stress that swinging movements can use a little bit of space or a lot of space. Momentum can help this action.
4	On the apparatus, experiment with different balances on different parts of your body. Try to use some twisting movements.	Revisiting balances and twisting on the apparatus are necessary to improve the range of the children's movements.

Suggested Assessment Activity

Demonstrate a movement that uses a little bit of space and another that uses lots of space.

LESSON 12

BALANCE AND COUNTERBALANCE

Appropriate grade levels: Fifth and sixth grades

Lesson length: Approximately 30 minutes

NASPE Standards: 1, 2, 5, 6

State Standards: _____

OBJECTIVES

The learner will:

1. Demonstrate different ways of balancing or holding another person's weight.
2. Use another person's weight as a counterbalance both on the floor and on large apparatus.
3. Create a partner sequence to show a balance and counterbalance with swinging two movements of the legs.

LESSON MATERIALS

A variety of large apparatus as available

Minutes (Approximately)	Scripted Movement Tasks	Cues/Comments for Teachers
3	**Individual Activity** Run and show any kind of jump with a double take-off (off two feet). Work very hard to get the maximum time in mid-air. Repeat with distance or height as the objective. Try to show a twist of your body in mid-air. Repeat. Using your hands on the floor to support you, show any kind of smooth swinging movements of the legs.	Encourage high jumps. Stress twists to the left and to the right. Describe some of the varied movements that students demonstrate. Choose several students to demonstrate their ideas.
8	**Partner Activity** Find a partner of about your own weight. Lift him or her a few inches off the ground. Change roles. Try different ways of holding or leaning against your partner. Lean away from your partner. Use your partner's weight as a counterbalance. Try different ways. Can you keep steady and move? Develop a sequence where each partner shows a swinging movement of the legs when the hands support the weight and then combine your movements to show a balance and counterbalance. Add your own linking movements and finish.	Stress safe lifting. Encourage holds using different parts of the body and different body surfaces. Have some students demonstrate their ideas of holding and leaning on a partner. For sequence work, emphasize smooth transitions as movements are linked.
15–17	**Group Activity** (with or without large apparatus) Without large apparatus: Working in groups of three or four, develop a sequence that includes the ideas of swinging leg movements and counterbalance. With any pieces of large apparatus, a common task or challenge can be used: Use a swinging leg action to mount the apparatus, change direction, and use a different swinging action to dismount. Individual challenges could also be used at different learning centers rather than a common challenge.	Sometimes it works well to assemble all available apparatus and then allow previous work to be adapted to the apparatus. In this lesson, for example, you might allow the pairs to choose the apparatus on which to try the "counterbalance" sequence. Possibly restrict the lifting or supporting situation to groups of three, and combine twos and threes and leg swinging movements.
2	**Final/Assessment Activity** Show group sequences **or** select good **or** interesting apparatus work for comment. ▪ "Put the apparatus away. Lying on the floor on your back, try to flatten your spine. Relax. Stiffen the whole body. Relax." ▪ "Find a partner. One partner lies stiff in a star-shape and resists; the other tries to tip and turn the partner over on to the tummy. Change roles."	Select interesting sequences to show the class for both teacher and students to assess.

Short Unit Plans

The next five short unit plans show how content material can be extended. Each unit has a lesson that serves as a beginning point. Each lesson is then expanded into a short unit. Each short unit has a series of initial tasks that are accompanied by "Cues/Points for the Teacher to Stress/Suggestions to Children" to assist a teacher who might be new to the Movement Discovery method of teaching. The suggested extensions allow the teacher to expand the movement tasks in a variety of ways over several more lessons depending on the interest, experience, and skill of the children.

These five units can be used for a *variety of grade levels*. They focus on children learning to transfer their body weight to and from different parts of the body while working for better control of the movements involved. Use of hands and feet, rocking and rolling movements, actions of stretching and curling the body, and moving with the feet together and apart are all movement ideas that can be explored over many lessons.

In the following lessons, you will notice that some of the tasks are the same. In fact, you should try out several lessons that are basically the same. Take note, as you observe and circulate, of the additional things you notice and how you are able to think of more cues. This exercise is intended to develop teachers' observation skills, their skill in building more tasks based on what the children do, and their ability to recognize how children's abilities improve over time.

Teach the first lesson and write a report to yourself describing how it went. Repeat. By the time you get to the third lesson, try to include examples of what a few individual children are doing. For the remaining lessons, observe and report on the same children as well as on yourself. At the end of five short units, record how (if!) your observa-

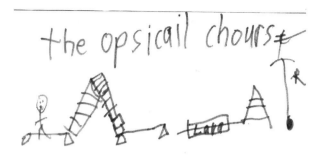

tional skills have improved, if your ability to think of cues has developed, and if you are more aware of what effects those cues have on the performance of the children.

Although there will be limits to what any particular child can do, even small changes in wording of tasks, different apparatus, and different combinations can greatly extend the range of responses made by one child. As stated previously, it is difficult to observe and even more difficult to monitor individual progress. The general impression of a Movement Discovery class is of tremendous variety. It takes many lessons to develop such a range of variety in one child. The interaction of a teacher with individual children also takes many weeks to develop. A teacher will circulate and offer comments and cues as appropriate, but there are usually 25 or more active children and all deserve the teacher's attention. In addition, their progress will need to be recorded individually. One way to uncover their progress in a Movement Discovery program is to allow the children to verbalize, draw, or record their own progress. Peers can also do this kind of assessment if time allows. This activity should *not* take away learning and activity time, which is precious in elementary schools, so do not perform this kind of recording and assessment in the gymnasium, but rather wait until you are back in the classroom.

UNIT PLAN 1

TRAVELING AND BALANCING USING DIFFERENT PARTS OF THE BODY

Appropriate grade levels: Second grade onward

Lesson length: Approximately 30 minutes

NASPE Standards: 1, 2, 5

State Standards: _____

OBJECTIVES The learner will:

Psychomotor
1. Demonstrate different ways of traveling on feet using different directions in space.
2. Practice balances using hands, feet, forearms, shins, and back.
3. Perform jumps with controlled landings in personal and general space.

Cognitive
1. Describe or report on why a large base is easier to balance on than a small base.
2. Make decisions about different ways to move on feet, which body parts to balance on, and which pieces of large apparatus to work on.

Affective
1. Be respectful of others' space while traveling on the floor and large apparatus.

UNIT MATERIALS

Large apparatus as available

Minutes (Approximately)	Scripted Movement Tasks	Cues/Points for Teacher to Stress/ Suggestions to Children
5	1. "Begin by facing another person. Now run about the general space being careful not to touch anybody. Look for free spaces to run." "Find several different ways of moving on your feet." "Move on your feet in a backward direction . . . then sideways."	Begin with a scattered formation. Remind children to run into free spaces, not in a circle. Vigorous activity should be encouraged where appropriate, but children should choose their own comfortable speed of movement. The teacher should describe the children's ideas as they are experimenting (e.g., "David is trying fast, hopping on one foot!") Stress the word "different" when moving on feet. Usual responses include running, hopping, skipping, leaping, jumping, and all kinds of stepping. The introduction of "direction" usually results in better use of space. When working with very young children the teacher could demonstrate an example of "backward" and "sideways" movements.
10	2. "Balance, rest, or take your weight on one part or several parts of your body and stay as still as possible." "Now try taking your weight on other body parts." "Which is easier to balance on, a large base or small base? Why?" "Take your body weight on two hands even if it is only for a short time. Keep your head up throughout (safety precaution to avoid overbalancing). When your legs come down, be sure your feet softly touch the ground first."	Stress "stillness." Allow children a short practice time. Children choose body parts for balance. Here the children work in a confined area or in their own personal space. Some quick demonstrations by the children may be used to share ideas and to indicate the variety of responses that are possible. The children can be guided to discover that generally the larger the base area, the easier it is to balance. Also, the flat parts of the body, or the parts that can be flattened (e.g., back, forearms, shins, hands, feet), are easier to balance on than the more rounded parts (e.g., head, elbows, knees). Always encourage controlled landings.
3	3. "See how high you can jump in your own personal space while lifting your body high into the air." "Run and jump to lift your body high in the air. Land and 'give' (bend your hips, knees, and ankles). Keep your head up."	Encourage maximum individual heights when jumping. All children need constant reminders to land softly on their feet with "give" in the hips, knees, and ankles. "Head up" is a safety precaution.

Minutes (Approximately)	Scripted Movement Tasks	Cues/Points for Teacher to Stress/ Suggestions to Children
12	4. "Move to any piece of the large apparatus. Find many different ways of moving freely on your apparatus without touching anyone." "I'm looking to see what parts of your body you're using!" "No one is allowed to wait for a turn; therefore, there must not be too many children at any one piece or group of apparatus." "After having a turn at one piece of equipment, move on to work on a different piece of equipment."	Children should never be given the responsibility of "spotting" other children. Emphasize children should do only those movements that they can do without help. In the early stages of work on apparatus it is essential to build up children's confidence and skill by allowing them to work at their own level of ability. This will also prevent accidents. Allow children plenty of time to discover what they can do on the different items of apparatus. If possible, allow the whole class to use similar apparatus in the early stages, for example, benches or mats or bars. This ensures that each child builds a considerable repertoire for using single pieces of apparatus. This will be of value later in group work.

Sample assessment

1. Circle which parts of your body you used for balances today. (Have a worksheet showing many body parts.)
2. Everyone show a movement on your feet that goes backward (and/or sideways). Use the class checklist to record results.

EXTENSIONS FOR TRAVELING AND BALANCING USING DIFFERENT PARTS OF THE BODY

Appropriate grade levels: Second grade onward

Lesson length: Approximately 30 minutes

NASPE Standards: 1, 2, 5

State Standards: _____

Initial Movement Tasks	Extensions to Initial Tasks	Cues/Points for Teacher to Stress/Suggestions to Children
1. "Begin by facing one other person. Now run about the general space being careful not to touch anybody. Look for free spaces to run." "Find several different ways of moving on your feet." "Move on your feet in a backward direction, then sideways."	1. "Move on two feet. Start by moving forward, then change to sideways and then back to forward and so on." "Move on one foot for a short distance, then on the other foot." "Move continuously from one foot to the other." "Move forward on one foot, and then change to the other foot and move backward." "Find parts of your body on which you can move, other than your feet." "What are some of the parts of your body on which you found you could move?" "Choose one way of moving and practice it. You choose which parts of the body to use. Then choose another part of the body, and practice moving that way. Now join the movements together to make a traveling sequence/movement sentence." (This very broad problem could be repeated for many lessons to encourage a wide range of responses.)	Changing the direction of one's movement increases the difficulty and requires greater body control. Specify any two directions here: forward, backward, sideways. Explore the combinations of direction. In gymnastic movement children should get off their feet and onto other body parts. Expect an answer like this: "We can move on our backs." The teacher could then suggest: "Try moving on your back, or on stomachs, or on sides of bodies, hands and knees, and so on." Try only two or three different methods of moving in any one lesson.
2. "Balance, rest, or take your weight on one part or several parts of your body and stay as still as possible." "Now try taking your weight on other body parts." "Which is easier to balance on, a large base or small base? Why?"	2. The initial problem is a broad one with many movement answers; therefore, you can experiment with some "limitations" that take some of the choices away. "Balance on several parts of your body." (Later substitute foot, shins, etc.) "Take your weight on, for example, your head, one hand, and two feet. Now find a different way of balancing on these same parts."	Repeat many times using other body parts. Include some demonstrations by the children. Children should be lead to discover that it is easier to balance on a broader base.

Initial Movement Tasks	Extensions to Initial Tasks	Cues/Points for Teacher to Stress/ Suggestions to Children
"Take your body weight on two hands even if it is only for a short time. Keep your head up throughout (safety precaution to avoid overbalancing). When your legs come down be sure your feet *softly* touch the ground first."	"Balance your weight on two body parts which are the same, for example, two hands, two shins, two forearms, etc. Experiment with placing parts of the body apart, together, one in front of the other, crossed, etc." "Balance on any two (or more) body parts, where you use a body part from the left and the right side of the body. Then try just using body parts from the same side of the body in your balance." "Which is easier? Using body parts from the same or opposite sides of the body?"	
3. "See how high you can jump in your own personal space while lifting your body high into the air." "Run and jump to lift your body high in the air. Land and 'give' (bend your knees/hips/ankles). Keep your head up."	3. "See how high you can jump in your own personal space while lifting your body high into the air. Show a stretched position in the air (or make your body into any shape while in the air or use different take-offs)." "Run and jump to lift your body high in the air. Land and 'give' (bend your knees/hips/ankles). Keep your head up. Show a stretched position in the air (or make your body into any shape while in the air or use different take-offs)." "Practice running and jumping, but turn in the air to land facing a different direction." "Practice jumps from one foot as well as two feet."	To improve the quality of jumping skills concentrate on one aspect of the jump: ■ Lightness ■ Height ■ Stretch ■ Shape ■ Take-off ■ Turns Use demonstrations by children to illustrate these qualities.
4. "Move to any piece of the large apparatus. Find many different ways of moving freely on your apparatus without touching anyone." "I'm looking to see what parts of your body you're using!" "No one is allowed to wait for a turn; therefore, there must not be too many children at any one piece or group of apparatus." "After having a turn at one piece of apparatus, move on to work on a different piece of apparatus."	4. "Go over and under many pieces of apparatus. Keep moving all the time." "Find different ways of getting on and off your apparatus. Be careful not to touch anybody as you are moving. (i.e., mounting and dismounting)." "Move along and around the apparatus in different ways." "Move through and around the apparatus. Keep moving."	Prepositional movement tasks allow children to choose the type of movement they will use, how fast to travel, etc. Allow the children to work out these problems on several different types of apparatus, for example, benches, ladders, mats, various heights of bars, etc.

USING HANDS AND FEET

Appropriate grade levels: Second grade onward

Lesson length: Approximately 30 minutes

NASPE Standards: 1, 2, 5

State Standards: _____

OBJECTIVES The learner will:

Psychomotor	1.	Demonstrate traveling and balancing, emphasizing the use of hands and feet, both on the floor and on or with large apparatus or small equipment.
Cognitive	1.	Create a movement "sentence" of jumps that are high and low either while traveling or stationary.
	2.	Discover a minimum of two ways to balance and travel on hands and feet.
Affective	1.	Show respect for others using the general space and large apparatus by working without bumping or touching others.

UNIT MATERIALS

Use any items of large apparatus that are available

Minutes (Approximately)	Scripted Movement Tasks	Cues/Points for Teacher to Stress/ Suggestions to Children
5	1. "Practice jumping up and down all about the general space, without stopping. This can be done on one or two feet. Do it lightly." "Now everybody practice light jumps up and down. Sometimes do low jumps and sometimes high jumps. Use your arms to get yourself up higher." "Create a sequence ('movement sentence') of jumps that go upward and downward either in personal or general space—for example, two low jumps, then one high jump."	Emphasize jumping lightly. Encourage use of all the available general space. The arms can be used to get greater lift in jumping. The teacher may have to suggest a sequence in the beginning—for example, two low jumps, one high jump (repeat). The idea of a "sequence/movement sentence" might need to be taught (i.e., join/combine some movements together so they become a whole without a break).
6	2. "Show an interesting balance on two hands and two feet. Change to another interesting balance position while still on two hands and two feet. Find a different way . . . and still another way." "Balance or make a base using two feet and one hand. Make a different base using the same parts." "Balance on hands. Lift your feet off the ground and every time you land, try to bring your feet down softly in a new place. Keep your head up."	Guide children to find multiple ways of answering the movement problem/task. Ensure that weight is taken frequently on the hands and in many differing situations to improve upper-body strength. Children should become increasingly confident and competent in the inverted position.

Minutes (Approximately)	Scripted Movement Tasks	Cues/Points for Teacher to Stress/ Suggestions to Children
6	3. "Move in different ways using your hands and feet. Now try a different way . . . and still another way." "Travel using just your two hands and two feet. Now try a different way . . . and still another way."	Encourage a wide range of responses. The use of demonstrations by children helps generate ideas for class members as they observe. For example, let two or three children show their movements or half the class show the others, and vice versa. The more times a movement task is repeated, the more new ideas the children will produce.
11	4. "Find different ways of getting on to your apparatus. Practice swinging, hanging, or climbing, being careful not to touch anyone. Jump to the ground softly. Remember to bend your knees when landing." "Find ways of moving on your apparatus using your hands and feet in different ways."	A variety of small equipment can be used if larger apparatus is not available (e.g., hoops, jump ropes on the floor). Stress to children that swinging, hanging, and climbing activities are extremely valuable for arm and upper-body muscular strength. Discuss "gripping" on apparatus. This action is very difficult to do on a flat surface like the floor or up a slide. Encourage the following movement variables to be explored: ■ Hands may lead while feet follow. ■ Feet may lead while hands follow. ■ Hands (and feet) may move together or alternately. ■ Hands may pass feet, and vice versa. ■ Hands and feet may be on the same or different levels.
2	**Sample assessment** Everyone show an interesting balance on hands and feet, and hold it for at least 4 seconds. Use the class checklist to record individual data. Everyone show the "jumping sentence" they created. Repeat it twice. Use the class checklist to record individual data.	

EXTENSIONS FOR USING HANDS AND FEET

Appropriate grade levels: Second grade onward

Lesson length: Approximately 30 minutes

NASPE Standards: 1, 2, 5

State Standards: _____

Initial Movement Tasks	Extensions to Initial Tasks	Cues/Points for Teacher to Stress/Suggestions to Children
1. "Practice jumping up and down all about the general space, without stopping. This can be done on one or two feet. Do it lightly." "Now everybody practice light jumps up and down. Sometimes do low jumps and sometimes high jumps. Use your arms to get yourself up higher." "Create a sequence ('movement sentence') of jumps that go upward and downward either in personal or general space—for example, two low jumps, then one high jump."	1. "Practice jumping in different *directions* about the general space. Sometimes jump sideways, backward, and forward." "Can you make a sequence of jumps in different directions?" "Travel on your feet and make a zigzag pattern on the floor as you move."	The teacher should make the class aware that feet can be used individually or together in both take-off and landing. Feet may catch each other (e.g., take off on the right or left foot and land with both feet together). Feet may pass (e.g., leaping from one foot to the other). Explore/stress the five basic jumps: from one foot to the other; from one foot to the same foot; from two feet to two feet; from two feet to one foot; from one foot to two feet. The teacher can suggest other floor patterns (e.g., curvy, straight). Visuals are helpful.
2. "Show an interesting balance on two hands and two feet. Change to another interesting balance position while still on two hands and two feet. Find a different way . . . and still another way." "Balance or make a base using two feet and one hand. Make a different base using the same parts." "Balance on hands. Lift your feet off the ground and every time you land, try to bring your feet down softly in a new place. Keep your head up."	2. "Balance on two hands and one foot. Hold the balance position for 2 to 3 seconds. Find at least two other ways of balancing on these body parts." "Try to hold your balance on one hand and one foot. Change to the other hand and the other foot. Use the right hand and the left foot, then the right foot and the left hand. Find other ways of balancing on these parts." "Take your weight on hands and land with one foot after the other." "Take your weight on hands and land on two feet together." "Take your weight on hands and get one foot (later two feet) high into the air." "Take your weight on hands and make one foot pass the other in the air."	Stress that children should increase the amount of time they balance on body parts, including hands. This will increase their balance skills in the inverted position as well as their upper-body strength. Expect vast individual differences in balances on hands from any group of children. Stress controlled, soft landings on feet.

Initial Movement Tasks	Extensions to Initial Tasks	Cues/Points for Teacher to Stress/ Suggestions to Children
3. "Move in different ways using your hands and feet. Now try a different way . . . and still another way." "Travel using just your two hands and two feet. Now try a different way . . . and still another way."	3. "Move on two hands and one foot. Find another way." "Move on one hand and two feet. Try these movements in different directions. Make a pattern on the floor by following different pathways." "Move from feet to hands, keeping hands far away from feet." "Travel around the general space sometimes with your feet near *to* your hands and sometimes with your feet far away from your hands." "Can you move with one foot or both feet lifted high?" "Can you move with a hand or hands lifted high?" "Can you move with either a foot or a hand lifted high and then change to move with the other one?" "Can you move with a foot (or hand) up high and then change to move with the same foot (or hand) down low?"	The more times a movement task is repeated, the more new ideas the class will produce. There are many patterns/pathways children can use. Prepare visuals of pathways/patterns for them to follow. Any work on hands can be tiring. Give children rest periods by using demonstrations of interesting ideas and good-quality movement.
4. "Find different ways of getting on to your apparatus. Practice swinging, hanging, or climbing, being careful not to touch anyone. Jump to the ground softly Remember to give in your knees when landing." "Find ways of moving on your apparatus using your hands and feet in different ways."	4. "Practice jumping over a piece of the apparatus, or on and off it. Include some turning jumps." "Try swinging or hanging in different ways using hands and other parts of the body. Experiment with different ways to grip." "With which parts of the body could you grip the apparatus?" "Find places to hang with your body in different shapes." "Try long, stretched, wide, rounded, and twisted shapes; shapes with feet together or apart; and crossed leg shapes." "Move on the apparatus sometimes with hands near feet and sometimes with hands far away from feet." "Travel on your apparatus with one foot or both feet high in the air." "Travel on your apparatus sometimes making a zigzag pathway and sometimes traveling in a straight line."	Stress use of feet in different ways for jumps. After the children experiment with "gripping," they should be able to answer the question asked. Answers would include toes, instep, back of knees, armpits, elbow joints, and front of hips.

ROCKING AND ROLLING MOVEMENTS

Appropriate grade levels: Second grade onward

Lesson length: Approximately 30 minutes

NASPE Standards: 1, 2, 5

State Standards: _____

OBJECTIVES The learner will:

Psychomotor 1. Demonstrate different kinds of rocking and rolling movements on different parts of the body on large apparatus and on the floor.

Cognitive 1. Discover (a) a minimum of four different leg positions for jumping and (b) different rolling and rocking movements.

2. Name and describe objects that rock and objects that roll.

Affective 1. Avoid making physical contact with students who are close to them while moving in general space.

UNIT MATERIALS

Use any items of large apparatus that are available

Minutes (Approximately)	Scripted Movement Tasks	Cues/Points for Teacher to Stress/ Suggestions to Children/Questions
5	1. "How many different ways can you jump? Try two or three different ways in your own personal space." "Jump up. Do something with your legs in the air."	Have *children* demonstrate some of the different ways they found to jump. Children can discover that legs may be: ■ Tucked—in front, to the side, behind ■ Apart—forward, backward, or sideways ■ Together and straight—in front, at the back, or to the side ■ One leg may be bent, one stretched ■ Crossed
6	2. "What are some things you know of that *rock*?" "Practice a rocking movement on your two feet. Rock forward, backward, and sideways. Experiment with your feet in different positions to each other." "Try a rocking movement on your back. Find another way of rocking on your back." "Rock on your tummy and your side. Use your hands on the floor to push and increase the size of the rocking movement."	Briefly use a gesture to illustrate a rocking action. Rocking on parts of the body is a good preparation for rolling. Children can discover surfaces that must be rounded for rolling. Children can experience rocking (forward, backward, and sideways) on two feet placed in different positions with respect to each other (e.g., apart, one in front of the other, together). Rocking may be forward, backward, or sideways. The body may be elongated or rounded. Children can discover these methods of rocking for themselves.

Minutes (Approximately)	Scripted Movement Tasks	Cues/Points for Teacher to Stress/ Suggestions to Children/Questions
6	3. "See how many different ways you can roll." "If you can, combine rocking and rolling on the floor."	Emphasize that rolling can be performed in a number of different ways. Allow the class complete freedom to practice rolls already mastered or to discover new ways of rolling. At first each child can attempt the ways he or she finds easiest. In the early stages, stress the point that in rolling, the body should be rounded and that pointed body parts should be tucked in.
13	4. "Find different places and different ways of rocking and/or rolling on the apparatus." or Mats (either individual or 6-feet by 3-feet tumbling mats): "Try three or four different ways of rolling across your mat." Benches (used either individually or in different groupings): "Get onto the bench in some way, move along or roll along the bench, and jump off." **Sample assessment** Worksheet displaying seven pictures: "Which of these seven objects can roll and which can rock?" Write the words "rock" and "roll." (Pictures: rocking horse, rocking cradle, rocking chair, ball, pencil, apple, watermelon) "On a sheet, draw four different positions or shapes your legs can be in when you jump in the air." Class checklist: Demonstrate two different rolls on the mat.	Children can experiment with various ways of rocking and rolling. Rocking can lead into a roll. Make some combinations of large apparatus available, and provide a variety of approaches and pathways. When grouping apparatus, arrange it so there are a number of starting and finishing points. Different arrangements of apparatus (e.g., benches, benches and mats, inclined benches) will also suggest various tracks or paths along which children can move.

EXTENSIONS FOR ROCKING AND ROLLING MOVEMENTS

Appropriate grade levels: Second grade onward

Lesson length: Approximately 30 minutes

NASPE Standards: 1, 2, 5

State Standards: _____

Initial Movement Tasks	Extensions to Initial Tasks	Cues/Points for Teacher to Stress/ Suggestions to Children
1. "How many different ways can you jump? Try two or three different ways in your own personal space." "Jump up. Do something with your legs in the air."	1. "Run and jump and do something with your feet in the air." "Run and jump and do something with your arms in the air." "Run and jump and do something with your knees in the air." Look for knees/legs. "Run, jump, land, and roll. Use your hands to make the action on the floor safer and smoother."	Try variations with the feet lifted high into the air in front of the body one after the other, kicked into the space behind, or brought to the side. Try variations with the arms crossed, together or apart, one or both high and/or low, and so on. Try variations with the knees together or apart, at the front or side of the body. Jumping can be practiced without a run-up. As soon as the class can manage the body safely doing this, then two ways of transferring weight can be combined: "Run, jump, and land." "Jump, land, and roll. Practice this until it becomes a smooth continuous movement."
2. "What are some things you know of that rock?" "Practice a rocking movement on your two feet. Rock forward, backward, and sideways. Experiment with your feet in different positions to each other." "Try a rocking movement on your back. Find another way of rocking on your back." "Rock on your tummy and your side. Use your hands on the floor to push and increase the size of the rocking movement."	2. "Practice rocking smoothly with your body curled." "Practice rocking smoothly with your body elongated or stretched." "Practice rocking forward and backward." "Squat down. Practice rocking from your feet along your back to your shoulders and onto your feet again."	Stress the body's shape as it is rolling. Having introduced the possibility that weight can be transferred onto feet at completion of a rocking action, the children may now experiment with the idea that as the feet and shoulders receive weight, the rest of the body may be redirected by a slight twist of the top or lower half against the fixed part (i.e., changing direction as you rock).

Initial Movement Tasks	Extensions to Initial Tasks	Cues/Points for Teacher to Stress/ Suggestions to Children
3. "See how many different ways you can roll." "If you can, combine rocking and rolling on the floor."	3. "Practice rolling sideways in different ways. Roll in one direction, then back in the opposite direction." "You can roll forward over one shoulder. If you'd like to try to get onto your hands and knees, lift a hand and with head following, lead your body through the space between the other hand and knee until the point of overbalance, and then roll on a shoulder." "Practice a rocking movement and then a rolling movement." "Rock and then follow with a jump or some other movement."	Elicit from the children that they can change their arm positions and leg positions when rolling sideways. If children want to learn how to roll forward, stress that they should crouch down, keeping the knees off the ground. Lift the hips and push off slightly from the feet. Look into the space between the legs. Shoulders should touch the ground first, not the head or neck. For most children it is easier to start on the feet and roll backward.
4. "Find different places and different ways of rocking and/or rolling on the apparatus." or Mats (either individual or 6-feet by 3-feet tumbling mats): "Try three or four different ways of rolling across your mat." Benches (used either individually or in different groupings): "Get onto the bench in some way, move along or roll along the bench, and jump off."	4. "Move along or over the apparatus. Finish your movement with a roll either on the ground or on the apparatus." "Jump from the apparatus, land on your feet, and then roll." Mats: "Roll on the mat. Vary your starting position and approach the mat from different angles." "Start away from the mat (say 3 yards). Move toward the mat in different ways and then roll across the mat." Benches: "Jump onto the bench, move along or over the bench, and roll on the ground to finish your movement." "Get onto the bench with hands touching first, travel along the bench, and get off with hands touching the ground first."	Provide a variety of approaches and pathways, as the physical environment is designed/constructed by the teacher. When grouping large apparatus, arrange it so there are a number of starting and finishing points. Different arrangements of apparatus will also suggest various tracks or paths along which children can move.

MOVING WITH FEET TOGETHER AND FAR APART

Appropriate grade levels: Second grade onward

Lesson length: Approximately 30 minutes

NASPE Standards: 1, 2, 5

State Standards: _____

OBJECTIVES The learner will:

Psychomotor
1. Demonstrate jumping and traveling in different ways while feet are together or far apart both on the floor and large apparatus.
2. Support partial weight of the body on the hands while the feet are together and/or apart in the air or on landing.

Cognitive
1. Demonstrate and describe the difference between feet together and feet apart.

Affective
1. Respect the personal space of other students by avoiding physical contact with those who are close to them while moving in general space.

UNIT MATERIALS

Use any items of large apparatus that are available

Minutes (Approximately)	Scripted Movement Tasks	Cues/Points for Teacher to Stress/ Suggestions to Children
5	1. In your own personal space, jump on the spot, keeping your feet close together in the air. Do many jumps like this." "Jump on the spot. Find different ways of making your feet go far apart in the air. Remember to try different ideas with feet apart."	Throughout this theme, the teacher will be constantly making reference to what the children's feet are doing. The teacher should encourage children to work with feet very close together or as far apart as possible so as to achieve flexibility effects. A wide range of responses to this problem should be encouraged. Always stress "soft feet" when jumping and landing. Bending ankles, knees, and hips produces "soft feet."
7	2. "Travel in general space keeping your feet together." "Find different *ways* of moving with your feet close together." "Travel about the area with your feet as far apart as possible." "Find other ways of moving with your feet far apart."	Encourage children to move on hands and feet, not just on their feet. Have children discover many ways of solving the problems stated. The children may move on different body parts, in different directions. They may travel by using jumping, sliding, pushing, stepping or rolling movements. If rolling movements have been explored, some children will probably move in this way, but they will be thinking about their feet being together or apart as they roll.

Minutes (Approximately)	Scripted Movement Tasks	Cues/Points for Teacher to Stress/ Suggestions to Children
4	3. "Keeping your hands on the floor, move your feet around them, sometimes having your feet close together and sometimes far apart." "Put your hands on the floor and lift or jump your feet in the air. Bring your feet down one after the other. Hands can be under or behind the body or at the side as well as in front."	Supporting weight on the hands and doing different movements with the legs and feet are very helpful in increasing upper-body muscular strength. Children should do this often for short periods of time because it is quite stressful for some children. Encourage soft landings when feet come down and contact the floor. This behavior encourages better body control from children. Bringing one foot down before the other is a different skill than bringing both feet down together. Encourage this variation. Children will become more versatile movers when the teacher changes these small elements of the tasks.
14	4. "Travel on, along, over, or across any pieces of large apparatus or small equipment keeping your feet together." "Travel with your feet apart using any piece of large apparatus or layout of small equipment."	Large apparatus and small equipment can be tried (e.g., jump ropes, beanbags, hoops, spots). Possible items of large apparatus to group in different formations: ■ two benches, mat, ropes ■ two mats, one vaulting stool, ladder ■ Inclined bench, trestle, sliding board, mat ■ Hoop, jump rope, hoop

Sample assessment

Everyone demonstrate two different ways to travel with feet together, either on the floor or on large apparatus.

Everyone demonstrate two different ways to travel with feet apart, either on the floor or on large apparatus.

EXTENSIONS FOR MOVING WITH FEET TOGETHER AND FAR APART

Appropriate grade levels: Second grade onward

Lesson length: Approximately 30 minutes

NASPE Standards: 1, 2, 5

State Standards: _____

Initial Movement Tasks	Extensions to Initial Tasks	Cues/Points for Teacher to Stress/ Suggestions to Children
1. In your own personal space, jump on the spot, keeping your feet close together in the air. Do many jumps like this." "Jump on the spot. Find different ways of making your feet go far apart in the air. Remember to try different ideas with feet apart."	1 "Run and jump off one foot, bringing your feet close together in the air." "Run and jump off one foot, parting your feet in the air." "Run and jump off two feet, finding different ways of having your feet together in the air" (e.g., feet can be together with both legs straight or both legs bent; feet can be in front, behind, or to the side). "Run and jump off two feet finding different ways of having your feet apart in the air" (e.g., one leg can be forward and one back; the legs can be stretched sideways, or one leg can be bent and one leg stretched).	An instant activity with cardiovascular endurance effects if children work for extended periods of time. Stress feet *far* apart to achieve maximum flexibility effects. Focusing on height and increasing the height of a jump, in addition to changing the position of the feet in the air, can improve jumping skills.
2. "Travel in general space keeping your feet together." "Find different ways of moving with your feet close together." "Travel about the area with your feet as far apart as possible." "Find other ways of moving with your feet far apart."	2. "Travel in general space, sometimes with your feet together and sometimes with your feet apart." "Move on your hands and feet, keeping your feet together. Try several different ideas." "Move on your hands and feet, with your feet as far apart as possible. Try several ways." "Move on hands and feet, sometimes with feet together and sometimes with feet apart." "Travel with your feet together (or apart, or change from one to the other) but try to travel sideways, backward, or forward, or just change the direction of your movement." "Keep your feet apart (or together, or change from one to the other) as you travel along different pathways on the floor. Try straight, curvy, or twisting pathways."	These original movement tasks can be repeated many times, depending on student interest. Encourage children to practice some of their specific movement ideas to improve the quality of the movement. The teacher can specify other body parts on which to travel after hands and feet have been tried. Specify a direction in which to move with feet together (or apart, or changing from together to apart). Children can choose the type of floor pathway to follow or the teacher can specify it.

Initial Movement Tasks	Extensions to Initial Tasks	Cues/Points for Teacher to Stress/ Suggestions to Children
3. "Keeping your hands on the floor, move your feet around them, sometimes having your feet close together and sometimes far apart." "Put your hands on the floor and lift or jump your feet in the air. Bring your feet down one after the other."	3. "Put your hands on the floor, and lift or jump your feet into the air. Land with your feet close together." "Take your weight on your hands and make your feet go apart in the air." "Try keeping your hands underneath your body and at one side, as well as in front of you."	Prompt children to keep their heads up. Some jumps of the feet will leave the floor for only a small distance, while other children can lift their feet high into the air. Expect these individual differences because arm/shoulder strength is varied.
4. "Travel on, along, over, or across any pieces of apparatus or small equipment, keeping your feet together." "Travel with your feet apart using any piece of large apparatus or layout of small equipment."	4. "Travel on the apparatus first with your feet together and then with your feet apart." "We will change the apparatus groupings and repeat the original tasks." "Travel on the benches with feet together and on the mat with feet apart." "Get off or get on with either your feet far apart or glued together." "Travel along, around, and over your layout of small equipment while keeping your feet either together or apart."	Repeat these tasks many times. Create interesting physical layouts. Children can make useful layout suggestions. Depending on which large apparatus is available in a school, supplement it with small equipment to ensure maximum activity time for all children. Tasks using prepositions offer scope for children to discover new movements while still allowing children much freedom and choice.

2 benches, mat, ropes

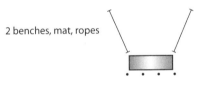

2 mats, 3 benches, bar (medium height)

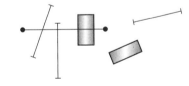

Inclined bench, window bars, mat

2 benches, 2 mats, table

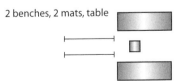

Suitable large apparatus and small equipment for work on this theme: inclined sliding boards, benches, mats, hanging ropes/rope ladders, horizontal or sloped ladders, bars of different kinds and heights, trestles, jump ropes, beanbags, hoops, spots.

STRETCHING AND CURLING ACTIONS

Appropriate grade levels: Second grade onward

Lesson length: Approximately 30 minutes

NASPE Standards: 1, 2, 5

State Standards: _____

OBJECTIVES The learner will:

Psychomotor   1. Demonstrate traveling movements with the body stretching and curling on large apparatus and on the floor.

Cognitive   1. Discover and show a variety of balances and grips where the body is flexed/curled and in stretched positions.

Affective   1. Work sensibly in the movement space without interfering with the actions of other members of the class.

UNIT MATERIALS

Use any items of large apparatus that are available

Minutes (Approximately)	Scripted Movement Tasks	Cues/Points for Teacher to Stress/ Suggestions to Children
5	1. "Travel about the space on your feet. Sometimes move with your legs bent and sometimes with your legs stretched."	Traveling on feet can be by stepping or running. Encourage a good stretch in the legs. Emphasis should be put on "lightness" as children travel on feet. Encourage vigorous activity. Share children's ideas by selecting several children to demonstrate their actions: "Sue, show us your idea with bent and stretched legs!"
6	2. "Rest your body weight on your feet and curl your whole body." "Curl up and rest on the side of your body." "Rest on other parts and curl or stretch your body (e.g., hands, shins, back, shoulders)." "Lie down on the floor and stretch your whole body. Turn on to your side and see if you can stretch further. Fully stretch to your fingertips and toes."	"Be still or balance on one or both feet and completely stretch out." Have the children hold their positions for increased lengths of time but avoid a series of static poses. Have the children experience the two extreme positions—body fully curled and fully stretched to fingertips and toes. Notice that sometimes a curl is opposite a stretch. They are experienced at the same time (e.g., lying on the side shows this clearly). Have children suggest parts of the body on which to rest. At first, it is probably better for the teacher to select parts of the body that might take weight (e.g., hands, shins, back, shoulders). After having experienced the extremes of curling and stretching, the children could experiment with other bases of support. Getting the body weight onto the hands in every lesson helps build upper-body strength. Expect only momentary weight bearing on hands in the beginning.

Minutes (Approximately)	Scripted Movement Tasks	Cues/Points for Teacher to Stress/ Suggestions to Children
4	3. "Move around the general space with your body curled, rounded, or flexed." "Move all around the gym with your legs stretched. Try several ways of moving like this."	Allow time for experimentation with "curled" and "stretched" moving around general space. Suggest rolling. Encourage smooth, slow movement; consecutive rolls; or rolls in different directions. Encourage movements on many different parts of the body while the legs are stretched (e.g., back, hands and feet, side, and front of body).
4	4. "Run and leap to show a fully stretched position in the air." "Try again, but show a different stretched position in the air."	Encourage "stretching," to include the fingertips and toes. Note the difficulties involved in curling once airborne. It is far easier to stretch in the air. Therefore, it may be better to postpone curling the body in flight.
11	5. "Find different ways of gripping the apparatus while curling the rest of your body." "Find different ways of gripping the apparatus while stretching the rest of your body." "Travel on your apparatus, curling and/or stretching your body as you move. Try your ideas on several different pieces of apparatus." "Invent a movement sequence using stretching and curling/bending movements on any piece of large apparatus." **Summative assessment (sample)** "Invent a movement sentence. Decide where you'll start and stop. Use minimum of two still positions, minimum of one jump, and traveling movements where your body is clearly stretched sometimes and bent/curled sometimes."	Allow children time to explore the possibilities of "gripping" on several different types of apparatus while they stretch and curl their bodies. The children need not be grouped for these tasks. Children can choose where or which pieces of large apparatus they want to practice their ideas.

EXTENSIONS FOR STRETCHING AND CURLING ACTIONS

Appropriate grade levels: Second grade onward

Lesson length: Approximately 30 minutes

NASPE Standards: 1, 2, 5

State Standards: _____

Initial Movement Tasks	Extensions to Initial Tasks	Cues/Points for Teacher to Stress/ Suggestions to Children
1. "Travel about the space on your feet. Sometimes move with your legs bent and sometimes with them stretched."	1. "Travel on your feet, keeping low to the floor so that your legs are bent. Try movements where both feet move together or the feet move one after the other." "Travel on your feet, stretching your legs as you move."	Encourage vigorous traveling movement. Children can be made aware of how the leg shape is changing, as they are moving. The comparatively simple actions of curling and stretching will have been performed already many times in response to activities on different themes.
2. "Rest your body weight on your feet and curl your whole body." "Curl up and rest on the side of your body." "Rest on other parts (e.g., shins, back, shoulders)." "Lie down on the floor and stretch your whole body. Fully stretch to your fingertips." "Be still or balance on one or both feet and completely stretch out." "Rest on your hands and try to stretch the rest of your body."	2. "Find many different parts of your body on which you can be curled. Hold each position for approximately 3 seconds before changing to the next curled position." "Take your weight on your shoulders and stretch the rest of your body" (an incomplete stretch only is possible). "Choose other bases and stretch the free parts of your body to the fullest." (Repeat many times.)	Repeat the task several times. Have children experience the two extreme positions—body fully curled and fully stretched, to the fingertips and toes! Repetition will improve the children's skill. After having experienced the extremes of curling and stretching, the children could experiment with other bases.
3. "Move around the general space with your body curled, rounded, or flexed." "Move all around the gym with your legs stretched. Try several ways of moving like this."	3. "Move around, sometimes being curled up and sometimes being stretched out. Practice your ideas." "Try other ways of moving in general space, being curled and then stretched. When using different body parts on the floor, try using your hands to help make a smooth transition."	Allow a period for experimentation. Have children repeat their ideas. Rolling is a possible response. Encourage smooth movement. Children can try consecutive rolls, rolls in different directions, or rolls with the body in different shapes. Encourage children to move on many different parts of the body while the legs are stretched (e.g., back, hands and feet, side, and front of body).

Initial Movement Tasks	Extensions to Initial Tasks	Cues/Points for Teacher to Stress/ Suggestions to Children
4. "Run and leap to show a fully stretched position in the air." "Try again, but show a different stretched position in the air."	4. "Run, leap, and stretch in the air. Then try other methods of stretching in the air." "Try different ways of running, leaping, and stretching in the air." "Run, jump, stretch, and turn in the air to land facing in a different direction."	The teacher should realize the difficulties involved in curling once airborne. It is far easier to stretch in the air. Therefore, it may be easier to curl only part of the body in flight.
5. "Find different ways of gripping the apparatus while curling the rest of your body." "Find different ways of gripping the apparatus while stretching the rest of your body." "Travel on your apparatus by curling and/or stretching your body as you move. Try your ideas on several different pieces of apparatus."	5. **2 mats, "A" and "B", spread apart or 2 jump ropes or 2 large hoops or 1 hoop and 1 jump rope:** "Travel along or across Mat A keeping the body curled. Travel along or across Mat B stretching." **Bench and/or balance beam and mat:** "Travel along the bench/balance beam first curling your body then stretching your body. Jump off the end and roll over the mat." **Bar(s) at hanging height:** "Move along either stretching your body or stretching and curling your body." **Vertical, hanging ropes:** "Climb the rope stretching and curling as you move up and down." "Hang from one or two stationary or moving ropes. Show some stretched and/or curled positions on the ropes." **Climbing frame, window bars, wall bars:** "Travel up and down, over or across the bars with your body stretching and curling."	These movement tasks can be used for many lessons. Where large apparatus is not available teachers should substitute with small equipment to ensure small groups and no lines of children waiting for their turn. When children have had sufficient time to experiment on single pieces of apparatus, more complicated arrangements, where they explore other curling and stretching possibilities, can be planned. Rather than using one task for all pieces of apparatus the teacher can plan more specific tasks for each piece or group of apparatus. Students would then be grouped for the different learning centers.

TABLE 11–1   Guidelines to Assess Your Teaching of Educational Gymnastic Lessons   Get a friend to observe you teach one or more of the preceding lessons. Have that person check off the boxes that you have addressed.

In every educational gymnastics lesson, where possible include vigorous running and jumping and taking the body weight on the hands.	Concisely worded movement tasks work best. Lengthy explanations reduce moving time.	There should be no lines of children waiting for their turn! Sufficient apparatus should be available so that each child can work almost continuously.	Plan the physical space carefully for a safe environment. Placement and arrangement of apparatus can be changed to stimulate more variety, originality, and difficulty in the children's movement skills.
Movement challenges preceding the equipment tasks prepare children with movement experiences, which will contribute to the safe, effective, and creative use of the equipment.	Give children CHOICE. They will tend to choose movement solutions within their own ability limitations; accidents are thus rare. Choice is a motivator, as it allows children to pursue their own interests.	Children must be taught to give very careful thought to the consequences of their actions. Teachers should praise appropriate, safe behavior.	When apparatus is introduced, a variety of surfaces, heights, and slopes should be provided where possible. This allows for new parts of the body to be used for balancing, weight bearing, and traveling.
Children can be trained to handle large apparatus safely and efficiently. Such lifting contributes to their muscular strength.	Educational gymnastics lessons must be activity lessons. Encourage maximum participation and effort. Frequently set movement tasks that require intensive efforts.	Appropriate, nonbulky clothing should be worn when working on large apparatus. Encourage bare feet indoors—never socks! They slip and slide easily, which is dangerous.	Children should work mainly individually. Partner work will increase the difficulty significantly.
A teacher must make sure that the apparatus being used is in sound condition.	Groups should be kept very small.	The general theme serves as a focus for the movement content of a lesson. Different skills and knowledge are learned from these themes.	Use a variety of small equipment if sufficient large apparatus is not available for educational gymnastics work.

Discovering Special Needs: Adaptations and Modifications

QUESTIONS TO DISCUSS

1. Share some of the experiences you have had with persons with disabilities. Mention some of the characteristics you have observed, including movement, cognitive, social, and emotional abilities.

2. What are some of the advantages of including students with disabilities in a class with their able-bodied peers? List at least four advantages, and compare your list with your partner's.

3. Under which circumstances would it be reasonable to provide instruction for some students with disabilities in a self-contained class? Discuss your ideas with a partner.

4. Describe any situations where you have observed teachers giving students choices in Physical Education. How well (or poorly) did those students handle the amount of freedom given to them? Discuss.

5. Try to observe students who are nonverbal and note how teachers communicate with them. Which types of communication aids have you noted that are effective? List as many as you can.

6. Observe teachers who employ a variety of instructional strategies when teaching students with diverse abilities. Which teaching methods appear to be effective with students with intellectual impairments versus students with motor impairments? Discuss this issue with another observer.

7. What role do the related service personnel play in the education of children with disabilities? Discuss the support services offered by physical therapy, occupational therapy, speech therapy, psychological services, audiology, orientation, and mobility training specialists.

8. What are some of the adaptations you have seen used in Physical Education to aid in the successful inclusion of students with special needs at the preschool and elementary levels?

9. List ways in which small equipment/apparatus can be created, used, improvised, modified, and customized for children with reduced strength, impaired coordination, balance challenges, or visual impairments. Compare your list with a partner's.

10. Why is movement in the water environment emphasized for children with disabilities? Which kinds of disabilities can benefit most from these movement experiences? Consider the practical implications of providing such experiences.

Physical Education should be an integral part of the educational program of all children with disabilities from the youngest possible age. Chapter 3, Discovering Capacity, has suggested that physical activity is essential as a basis for all mental/cognitive development in human beings. It is not the intent of this chapter to prepare teachers to teach all children with disabilities, including those with severe disabilities. Instead, this chapter suggests adaptations that teachers might use in a variety of physical activity settings where movement, fitness, and games and sports skills are being taught. It is beyond the scope of this text to try to address every disability or medical condition a teacher might encounter in a Physical Education class.

It has been emphasized consistently that able-bodied or typically developing children have different abilities, needs, and interests. The same is true for children with disabilities: They also have different needs and interests in addition to the many variations in their cognitive, social, emotional, communication, and movement abilities.

Choosing Instructional Strategies for Diverse Students

The Movement Discovery approach has as its basis individualized instruction, choice, variety, and individual progression. As a consequence, it is well suited to be used in either an inclusive Physical Education environment or a self-contained, small-group placement that exclusively serves children with more severe disabilities. The range of activities and movements that children

Anecdote 12–1

Amy is a nonverbal student who is regarded as having severe intellectual impairment. Expectations in the self-contained school she is attending are quite low. When she came to a Movement Discovery type of Physical Education program, some interesting things happened. Amy's new teachers led her to a variety of climbing apparatus and "told her" to get climbing as they pointed to and tapped the trestles, bars, benches, and hanging ropes. They beckoned her with hand gestures to come toward them. To their great surprise, Amy started moving toward them as if she understood. After she had traveled from one end of the apparatus to the other, she was encouraged to "Do it again!" With some physical assistance and gesturing, she headed back to her "start" and moved along all the apparatus again.

produce when challenged continually surprises teachers—whether the children have disabilities or not. Try allowing choices before employing teacher intervention.

Guided discovery/limitation and free exploration/indirect methods involving choice will be effective instructional strategies in a variety of curricular areas for the majority of students with disabilities. The teacher will likely need to give much direction and structure, including total or partial physical assistance, to more severely involved students. Remember the stimulus that apparatus offers to all children, and allow its use in a safe environment. Exploration will be the first stage. Children with exceptionalities can also be held accountable for their own safety when given free choice.

Teachers of children with special needs will need a repertoire of effective communication and pedagogical strategies. Communication with some children with disabilities will need to occur without the use of words. Visual communication aids that can be constructed using the program "Boardmaker" and/or various clip art computer programs and sign language may also enhance communication.

Free choice and individual activity should be offered, but teachers must be tolerant of limitations caused by the children's disabilities. The direct style of teaching, where the teacher gives all the direction and structure, will be useful for many severely involved students who do not have—and may never have—the ability or possibility of coming up with ideas on their own. At the same time, the changing dynamics of the learning environment may mean that complete freedom and choice or the indirect/free exploration method may be very effective with children who have the possibility of choosing things they like to do or can do. Teachers may limit some children because they have low expectations of a disabled child. Give children the opportunity to challenge themselves before setting too many limitations. Some children may frequently change from one activity to the other to stay interested and engaged.

When deciding on pedagogical strategies to use with an individual child or a group of children, the teacher should be ready at all times to adjust instructional tasks based on the responses of the children. Some children

with disabilities will need instructional task limitations on the size of the group or the number of people with whom they must work or cooperate. For others, limitations or choices in terms of the equipment to use will be very important for their successful participation. Thus the limitation method of teaching will be used predominantly because the teacher will be able to vary the amount of freedom and choice that the children can handle.

If a child needs more structure or teacher direction to learn, then the teacher should be ready and able to provide assistance. When a child with a disability has the ability to critically think and problem-solve, however, then those skills should be included in the Physical Education experience. Less teacher direction will be more appropriate for such children.

Instructional Settings/ Placements and Supports

Children with disabilities should be educated with students without disabilities in the regular Physical Education program to the maximum extent possible. This is a legal mandate in the United States, established by the Individuals with Disabilities Education Improvement Act (IDEA). Answers to many questions about students with disabilities can be found in the regulations published in the *Federal Register* (2006), a daily U.S. government publication. The American Alliance for Health, Physical Education, Recreation, and Dance (AAHPERD, 2004) has also published a very helpful pamphlet on including students with disabilities in Physical Education.

All children should have the choice of the most appropriate instructional setting in addition to the opportunity to participate in developmentally appropriate and meaningful physical activity that is sensitive to the multiple needs, learning styles, and experiences of the child. Sometimes it will be necessary to offer "supports" to enable children with disabilities to be successful in Physical Education. These supports might take the form of one-on-one assistance, peer helpers, itinerant adapted Physical Education specialist teachers, specialized equipment, or other assistive technology, and are offered on a needs basis. Physical therapists, occupational therapists, and speech therapists are also support personnel, just like movement specialists. Consultation with these related-services professionals regarding the best positioning of some children for optimal function is advised. For example, hand-function issues, including grasping and releasing, can be addressed by the occupational therapists in your school system. Speech therapists can provide valuable information on language (both receptive and expressive), assistive technology communication devices, and other communication challenges.

All children need the proprioceptive, vestibular, and kinesthetic sensory input that development requires. The goals for children with disabilities when engaging in Physical Education are that they will be interested in movement, that they will enjoy the experience, that they will develop their strengths and abilities to the fullest extent possible, that they will become physically educated in personally meaningful ways, and that they will learn skills that will encourage them to be physically active for a lifetime.

Ways to Adapt Environments to Increase Success for All Children, Including Those with Special Needs

The adaptations suggested here can be considered for students displaying challenges as they participate in varied movement and fitness activities.

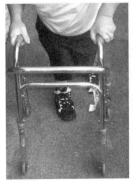

The Student with Cardiovascular and/or Muscular Endurance Limitations

- Adjust the amount of activity time required.
- Adjust or eliminate speed requirements.
- Include or permit rest periods of different lengths.
- Reduce the playing field size or length of games/sports.
- Shorten activity distances.
- Use deflated, slower-moving balls.
- Use walking instead of running.
- Allow the student to change body positions: standing to sitting; sitting to lying down/all fours.
- Use walls, corners, and protected areas.
- Use walkers, canes, or quad-canes for long distances.
- Use a helper (peers or a teacher's aide) to retrieve balls.
- Attach the ball to a string for easy retrieval by a wheelchair user.
- Attach balls on strings to the wrist/arm, pole, fence, or wheelchair.

The Student with Muscular Strength Limitations

- Use lighter equipment (e.g., sticks, bats, balls, balloons).
- Reduce the length or weight of hitting/striking implements.
- Adjust the weight of objects to be held or lifted.

- Assist gripping of implements by using Velcro straps to secure the child's hand to the handle.
- Suspend balls on strings or elastic bands.
- Allow stationary balls on cones or use of a tee-ball stand.
- Permit choice of shorter distances to propel objects.
- Reduce the amount of time spent on an activity.
- Reduce the number of repetitions.
- Eliminate or reduce speed requirements in activities.
- Allow the student to choose the working position—for example, propped against the wall, sitting, straddling a bench or foam roll, kneeling, or laying down (prone, supine, side).
- Allow the student to use a wheelchair, walker, or cane to ambulate.
- Lower the goal or target.
- Use softer, slower, lighter, or larger balls.
- Modify grasps.
- Use an inclined ramp or chute to deliver a ball to a target.
- Allow the student to use a head-pointer where use of hands is not possible.
- Provide different amounts of physical assistance (from partial to full assistance).

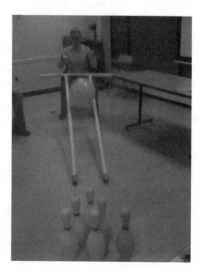

The Student with Balance Limitations

- Increase the width of the apparatus (e.g., beams, ladders, slides, benches).
- Provide apparatus with a variety of heights, slopes, and widths for all to use in educational gymnastic movement.
- Allow students to use physical supports (e.g., walkers, canes, quad-canes, bars, chairs, prone and supine standers, gait-trainers).
- Use a partner or buddy system.
- Provide different amounts of physical assistance (from partial to full assistance).
- Encourage use of environmental supports such as walls and poles.
- Use sitting postures if the child's standing balance is poor.
- Utilize stationary positions for striking (sending) and catching (receiving) objects.
- Use suspended balls and other objects.
- Allow the ball to remain stationary (e.g., use of tees or placement of the ball on the ground).
- Have "safe" areas in games and sports activities.
- Avoid slippery working surfaces and uneven, sloping outdoor surfaces.
- Include different activities that challenge balance skills so as to improve balance.

The Student with General Coordination Limitations

- Increase the sizes of targets and goals for greater success in aiming.
- Include a choice of lower nets and goals for everyone in games and sports.
- Adjust or decrease distances for propelling and sending objects.
- Increase the size of objects to hit, send, or catch (e.g., ball, puck, birdie).
- Use stationary rather than moving balls or other objects to push, strike, or send.
- Offer all students a choice of hitting implements, particularly those with larger hitting surface areas.
- Offer all students a choice of softer, slower, or lighter balls of different sizes to throw, catch, kick, strike, and roll.
- Use suspended balls or objects, or place stationary balls on tees or cones.
- Use slower-moving objects to catch (e.g., balloons, scarves).
- Slow the activity pace.
- Modify body positions.
- Modify grasps.
- Use walls, corners, and protected areas.
- Use partner assistance (e.g., to retrieve balls).
- Designate "safe" areas for some students.

The Student with a Visual Impairment

- Use beepers for targets or bases.
- Use beeper or bell balls.
- Provide a raised boundary of the playing area for tactile identification.

The Student with a Latex Allergy

- Remove all Physical Education apparatus containing latex or rubber.
- Have available plastic balls, vinyl balls, or balls covered with fabric.

The Student with a Specific Medical Condition That Affects Participation in Physical Activity

- Check with the child's doctor for specific activity restrictions and vary the activities offered accordingly.
- When an activity is contraindicated or prohibited for any student, offer a choice of activities for all children.

The adaptations suggested here can be used for a whole class, for several students, or for one student only. Adaptations and availability of choices increase opportunities for success and satisfaction for all students and provide new skill and fitness challenges, particularly in inclusive environments.

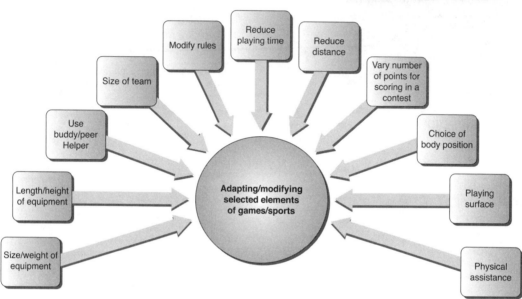

FIGURE 12–1   Adapting/Modifying Selected Elements of Games/Sports

Adapting/Modifying Selected Aspects of Games/Sports

Larger Objects		
Activity	**Modifications**	**Consequences**
Catching activities	Larger balls	Easier to catch than small balls; more contact area
Throwing/striking activities	Bigger targets	Larger area at which to aim; increases success
Volleyball-like games	Foam, vinyl, SloMo, or beach balls	Softer to strike; ball moves more slowly than regulation ball, thereby slowing down the game; area of contact is increased, enhancing success and requiring less finger strength to control ball
Badminton-like games	Balloons, bigger birdies	Travels slowly; more time to aim and hit, thereby increasing success
Tennis-like games	Larger ball than tennis ball	Larger surface area for contact

Activity	Modifications	Consequences
Softball-like games	Larger ball than softball	Larger surface area for contact; ball won't travel as far; success is enhanced; tempo of game is reduced
Soccer-like games	Larger/softer ball	Hurts less when it hits a player; larger surface area for better contact by feet
Softball-like games	Balloon or beach ball	Speed of the object and tempo of game are reduced
Soccer-like/ basketball-like games	Larger goal area/ larger hoop	Increasing the goal area requires less accuracy in kicking/throwing

Reduce Size of Playing Area

Activity	Modifications	Consequences
Soccer-like/ basketball-like/ football-like games	Reduce size of field	Less distance to cover; ball moves from one end of field to other more rapidly; more practice time
Badminton/volleyball/ tennis-like games	Reduce size of court	Less distance to cover; less mobility required

Lighter Equipment

Activity	Modifications	Consequences
Varied striking activities	Use lighter striking implements	More easily manipulated; easier to strike
Varied throwing activities	Use lighter balls (often smaller balls for small hands)	Easier to "send"; easier to throw with one hand
Varied catching activities	Use lighter balls (often larger balls for small hands) or balloons or scarves	Easier to "receive"; safer if catch is missed and ball hits face; move more slowly for tracking
Softball-like games	Use lighter bat, which is often shorter	Bat can be moved more quickly so there is greater opportunity to strike the ball
Soccer-like games	Use lighter ball or smaller ball	Ball speed is reduced; successful contact is more likely
Bowling/bocce	Use lighter balls	A weaker person has greater control of the ball
Tennis-like games	Use lighter, shorter racket, often with a smaller grip or Velcro strap to hold the racket to the wrist	Perform more accurate hits; a weaker person can control the racket

Increase/Decrease Size of Team

Activity	Modifications	Consequences
Games children create	Fewer players	Easier social situation; fewer players to avoid in space; more opportunities for skill development and practice
Other team sports	Fewer players	Less cooperation needed; often fewer arguments among team members

(continues)

Activity	Modifications	Consequences
Volleyball-like games	Add more players	Less area for each person to cover
Soccer-like games	Add more players	Distance each person must cover in team play is reduced
Softball-like games	Add more fielding players	Less area for each person to cover
Handball/ tennis-like games	Play triples	Less area for each person to cover

Make Minor Rule Changes

Activity	Modifications	Consequences
Bowling/bocce	Use two hands instead of one hand	Assists child with less strength
Softball/baseball-like games	Use a stationary ball on a batting tee	Stationary target is easier to hit
Games using bases	Use beepers	Assists child with visual impairment locate the bases using auditory cues
Tennis-like games	Allow two bounces of ball	Wheelchair user has more time to get to the ball
Tennis-like games	Start serving inside the baseline	More success with accurate serve
Wrestling	Use physical contact on takedown for a blind person	Blind person will always be in physical contact with opponent; enables him or her to know where opponent is at all times
Volleyball-like games	Allow the person with impairment in the arms or hand to carry on a volleyball hit	Greater success in game
Soccer-like games	Increase size of goal area	More chances to score goals
Basketball-like games	Use two-hand dribble	Assists the child who has difficulty controlling a big ball
Basketball-like games	Use lower goal (hoop)	More chances to score goals
Net-type games	Use lower net	Greater chance of getting the ball/object over the net
Gymnastics	Strap impaired legs together for aerial work	Strap controls the legs when the body moves

Reduce Playing Time

Activity	Modifications	Consequences
Any field, court, wall, net games that children create	Children or teacher can reduce the number of minutes of play between rest periods	Reduces fatigue
Hockey/lacrosse/ basketball/ soccer-like games	Substitute every 3 or 4 minutes	Reduces fatigue by allowing increased rest periods

Activity	Modifications	Consequences
Swimming	Swim beside pool edge and rest at prescribed distances of travel or time intervals	Reduces fatigue

Reduce Distance

Activity	Modifications	Consequences
Track and field running events	Decrease distance to run	Reduces fatigue
Baseball/softball-like games	Shorten distance between bases	Leads to more success because there is less distance to cover to get to the base; more chance of scoring runs
Volleyball-like games	Serve closer to the net / Use smaller court size	Better chance of getting object over the net; more hits for everyone in the game; less court to cover
Badminton/tennis-like games	Begin the game inside the baseline rather than on the baseline / Use smaller playing area	Better chance of getting the object over the net; game moves along faster; less distance to travel
Golf-like target games	Shorten the distance to holes	More opportunities to send the object at the target (hole)
Softball/baseball-like games	Shorten pitching distance	More chance of the ball reaching the batter

Reduce Number of Points Required to Win Contest

Activity	Modifications	Consequences
Handball/paddleball/tennis-like games	Fewer points needed to win	Physical endurance will not be a factor in the outcome of the game
Basketball-like games	Play until a specified number of points is made	Shortens game; more success for all

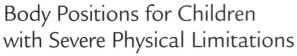

Assignment 12–1

The games and sports activities in the table do not represent an exhaustive list. Prepare a grid similar to the one shown here and list additional "Activities" with possible "Modifications" and "Consequences." Where you have access to children of different ages, try some of the adaptations that are listed and add additional consequences to the list.

Body Positions for Children with Severe Physical Limitations

Use scooter boards or long padded rolling boards, rolls of various diameters, foam wedges of different inclines and sizes, benches of different widths, prone and supine standers, gait trainers, and other supportive devices to assist children with severe physical limitations in engaging in Physical Education activities. Some activities can be done from a child's customized (and comfortable) wheelchair.

Use of a mat on the floor and a small roll or wedge under the chest provides the following benefits:

- Better head lift
- Easier head lift
- Enhanced eye–hand coordination
- Avoidance of pathological postures

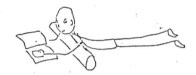

A bench in place of a chair or wheelchair offers the following benefits:

- A more secure base
- Workspace at a lower level
- Encouragement of midline head alignment
- Weakening of adductor spasticity
- Symmetrical back extension

A prone board against a table can provide the following benefits:

- Experience of the upright position
- Prevention of hip flexion contractures
- Physiological weight bearing
- Hand and arm freedom in assisted standing
- Standing without the need for equilibrium response

Anecdote 12–3

In a small, rural school, the students made balls for their Physical Education lessons. They stuffed molded newspaper into the toes of socks or stockings. They then twisted the covering and retwisted it, finally sewing the remainder of the cover into the ball itself. The children decided to leave some of the balls with "tails" attached. The younger children were allowed to grab the ball by the tail. Older children had to catch the ball.

Movement Discovery as a teaching method allows each individual to work at his or her own level. The challenges used stimulate exploration and allow different responses. This approach requires each person to assess and improve his or her own capacity. It is by nature inclusive. The inclusion of children with disabilities in the class simply means that the range of responses will be greater. Because most children will be active, they will not readily notice other abilities. Many children accept children with different abilities without comment. Children with disabilities can also be used, as others are, to "show" interesting ideas.

Many teachers report that children have no difficulty in allowing different rules for different individuals in a group game (e.g., in a group game of "volleyball" or "tennis," some children are allowed to "serve" from inside the back line if they so choose). It is perhaps worth mentioning that this approach is also very well suited to a small, rural, all-age school where widely different age levels join together for a Physical Education lesson. Children understand the need to "adapt" and will make their own rules so that all children are included and treated fairly.

Inclusive Language in Inclusive Environments

When designing movement activities for children with special needs who are included in the Physical Education class, think carefully about the wording of your movement tasks/activities. These tasks should be described using wording that does not single out a child as being different or exclude the child from participating in the activity because of his or her special needs. The following examples illustrate this point.

Example 1: If one of the objectives or tasks planned is to "Jump off different pieces of apparatus," then children in the class who cannot jump because of mobility impairment or other lower-limb disability, such as spastic diplegia, might be excluded from participation. The teacher could very easily change the wording of the task to say something like this: "Find different ways to get off the various pieces of equipment." This instruction would allow children who can jump, to jump, while those who cannot jump might find their own way to slide off or step off with their hands first, for example.

Example 2: Suppose the task is "Run around all the cones, spots, and other markers in the room." A child who uses a wheelchair cannot run, but can travel or wheel. This type of traveling activity could be reworded as follows: "Move or wheel around all the markers in the space."

Example 3: Suppose the task is stated as "Everyone collect a hockey stick. If you are short or weak, get a shorter/lighter hockey stick." This type of wording causes the child with dwarfism, or the child with a health impairment that causes weakness in the body, to stand out or be singled out from the able-bodied classmates. Instead, the task could be reworded in this way: "There are many different kinds of hockey sticks. Select the one that works best for you!"

An inclusive Physical Education program, designed and taught by Boucher and Wiseman, among others, was filmed in 1977 and funded by the Bureau of Education for the Handicapped, U.S. Office of Education (now U.S. Office of Special Education). The film depicted children of ages ranging from 3 to 12 years being taught together in the same Physical Education class. Twelve of the children had special needs, and approximately eight others were able-bodied. This film provides an early demonstration of the use of the Movement Discovery method with children with special needs. Another film targeted for parents of children with disabilities, made by Boucher and Tripp (1992), also demonstrates this Movement Discovery method being used with students from the early childhood years through high school.

Creating, Customizing, Adapting, and Improvising Equipment

Any teacher can quickly acquire an abundant supply of free or inexpensive, small equipment for use in Physical Education lessons.

BALLS

It is essential that every child in the class have some kind of ball. Make balls of different weights, sizes, colors, textures, and shapes.

- Lightweight balls can be made from plastic, foam, Styrofoam, or other synthetic materials. When empty, the "oranges" and "lemons" used to hold juice make excellent light balls for children; the bright colors add interest. A colored plastic bag filled with peanut/Styrofoam packing material makes a great ball, either large or small.

- Old tennis balls and balls used in racquetball are often readily available from a local club.

- Newspaper balls can be made by pressing the paper into a ball shape and inserting it into the toe of an old nylon stocking or sock. The material is then twisted, turned inside-out, and refolded over the ball until the final end or tail is stitched back on to the material already covering the ball. This ball will even bounce and roll if the paper is dampened and molded before being allowed to dry. Children can easily make this equipment.

- Brightly colored yarn or wool can be made into a ball by using a double cardboard circle with a hole in it or a fan-shaped segment with a "center." Wool is then wound and rewound over this core and tied securely in the center after the outside edge has been cut and the two pieces of cardboard pulled gently apart:

1. Obtain two cardboard circles (at least 3 to 5 inches in diameter).

2. Bind the circles with wool, yarn, or another material.

3. Cut between the two cardboard circles.

4. Separate the circles and tie them firmly in the center.

5. Fluff out and trim the ball after removing the cardboard.

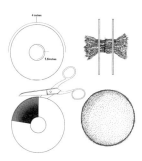

For students with visual impairments, different small-sized bells and commercially produced beepers can be inserted inside or attached to different kinds of balls.

Balls attached to strings, elastic bands, or ropes can be suspended from pulleys, climbing frames, tree branches, and basketball hoops. These are particularly useful for students who use wheelchairs or children with mobility impairments who are unable to retrieve balls at a distance.

HITTING IMPLEMENTS

Bats can be shaped out of plywood or pine and finished with polyurethane. Suitably shaped driftwood or sticks also make good bats. Round or square bats can be made.

It is important to have hitting implements that are of different weights because children vary dramatically in their grip strength and ability to hold something with which to hit objects. Some students with disabilities may not be able to grip a bat, racket, or stick and, therefore, may need a Velcro fastening device to secure the hand and implement together.

Stocking Bats

Various shapes, sizes, and colors can be constructed by children, teachers, or parents. Take a wire coat hanger and pull it into a diamond, circular, or square shape. Insert the coat hanger into an old nylon stocking, net, or other light, stretchy material. Tie a knot in the top, turn it inside out, and pull the fabric tightly down into the handle and tie it off. Make a handle out of a dowel

or ½- or ¾-inch PVC pipe of various lengths. Bind the handle with duct, masking, or colored tape to ensure there is no wire protruding.

Bottle Bats

Use 1- and 2-liter plastic soda bottles. Secure a wooden dowel or PVC pipe for a handle. A wood screw works well to secure the bottle to a dowel. Place duct tape around the mouth of the bottle to prevent the handle from pulling out.

CATCHING IMPLEMENTS

Large plastic bleach bottles can be cut to form a scoop. The handle should be left intact and a smooth cornered cut made to remove the base and a section of the lower half of the bottle.

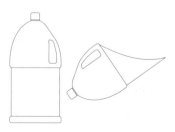

A stocking bat can be adapted to form a crosse for lacrosse by adding a longer handle and substituting nonstretchy material for the stocking. Plastic containers of all kinds can be used to "catch" balls.

MARKERS

Collect enough for two to three per student. Soda bottles (different colors), bleach and detergent bottles, and milk/water bottles can be left empty or filled with sand, water, small stones, or colored paper. Markers may also be made out of Pringle chip cans, paper rolls, paper plates, corrugated cardboard shapes and structures, or cardboard boxes. These items can be decorated. Old traffic cones may also be used as course markers.

OBSTACLES FOR JUMPING

Plastic bottles with a groove in the top of a handle can be used to support dowels, sticks, or canes. Make sure the dowel will fall off easily.

PUCKS AND OTHER OBJECTS TO STRIKE OR PUSH

- Small plastic chip-dip, margarine, and butter containers can serve as pucks. They may be weighted or put together to make pucks to be pushed or struck.

- Cardboard boxes of all sizes are useful for kicking, striking, and pushing.

- Broken plastic birdies from the local badminton club are useful.

- Different-sized round shapes, oval ellipses, or even discs or cubes can be cut out and used for pushing and striking. Some of these items can even be used indoors in the regular classroom.

NETS

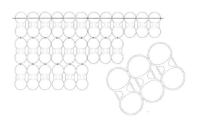

The six-hole plastic holders for soda cans can be stapled or tied together to make nets of different sizes. These nets can be threaded on string or rope and attached to chairs, fences, or poles (PVC/wood). They may be used either indoors in the gym or classroom and outside. These constructions also work well for "net" games in the water. Note the variety of small "nets" suitable for small-sided games in the elementary school depicted in the photos.

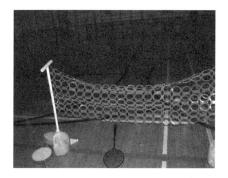

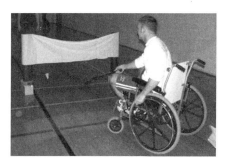

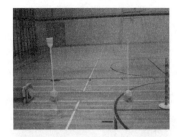

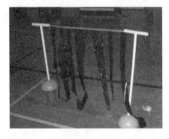

TARGETS

Targets add challenge and interest for aiming practices. Use colorful cloth bed sheets, all kinds of fabric, plastic pieces, tablecloths, or pieces of corrugated cardboard from free boxes to construct targets. Note that fabric can be folded away for easy storage. Targets can be designed and decorated using a theme from a story or poem, the alphabet, numbers, colors, shapes, or other ideas. Bells, streamers, and holes add interest.

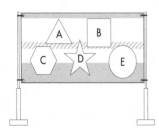

HOOPS

Hoops of different sizes can be made from ¾-inch black polyethylene plumbing pipe. Eight feet of pipe is a good length for a hoop; the pipe is easily cut with a hacksaw or a pipe cutter. After the pipe ends are heated in very hot water or using a hairdryer, a ¾-inch coupling is inserted inside one end of the pipe. The opposite end is then curved around and attached to the other end of the coupling. Have a few small hoops and a few giant-sized hoops. All of the necessary supplies are easily obtained from any store selling plumbing supplies.

A wooden dowel can also be used to join piping. It can be bound with masking or duct tape so that it becomes flush with the surface of the tube, or the piping can be stapled.

Hoops can serve as goals and targets in games. They can also be twirled using different parts of the body, rolled, jumped over or through while rolling, and spun. Back spinning also is easily learned.

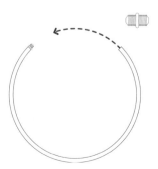

GOALS

Cardboard boxes, soda bottles, and ½-inch PVC pipe structures can all be used as goals in games. A 5-foot length of ½-inch black polyethylene pipe is a good choice for a small-size "basketball" hoop. A ½-inch plastic tee is used to join the polyethylene pipe so that it has a circular shape. The third hole in the tee is used for inserting a ½-inch PVC pipe length or a wooden dowel so the "goal" can be placed at different heights for very young children. The resulting goal is both portable and lightweight.

INDIVIDUAL MATS

High-density ½- to ¾-inch foam works best for use as individual mats. Suitable sizes range from approximately 2 feet by 3 feet to 18 inches by 2 feet, 6 inches.

Carpet pieces and ends can often be acquired free. Other matting may be given a plastic base for use on damp playground surfaces. Sheets of cardboard or foam rubber can be used indoors. Small mats can be woven from newspaper that is covered with varnish or polyurethane to enhance its durability.

ROPES

Ropes can be used for jumping, for boundaries, and for nets. They can be made from any kind of rope or sash cord where the ends are knotted, bound, spliced, and dipped in plastic or burned. Strips of material from disused clothing can be braided to form ropes, as can old nylon stockings. These ropes are fairly heavy and swing well, so they are sometimes preferred by children over the commercially produced nylon ropes, which are light, hard on the hands when turned, and sharp when they hit the legs. Ropes need to be at least 6 feet long; long ropes allow for skipping or jumping with stretched arms. A few ropes should be 12 feet for group skipping.

BEAN BAGS

Children can make their own bean bags, provided they can learn a strong backstitch or operate a sewing machine. Closely woven strong material is important if the contents are dried peas, lentils, or small beans. Other fillings may include Styrofoam packing piece scraps (very light); apricot, peach, plum, or cherry stones; pebbles; small pieces of bark; corn; acorns; and even coarse sand or gravel. The usual size of a bean bag is a 6-inch square. Bags must not be filled too full; that is, they should be only half or three-fourths full. A few extra-heavy or fully stuffed bean bags can be used as a "shot" when learning to putt the shot in track and field activities.

RINGS

Quoits or rubber rings make useful objects to throw or toss but unless acquired cheaply are probably not worth a special outlay. A floor hockey disc can be improvised from them or made by binding any 6-inch disc firmly. (Use a rubber car tire for the base, plus a thick strip that overlaps.) This kind of item can also serve as a discus in track and field activities if it is fairly heavy.

CANES

Canes or thin sticks are useful as obstacles to jump over (hurdling), throwing implements (javelin), or markers for boundaries, goals, or lines.

CAR TIRES

Both inflated inner tubing and outer casings of car tires are very useful in Physical Education classes. The inflated inner tube can serve as a home-made trampoline if large enough, and most tires will roll. In addition, tires are heavy to manipulate (good strengthening work) and fun to use in groups. Although they take up significant storage space, only a few are needed. Six or seven tires, for example, can be used in the group work section of a lesson.

WALLS

Walls are not normally thought of as a piece of apparatus, but a number of skills can be tried using a vertical surface (e.g., hitting and throwing practices). Some schools attach ledges and pegs to create climbing walls. A doorframe or corner angle can sometimes be climbed.

COMBINATION WOODEN/METAL CLIMBING/ HANGING/SWINGING STRUCTURES

Many interesting structures can be constructed from lumber (4 inch by 4 inch and 6 inch by 6 inch) and standard galvanized water pipe (1½- to 2-inch diameter supports). Ladder structures, balance beams, ropes, horizontal and vertical surfaces/platforms, and hanging bars are all possibilities.

OUTDOOR STRUCTURES

Hills, fences, walls, ledges, trestles, stages or platforms, ladders, oil drums, trees, steps, gates, balance ledges, boxes, benches, and tables may serve as improvised equipment but must be checked carefully for safety hazards.

BOWLING

Collect old pins from bowling alleys. Construct lanes, using folded gymnastic mats to separate the lanes. Wooden 2-inch by 4-inch frames can be used to support the mats. Lengths of PVC pipe of 4- to 5-inch diameter can be cut in half to form a "return." Long pieces of pipe can be taped to the floor.

For younger children, plastic bottles (with numbers, alphabet letters, colors, or shapes on them) can serve as bowling pins.

MINIATURE GOLF

Collect old golf clubs. Long handles can be cut down to suit children of different heights. Lengths of 2-inch by 4-inch wood can serve as boundaries for a variety of "holes." Vary lengths, shapes, and terrain of the holes. Carpet (indoor/outdoor) can be cut to fit inside the wooden boundaries, and bumps, slopes, and finishing holes can be positioned in different ways. Finishing holes can be constructed from 4- to 5-inch diameter PVC pipe cut in 2-inch lengths and mounted into foam lengths and placed under the carpet. Holes can be made using steel cans.

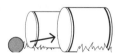

CARDBOARD BOXES FOR OBSTACLES AND TARGETS AND DANCE PROPS

Abundant free cardboard boxes of different sizes are available everywhere! These can be used as obstacles to improve body management skills as children can get in and out, over and under, and through them. They can also be decorated as targets for aiming practices. Holes cut in the boxes can be used for sending objects "through" (e.g., a bean bag or ball of some kind). Decorated boxes can be used as props for creative dance (e.g., fire trucks, shelters, and storefronts).

WOODEN LOGS, TELEPHONE POLES, AND TREE TRUNK LENGTHS

Construct "adventure" playgrounds for stepping, jumping, climbing, and balancing. Eliminate all splinters. These items should be permanently fixed in a playground.

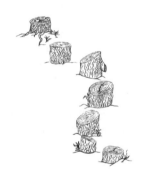

JUMPING PITS

Jumping pits can be considered as an item of apparatus. They are very useful for group work in an outdoors lesson.

HURDLES

Hurdles make use of sticks (hockey sticks) or dowels placed on low cones, stools, or blocks. They should fall off easily when knocked.

SHOT

A shot can be improvised by filling an old small rubber playground ball with sand.

POLE

A pole for vaulting can consist of any sturdy wood or plastic pole with a rubber tip to prevent sliding. A pole that is 4 or 5 feet high is typically the most useful choice.

SOCCER CLAW

A soccer claw can be created out of PVC pipe and attached to a wheelchair. Students without use of feet can participate using a manual or electric wheelchair in a floor-hockey-like and soccer-like game that uses a ball. This device was created and fabricated by Williams (2003, pp. 32–33).

Movement in the Water

In the IDEA legislation of 2004, reference is specifically made to content areas of Physical Education that must be offered to students with disabilities. The Rules and Regulations (U.S. Department of Education, 2006, pp. 46761–46762) state that under "§300.39 Special Education (b) (2) Physical Education means (i) the development of (A) physical and motor fitness; (B) fundamental motor skills and patterns; and (C) *skills in aquatics* [emphasis added], dance, and individual and group games and sports (including intramural and lifetime sports)."

Wherever a water environment is available, the physical educator should try to incorporate movement in the water, water aerobics, games in the water, and swimming into the Physical Education program. The purpose of this section is not to outline how to teach swimming, but rather to suggest some possibilities for learning to manage the body in the water. Early water experiences lay the foundation for building children's confidence to move in the water, to enjoy "deeper" water, and later to swim and participate in the myriad of water activities available in the community throughout life. Many schools with programs for children with severe disabilities have warm, small, shallow learner pools. Warm water (92°F) is a wonderful medium for children who have

any kind of mobility impairment. They will often be able to do movements in the water that they may never be able to do in their everyday lives on land.

EARLY WATER EXPERIENCES

With very young infants, water can be dribbled on their ears and eyes. Moving the baby around on the back and tummy so that the water swishes and splashes is a great way to start! When the climate is appropriate, toddlers should be introduced to all kinds of water play. Small, shallow plastic pools and hosepipes are readily available for outdoor play both at home and in day care centers. In addition, the bathtub can be used indoors. These kinds of settings lend themselves to many beneficial and enjoyable activities that are rich in sensory stimulation.

Parents should be encouraged to provide toys that allow children to experiment and discover some of the properties of water. Activities such as pouring and transferring liquids, as well as working with objects that sink and float, are favorites of young children. It is easy to collect different-sized containers, bottles of different shapes and colors, plastic tubing, plastic sieves, boats, stones, and pieces of wood of different weights and density for children to discover what they can do with them in the water. "Water play" should be part of every quality preK program; it is important for the child to experience being in water. Sprinklers can be used to provide a range of sensory experiences.

WATER EXPERIENCES IN SHALLOW AND DEEP POOLS

The same Movement Discovery approach recommended throughout this text can be used in the water. Individualizing instruction for children who are at different stages and ages allows these children to be taught together. Often local school authorities require that teachers working with children in the water, or other lifeguards present in the pool, should have Water Safety Instructor or Royal Life Saving Society certification (or comparable certification) for liability purposes.

Children who are fearful of the water will need more personal help. They often need to proceed at a slow pace until their fears can be overcome. Some children dislike water in their eyes, so introduce it early on. The child can splash himself or herself and when underwater "look" both down and up.

CREATE AN INTERESTING WATER ENVIRONMENT

All of the following items can be used to create an interesting water environment:

- Things that float and sink (e.g., diving sticks, diving rings, toy diving fish that sink slowly, disks, hoops, beach balls, plastic balls of different sizes that float)

- Kickboards

- Different-shaped "floats"

- Personal flotation devices (head floats, whole-body floats, sectional rafts)

- Water walking aids

- 3-inch foam noodles of different colors (approximately 4 feet long)

- Hoops

- Low water basketball goals

- Nets

- Plastic ropes

- ¾- to 1-inch dowels with polyfoam floats on each end

- Plastic tubing

- Sieves

- Plastic milk jugs

- Plastic bottles of all shapes and sizes

- Water weights

WATER CONFIDENCE ACTIVITIES: ADJUSTING TO THE WATER

Some children will find coming to the side of a pool difficult. Let them watch. Go slowly. Encourage them to come and sit on a chair near the pool as a transition.

Other children will eagerly sit on the side of the pool. They are ready to enjoy the challenge of the water!

The example activities listed under each heading in this section are not presented in any "magical order." Pick those that are appropriate for your learners.

Activities to Do from the Side of the Pool

- Put toes in the water

- Gently move the water with feet

- Splash the water with feet

- Make a lot of splash with feet

- Bend down and put one or both hands in the water

- Move your hand around any way in the water

Entering the Water

Children can choose how they'll get in:

- By moving down steps or a ramp with or without help

- By sliding off the edge of the pool into the water

- By jumping in

- By wheeling or being wheeled down a ramp

Observe the initial confidence level of the group as children are getting into the water as well as in the water. Assess their competence and previous experience, and identify fear problems. Divide groups into swimmers and nonswimmers, if appropriate. Remember that height on land may need to match water depth on an individual basis.

An Initial Session

Activities should be chosen to allow for a range of different experiences—for example, general free exploration of movement in the water environment; jumping in; going underwater; breathing; moving arms, legs, and the whole body in different ways; and a variety of individual water confidence games. Challenge children to "discover" for themselves the different things they can do in the water. Subsequent classification into subgroups will allow swimmers to concentrate on activities mostly relevant to various strokes and nonswimmers to build skill and knowledge relevant to becoming water-borne.

A note about *floats* (either on the arms or around the body) for able-bodied children: The authors believe that it is far better to have children do early work in the pool without these swim aids. They give children a false sense of security and hinder natural movement of the body in the water. It is better that children learn to naturally balance and maneuver themselves with their arms and legs. At the same time, be aware that children with severe physical challenges or medical conditions may not be able to go underwater. They can often enjoy the sensation of movement in the water by using whole-body flotation devices and head floats.

Water Confidence Activities Above the Water and Traveling in Shallow Water

- Travel in different ways across the pool while trying to keep the shoulders below the water.
- Move around the pool using little (low) and big (high) jumps.
- Travel across the pool with bent legs, straight legs, and arms out of the water.
- Collect an object from the side of the pool and carry, push, or pull it to another area of the pool and place it on the side (e.g., rope, hoop, ball, ring, kickboard).
- Jump up and down on one foot; two feet; with deep knee bends; push from the balls of the feet; with an arm swing.
- Move around using first big steps, then tiny steps.
- Bounce about in the water.
- Experiment with ways to turn or spin yourself around in the water.
- Travel when the body is in a "ball" or a "log".
- Travel using movement of arms and hands to "pull" and "push".
- Use arms and hands to "push" and "pull" water; experiment with "flat hands" and "cupped hands".
- Travel in a small circle.
- Pull or push yourself using arms only; try it with hands close to the body and away from the body.
- Move on your side with one ear in the water; repeat on the other side of the body
- Jump and "pull" water to the side of your body.
- Hop on one foot a couple of times, then change to hop on the other foot.
- Get from one side of the pool to the other with part of one foot out of the water most of the way.
- Travel backward with the shoulders under the water, to get to the other side of the pool.
- Move sometimes forward, sometimes backward, and sometimes sideways to get across the pool; experiment with changing directions.
- Move as fast as you can to get to the other side.
- Move slowly and smoothly so that you make no splash.
- Move making lots of splash or waves as you go.
- Change the pathway you travel to get across; go in a straight line, then in a curvy line.
- Travel about the pool with the arms under the water and chin as close to the water as possible.
- Get in and out of the pool several times
- Find different ways to get in and out of the pool.
- Move your body up and down as you travel about the pool.
- Blow bubbles with your mouth or your nose as you move around.
- Hold your nose to make bubbles with your mouth.
- Close your mouth and make bubbles with your nose.
- See if you can blow a lightweight ball that floats across the pool.
- Throw a ball away from you and then go and get it.
- Hold onto something (kickboard, float, bar, poolside) and try to slowly lift your feet off the bottom of the pool.
- Play throw-and-catch with a ball or ring with a partner.
- Pull the water with your hands and arms, first close to the body and then away from your body.
- Push the water away from you with your hands.
- Move on your side.
- Kick your legs in the water.
- While stationary, make waves and splash the water.
- Experiment with using the arms and legs as "paddles," "fins," "sculls," "wheels," "oars," "propellers," and so on.

CHANGE BODY POSITIONS AND STAND UP IN THE WATER

As children perform these activities, they will discover how the body can change position in the water and how they can propel themselves about. Different water skills can be explored from the front, back, side, and upside-down positions.

Practicing standing up in the water from different horizontal positions—either front, back, or side—is important for safe working in the water.

- Hold onto the side of the pool; let your legs float up, and then stand up.

- Roll from side to side in the water.

- Roll over from the back to the front of your body and then back again.

- Get yourself "upside-down" in the water.

- Hold onto a kickboard and change the position of your body in the water.

- Find ways to balance yourself using different body parts on the kickboard (e.g., on your stomach, sit on it, stand on it).

- Try "stretched" body positions and "curled-up" body positions.

Discover Movements to Do Under the Water

- Put one ear, and then both ears, under the water.
- Put the back of your head in the water.
- Lower yourself so your nose is just under the water. Look around!
- Try to open your eyes under the water.
- Blow bubbles under the surface of the water.
- Go deeper and blow bubbles. Come up for a breath, and then go down again blowing more bubbles. Do the same, only this time with your mouth closed.
- Try to go down and sit on the bottom and then come up. Experiment with staying down for longer periods of time.
- Count the number of seconds you can stay underwater. See if you can beat your own score next time.
- Throw a diving stick, fish, ring, or disk so it sinks. Get the item off the bottom somehow. Use your feet or hands.

- Try to stoop down and pick up a diving toy (disk, ring, fish, stick) with your hands.
- With a partner, hold hands. One partner should go under to count the number of fingers held up by the other partner.
- Let your partner throw a diving toy while you try to grab it before it hits the bottom of the pool.
- Step through a series of hoops suspended under the water.
- Go under your partner's legs, which are spread apart.

Teachers can suggest that children practice "ways of breathing" as homework in addition to "opening the eyes" in water (e.g., in the bathtub). In hot weather, playing with the water from sprinklers (e.g., running through the spray, standing in the spray with your back or front to it, letting water run down the face) is an excellent experience.

FLOATING

Buoyancy is such an important skill in the water. When children gain confidence, trust their bodies, and discover they can float, they generally move forward very quickly in their skills in the water.

Some Variations of Floating to Discover and Vary

- Float on your front, with feet off the bottom of the pool.
- Float on your back, with feet off the bottom of the pool.
- Make your body into different shapes as you float (e.g., long, wide, bent) on your side.
- Float in stretched-out shapes.
- Make your body into a rounded shape to float.
- While on your back, count to 5 without moving arms or legs.
- Count to 5 while floating on your front with your face in the water and feet off the bottom.
- Float first on your back, then change to your front, and finally return to your back; stand up.
- Float for a very long time without moving any parts of your body. You count the number of seconds!

GLIDING

Gliding involves pushing off the side of the pool and moving through the water without kicking or moving the arms. It is also a very important skill for swimming.

Some Variations of Gliding Skills to Discover and Practice

- Push off and glide as far as you can on the front of your body, with your head in the water; then stand up. Keep your body as streamlined as possible. Blow bubbles as you go.
- Glide on your back. Hold on to the edge of the pool, with your feet up on the wall, and push off on your back. Glide as far as you can without kicking and then stand up.
- Practice gliding as far as you can after you give a good push-off. Repeat this action many times, seeing if you can go farther each time.
- Glide on your front or your back. When you've run out of momentum, try to kick or move your legs in some way and keep going.
- Glide as far as you can, then just use your arms to keep going.
- Glide and make no splash.
- Glide on your side, then move your arm in the water to go farther.

ENTERING THE WATER HEAD FIRST

To enter the water with the head first, children must inhibit the head-righting reflex; that is, they must learn to keep the head down. Our normal reflexive response to the "head going down" situation is to bring the head up toward the upright posture and into midline. Deeper water is also needed to work on these skills because when the head stays down the body continues to go down until the head is raised upward.

Here are some tasks to practice when entering the water head first:

- Sit on the side of the pool, lean over with arms extended toward the water, and slide in head first, trying to keep your head down all the way.

- Try entering head first from a kneeling or half-kneeling position.

- Practice entering from higher and higher positions.

- Put your arms and hands ahead to make a "hole" in the water for your head and body to go through.

DIFFERENT LEG MOVEMENTS AND KICKS

Often the "dog-paddle" stroke makes an easy transition to the front crawl. Using the legs and arms in different ways for propulsion builds skill in the water. The more skillful children will master all the different kicks and arm movements used in the various swimming strokes used by competitive swimmers, synchronized swimmers, and water polo players.

Some Variations to Practice with Legs, Feet, and Kicks

- Use your legs to make you go around in a circle in the water.
- Go across the pool with your feet going first.
- Hold a kickboard with your hands and move around the pool using your legs in different ways.
- Put the kickboard on your chest while you're on your back and kick your legs so you move about the pool.
- Work on your front holding a kickboard and practice kicking movements to take you across the pool.
- Try moving around where both legs and feet do the same movement.
- Try moving about where the legs and feet do different movements.

DIFFERENT ARM MOVEMENTS AND STROKES

Some Arm Movements to Vary and Practice

- Go all the way across the pool using different arm movements. Try some little movements and some bigger movements.
- Pull the water with your hands and arms to get across from one side of the pool to the other. Sometimes travel fast and sometimes move more slowly.
- Make four different arm actions before your legs kick.
- Try moving around where both arms and hands do the same movement.
- Try moving about where the arms and hands do different movements.

Children can try many ways of putting things together, using floats or kickboards to facilitate buoyancy, and pushing off from the side of pool to get momentum. They can combine many different body actions to form a sequence in the water. Allow choice and encourage the discovery of new inventions; allow copying of others' ideas.

Some of the activities can be done in twos, threes, and small groups. Allow matching patterns, competitions, tandem swimming, making up a sequence of different moves, inventing a game, inventing a "fish dance" or "the story of a frog, a crab, and a dolphin," and other types of creativity. With able-bodied children, do not allow holding or physical manipulation of another child unless children are cooperative and genuinely helpful to each other.

If children actually swim, encourage them to do so in a variety of ways, as well as allowing them to concentrate on becoming more efficient. Endurance will be improved when children are encouraged to "keep going" for longer distances and longer periods of time. They can challenge themselves.

Allow a period of free practice or individual work on self-devised activities either at the beginning or at the end of each session. This is valuable both as a mental and physical warm-up and as a culminating, concluding, assessment activity.

The discovery approach will facilitate the children thinking about how they can move in the water environment:

"See if you can . . ."

"What other ways can you . . ."

"What happens to the water when . . ."

"How does it feel when . . ."

"Try to . . ."

"What else can you do . . ."

"Find another way to . . ."

"Spin and roll . . ."

"Stand on your hands or get upside-down . . ."

Basically, a limb or head is "heavier" when out of the water. Gymnastic and dance-like skills, such as seen in synchronized swimming, can be performed in the water. Many recreational and lifetime activities involve the water. For example, canoeing, rafting, wind-surfing, kite-surfing, sailboarding, surfing, kayaking, water skiing, kneeboarding, disc-spinning, boogie-boarding, sailing, snorkeling, scuba diving, and fishing. All require the skill of swimming for safety reasons.

Encourage children to discover how their bodies behave differently in water. Allow them to discover how the water behaves as it is moved in different ways.

Assignment 12–2

Design an individual record booklet in which children can keep a log of what they learn in the water. Have children set their own "challenges" and "targets" for each lesson for a series of six lessons.

Water temperature is a highly significant factor when working in the water. Therapists use very warm water to facilitate movement in the water with persons with disabilities. Cold water will cause tension and increase spasticity with children with cerebral palsy. Relaxation is needed to learn to swim.

Recommended Sources of Information on Adapted Physical Education

If you need more help in working with children with disabilities, the following texts and resources are recommended:

■ Auxter, D., Pyfer, J., & Huettig, C. (2001). *Principles and methods of adapted physical education and recreation.* Boston: McGraw-Hill.

■ Block, M. (2009). *A teacher's guide to including students with disabilities in general physical education* (3rd ed.). Baltimore, MD: Paul H. Brookes.

■ Hellison, D. (2003). *Teaching responsibility through physical activity* (2nd ed.). Champaign, IL: Human Kinetics.

■ Lieberman, L., & Houston-Wilson, C. (2009). *Strategies for inclusion: A handbook for physical educators* (2nd ed.). Champaign, IL: Human Kinetics.

■ National Consortium for Physical Education and Recreation for Individuals with Disabilities. (2006). *Adapted physical education national standards* (2nd ed.). Champaign, IL: Human Kinetics.

■ National Dissemination Center for Children with Disabilities NICHCY Publications: http://www.nichcy.org/InformationResources/Pages/NICHCYPublications.aspx (free)

■ Sherrill, C. (2004). *Adapted physical education and recreation: A multidisciplinary approach* (6th ed.). Dubuque, IA: Wm. C. Brown Company.

- Williams, B. (2003). *Assistive devices, adaptive strategies, and recreational activities for students with disabilities.* Champaign, IL: Sagamore Publishing.

- Winnick, J. (2005). *Adapted physical education and sport* (4th ed.). Champaign, IL: Human Kinetics.

Sources of Adapted Equipment

Toy stores and pet stores carry a variety of inexpensive smaller, durable balls, including balls with bells and interesting surface textures. These can be used in a sensory stimulation Physical Education program for some students with severe and profound disabilities.

Some vendors have specialized catalogs serving the Physical Education profession. These catalogs can be found on the Web.

Teachers can buy a wide variety of good-quality Physical Education supplies from other general vendors.

Summary

Physical Education and variety of movement learning experiences must be part of the total education program of all children, including those with disabilities. A variety of instructional strategies using the Movement Discovery approach may be employed to serve the educational needs of special needs children. Individualized instruction, which incorporates choice and varying degrees of freedom along with teacher direc-

tion, can be used in a dynamic way when working with these children.

Many elements of games and pre-sports may be modified to enable children with diverse abilities to participate. For example, educators may prescribe use of adapted/modified equipment, larger objects, lighter equipment, increased/decreased team size, reduced size of playing area, minor rule changes, reduced playing time, reduced distance, and reduced number of points required to win a contest.

Movement experiences in the water focus on confidence-building activities, changing the body's position and shape, traveling in different ways using different forms of propulsion, and increasing sensory stimulation for children with diverse abilities.

References

American Alliance for Health, Physical Education, Recreation and Dance. (2004). *Including students with disabilities in physical education.* Reston, VA: Author.

Boucher, A. (1977). *Movement toward control* [film]. Washington, DC: Bureau of Education for the Handicapped, U.S. Office of Education.

Boucher, A., & Tripp, A. (1992). *Disabled children in physical education: Parent awareness and advocacy* [film, book]. Rockville, MD: Disabled Sports USA.

Federal Register. (2006, August 14). Regulations for PL 108-446, Individuals with Disabilities Education Improvement Act of 2004.

U.S. Department of Education. (2006). IDEA 2004, Part 300: Assistance to states for the education of children with disabilities. Washington, DC: Author.

Williams, B. (2003). *Assistive devices, adaptive strategies, and recreational activities for students with disabilities.* Champaign, IL: Sagamore Publishing.

Conclusion

In this book, much consideration has been given to the nature of young children and the processes by which they grow, learn, develop, and become more skillful. Throughout the discussion presented here, we have emphasized the need for an individualized discovery teaching method. This process is inevitably present in preadolescent children, and the educational profession would do well to capitalize on its promise. A great deal of material suitable for preschool and elementary school Physical Education lessons has been presented. Due to the individual nature of learning, the results obtained with such a curriculum will inevitably vary. To a certain extent, this material is "new" every time it is used, because the responses vary with the particular teachers and children.

The future of good Physical Education in early childhood years lies in your hands, dear reader. You are asked to

pass on your experiences and learning to benefit the profession. Comments about the approach suggested here, both positive and negative, are most welcome. Films, pictures, children's comments and drawings, anecdotes, and video clips are also most important in inspiring others to follow suit and should be sent to the following Jones and Bartlett Web address: info@jbpub.com. Your contributions will be acknowledged and permission will be sought if Jones and Bartlett wishes to include those materials in future editions of this book. It is also hoped that future students, members of the teaching profession, and physical educators interested in research will focus those efforts on the area of Physical Education teaching method and skill measurement.

In the preface, we were reminded that the obesity epidemic has reached crisis proportions in Western society. If you engage in a balanced program of Movement Discovery in your teaching career, your experience will truly be vital in combating this trend. Longitudinal studies are urgently needed to develop preventive initiatives, which should include Physical Education programs in addition to work with families on nutrition and the sedentary behaviors of children.

The final reminder, perhaps, is that we should always focus on the child. The weakness of enthusiasm is that it sometimes gets put before the interests of the intended recipient. Many children today live with pressures we do not know about. Too many forces clamor for a child's interest, and forced participation may result in "turn-off." Human beings need time to be themselves on their own terms. They sometimes need to ignore the "world," however it presents itself.

Appendix 1

Additional Historical Roots

This appendix provides additional historical material for those who are interested. Many areas in the United States have strong European traditions and much of this material looks at European developments. It is also possible that professors will use historical study as a basis for longer projects or term papers. This material may be useful for that purpose.

Some of the earliest forms of Physical Education were connected with religion. There was, for example, an ancient Chinese system of exercises or medical gymnastics called Cong-fou dating from about 2700 B.C. The purpose of Cong-fou was the perfection of self. By practicing various postures and breathing exercise, the soul was prepared to enter into relationship with the spirits. Many systems of yoga use similar techniques. The body is thought of as an important tool whereby immortality can be approached. This idea need not be thought of as pertaining solely to the ancient world.

> To man, propose this test—-
> Thy body at its best,
> How far can that project thy soul on its lone way?
> —*Robert Browning* (1812–1883)

If dancing is included in Physical Education, then there is a long history of religious ceremonies and rituals that could properly be called Physical Education activities, ranging from primitive and pagan customs to Christian and Judaic practice today. A procession in an early Christian church was probably rhythmic and included dancing in the spirit. Modern Judaism includes an ancient tradition of dancing with the Torah scrolls.

The ancient Egyptian tomb of Beni-Hassan (2500 B.C.) contains some delightful wall paintings showing acrobats and various ball games. Gardiner (1965) has reproduced several of these paintings. You can view many of these drawings on different Web sites if you go to Google Images.

Ancient Cultures

Communities in ancient times also needed physical fitness just to survive. Although ancient lifestyles required physical strength and endurance and physical skills just to eat and live, there are also records of sport and dance that did not serve a utilitarian purpose. In any museum you will see delightful pictures of a variety of physical activities. A study of native/indigenous cultures will uncover many sports, games, contests, and dances.

Greece

Physical Education was always a fundamental part of classical Greek education. Greek literature gives the impression that ordinary people valued the sense of physical well-being that exercise can give. *Palaestrae* (exercising yards) were fairly common in the cities of the Greek world. Youths exercised naked in the palaestra, and much of Greek sculpture shows an admiration for a well-developed human body. There were, of course, slaves and serfs supporting the leisured class in Greek society.

Rome

Under the influence of Rome, several systems of exercise were developed. Galen (A.D. 130–201) probably relied on some earlier work while producing one of the most interesting of these systems. Galen may not have had much influence during his lifetime, but his writings survived and were studied with renewed vigor during the Renaissance. Galen anticipated a much later theory of gymnastics and classified exercises according to their effect on the body.

Military Influences

From earliest times, any systematic Physical Education (mostly of male youths and young adults) was probably undertaken for military purposes. Tribes, nations, and communities fought one another regularly, so it was important for warriors to develop physical strength, specific skills, and endurance. Marathon runners carried messages, a well-thrown discus or javelin could kill an enemy, and wrestling was useful in close fighting.

Christianity

Christianity teaches that the body is the temple of the Holy Spirit and, as such, is honorable. Even so, Christian teaching was largely the reason that Physical Education suffered a decline from the early emphasis of Greece and Rome. Some of the worst abuses arose as an outgrowth of asceticism. This was unfortunate, in part because the word "ascetic" was originally used to denote athletic training. In fact, it seems likely that St. Paul would have been an athlete in his youth in Tarsus. As a tent maker, he would have probably attended "games" such as the biannual Isthmian games near Corinth (where the winners were crowned with a perishable wreath of withered celery!). Although Paul used athletic metaphors in his writings, in translation and Christian interpretation it became common practice to think of subjugating the body. In fact, many early Christians became fanatical in their asceticism, and monastic tradition frequently led to contempt for the physical life of the individual. Some Christians even managed to persuade themselves that sickness of the body was in some way good for spiritual progress. This idea may persist today, as some individuals tend to cling to physical weakness.

Medieval European life after the downfall of the Greek and Roman Empires is sometimes referred to as the Dark Ages. Much of life centered on the church; in a Christian church that had an ascetic viewpoint, Physical Education would not have been valued.

The Renaissance and Subsequent Developments

The Renaissance in Europe was interested in the classical world of Greece and Rome. It also led to much philosophical thought. Humanism, for example, is interested in the whole person and sees Physical Education as an important part of education. Although during the Renaissance scholars rediscovered an interest in the human body and new philosophies abounded, the classical dualism of mind and body was largely perpetuated. The philosophers Descartes and Locke were concerned with the relationship between the separate entities of body and mind. Spinoza and Leibnitz rejected the idea of separation—a view that influenced Rousseau, who taught that self-realization in a unity of mind and body could be achieved. In Rousseau's *Emile,* published in 1762, the writer postulated that the natural development of the child required Physical Education. Rousseau attributed a "therapeutic" value to sports and games. He also saw the possibility of sport as a means of indoctrination and suggested that participation might have "moral" effects. His work has had modern-day echoes: Did the Hitler Youth Movement use sport to indoctrinate participants? Does mass uniform physical activity, such as that used in Communist regimes, imply a moral virtue?

Rousseau had a great influence on education in general, but from a Physical Education point of view, one of the most important of his followers was J. S. Basedow. Basedow set up a Philanthropist school in Dessau, Germany, that became a prototype for many others. At one of these schools, a Physical Education teacher called Johann Christoph Friedrich Guts Muths (1759–1839) was part of the staff.

Guts Muths had a very great influence on Physical Education both during his lifetime and subsequently. Guts Muths' work formed a comprehensive system. He taught for 53 years in one school and drew his inspiration from children and Rousseau's "back to nature" philosophy. His classes included jumping, climbing, and "natural" activities as well as sports, games, and outdoors excursions. Guts Muths also used trees, ropes, bars, and boxes and created an environment that stimulated exploration and gross motor activity.

Guts Muths' classification of exercises reflects Galen's writings. His own ideas about Physical Education were widely published and comprehensive. He not only included lists of activities, but also answered critics of "the natural way" and made suggestions for the training of teachers. It is unfortunate that among those who followed Guts Muths' lead, none really maintained the comprehensive and "natural" features of his system. It would be difficult to find in our modern schools a Physical Education program that provides so fully for the needs of children. Guts Muths' work probably influenced Pestalozzi, who also focused attention firmly on young children, their activity, and individual differences. Indeed, the development of curriculum and method in kindergartens and nursery schools in their early years may have shown a better understanding of the comprehensive nature of Physical Education and its relevance to the whole child than does our present system.

Perhaps the main reason why Guts Muths' Physical Education philosophy developed into different gymnastic systems is to be found in the political climate that prevailed during his lifetime. Three of the greatest of his followers were Pehr Henrik Ling (1776–1839), a Swede; Franz Nachtegall (1777–1847), a Dane; and Friedrich Ludwig Jahn (1778–1852), a Prussian. Their views differed widely. Europe was in turmoil after the Napoleonic Wars, and military defeat frequently leads to reexamination of the fitness of a nation. Ling and Jahn, in particular, were intensely patriotic and saw a need for raising the level of military preparedness to defend the Fatherland. To meet this need, Ling developed a system of exercises based on anatomy and physiology. Although this Swedish system became widely known, due to the very great veneration in which Ling was held, it became somewhat rigid and stereotyped and was only adapted to more modern needs in the twentieth century.

Nachtegall was a pioneer in the field of organized Physical Education. He was successful in organizing regular instruction in schools, setting up a Military Gymnastic Institute, and establishing teacher training courses. He also set up a special course for women teachers.

Although both Nachtegall and Ling had been influenced by the "natural" and comprehensive work of Guts Muths, they left behind classified and organized systems of gymnastics that were largely, but not entirely, freestanding exercises or calisthenics. Jahn, in contrast, developed apparatus and skill activities, but the same process of systematization took place.

From the natural activities and natural apparatus used by Guts Muths, Jahn developed what is now known as Olympic gymnastics or competitive gymnastics. He introduced the horizontal and parallel bars. He derived the former from observing how his pupils delighted in swinging on the branches of trees; the latter was essentially an extension of the pommels of the horse. In the course of 5 years of excited experiment, he and his assistants worked out an elaborate system of spectacular exercises on these two pieces of apparatus. That development has continued as evident in how Modern gymnastics constantly introduces new skills but uses specific apparatus. Jahn's system of "Turnen" was practiced widely by youths and adults and the "Turnplatz" became a common feature in Germany. Early on, this movement became strongly linked with political and nationalistic ideas and, for these reasons, ultimately had a checkered career. It was partly due to political persecution that many idealistic "Turners" emigrated.

An Immigrant Society

For immigrants who sought a new beginning on the North American continent, an individual's working life was probably physically exhausting. Sport and dancing probably existed in rural areas and at community events but would also have depended on the amount of leisure time available and the wealth and social status of the participants. Any systematized training would likely be linked with skills useful in battle, archery, and horse riding and later the use of guns and target practice. Foot soldiers needed endurance as well as speed.

Part of the Puritan tradition in early settlements in North America tended to frown on jollity and dancing and physical pleasure that was not utilitarian. The work ethic did not allow for "wasting" time.

The United States has always been a haven for Germans looking for new lives; it was particularly a target for German immigrants from 1840 to 1890, when large numbers arrived in the United States and sought to perpetuate their culture. Part of this way of life was "Turnen." Although initially it flourished in isolation, this philosophy eventually became linked with education and found its way into U.S. Physical Education as gymnastics.

The Swedish system also "emigrated" to the United States, albeit largely sponsored by private benefaction. It secured support, perhaps more from women than from men. Many of the pioneers in Physical Education in the United States obtained medical qualifications (Dr. Hitchcock, Dr. Sargent, Dr. Hartwell), and a system based on anatomy and physiology was especially attractive to them.

The intense national feeling and political involvement of the German Turners alienated some people. In fact, one reason why the German Turners had to adapt and systematize their work before it was included in U.S. school systems was because of the opposition they encountered. Particularly outspoken on this issue was Dio Lewis (1823–1886). Lewis was an American, an individualist, unorthodox in his views, energetic and dynamic. His criticism emphasized that German gymnastics was unsuitable for women, the elderly, and young children. To counteract the influence of the Turners, Lewis introduced his own system of exercise and invented a tremendous variety of activities, often using cheap, homemade equipment. He used beanbags! Lewis's system was introduced into some schools in the 1860s. Although his personal interest in Physical Education was brief, he succeeded in influencing the course of the development of an American system of gymnastics.

Dr. Sargent and Dr. Hitchcock also set up "systems." At Amherst College, Dr. Hitchcock extended his marching and calisthenics to include simple apparatus and games. He was also a pioneer in anthropometry. At Harvard University, Dr. Sargent, who was also interested in measurement, developed a variety of apparatus reminiscent of the medieval rack and wheel. However limiting his view might seem to modern physical educators, at the Boston Conference in 1889 organized by the newly formed American Association for the Advancement of Physical Education, it was Dr. Sargent who spoke the following words:

What America most needs is the happy combination which the European nations are trying to effect: the strength-giving German gymnasium, the active and energetic properties of the English sports, the grace and suppleness acquired from French calisthenics, and the beautiful poise and mechanical precision of the Swedish free movements, all regulated, systematized and adapted to our peculiar needs and institutions. (Weston, 1962)

At the second conference of the American Association for the Advancement of Physical Education, the American Turners were given admission to the Association through the efforts of Dr. Hartwell. The 1860s also marked the widespread acceptance of free public education in the United States, which in turn led to the expansion of university and college curricula. The YMCA and YWCA were active organizations during this period, and their influence spread widely. America had already begun to develop and adopt various sports and games; these, too, influenced Physical Education curricula. Access to a college or university education was a reality in the United States long before this idea was embraced in most parts of the world.

Into this battle between proponents of the systems came an interesting echo of Guts Muths. Just as Rousseau had paved the way for a philosophical reconsideration of the value of education, so John Dewey set the atmosphere for another manifestation of "natural gymnastics." His work probably represented a reaction against "the systems" and was a swing away from everything stereotyped and nonfunctional. Dr. Thomas D. Wood and Dr. Clark Hetherington seem to have been the main proponents of this approach. They emphasized the value of sports skills and athletics as well as the "natural" activities of tumbling and use of large apparatus as obstacles. In theory, many of their statements are in line with current thought:

> The naturalized method is definite; the procedure grows out of the problems and situations which arise with each class and group of children, and is different in each case, depending on the interests, initiative and originality of the children in each particular class, as well as on the intelligent and wise leadership of the teacher. (Wood & Cassidy, 1927, p. ix)

To a modern reader, this perspective likely sounds wonderful. However, it is disappointing to see isolated skills, group games, and mimetics suggested as part of this "New Physical Education." This approach did not lead to problem solving on an individual basis, and it had little room for individual responses. Although the idea of matching the curriculum to the specific group of children was present, discussion and decisions of the group more often prevailed. One could almost apply the following "rule of thumb" in regard to this system: "If all children are doing the same thing in the same way at the same time, it represents uneducational practice." One of the difficulties associated with individual and small-group responses is that they can look chaotic to an unenlightened observer. The issues of "control" and "discipline" for some reason often focus on the teacher in a dominant role. In this text, you are encouraged to use a teaching method that develops control and discipline within individual children. Self-control and self-discipline are needed throughout life and can be developed early.

The Industrial Revolution and Subsequent Developments

A major change in society took place around about this time. The Industrial Revolution had a tremendous impact on the physical demands placed on workers. Few workers today need physical strength and endurance to perform their work, especially in the Western world. One of the characteristics of an industrialized society is the growth of spectator sports. The development of spectator sports not only had an insidious effect on reserving strenuous activity for the few, but also affected educational programs in schools. Much of a curriculum in education is influenced from the top down.

Professional educational organizations tend to ask what will be needed in adult life. Curricula are then developed to prepare all students for this future, even though many will never use such knowledge and skills. But school life does prepare us for later life. Physical benefits acquired in a Physical Education curriculum can easily be lost if activity or sport does not continue once the person leaves school.

U.S. Physical Education has also been strongly influenced by what may be called "carry-over" or recreational interests. The playground movement, which was founded in 1906, suggested that activities and sports that have a high "carry-over" to later life should be included at the secondary education level. Many municipal recreation centers were constructed as part of this movement, and some schools began to serve as after-hours recreation centers.

In the United Kingdom, the Industrial Revolution created a large middle class. The newly wealthy families soon turned their attention to the education of their children—primarily their sons. They built upon ancient tradition and the educational institutions founded by the aristocracy. More universities were founded, and the "public school" ideal flourished. Despite their name, these institutions were actually private, expensive, and residential. With an environment that included extensive grounds and playing areas and a timetable that needed to occupy the students for many hours a day including weekends, team sports flourished. In Great Britain, the climate allows for almost year-round vigorous activities outdoors, which also promoted emphasis on physical fitness. Most public schools were single-sex institutions and produced many of the men who later held top positions in medicine, law, business, education, and government. (Today almost all of these schools are coeducational.) "Fair play," "the old school tie," and "character training" were phrases that echoed around the British Empire, and its "sporting behavior," "gentlemanly conduct," and "play the game" attitude were often emulated in distant cultures.

Some of the character training that was associated with public school sports probably derived from the fact that originally the organization and management of games were in the hands of the boys themselves and, therefore, offered many opportunities for decision making, cooperation, and leadership. Competition was often intense, but great emphasis was also put on engaging in "fair play," being a "good sport," and being a "good loser." Players shook hands with their opponents after the game and often congratulated them if they had won or played well. "Good game" was heard more often than "What was the score?" in the changing room. Questioning the official decision was unthinkable ("The umpire is always right"; "The umpire's decision is final"); even if a game was lost by a wrong decision, it was not to be challenged. "Playing the game" was more important than winning: "Play up, play up, and play the game."

Today, it hardly seems possible to believe that character training and moral value can be part of the playing of sports themselves. One has only to watch both players and supporters at any major top-level sporting event to see cheating, abuse of officials, violence, and vicious behavior.

Private schools for girls were also found in Great Britain. As women began to seek opportunities for further education, the teaching profession itself grew. Of specific interest was the development of private colleges for women teachers that focused on Physical Education, sometimes including physical therapy. These colleges created something of a female "elite"—the English "gymmistress"—who taught in both private and public schools, usually at the secondary level, and quite often traveled the world. Girls' Physical Education developed largely separately from that of boys, who were often taught by ex-army drill sergeants and had a strong emphasis on team games and sports in emulation of the public schools.

In the English system, Ling and Nachtegall influenced the gymnastics programs more than Jahn. Swedish apparatus (balance beams, wall bars, and a padded box) was more likely to be found in school gymnasia than German equipment (rings, parallel bars, horizontal bars, and pommel horses). German apparatus was more likely to be found in clubs and YMCAs and some of the residential private schools for boys.

It is perhaps obvious that the German influence is the driving force behind our current Olympic gymnastics. Most preparation of Olympic gymnasts takes place in clubs rather than in schools. Women use what could be called German apparatus, albeit without rings and the pommel horse. The parallel bars have been separated into "high-low" (uneven bars), and a balance beam has been included. Interestingly, instead of a pommel horse, a Swedish-type padded box is used for vaulting. One event in women's competitive Olympic gymnastics is the individual event of "rhythmic gymnastics," which entails using small equipment. There is a long history of unison dance-like gymnastics using small equipment that also reflects a largely German influence and comes from women.

The political and educational climate that produced "natural gymnastics" represented a reaction against what was perceived as a too rigid and competitive system. There was also a desire to include children and women in physical education programs.

> The system of naturliches Turnen which Gaulhofer and Margarete Streicher developed in Austria had a great influence upon gymnastics in schools. They too distrusted both sport and orthodox Turnen; sport they considered to lay excessive emphasis upon measurable achievement, and Turnen they dismissed as acrobatics. Their point of departure was the study of children's own movement-impulses and spontaneous play. (Bennett, 1972, p. 125)

In using gymnastic apparatus, the children were allowed to find their own ways to use it. It was Streicher who used the description of gymnastics as "games with gravity."

Other German educators were interested in more fluid and artistic forms of movement. For a while in the 1920s and 1930s, many systems of rhythmic gymnastics and simple group participation developed as part of this philosophy. Examples of progenitors and their creations include Dalcroze (1865–1950) and eurythmics; Duncan (1878–1927) and Greek dancing; Bode (1881–1971) and expression gymnastics; Gaulhofer (1885–1941) and natural gymnastics; Medau (1890–1974) and Medau movement; and Streicher (1891–1985) and natural gymnastics. These systems never penetrated the school systems in the United Kingdom or the United States, but were popular as forms of group recreation (e.g., Keep Fit associations, Women's Leagues of Health and Beauty). Perhaps this idea persists to some extent today: Does synchronized swimming provide the same kind of satisfaction for its performers? During the early years of the twenty-first century, many TV programs showed groups following a leader who performed exercises to music. Was this just for "fitness"? Is participation in this type of program still popular? Consider the mass exercise performed at the opening ceremonies for the Olympic Games.

Although the focus of this text is on elementary school Physical Education programs, it is important to realize how our society has evolved so as to cause individuals to persist with physical activity on a regular basis in adult life. Attractive recreational opportunities may offer a vehicle to control obesity in society and to maintain fitness and physical well-being.

For students particularly interested in the historical development of Movement Discovery (Movement Education, Educational Gymnastics, Movement Exploration, Fundamental Movement, Basic Locomotor Skills, Movement Fundamentals, Basic Movement), the articles by Howard (1967) and Ludwig (1968) in the *Journal of Physical Education and Recreation* are most important. The American Physical Education women who visited Britain were eminent and distinguished and had wide influence at the national, state, and university levels in the United States. These women were taken to see work in the United Kingdom approved by eminent professional Physical Education women there. There was a degree program in the University of Birmingham, United Kingdom, at the time (co-educational), but the tour group visited only private women's Physical Education colleges and observed work in specially selected schools. An historical study that taps into these exchange personnel could still get first-hand accounts of some of the participants.

References

Bennett, B. (Ed.). (1972). *The history of physical education and sport.* Chicago: Athletic Institute.

Gardiner, E. N. (1965). *Athletics of the ancient world.* Oxford, UK: Oxford University Press.

Howard, S. (1967, January). The movement education approach to teaching in English elementary schools: A report based on observations of participants in the Second Anglo-American Workshop on Movement Education. In *Journal of Health, Physical Education and Recreation*, 14–16. Reston, VA: AAHPERD.

Ludwig, E. (1968, March). Toward an understanding of basic movement education in the elementary schools. In *Journal of Health, Physical Education and Recreation*, 10–13. Reston, VA: AAHPERD.

Weston, A. (1962). *The making of American physical education.* New York: Appleton-Century-Crofts.

Wood, T. D., & Cassidy, R. (1927). *The new physical education.* New York: Macmillan.

Appendix 2

Anecdotes

Anecdotes are true stories included to provoke discussion. The purpose of including them in this book is to stimulate student input and to help improve observational skills and understanding. These short tales help to remind us of real situations. So often in teacher education, the focus is on what is *not* desirable at the expense of what *is*. Problem solving should be related to real problems, not hypothetical cases. All of our anecdotes are true. It is suggested that readers submit anecdotes and observations to the publisher for use in the future.

The incidents described in this appendix may have happened any time between 1950 and 2009. They come from practitioners in the United States, Canada, the United Kingdom, and Australia. Each has at least one implication that augments a point made in the text. Anecdotes 1–29 are included in the main chapters of the text, while Anecdotes 30–44 are included as additional material to discuss, but are not included in any of the preceding chapters.

ANECDOTES INCLUDED IN THE TEXT

1. A Physical Education teacher had lost touch with a Greek couple with whom she had stayed 5 years previously. While driving through the Greek countryside near the town where they lived, she passed a woman dressed in a long dress with a large hat (no features were visible) working in an olive grove. The sight was momentary, but something about how the woman moved as she threw a branch aside reminded the driver of her friend. She called at the house, but no one was home. On impulse, she went back to the olive grove and stopped. Three friends were reunited because of the teacher's movement memory. (**Anecdote 1–1**)

2. An observer watched two boys aged approximately 12 years using a climbing frame, climbing up and jumping off. One boy went confidently to the top and jumped to the ground. His friend was jumping from lower down. "Come on up," said the one and the second (halfway) boy did. "It's easy," said the confident boy and jumped. The second boy looked and hesitated. The confident boy repeated the activity. The second boy again hesitated. "Chicken," shouted the confident boy. The second boy looked around as if admiring the view and then climbed down to the halfway bar where he had been previously and jumped from there. (**Anecdote 1–2**)

3. A supervisor of student teaching went to a British infant school to watch a lesson and entered by a side door. Looking around, she was asked by a 5-year-old girl, "Are you looking for Miss [Principal's] office?" Affirming that she was, the visitor was then offered a hand. "Come along then," said the child, who led the way to the correct office. Before she could be thanked, the child disappeared into the washroom. (**Anecdote 1–3**)

4. A demonstration of Movement Discovery was being given, and any professors, students, teachers, principals, supervisors, and interested professionals were invited to attend. During the demonstration, a class of first-grade children was observed just finishing a lesson; the children were separated into four groups, with each group using different small apparatus. A middle-aged woman walked in and sat down to watch the "chaotic" scene. After approximately 3 minutes she

approached the teacher and said, "This is what I want my teachers to do. Where can I find out about this?" (**Anecdote 1–4**)

5. An investigation was made into the obesity and inactivity of a teenaged girl. Her mother protested that she had always been a "couch potato." It was discovered that the girl's hip joints were not properly formed due—the doctors thought—to lack of weight bearing by the legs during childhood. (**Anecdote 2–1**)

6. An adult gave a light, small, plastic hockey stick and ball to a 6-year-old girl and said nothing. Initially the little girl used the stick as a fishing rod behind a sofa. She later swung it and in the space of three minutes discovered what an adult would call "dribbling" (hands apart on the stick), hitting (hands together), hitting for distance, and aiming for a target. (**Anecdote 3–1**)

7. A frustrated track and field coach described teaching a 12-year-old boy to high jump. The youngster was a "natural" with tremendous ability to use his body, even though he could not read or write. The objective was to learn the Western roll technique (the strategy used before the days of the "Fosbury flop"). Everything had been tried—watching an expert, drawing a diagram, practice galore with a reasonable response, holding the "position" in a stationary position on the floor, and so on. Finally, the coach said, "Reggie, next time you do it, kick your chin with your knee and reach with your arms for my hankie." He put his handkerchief in the appropriate corner of the pit. Result: a "perfect" Western roll. (**Anecdote 3–2**)

8. A frustrated tennis coach filmed a young adult serving on a tennis court. The performer did not fully extend his arm at the point of impact. When the student saw the video, he exclaimed, "But my arm is bent!" After the coach reminded him of the many times he had been told precisely that, the student replied, "But it didn't feel bent!" (**Anecdote 3–3**)

9. A parent approached the local top-level field hockey coach and said she had just agreed to coach a team made up of girls, all younger than age 15 years. Because the team was due to play in a tournament in 6 weeks, the new coach asked desperately which skills should be practiced as a top priority. She was told to do anything she liked but to insist on one thing—speed. Whatever was practiced had to be done quickly. Although the young team's style and "form" were very poor, they eventually won the tournament. (**Anecdote 3–4**)

10. Julie, a fourth-grade student, asked a classroom teacher about how worms reproduce. Julie had noticed baby worms in the classroom wormery on the science table. The teacher showed her the chart on the wall above the wormery showing the internal organs of a worm and carefully explained it. "But that's not a worm," Julie objected. The teacher persisted and Julie considered the evidence. Finally, she stated firmly, "No! That's not a worm. It's too big." (**Anecdote 3–5**)

11. Andrew (aged 3 years) was sent to his room after misbehavior when company was present. After a while (while his mother and two adults watched with astonishment), Andrew emerged from his room with his eyes shut. He headed for the door into the garden. When he bumped into a sofa, he opened his eyes. Upon seeing the adults, he was "horrified" and quickly closed his eyes again before continuing out. Andrew believed he could not be seen if he could not see. (**Anecdote 3–6**)

12. An 8-year-old boy had a bad experience with fire and was afraid of it. Upon learning to ride a two-wheeled bicycle for the first time, he was thrilled. Flushed with success, he turned to his father and asked, "Daddy, can I have a box of matches?" (**Anecdote 4–1**)

13. A professor was giving a demonstration lesson with kindergarten children, who were individually exploring large apparatus and a climbing frame. Preservice college students sat around the walls watching and taking notes. A worried student who was looking for the professor approached her to ask a question and was incredulous when he received the reply, "I'm busy." The student merely saw children playing in a gym. (**Anecdote 4–2**)

14. A beginning teacher had a class of 12-year-old students. When recess came, the teacher allowed them to go out into the hallway without lining up. The principal happened to see unruly behavior and brought them *all* back to line up (complaining to the teacher). The teacher apologized and said she would do something about it but asked the principal if she could do things her way. Because the teacher agreed the children had behaved badly, the principal grudgingly agreed.

    The teacher made sure the children were busy on individual activities when the bell rang for recess. Ignoring it for a few minutes, she said, "If you have finished your work, you can tidy your desk and go out to recess." (One or two rushed out.)

    After a few weeks the teacher checked with the principal if "her" class was behaving well in the hallways. (By this time, she sometimes had to insist that students go out to recess instead of continuing to work.) The principal agreed her class behaved well but said, "I could have done it more quickly." Later, when writing a recommendation for this teacher, he said, "She prefers the unorthodox approach." (**Anecdote 5–1**)

15. A preservice student was sent to observe a kindergarten teacher who had the reputation of being the best in the school district. Parents competed to get their child into her class. The student returned to say, she did not agree with that judgment. "The teacher sat at her desk most of the time, and when the children went to her for help, she sent them away to do it themselves," the student reported. The preservice observing student had focused on the teacher and failed to observe the children, who were largely confident and active and busy enjoying a range of self-directed learning. They sometimes asked for help knowing it would be forthcoming, but then went away to solve the problem for themselves. (**Anecdote 5–2**)

16. An elementary Physical Education teacher was offered $5000 by a climbing apparatus company representative to buy climbing frames, A-frames, trestles, and other portable hanging, sliding, swinging, and climbing equipment for his son's elementary school. The Physical Education teacher declined the offer, saying all he wanted was some more balls, not trestles and bars. The teacher ended up with nothing new. The school had no educational gymnastic equipment at all. (**Anecdote 5–3**)

17. An elementary school principal was given $1000 to spend on Physical Education equipment. He had noticed that when playing softball, many students were afraid to catch the ball. He decided to buy enough softball mitts so that every child in the class could have one. When asked how many balls were available for softball, he replied, "Two." (**Anecdote 5–4**)

18. First-grade boy to visiting Physical Education teacher: "Miss, I think you're a good teacher." "Thank you Johnny. Why is that?" "Because you always use lots of stuff." (**Anecdote 5–5**)

19. A young second-grade teacher was hired in the middle of the school year to take over a class whose teacher had resigned upon becoming pregnant. The principal warned the new teacher that it was a poor class; there was much absenteeism, lateness, and lack of enthusiasm for school. The county supervisor told the teacher that the students' reading ability was very poor and below level. When a reading lesson was announced, the children asked, "Do we have to?"

The teacher had enjoyed good success previously in teaching Physical Education with a discovery approach. Although the school's facilities were poor, she managed to obtain enough small balls for the class to play with them, and she took the children to a park adjacent to the school. When it snowed, she obtained sheets of plastic so that the class members could slide down inclines.

Avoiding the use of reading books, the teacher introduced morning and afternoon lessons in Physical Education, enriching the lessons with much oral language, art, and movement. It was the time of the first moon walk, so the class made lunar module constructions with toothpicks and orange peel and looked at the pictures the teacher obtained from NASA. Much discussion and excitement were generated in the classroom, and absenteeism and lateness improved greatly. After about a month, more formal reading materials were gradually introduced and the children eagerly participated in lessons.

When the county supervisor came to observe near the end of the school year, she complimented the new teacher by saying she must be a magnificent reading teacher: The children were now reading at or above grade level and showed interest in learning. The new teacher responded by saying she was not a great teacher of reading, but rather cared more that children were interested in school and learning. (**Anecdote 5–6**)

20. A beginning teacher went to the fully equipped gym at her new school—a secondary school that took many children who were refused entrance to other schools on the grounds of bad behavior—to teach her first Physical Education lesson. When she arrived, she discovered that the boys had not been told that their lesson that day was to take place in the hall. The two mixed classes had taken out all available large apparatus and were using it vigorously with a great deal of pleasure and noise.

Slamming the door, the teacher announced in her loudest voice, "Stop what you are doing and stand still!" There was no response; the teacher doubted that she had even been heard. Discarding the thought "What do I do now? They never told me about this at college," she proceeded to the row of climbing ropes that bisected the room and physically dragged them to the sides. (Various students dropped off the ropes during this process.) It made a noise and some students became aware of her presence, a new teacher neatly dressed in her gym uniform. When all students were sitting on the floor, the novice teacher sent the boys to the hallway, where their own teacher awaited them. She then got the ropes out again, required all girls to attempt to climb them, and encouraged much activity on all other apparatus. After several minutes when the girls were visibly tiring, she put apparatus away and sat the class down to introduce both herself and the program. Safety and the conduct of a Physical Education lesson were included. (**Anecdote 5–7**)

21. Paul, aged 12 years, caused major disruptions in class. The class "clown," he had recently failed an examination that would have set him on the road to follow his

father into the police force. Paul dropped books, fell off his chair, made smart comments, and generally wreaked havoc in the classroom, much to the delight of his classmates, who responded uproariously and egged him on.

Shortly after the beginning of the school year, Paul got sick and ended up in the hospital. The teacher made all classes write letters to Paul, which she promised she would deliver without reading. (She later discovered that one letter began, "Dear Paul, I am writing to you because Miss Blank says we have to.")

When Paul returned to school, he began to work and by the end of the year earned good grades. His parents thanked the teacher with tears in their eyes for turning Paul around. The teacher said she had done nothing other than to treat Paul the same way as the other children. (**Anecdote 5–8**)

22. A 12-year-old girl began to cause disruption in the class whenever a particular new teacher taught. The new teacher was very overweight, and the student had a mother who was "fat." The girl was a leader in the class. When asked why she caused so much trouble (she had been sent to the principal by the new teacher), she replied, "Because she's fat." (The student was ashamed of her mother.) Later the girl admitted that the new teacher had tried to befriend her and the student thought this was wrong; the girl believed that a teacher should treat all students in the same way. (**Anecdote 5–9**)

23. A new teacher found no climbing equipment at her school, so she proceeded to have a fund-raiser to buy it. Within 3 months she had purchased and was using in her lessons the wall frames, trestles, bars, and some mats. The teacher enthusiastically started teaching educational gymnastics. Her supervisor of Physical Education came to observe and told her that using the apparatus was unsafe. The new teacher was distressed and asked one of her former professors to come and evaluate what she was doing. She was told she was doing an excellent job. After a year, the teacher transferred out of the county school system and into the school system of an adjoining county. She proceeded to do another fund-raiser for climbing apparatus at her new school. She went on to be a State Elementary Teacher of the Year in Physical Education. (**Anecdote 5–10**)

24. A male college preservice student was most skeptical that creative dance could be used with preteen boys. As a compromise, he agreed to call it "fitness training" and try it out on his Boy Scouts troop. He came back the next day thrilled. "They love it," he said. The children asked if they could do it again. When this young man was in his first elementary school teaching position, he was appointed as a music teacher. He had the

whole school moving throughout the building to music going up and down staircases, along corridors, out the doors into the playground, and into a hall—a regular symphony of activity. The principal was thrilled (no reports from other teachers!). (**Anecdote 8–1**)

25. Nicholas, age 6 years, had been a page at a family wedding celebrated in a garden. He was still dressed in white shirt and kilt. Now evening had come, and many of the guests were dancing to a band. Nicholas found a corner where he could not be seen and proceeded to dance using all kinds of gestures and unstructured body movements. He stayed mostly in one place. Some of his movements seemed designed to make his kilt flare out and twirl. He was totally absorbed in his own world. (**Anecdote 8–2**)

26. Keith, a second-grade student, was in danger of failing his year and having to repeat grade 2 because of poor written work and manual dexterity. His classroom teacher reported that his handwriting was atrocious. In a week of Movement Discovery body management activities in the gym, Keith used his shoulders and arms to support his body weight and climbed on large apparatus. His improvement in classroom work was so dramatic that he passed his year (demonstrating proximo-distal neurological development). (**Anecdote 10–1**)

27. Amy is a nonverbal student who is regarded as having severe intellectual impairment. Expectations in the self-contained school she is attending are quite low. When she came to a Movement Discovery type of Physical Education program, some interesting things happened. Amy's new teachers led her to a variety of climbing apparatus and "told her" to get climbing as they pointed to and tapped the trestles, bars, benches, and hanging ropes. They beckoned her with hand gestures to come toward them. To their great surprise, Amy started moving toward them as if she understood. After she had traveled from one end of the apparatus to the other, she was encouraged to "Do it again!" With some physical assistance and gesturing, she headed back to her "start" and moved along all the apparatus again. (**Anecdote 12–1**)

28. Todd was special—a "little person" with achondroplasia. He had a very long trunk, short limbs, and a large head. At age 3 years, he could not lift his body from the floor. Although Todd could not walk, he traveled on the floor using his elbows, knees, and a wriggling movement of his body. He had been told that when a special visitor came to see him, she would sing to him. She came and sang. For a few minutes, Todd listened totally still. He then shook his head and shoulder vigorously while turning it slowly to the left, and then he repeated the movement to the right. He then slowly stretched out one leg. There was

something special about the quality of his movement, which was intentional and deliberate. His mother watched in wonder. Finally, she said with tears in her eyes, "He's dancing." (**Anecdote 12–2**)

29. In a small, rural school, the students made balls for their Physical Education lessons. They stuffed molded newspaper into the toes of socks or stockings. They then twisted the covering and retwisted it, finally sewing the remainder of the cover into the ball itself. The children decided to leave some of the balls with "tails" attached. The younger children were allowed to grab the ball by the tail. Older children had to catch the ball. (**Anecdote 12–3**)

ADDITIONAL ANECDOTES NOT IN THE TEXT

30. An elementary school's teaching of mathematics was inspected by "government officials" assessing the teaching of mathematics throughout the school (kindergarten through grade 6). At the final evaluation, the inspectors commended one particular teacher as having the only worthwhile mathematics program. After the inspectors had left the room, the other teachers turned to the commended teacher and asked, "Are you using the curriculum guide?" The reply: "What curriculum guide?" As a new immigrant from another country, it had not occurred to her that a curriculum would be decided at the top level and required to be followed. She was used to matching her lessons to the children's level.

31. A third-grade girl said (happily), "I have more friends now we have Physical Education lessons."

32. A female playground supervisor at recess saw a young boy trip and fall. "Up you get, Johnny," she called. "You're okay." Later a girl fell. The supervisor went over to the girl and helped to "dust her off." She then sent the girl to the office to see if further attention was needed.

33. During the era in tennis when the double-handed backhand was just emerging and players using this stoke were winning Wimbledon and other major tournaments, a teacher intern in Physical Education was told that the correct way to teach a backhand stoke was using only one hand to hold the racket. The university supervisor questioned the supervising teacher and mentioned that it would be appropriate for the students to use both methods. The mentor teacher insisted that the double-handed backhand was *not* the correct way to perform a backhand stroke in tennis.

34. A junior team was entered in the local county sports events (track and field). Their teacher insisted that in hurdles races, it was not important if hurdles were knocked over. The "whole" skill was presented as running continuously to keep going over every hurdle. After the team won every hurdles race in the competition, the trophy was theirs.

35. An athlete discovered a new way to throw a javelin. He threw it using the technique used to throw a discus. He broke all previous records by a huge margin. Unfortunately, the method had to be outlawed to save the necessity of building new stadiums or rebuilding existing ones to accommodate the new distances.

36. A college basketball player with top "statistics" in "steals" was asked how he managed to steal the ball from the opponents on so many different teams. "I watch their eyes," he replied. This young man had somehow learned to interpret minute eye movements. He also had a fast reaction time!

37. In a Saturday morning gym class, a father arrived and placed his 3-year-old daughter on top of an old gym horse (between the pommels). He then started to walk away until challenged by the teacher. "How is she supposed to get down?" was the question. He looked at the teacher as if to say, "That's your job." The teacher continued: "You put her there; you get her down. If she had got there herself, I know she could get herself down." The father retrieved his daughter and put her on the floor.

38. A Saturday morning children's gym class for 3- to 8-year-olds was held in a gym that had a climbing frame (with net, ropes, and bars) pulled out from the wall. A gym bench was hooked halfway up one frame, providing an inclined surface. One girl climbed up to the top and decided she did not want to continue through to the other side. She stopped and looked behind her. Unfortunately by now several other children had followed her—about four or five of them. She looked ahead once again, but definitely did not want to go on. When she stopped, the other children had to stop as well. They looked up and down. The one at the bottom had to lean far out to see "the problem" at the top. He backed down and got off the apparatus, followed by all ahead of him. When the girl was finally down, the rest went back up. Not one word was spoken.

39. In a Saturday morning gym class where young children had access to a great deal of large gymnastic apparatus, Chris, a 6-year-old boy, spent most of the time lying on the floor looking at the ceiling. He would occasionally look vaguely at the other children but never interacted or spoke. Sometimes he was active on his own. After several weeks, he came to the teacher, made no eye contact, but pulled on her sleeve. "Oh, Chris," said the teacher. "You want to show me something?" He made a vocal sound (a bit like "Uh-huh"). He led her to piece of apparatus and he then proceeded to

climb slowly to the top. This incident happened in the 1970s, before autism was a recognized diagnosis. Chris's mother, who was watching, had previously commented that she had noticed that the teacher had treated him "the same as the other children."

40. Recorded in *Sports Illustrated,* November 15, 2004, page 83, is an article written by Tim Layden entitled "Get Out and Play!": "The children played games that they themselves suggested, and SOMETHING EXTRAORDINARY happened: They loved exercising."

41. At the elementary school, a flight of improvised hurdles (canes resting on low traffic cones) was left at one side of the play area during recess. A former female student was visiting from her middle school when she saw them and went to use them. She kicked off her shoes and, with a smooth continuous action, earrings flying, long blonde hair flowing, and an even pattern, she cleared them all. An observer thought she derived a sensual pleasure from it.

42. An argument developed between a gymnastics coach and a proponent of a Movement Discovery approach to learning physical skills. It was decided to use a motley group of adults (classroom teachers taking a Physical Education methods course!) to compare teaching methods. There was 30 minutes available for the experiment. Because there were two horizontal bars in the room, the "kip" (under grasp upstart) was selected as the skill to be taught. This involves standing with the bar at chest height, with an under-hand grasp (hands facing performer) swinging the legs forward and back up over the bar to end in a balance position on the top of the bar. Two teams were picked roughly according to ability, and teaching and practice began. The gymnastic coach explained, demonstrated, and set to work, with one student at a time attempting the skill at the bar, while the others watched. Sometimes manual assistance was given and principles of momentum explained. The Movement Discovery teacher set out various pieces of equipment, including a gym mat, a bench, hula-hoops, and the horizontal bar. She required everyone to have a turn at the bar, but students were told to do anything they liked with any piece of equipment. They had to "keep busy" and not be inactive.

After 30 minutes, the class was stopped for the test. The test was demonstrated and the groups had alternate attempts to succeed. No one succeeded in performing the test. What was most noticeable was the way individuals approached the test. The Movement Discovery group was relaxed and casual, and two of them very nearly succeeded. The coached group was tense and slower, obviously trying to remember what they had been taught before trying. One of the coached group complained that he had not had fun with the hula-hoops!

43. A future secondary school wrestling coach participated in a creative dance lesson for the first time in a college methods class. "I haven't had so much fun since I was in church," he commented. (He was a member of a Pentecostal "Holy Roller" congregation.)

44. A teacher asked a sixth-grade class to give a definition of "infinity." One boy replied, "It's like the boy on the cereal box." The teacher did not follow up on this response, but asked a girl who gave a word-for-word definition as taught by the teacher. An interested observer asked the boy after class what he had meant by his answer. The boy replied that on the cereal box was a picture of a boy looking at a picture of the cereal box, which showed a picture of a boy looking at a picture of a cereal box, which showed . . . and so on. The observer was impressed by this definition in the boy's own words, which showed his understanding.

Teacher Education
National Standards

The National Standards included in this appendix are intended for Physical Education teachers as well as for early childhood professionals. Physical Education standards for both preservice and in-service teachers are outlined here, in addition to the 2006 Adapted Physical Education National Standards.

For those professors in Physical Education teacher education programs in the United States, the following 2008 initial standards pertain to preservice teacher preparation in Physical Education. The 2008 Initial Standards in Physical Education Teacher Education are available for download as a .pdf file from the National Association for Sport and Physical Education Web site (NASPE, 2008) and are also contained in the NASPE text (NASPE, 2009).

2008 Initial Physical Education Teacher Education Standards

STANDARD 1: SCIENTIFIC AND THEORETICAL KNOWLEDGE

Physical Education teacher candidates know and apply discipline-specific scientific and theoretical concepts critical to the development of physically educated individuals.
Elements—Teacher candidates will:

  1.1 Describe and apply physiological and bio-mechanical concepts related to skillful movement, physical activity, and fitness.

  1.2 Describe and apply motor learning and psychological/behavioral theory related to skillful movement, physical activity, and fitness.

  1.3 Describe and apply motor development theory and principles related to skillful movement, physical activity, and fitness.

  1.4 Identify historical, philosophical, and social perspectives of physical education issues and legislation.

  1.5 Analyze and correct critical elements of motor skills and performance concepts.

STANDARD 2: SKILL AND FITNESS-BASED COMPETENCE*

Physical Education teacher candidates are physically educated individuals with the knowledge and skills necessary to demonstrate competent movement performance and health-enhancing fitness as delineated in the NASPE K–12 standards.
Elements—Teacher candidates will:

  2.1 Demonstrate personal competence in motor skill performance for a variety of physical activities and movement patterns.

  2.2 Achieve and maintain a health-enhancing level of fitness throughout the program.

  2.3 Demonstrate performance concepts related to skillful movement in a variety of physical activities.

STANDARD 3: PLANNING AND IMPLEMENTATION

Physical Education teacher candidates plan and implement developmentally appropriate learning experiences aligned with local, state, and national standards to address the diverse needs of all students.

Elements—Teacher candidates will:

3.1 Design and implement short- and long-term plans that are linked to program and instructional goals as well as a variety of student needs.

3.2 Develop and implement appropriate (e.g., measurable, developmentally appropriate, performance-based) goals and objectives aligned with local, state, and/or national standards.

3.3 Design and implement content that is aligned with lesson objectives.

3.4 Plan for and manage resources to provide active, fair, and equitable learning experiences.

3.5 Plan and adapt instruction for diverse student needs, adding specific accommodations and/or modifications for student exceptionalities.

3.6 Plan and implement progressive and sequential instruction that addresses the diverse needs of all students.

3.7 Plan and implement learning experiences that require students to appropriately use technology to meet lesson objectives.

STANDARD 4: INSTRUCTIONAL DELIVERY AND MANAGEMENT

Physical Education teacher candidates use effective communication and pedagogical skills and strategies to enhance student engagement and learning.

Elements—Teacher candidates will:

4.1 Demonstrate effective verbal and nonverbal communication skills across a variety of instructional formats.

4.2 Implement effective demonstrations, explanations, and instructional cues and prompts to link physical activity concepts to appropriate learning experiences.

4.3 Provide effective instructional feedback for skill acquisition, student learning, and motivation.

4.4 Recognize the changing dynamics of the environment and adjust instructional tasks based on student responses.

4.5 Utilize managerial rules, routines, and transitions to create and maintain a safe and effective learning environment.

4.6 Implement strategies to help students demonstrate responsible personal and social behaviors in a productive learning environment.

STANDARD 5: IMPACT ON STUDENT LEARNING

Physical Education teacher candidates utilize assessments and reflection to foster student learning and inform instructional decisions.

Elements—Teacher candidates will:

5.1 Select or create appropriate assessments that will measure student achievement of goals and objectives.

5.2 Use appropriate assessments to evaluate student learning before, during, and after instruction.

5.3 Utilize the reflective cycle to implement change in teacher performance, student learning, and instructional goals and decisions.

STANDARD 6: PROFESSIONALISM

Physical Education teacher candidates demonstrate dispositions essential to becoming effective professionals.

Elements—Teacher candidates will:

6.1 Demonstrate behaviors that are consistent with the belief that all students can become physically educated individuals.

6.2 Participate in activities that enhance collaboration and lead to professional growth and development.

6.3 Demonstrate behaviors that are consistent with the professional ethics of highly qualified teachers.

6.4 Communicate in ways that convey respect and sensitivity.

For teachers already in the field of Physical Education, the following voluntary national standards for K–12 Physical Education reflect current thinking on what students should know and be able to do as a result of a quality Physical Education program. More details can be found in the texts *Moving into the Future: National Standards for Physical Education,* second edition (NASPE, 2009) and *National Standards & Guidelines for Physical Education Teacher Education,* third edition (NASPE, 2009). The latter addresses both initial and advanced PETE Standards in addition to some sample rubrics and guidance for writing assessments.

National Standards for Physical Education

Physical activity is critical to the development and maintenance of good health. The goal of Physical Education is to develop physically educated individuals who have the knowledge, skills, and confidence to enjoy a lifetime of healthful physical activity. A physically educated person:

Standard 1: Demonstrates competency in motor skills and movement patterns needed to perform a variety of physical activities.

Standard 2: Demonstrates understanding of movement concepts, principles, strategies, and tactics as they apply to the learning and performance of physical activities.

Standard 3: Participates regularly in physical activity.

Standard 4: Achieves and maintains a health-enhancing level of physical fitness.

Standard 5: Exhibits responsible personal and social behavior that respects self and others in physical activity settings.

Standard 6: Values physical activity for health, enjoyment, challenge, self-expression, and/or social interaction.

The purpose of the standards is to define what a student should know and be able to do as a result of a quality Physical Education program. They provide a framework for developing realistic and achievable expectations for student performance at every grade level. These expectations are the first step in designing an instructionally aligned program.

Many states and local education authorities in the United States have used the national standards to develop standards, frameworks, and curricula. Others have revised their existing standards and curricula to align with the national standards. NASPE (2004) states that, "National physical education standards bring accountability and rigor to the profession."

Standards for Adapted Physical Education

The need for national standards in Physical Education arose when the Individuals with Disabilities Education Act (IDEA, 2004) included the discipline of Physical Education under the definition of special education in this law. Physical Education was the only specific curricular area identified in this federal legislation. Thus the 15 standards were developed to identify what an adapted physical educator should know in order to provide services to children with disabilities. The National Consortium for Physical Education and Recreation for Individuals with Disabilities spearheaded the effort to develop these standards and to develop a national certification examination to measure knowledge of the standards.

STANDARD 1: HUMAN DEVELOPMENT

The foundation of proposed goals and activities for individuals with disabilities is grounded in a basic understanding of human development and its applications to those with various needs.

STANDARD 2: MOTOR BEHAVIOR

Teaching individuals with disabilities requires knowledge of typical physical and motor development as well as the influence of developmental delays on these processes. An understanding of how individuals learn motor skills and an application of the principles of motor learning are essential to planning and teaching.

STANDARD 3: EXERCISE SCIENCE

This standard focuses on the principles that address the physiological and biomechanical applications encountered when working with diverse populations, including modifications to activity.

STANDARD 4: MEASUREMENT AND EVALUATION

Understanding the measurement of motor performance is, to a large extent, based on a good grasp of motor development and the acquisition of motor skills covered in other standards.

STANDARD 5: HISTORY AND PHILOSOPHY

This standard traces legal and philosophical factors involved in current-day practices in adapted physical education (APE). A review of history and philosophy related to special and general education is also covered.

STANDARD 6: UNIQUE ATTRIBUTES OF LEARNERS: CONSIDERATIONS FOR PROFESSIONAL PRACTICE

This standard refers to information based on all the disability areas found in the Individuals with Disabilities Education Improvement Act (IDEA as amended in 2004).

STANDARD 7: CURRICULUM THEORY AND DEVELOPMENT

Certain curriculum theory and development concepts, such as selecting goals based on relevant and appropriate assessment, must be understood.

STANDARD 8: ASSESSMENT

Assessment goes beyond data gathering to include measurements for the purpose of making decisions about special services and program components for individuals with disabilities.

STANDARD 9: INSTRUCTIONAL DESIGN AND PLANNING

Many of the principles addressed in other standards are needed to successfully design and plan adapted physical education programs to meet the unique needs of individuals with disabilities.

STANDARD 10: TEACHING

Many of the principles addressed earlier in such standard areas as human development, motor behavior, and exercise science are applied to this standard to effectively provide quality Physical Education to individuals with disabilities.

STANDARD 11: CONSULTATION AND STAFF DEVELOPMENT

This standard identifies key competencies an adapted physical educator should demonstrate related to consultation and staff development, in particular the dynamics of interdisciplinary cooperation particularly with those in the general education program.

STANDARD 12: STUDENT AND PROGRAM EVALUATION

Program evaluation involves evaluation of the entire range of educational services. Student assessment is only a part of this process.

STANDARD 13: CONTINUING EDUCATION

This standard focuses on ways teachers of APE can remain current in their field by taking advantage of professional development opportunities.

STANDARD 14: ETHICS

This standard has been developed to ensure that teachers of APE adhere to the highest ethical standards.

STANDARD 15: COMMUNICATION

This standard includes information on how to effectively communicate with families and other professionals, using a team approach to enhance program instruction for individuals with disabilities.

Standards for Programs Preparing Early Childhood Professionals

All National Association for the Education of Young Children (NAEYC) position statements, including the Standards for Professional Preparation Programs, can be downloaded from this organization's Web site: http://www.naeyc.org/about/positions.asp. At the time of this book's writing, the newest draft of NAEYC Professional Preparation Standards (2009) were in revision. Physical Education is listed in Standard 5. These six standards are summarized in the remainder of this section.

STANDARD 1: PROMOTING CHILD DEVELOPMENT AND LEARNING

Students prepared in early childhood degree programs are grounded in a child development knowledge base. They use their understanding of young children's characteristics and needs, and of multiple interacting influences on children's development and learning, to create environments that are healthy, respectful, supportive, and challenging for each child.

STANDARD 2: BUILDING FAMILY AND COMMUNITY RELATIONSHIPS

Students prepared in early childhood degree programs understand that successful early childhood education depends on partnerships with children's families and communities. They know about, understand, and value the importance and complex characteristics of children's families and communities. They use this understanding to create respectful, reciprocal relationships that support and empower families, and to involve all families in their children's development and learning.

STANDARD 3: OBSERVING, DOCUMENTING, AND ASSESSING TO SUPPORT YOUNG CHILDREN AND FAMILIES

Students prepared in early childhood degree programs understand that child observation, documentation, and other forms of assessment are central to the practice of all early childhood professionals. They know about and understand the goals, benefits, and uses of assessment. They know about and use systematic observations, documentation, and other effective assessment strategies in a responsible way, in partnership with families and other professionals, to positively influence the development of every child.

STANDARD 4: USING DEVELOPMENTALLY EFFECTIVE APPROACHES TO CONNECT WITH CHILDREN AND FAMILIES

Students prepared in early childhood degree programs understand that teaching and learning with young children is a complex enterprise, and its details vary depending on children's ages, characteristics, and the settings within which teaching and learning occur. They understand and use positive relationships and supportive interactions as the foundation for their work with young children and families. Students know, understand, and use a wide array of developmentally appropriate approaches, instructional strategies, and tools to connect with children and families and positively influence each child's development and learning.

These methods include:

- Fostering oral language and communication

- Making the most of the environment and routines

- Capitalizing on incidental teaching

- Focusing on children's characteristics, needs, and interests

- Linking children's language and culture to the early childhood program

- Teaching through social interactions

- Creating support for play

- Addressing children's challenging behaviors

- Supporting learning through technology

- Using integrative approaches to curriculum

STANDARD 5: USING CONTENT KNOWLEDGE TO BUILD MEANINGFUL CURRICULUM

Students prepared in early childhood degree programs use their knowledge of academic disciplines to design, implement, and evaluate experiences that promote positive development and learning for each and every young child. Students understand the importance of developmental domains and academic (or content) disciplines in the early childhood curriculum.

They know the essential concepts, inquiry tools, and structure of content areas, including academic subjects, and can identify resources to deepen their understanding. Students use their own knowledge and other resources to design, implement, and evaluate meaningful, challenging curricula that promote comprehensive developmental and learning outcomes for every young child.

Early childhood curriculum content includes the following components:

- Learning goals, experiences, and assessment in academic disciplines or content areas, including language and literacy; the arts—music, creative movement, dance, drama, and visual arts;

mathematics; science; physical activity, *physical education*, health, and safety; and social studies

- Comprehensive developmental and learning outcomes: security and self-regulation; problem-solving and thinking skills; academic and social competence

STANDARD 6: BECOMING A PROFESSIONAL

Students prepared in associate degree programs identify and conduct themselves as members of the early childhood profession. They know and use ethical guidelines and other professional standards related to early childhood practice. They are continuous, collaborative learners who demonstrate knowledgeable, reflective, and critical perspectives on their work, making informed decisions that integrate knowledge from a variety of sources. They are informed advocates for sound educational practices and policies.

All the Standards listed in this appendix are current at the time of writing this text. Readers should know that national organizations do change these standards on a regular basis. It is wise, therefore, to check the appropriate organization's Web site for any updates or revisions.

References

National Association for the Education of Young Children (NAEYC). (2009). Standards for programs preparing early childhood professionals. Washington DC: Author.

National Association for Sport and Physical Education (NASPE). (2004). *Moving into the future: National standards for physical education* (2nd ed.). Reston, VA: Author, AAHPERD. Retrieved December 25, 2009, from http://www.aahperd.org/naspe/standards/nationalStandards/PEstandards.cfm

National Association for Sport and Physical Education (NASPE). (2008). *2008 initial standards in physical education teacher education.* Reston, VA: Author, American Alliance for Health, Physical Education, Recreation, and Dance. Retrieved December 25, 2009, from http://www.aahperd.org/naspe/standards/nationalStandards/PETEstandards.cfm

National Association for Sport and Physical Education (NASPE). (2009). *National standards & guidelines for physical education teacher education.* (3rd ed.). Reston, VA: Author, AAHPERD.

National Consortium for Physical Education and Recreation for Individuals with Disabilities. (2006). *Adapted physical education national standards* (2nd ed.). Champaign, IL: Human Kinetics.

Photo Credits

Chapter 1
Page 5 (top) © Felix Mizioznikov/ShutterStock, Inc.; **page 5 (middle)** Courtesy of Andre Stringer; **page 5 (bottom)** © Sergey Lavrentev/ShutterStock, Inc.

Chapter 2
Page 13 Courtesy of Todd Stringer; **page 14 (bottom left and top right)** Courtesy of Andre Stringer

Chapter 3
Page 24 (top left and right) Courtesy of Andre Stringer; **page 24 (bottom right)** © Felix Mizioznikov/Dreamstime.com; **page 25** © Kitti/ShutterStock, Inc.; **page 29, page 30, page 32** Courtesy of Andre Stringer

Chapter 4
Page 34 Courtesy of Gerstung Intersport; **4–1** Courtesy of Todd Stringer; **page 43 (bottom)** Courtesy of Gerstung Intersport; **page 44 (right)** © Tony Wear/ShutterStock, Inc.; **4–2** Courtesy of Todd Stringer; **page 49 (top and bottom)** Courtesy of Gerstung Intersport; **4–4** Courtesy of Todd Stringer

Chapter 5
Page 60, page 79 (bottom right) Courtesy of Gerstung Intersport; **5–10** Courtesy of Todd Stringer

Chapter 6
Page 91 (right), 6–2 Courtesy of Todd Stringer; **page 106** © Barsik/Dreamstime.com; **page 107 (left)** © Stavchansky Yakov/ShutterStock, Inc.; **(right)** © Fancy/Alamy Images; **page 109 (left)** © Orange Line Media/ShutterStock, Inc.; **(right)** © JJ pixs/ShutterStock, Inc.; **page 110** © Kuzmin Andrey/ShutterStock, Inc.; **page 111** © Photodisc; **page 112 (left)** © Kapu/Dreamstime.com; **(top right)** © Bartlomiej Nowak/ShutterStock, Inc.; **6–10** Courtesy of Todd Stringer

Chapter 7
Page 125, page 133 Courtesy of Todd Stringer

Chapter 8
Page 144, page 151 Courtesy of Gerstung Intersport; **8–1, 8–2** Courtesy of Todd Stringer

Chapter 10
Page 182 (bottom left) © Timofeyev Alexander/ShutterStock, Inc.; **page 182 (right)** © Lastdays1/Dreamstime.com; **page 183 (top left)** Courtesy of Gerstung Intersport; **10–1** Courtesy of Todd Stringer; **page 190 (bottom left)** Courtesy of Gerstung Intersport; **page 190 (right)** © Olivia Drew/National Geographic/age footstock; **10–2, 10–3** Courtesy of Todd Stringer; **page 197 (middle left)** Courtesy of Gerstung Intersport; **10–4, 10–5, 10–6, 10–7, 10–8, 10–9, 10–10** Courtesy of Todd Stringer

Chapter 11
Page 208 (left) Courtesy of Andre Stringer; **page 212** © Ruslana Stovner/Dreamstime.com; **page 214** © Paul Moore/Dreamstime.com; **page 249** Courtesy of Todd Stringer; **page 251 (right)** Courtesy of Gerstung Intersport

Chapter 12
Page 265 Courtesy of Todd Stringer and Nathan Hess; **page 266 (bottom left), page 266 (second right), page 266 (third right), page 266 (bottom right), page 267 (middle left), page 267 (top right), page 267 (second**

Index